Shadows of the Sacred

Seeing Through Spiritual Illusions

Shadows of the Sacred

Seeing Through Spiritual Illusions

Frances Vaughan

Foreword by Ken Wilber

QUEST BOOKS

The Theosophical Publishing House

Wheaton, Illinois, U.S.A.: Adyar, Madras, India

The Theosophical Publishing House
P.O. Box 270
Wheaton, IL 60189-0270

A publication of the Theosophical Publishing House,
a department of the Theosophical Society in America.

*This publication made possible with
the assistance of the Kern Foundation*

Library of Congress Cataloging-in-Publication Data

Vaughan, Frances E.
   Shadows of the sacred : seeing through spiritual illusions / by Frances
Vaughan.
      p.   cm.
   Includes bibliographical references and index.
   ISBN 0-8356-0723-2
   1. Spiritual life.   2. Theosophy.   I. Title.
BL624.V377   1995
299'.934—dc20   95-7201
                                                                        CIP

9 8 7 6 5 4 3 2 1 * 95 96 97 98 99

Printed in the United States of America

For Roger

Contents

Foreword by Ken Wilber / ix

Preface / xv

Acknowledgments / xvii

Introduction / 1

1. Golden Chains on the Spiritual Path / 3

2. Living in Two Worlds: The World of Ego and the World of Soul / 29

3. Sex and Death: Eros and Thanatos / 49

4. The Path of Love / 81

5. Awakening Soul: Ancient Wisdom and Modern Science / 108

6. Soul and Gender / 138

7. Healing and Empowerment / 152

8. The Myth of Enlightenment / 196

9. Spiritual Freedom / 224

10. Spiritual Practice in Daily Life / 253

Notes / 289

Index / 307

Foreword

by Ken Wilber

FRANCES VAUGHAN IS THE WISEST OF THE Wise Women I know. Such a wonderful concept: the woman who is wise, the woman who has more wisdom, perhaps, than you or I, the woman who brings a special knowledge, a graceful touch, a healing presence, to her every encounter, for whom beauty is also a mode of knowing and openness a special strength—a woman who sees so much more, and touches so much more, and reaches out with care, and tells us that it will be alright, this woman who is wise, this woman who sees more.

The woman from whom we all can learn. I suppose there are some in our society who object to distinguishing between male and female persons; the gender wars are intense nowadays, and any "differences" ascribed to men and women are looked upon suspiciously, as perhaps a prelude to some oppressive agenda. The "differences" between male and female are just so much propaganda, the argument goes, designed to keep women barefoot, pregnant, and in the kitchen. But if the differentiation between the male and female value sphere is an oppressive plot, it goes back to day one. From the earliest foraging cultures to the first horticultural societies, and from there to the great agrarian Empires that ran from the Aztecs and Incas to the Khans and Ottomans, Romans and Greeks, Egyptians and Chinese: in virtually all known societies to date, the male and female value spheres were indeed thought to be quite different. Some of these societies—such as the horticultural planting communities ruled by the Great Mother— valued the female sphere more or less equally with the male sphere (as did many earlier foraging societies.) Other cultures—particularly the agrarian Empires and the cultures of horse and herding—placed an almost exclusive emphasis on the male value sphere: the deities were purely male and the values were those of the warrior or princely aristocrat (the "patriarchy").

Looking back on history, we moderns feel sadness, sometimes outrage, that some cultures so disproportionately championed the male sphere over the female sphere, but the point for now is that, regardless of emphasis, in all of these cultures (foraging to horticultural to agrarian, matrifocal or patrifocal)—in all of these cultures, the male and female values spheres were crisply differentiated, and these differences show a surprising consistency—sometimes monotonously so—across cultures.

And indeed, in recent times, the radical feminists, the spiritual feminists, and the ecofeminists, in their own various ways, have all embraced the female value sphere as indeed embodying a universal sphere of values, a sphere significantly different from the male sphere, and a sphere that has been severely undervalued during the last several thousand years of agrarian/herding/patriarchal cultures. And there is much truth to this, I think.

But what, indeed, are these values, in both the male and female sphere? Perhaps the simplest way to summarize the evidence is in terms of the two major types of love—Eros and Agape—and the two major types of action—agency and communion. Eros is the love of the lower reaching up for the higher, always ascending, always yearning for more, always seeking, often recklessly, restlessly, for more; whereas Agape is the love of the higher reaching down to the lower, embracing it in compassion and acceptance, tenderness and care (thus Eros tends always to aim high, for the sky and Heaven, and Agape always reaches down and embraces gladly the body and the Earth). Agency is a type of action and being that stresses the individual, the separate and autonomous agent, the isolated, the singular; whereas communion stresses relationship, network, linking, joining.

It's not that one form of love or action is better or nobler or more desirable than the other. It's more the primordial yin and yang: interpenetrating each other, relying on each other, generating each other, and—ideally—balancing each other.

Without in any way pigeonholing men and women, or implying that distinctions are etched in concrete, the evidence strongly suggests that, across cultures and virtually from day one, the female value sphere has been pictured as emphasizing Agape and communion, whereas the male sphere has been seen as emphasizing agency and Eros.

And, indeed, these are the main differences in values that Carol Gilligan, for example, has detected in men and women's responses to moral dilemmas: males have a tendency to emphasize individual rights and legalistic justice (agency), whereas females tend to emphasize care and responsibilities (communion). Likewise, the theological ("thealogical") and spiritual feminists have tended to summarize the entire thrust of "feminine spirituality" as "the Divine embodied" (Agape incarnate!), bringing heavenly wisdom down and into relationships, into the Earthbody, into the day-to-day living of the Divine (whereas most forms of "male spirituality," from shamans to yogis and saints, have almost always sought "journeys" to the "other world," the upward yearning Eros looking for ways beyond the everyday Earthbody, for their kingdom is not of this world.)

Every single major world religion (Christianity, Islam, Judaism, Hinduism, Buddhism and even later Taoism) arose during the time of the great agrarian empires (and/or the horse and herding cultures.) Which means that *every single major world religion* arose in a climate that highly valued the male sphere of Eros and agency (go off in a cave, or into the desert by yourself, and ascend!)—and thus they either indirectly devalued, or frankly oppressed, the female value sphere of Agape, of Earthbody, of communion with nature and with others, of embodiment, and most of all, of *being-in-relationship.*

This, of course, does not mean that the great patriarchal wisdom traditions have nothing to teach us, any more than it means we shouldn't use the wheel because a man invented it. It does mean, however, that there is a whole value sphere yet to be, literally, unearthed in the modern era. The great traditions do not need to be simply jettisoned—that would be catastrophic—but they need desperately to be supplemented.

And that means, above all, that we are desperately in need of, yes, the Wise Woman.

Frances is such a one: the woman who brings wisdom into the world and does not flee the world for wisdom somewhere else. The woman who teaches individuality, but set in its larger and deeper contexts of communion: communion with others, with body, with Spirit, with one's own higher Self, the Spirit that manifests its very being in relationships. And that is how I think of Frances most often: the wise woman who teaches sane and sincere relationship, the woman who sets us in our deeper contexts, this wise woman who I am proud to know.

But it is not just as a Wise Woman that Frances comes to us. When historians from Toynbee to White remarked that the introduction of Buddhism to the West would likely be regarded by future generations as one of the great turning points in civilization, I think they were onto something important. Perhaps Buddhism *per se* will not become a culture-wide movement, but the point, I think, is that the introduction or discovery (or rediscovery) of some form of genuinely *transpersonal endeavor* is crucial to the future of Western culture.

In the West, where psychology (and psychiatry) have completely replaced religion as the dominant sciences of the soul, it is the school of
transpersonal psychology that carries most clearly the banner of genuine
contemplative spirituality. Drawing on the great mystical and contemplative
traditions (but not limited to them), transpersonal psychology weaves
ancient insights with modern psychotherapeutic techniques, creating a
unique synthesis and amalgam of ancient wisdom and modern truths.

And Frances is one of the relatively few transpersonal psychologists
actually "in the trenches," as it were—working with clients, day to day, on
a professional basis. Not only has she been trained in several contemplative
traditions (from Christian to Zen to Hindu and Sufi), and not only has she
received her "orthodox" training from the highly regarded California School
of Professional Psychology, but she brings that combined wisdom to the
actual day-to-day details of the therapeutic situation.

The book you are holding in your hands is, so to speak, dispatches from
the front lines, which is why it is so incredibly important as a document. It is
what Frances and her clients have taught each other about sane living, sane
relationships, care and compassion, dignity and grace, in and through the
most difficult of times that bring people to the office of a therapist, looking
for a kind ear and a sense of gentle direction. They have lost their way a bit,
in this society that doesn't particularly care, perhaps even lost their soul,
and they come quietly and confused, and can you please help me?

In the type of transpersonal practice that Frances (and a handful of
others) are attempting to forge, we see the emergence of whatever it was
that Toynbee and White recognized as so crucial: some sense of the transpersonal, some sense of the Mystery of the Deep, some context beyond the
isolated me, that touches each and every one of us and lifts us from our
troubled and mortal selves, this contracted coil, delivers us into the hands
of the timeless and very Divine, and gracefully releases us from ourselves:
where openness melts defenses and relationship grounds sanity, where
compassion outpaces the hardened heart and care outshines despair: this
is the opening to the Divine that Frances teaches each of us.

One of Frances's clients once told her that she (Frances) had helped to
midwife, to deliver her soul. I think that somehow says it all. To midwife the
Divine—already present in each, but perhaps not shining brightly; already
given to each, but perhaps not noticed well; already caring for the world,
but perhaps forgotten in all the rush: this opening also Frances teaches us.

Like all dispatches from the front, the following notes are not linear.
They are not in the form of a logical argument where one enters the tunnel

at point A and is coerced through an argument to come out at point B. They sometimes meander, these notes. They sometimes bounce around. They follow the contours of real-life terrain; they are conversations with her clients, conversations she is having with us as well, following the ups and downs of real thought and genuine dialogue, and not the stiff lines of geometric proof.

And so, if I may suggest, let these notes wash over you, wash through you, and follow gently the curves of terrain, and don't force it into a linear argument. It is a new and strange and wonderful terrain, this transpersonal journey, and your tour guide has seen it all, and lived it all, and lived to tell the tale. And there, just there, is the definition of the Wise Woman.

Let us both, you and I, take the hand of the Wise Woman, and walk with her through the land of our own soul, and listen quietly to the tale she has to tell. And know that a surer pair of hands we are not likely to find in this lifetime.

Preface

IN RECENT TRAVELS ALL OVER THE WORLD
I have seen new forms of spirituality appearing everywhere. As people
become more conscious that problems such as pollution, overpopulation,
war, depletion of resources and the devastation of the planet are human
caused, there is a growing awareness of the urgent need for changing human
consciousness and behavior.

Sometimes the signs of spiritual renewal look like passing new age fads.
Sometimes they seem quite conventional, espousing traditional religious
forms. Sometimes they appear to be secular and humanistic, sometimes
idealistic, sometimes wise and sometimes foolish. Regardless of how they
appear at first glance, the stirrings of the human soul are unmistakable.
Even in places such as China and Eastern Europe, where people have lived
for decades under repressive political regimes, new interest in spirituality
is bursting forth.

In the United States the worlds of academia and professional psychology, with which I am familiar, seem to be lagging far behind the general
population in recognizing the importance of healthy spirituality for both
personal and planetary well-being. I have watched the growing popularity
of transpersonal psychology over the past two decades. I see that the
transpersonal movement, which attempts to integrate psychology and spirituality, has now moved out into the world at large. Transpersonal studies
are emerging in many different disciplines, and people everywhere are
realizing that the shadow side of spirituality cannot be ignored.

The perennial quest for happiness, meaning and a sense of belonging
cannot be divorced from spirituality. Yet few people seem to recognize
that spiritual freedom is essential to a free, democratic society as well as
to personal well-being. Even in a democracy with relatively few external
constraints on personal freedom, many people fail to exercise freedom in
choosing beliefs and a spiritual path.

As a psychotherapist I have spent many hours with people who want
to change and who know that many obstacles to change are internal

rather than external. As a teacher and workshop leader I have also learned how people who embrace a spiritual discipline can feel empowered and transformed by it. The people I have met in many different contexts have taught me a lot about the power of illusions and what it means to awaken the soul and consciously choose a spiritual path. I have worked with some people who have devoted themselves to a religious life for many years and with others who have been dedicated to a spiritual life in an invisible way. Some live peacefully in accordance with their spiritual vision every day, while others struggle with inner conflicts and their own shadows.

I have observed that when people are ready to take their spirituality seriously, a path unfolds before them and their inner world can be transformed from a battleground to a sanctuary. In this book I offer some of the ideas and processes that have been helpful to me and to others whose awakening I have witnessed.

Acknowledgments

THIS BOOK WOULD NOT HAVE BEEN WRITten without the support of family and friends who have encouraged me along the way. I am also indebted to my clients who have explored the world of soul with me and who have shared so much. I want to thank them all and, in particular, those who have graciously granted me permission to retell their dreams and experiences. The examples I have used are drawn from real-life experiences, but some are composites, and identifying details have been changed to protect privacy and confidentiality.

I specially want to thank those individuals who read portions of this manuscript and who gave me constructive critical feedback: Roger Walsh, Ken Wilber, Angeles Arrien, Roxanne Lanier, John Levy, Loretta Barrett, John White and my editor at Quest, Brenda Rosen. Each one has contributed valuable time and attention to this endeavor. I am also grateful to Judith Skutch Whitson for granting me permission to include some quotations from *A Course in Miracles*.

I also want to thank some of my teachers who have guided my soul's journey through valleys of the shadow to realms of light and joy. Their kindness, their vision and their love has been an inspiration to me across the years. First among them are my parents and my two children, Robert and Leslie Clark. Others, in alphabetical order, are those whose influence has shaped this book: Angeles Arrien, the Dalai Lama of Tibet, Ram Dass, Christina Grof, Stan Grof, Lex Hixon, Jack Kornfield, Sonja Margulies, Huston Smith, William Thetford and Ken Wilber. I am also grateful to many other women and men who have been my companions at different times on this fantastic voyage, and whose friendship I shall always treasure.

Introduction

WE LIVE IN A WORLD OF DANGEROUS ILLU-
sions. False promises of happiness from the latest consumer products or
security from a bigger arsenal of weapons mislead us into believing that
peace is possible if we can only accumulate more money, more power or
more control over nature. These are some of the illusions we pursue when
we identify with an isolated, skin-encapsulated ego.

Contemporary global culture is predominantly egocentric and materialistic, plagued by alienation and violence. The pervasiveness of social injustice and ecological disasters can easily lead to a sense of futility and despair.
Some people hide from despair in addictions and obsessive preoccupation
with material possessions; others seek solace in beliefs that promise escape
or immortality.

Since the major threats to life on earth are caused by human behavior,
the need for changing consciousness is urgent. Global crises reflect values,
beliefs and attitudes that seem to ignore our relationship to nature. Unexamined beliefs can be dangerous to ourselves, our children and the earth.
Future generations will bear the burden of our addictions and illusions that
promise salvation while threatening annihilation.

Postmodern worldviews give scant support to the notion of a spiritual
reality. Yet a restless and pervasive hunger for living spirituality has led to
widespread interest in new religious movements, ancient esoteric traditions
and a variety of psychospiritual techniques that promise liberation or
enlightenment. The spiritual quest is no longer the property of organized
religion, nor is it the privilege of a few individuals who have made a formal
commitment to religious life.

Illusions about spirituality have long been debunked in scientific circles.
The materialistic worldview that assumes consciousness is only a byproduct
of randomly generated matter is seldom questioned in secular society.
Religion, then, is presumed to be an opiate of the masses and spirituality
no more than a palliative for those who cannot face the existential reality

1

of our inevitable death. Perhaps the most dangerous illusion is the belief that human beings are free of illusions as they persist in pursuing money, sex and power, while their souls are consumed by greed, guilt and anger.

On the other hand, some illusions seem to serve a useful purpose on a path of awakening that leads from ignorance to understanding and from bondage to freedom. A person on a spiritual path who is primarily identified with the soul rather than the ego may begin to question the values and motivations that seem to keep the soul in bondage.

It seems to me that the soul on a spiritual path must traverse both the outer world of ego and the inner world of soul before reaching liberation. Sometimes illusions that help to extricate us from bondage to the world of ego can entangle the soul in shadowy, distorted forms of spirituality that do not lead to freedom. Some of the most pervasive distortions are associated with the yearning for safety, the denial of death, the search for love, beliefs about the soul and the fascination with empowerment and enlightenment.

In this book I want to share reflections on widespread beliefs about the spiritual path and the nature of the soul. In my own life this exploration has led me from the world of ego through the world of soul to a profound appreciation of spiritual freedom. On the way to freedom I think everyone encounters both the personal shadow, those aspects of the self that are feared and despised, and the shadow side of idealized spirituality. This encounter stirs some of our most deep-seated fears and desires related to love, sex and death. When we are willing to face our fears and make an effort to see through self-deception, a deeper awareness of the mystery of enlightenment leads us back to the practical task of nurturing spirituality as a source of healing and wholeness for ourselves and the earth.

CHAPTER 1

Golden Chains
on the Spiritual Path

*The soul that is attached to anything, however much good there
may be in it, will not arrive at the liberty of divine union. For
whether it be a strong wire rope or a slender and delicate thread
that holds the bird, it matters not, if it really holds it fast; for,
until the cord be broken, the bird cannot fly.*

—St. John of the Cross

THE SEEDS OF GRASSROOTS SPIRITUALITY
seem to be springing up everywhere through the cracks in the old order.
Evidence of spiritual renewal can be found in many segments of society
amidst the crumbling ideologies of the modern era. As the race between
consciousness and catastrophe accelerates and people struggle to make
sense of a rapidly changing world, they are increasingly dissatisfied with religious dogma that seems irrelevant to contemporary life. Yet the search for
meaning and authentic spiritual experience seems increasingly widespread.

The quest for wholeness brings us face to face with our personal shadows
as well as the collective shadow that is reflected in the hypocrisy, greed,
violence and other excesses of our culture. In the analytical psychology
of Carl Jung, the shadow is defined as those repressed elements of the
personality that are unacceptable to the ego, with which we do not wish to
be identified. The cultural shadow is constellated when a culture represses
awareness of what it does not want to see in itself. Although we usually
think of the shadow as negative, it also contains positive aspects that we

have denied. In our search for healing and wholeness we need to integrate those aspects of ourselves that are hidden in the shadow.[1]

The shadow side of spirituality has been all too evident in holy wars and fanaticism all over the world throughout history. It is always easier to see the shadow in others than in ourselves. In this century Americans have projected the collective shadow onto all German and Japanese people during World War II, then onto the Soviet people during the Cold War, seeing them as evil until our nations made peace and we recognized that we could be friends with the people. Now that we do not have a foreign enemy we are forced to face our own dark side at home.

Many people have seen the personal shadow side of spiritual leaders who preach moral virtue and behave in socially unacceptable ways, ranging from alcoholism to misuse of funds to sexual misconduct. The destructive power of the unacknowledged shadow is starkly evident in such cult behavior as the mass suicide in Jonestown or the more recent tragedy in Waco, Texas, when the Branch Davidians chose death rather than surrender to civil authorities. I remember talking with two survivors of Jonestown and other former cult members as part of a research project in new religious movements about a decade ago. What impressed me most about them was the idealism that had blinded them to the shadow side of their leaders and their organizations.

We wonder how intelligent people could be led astray until we remember that we are all vulnerable to collective projections of the shadow if we do not acknowledge our own. It is more difficult to admit that any one of us may fall prey to our own dark side if we have suppressed it and are not aware of it. I agree with Jung's statement that we do not become enlightened by imagining figures of light, but by making the darkness conscious.[2] An authentic, vital spiritual life calls for bringing our shadows to light and discovering what they reveal.

OLD MYTHS AND NEW REALITIES

Ancient beliefs identified the shadow with the soul. The Romans believed that the "shade" went to the underworld Land of Shades after death. In pagan Europe the ghosts of ancestors were also described as shadows. In medieval Europe soullessness was indicated by lack of a shadow, and those who gave their souls to the devil could be distinguished by lack of a shadow. The most famous shadowless person was Peter Schlemihl, a fool in Jewish folklore who was tricked by the devil into parting with his shadow.[3]

In our materialistic, secular society the soul has been relegated to the shadowlands of the unconscious, along with all the other unacceptable parts of ourselves. Whether we think of the shadow as the unacceptable "other" in the psyche or the voice of the soul that has been repressed, it makes itself known to us whenever we turn attention to the inner world in search of spiritual renewal. Authentic spirituality cannot ignore the shadow.

Authentic spirituality implies awareness of who we are as whole human beings—including body, emotions, mind, soul and Spirit—existing in a web of interdependent relationships with the earth and the cosmos. Authentic spirituality contributes to a sense of freedom and inner peace, and to love, service and responsibility in the world. I believe authentic spirituality is a powerful force for healing and social change.

I think of spirituality as a subjective experience of the sacred. As an integral part of human life expressed in many different ways, spirituality certainly is not the exclusive property of any particular group or religion. It exists both within and outside of religious traditions, in the hearts and minds of men and women everywhere.

Historically, questioning conventional beliefs involved considerable risk; innumerable lives have been sacrificed in defense of both religious and secular ideologies. The collective myths that give meaning to existence are often sacrosanct, and many people are willing to die—or kill—to defend them.

In our pluralistic postmodern world, however, we have the opportunity to explore a variety of different beliefs. Many people who say they are on a spiritual path today are not formally affiliated with traditional religions. In this climate, where one person's religion is another's myth, and what is true from one perspective is an illusion from another, the spiritual path itself may appear to be only an illusion. Yet, in my experience, the path can lead a seeker from fear to love and from bondage to freedom.

My own journey on the spiritual path, as an explorer, an educator and a psychotherapist, has given me many opportunities to communicate with people of different cultural backgrounds about their deepest hopes and fears. It has offered me a way of understanding how spirituality contributes to healing and joy in our lives. Spiritual practice has also deepened my appreciation of nature, beauty and the arts, as well as expanding my capacity for love and compassion. As long as I am open to learning, the boundaries of my world seem to keep expanding into a vast spiritual universe.

My curiosity about the world and human nature has led me to explore many paths. I appreciate ways that lead to wholeness, where no part of what we are is excluded. Whereas unhealthy forms of spirituality tend to deny the shadow and imprison the soul, healthy spirituality does not deny the existence of any part of our humanity, nor exclude any aspect of reality.

Although I like to think of myself as a person who is in touch with reality rather than living in a dreamworld of illusion, I have found that the task of differentiating truth from illusion on the spiritual path is not always easy. Illusions may be defined as perceptions or images that deceive the mind and are confused with reality.

When we are unconscious of how beliefs shape perceptions, we tend to see only what conforms to our worldview. Sometimes we seem to live in a dreamworld, mistaking illusions for reality and partial perceptions for truth. I have come to accept the fact that perceptions are always partial and often distorted, and to allow that there is always more than one way of interpreting what I see.

The wisdom teachings of various spiritual traditions say that it is possible to awaken from dreams of fear and isolation to a reality of peace and joy. To discover for myself whether this is true, I have found it necessary to question many myths and assumptions that others seem to take for granted. For example, I have often questioned the relative merits of traditional forms of spiritual practice while also recognizing their value.

I have learned a lot from reading myths as metaphors of human experience. It was a revelation to me when I realized that many myths and stories reflected psychological truths about the inner world rather than literal facts. I now think of them as collective dreams that reflect the human condition and, like most dreams, they can be interpreted in various ways. Unfortunately, when myths are taken literally, they become dogma. Furthermore, myths that are helpful at one stage of the journey may later become inappropriate and constricting. The same myths that point the way to liberation can become limiting beliefs if one fails to see that they point to a reality beyond themselves.

Recognizing that symbolic representations of reality, like personal perceptions, can only be partial, I can appreciate them without mistaking them for absolute truth. If we fail to recognize the relative nature of these representations, it is easy to become enmeshed in a web of illusions. These entangling illusions are known as golden chains that attract attention at first glance and yet may prevent liberation if we become attached to them.

The term *golden chains* has been used in different traditions to refer to subtle distractions and temptations that may be encountered on the path. In Zen Buddhism, for example, golden chains are *makyo*, the fascinating visions that obscure the true nature of mind and reality. In some traditions golden chains refer to attachments to particular forms of practice, or attachment to piety and self-righteousness. Sometimes attachment to a teacher can also become a golden chain. Any beliefs or practices that cannot be questioned tend to become golden chains that constrict awareness and inhibit spiritual freedom.

Paradoxically, golden chains also serve a purpose on the path. As positive illusions they attract attention and provide images that engage the imagination and give form to intuitive perceptions. When used skillfully they can be instrumental devices for healing and spiritual awakening.

Medical research indicates that positive beliefs and illusions can contribute to both physical and psychological well-being. For example, in a book entitled *Positive Illusions: Creative Self-Deception and the Healthy Mind,* Shelly Taylor argues that overly positive self-evaluations and unrealistic optimism appear to promote mental health, including the ability to care about others, to be happy and to engage in productive and creative work.[4]

Philosopher Huston Smith calls positive spiritual illusions "celestial mirages" which, he says, are designed to "catch as in a golden net the greatest possible number of creatures plunged in ignorance, suffering, and darkness."[5] At one stage such illusions can provide spiritual nourishment. At a later stage they can become spiritual junk food that fails to satisfy the hunger of the soul.

When such expedient, provisional means of instruction are mistaken for final truth and turned into dogma, they can become a prison for the soul and inhibit further growth. Those who aspire to spiritual freedom and seek truth rather than illusion must be willing, eventually, to relinquish even the finest golden chains on the spiritual path. Kalu Rimpoche, a Tibetan sage, said,

> We live in illusion, the appearance of things.
> But there is a reality. We are that reality.

SYMBOLS AND METAPHORS OF THE PATH

The "path" is a metaphor of spiritual growth that appears in some form in all cultures, giving life a sense of purpose. For some, the spiritual path is the unfolding of the soul's relationship to God. Others who travel the path may be agnostic, nontheistic (e.g., Buddhism) or polytheistic (e.g., Hinduism and shamanism). The path may then be regarded as a process of awakening, of recognizing one's Buddha nature or reclaiming the true Self.

Those who do not understand the path may dismiss it as an illusory compensation for an empty life, an avoidance of existential realities or "an opiate for the masses." I have met many people who felt this way about spirituality until they had an experience that changed their minds. For some this might be falling in love; for others, a close encounter with death. Whatever the initial opening to a spiritual reality, those who explore a path are drawn deeper into life's mysteries.

Metaphorically, a path suggests an intimate, personal journey. I walk a path by my own efforts. I may find companions along the way, yet their path is never identical to mine. A path is not a freeway. Riding a bus, a train or an airplane is not the same as exploring a path. Collective modes of transportation are efficient for getting to a predetermined destination, but the solitary path of the inward journey takes us into another dimension of consciousness where perception of the world is transformed. When this happens, the world which seemed to be a terrifying, insane place of ignorance and delusion may be perceived as a sacred place of beauty and harmony. For heaven is spread upon the earth, but most of us do not see it.[6]

Once embarked on a spiritual path, a seeker may discover a previously unsuspected realm of subtle, psychic realities. Exploring these realms means encountering all that we are, including those aspects of ourselves that have been disowned. Any part of the psyche that has been denied, suppressed or ignored can then be reclaimed and reintegrated in a new vision of wholeness.

In exploring various paths, I have found it helpful to learn the language of symbols that speak for the soul in dreams, reverie and contemplation. Symbols are a universal language that both reveal and conceal the reality they represent. Although the meaning of symbols may seem obscure at first, people who spontaneously envision symbols are often intuitively able to decipher their meaning, and the art of interpretation improves with practice. Symbolic realms of perception become increasingly meaningful when a person turns attention to the inner life.

Symbolic perception appears to mediate spiritual experiences for people in all cultures regardless of race, gender, age or socio-economic status. Certain archetypes, such as mother and father, appear in some form in all cultures. However, what symbols are perceived, and their interpretation, are largely determined by cultural expectation. Thus a Tibetan encounters peaceful and wrathful deities, while a Christian sees angels, demons, Jesus or Satan. Beyond form, anybody may see white light.

CONSCIOUS EVOLUTION

Paradoxically, turning attention to the inner life can make us acutely aware of the beauty and fragility of the earth. Since our collective habits of behavior appear to be leading toward annihilation, recognition of our capacity for conscious evolution has become an increasingly compelling necessity. Spiritual awareness of our relationship to the whole earth can no longer be considered the prerogative of a few introverted individuals. Although it may take a leap of faith to believe that a radical shift in human consciousness is possible, this global mind change may be necessary to shift our collective trajectory from self-destruction to self-renewal.

From the perspective of deep ecology—the discipline that studies fundamental questions about the human relationship to nature—human beings need to shift their sense of identity from an *egocentric* view of themselves to an *ecocentric* view that recognizes their essential interdependence. This is one of the central tenets of deep ecology:

> Spiritual growth, or unfolding, begins when we cease to understand or see ourselves as isolated and narrow competing egos and begin to identify with other humans from our family and friends to, eventually, our species. But the deep ecology sense of self requires a further maturity and growth, and identification which goes beyond humanity to include the nonhuman world.[7]

Deep ecologist Arne Naess says that if we wish benevolent action to flourish, we need to understand how people become benevolent through natural inclination.[8] This is a process of psychological and spiritual maturation whereby they outgrow their exclusive identification with a separated, isolated ego.

Benevolent action cannot be coerced. A level of consciousness from which altruistic action flows naturally depends on a shift in motivation from fear and greed to love and compassion. This shift in motivation is an essential part of spiritual development that fosters compassionate action in the world. Conscious evolution implies that this process can be intentionally accelerated.

Many spiritual paths offer guidelines for this transition from egocentric self-absorption to an expanded empathic identification with all creatures as well as deepening awareness of the meaning of spiritual life. More widespread appreciation of spiritual paths that help replace egocentric behavior based on ignorance and fear with understanding, compassion and generosity could, therefore, make a significant contribution to a sustainable society and a livable world.

Sometimes conscious evolution and empathic identification with others begins with a personal crisis. Claire, for example, was a woman in her early forties who came to see me when her husband died suddenly of a heart attack. She found herself alone, going through the predictable stages of disbelief, rage and grief. During her mourning she struggled with depression and a sense that her life had lost its meaning. In time, she was gradually able to accept the reality of death, and she began a meditation practice that gave her new ways of thinking about dying. The meditation also gave her a taste of freedom and inner peace she had never known before. She became actively involved in hospice work and discovered that her own confrontation with deep sorrow had given her a way to connect with others that she would never have thought possible before her husband died. Over the next few years Claire's spiritual practice deepened and she grew into a woman of wisdom, whose presence and compassionate work brought comfort and solace to many who were facing grief and loss.

From Claire and others I have learned that despair in the face of tragedy is not insurmountable. Healing is always possible. Although spiritual practice may initially be sought for relief of personal pain, if we continue on the path, increasing illumination can expand awareness of spiritual dimensions of healing.

When life is regarded as a conscious evolutionary journey, personal melodramas become relatively less important, while myths and stories that point beyond ego become increasingly meaningful. Awareness of this symbolic dimension reminds us that we are connected to the whole human race and the cosmos. Our personal experience can then be perceived as a microcosm of the whole human experience, and our pain reflects the pain of the world. Recognizing shared spiritual experiences also helps us understand how we participate in the creative intelligence of the universe, and thereby contribute to conscious evolution.

PATHS OF THE SOUL

People who follow a spiritual path often become increasingly identified with being a soul rather than an ego. As explained in the next chapter, this identification tends to be more encompassing of human possibilities and imbues life with new meaning.

Many different spiritual paths are currently available. Among those symbolically portrayed as leading up a mountain, some are hard and narrow, others soft and gentle. Some are more scenic and meandering than others, and many seem to spiral into new ways of perceiving reality. All ostensibly lead to a summit of spiritual maturity, described by such terms as enlightenment, salvation or liberation. Other metaphors of spiritual development include escape from captivity followed by a sojourn in the wilderness, winding from the periphery to the center of a labyrinth, or cultivating a garden.

In Dante's classic allegory *The Divine Comedy*, the journey begins with waking up in the middle of a dark wood. The first stage of the journey is a descent into hell. Metaphorically we can read this as an encounter with the shadow, a witnessing of the suffering of souls trapped by their own desires. This is followed by ascent of the mountain of purgatory where purification takes place and culminates in paradise.

Although paths differ in some respects, they also share some features in common. First of all, they can be grouped into paths of attainment and paths of surrender. Paths of attainment point to stages of spiritual development and give instructions for progress on the path. Paths of surrender, such as some devotional paths and those that are called "always, already" paths, may tell you there is nothing to attain; you are already that which you are seeking. You have only to wake up to who and what you are to discover that Spirit, as the ground of being, is always present wherever you are, whether you know it or not. Attainment demands effort and discipline; surrender demands patience and self-containment.

In Buddhism these two approaches are quite distinct. For example, teachings that emphasize stages of attainment through practice are distinguished from those that emphasize waking up to the realization of our inherent Buddha nature. The former are teachings of gradual enlightenment; the latter are called teachings of sudden enlightenment. These two ways of teaching can be viewed as complementary rather than conflictive.

Paths of attainment provide expedient teachings that help you take one step at a time, assuring you that if you make sufficient effort you will reach liberation or enlightenment. They cultivate discipline and may include practices of renunciation and purification. The paths of surrender, or always, already paths, emphasize the final teachings which remind you ·that what you are seeking is already hidden in the depths of your own being. *Tat tvam asi*, thou art that. Love, lover and beloved are one.

Although these two approaches differ in their methods of instruction, both are necessary. Effort, patience and surrender are all required for letting go of limited self-concepts, integrating the shadow and awakening to a spiritual reality.

Other distinctions can be made between paths of knowledge, paths of love and paths of service, to name a few. One thing they have in common is that they all progress through stages of spiritual development as part of the evolution of consciousness. Each one involves both effort and surrender at some point along the way. Stages are mapped metaphorically according to the cultural context in which they are rooted.

For example, in the Indian tradition of kundalini yoga, the evolutionary process of awakening consciousness is symbolized by a snake. In an unawakened state the serpent is portrayed as coiled at the base of the spine. When it awakens, the kundalini energy represented by the snake moves up the spine, opening the psychic energy centers called chakras. At the level of the first chakra, consciousness is concerned only with basic survival. At the level of the second chakra, consciousness is preoccupied with sex and personal relationships. The third chakra, located at the solar plexus, is associated with power. These three levels have been characterized as "me" consciousness, "you and me" consciousness and "we all" consciousness, respectively, each one of which encompasses a larger reality. In psychological terms, awakening of the first three chakras corresponds to ego development. The person or culture that has evolved only as far as the third chakra is likely to be predominantly concerned with money, sex and power.

The fourth chakra, at the level of the heart, is associated with love and the awakening of spiritual values. When consciousness reaches the level of the heart, love becomes a compelling force and a powerful motivation. At this point concern for the welfare of others may take precedence over personal desires. At the level of the fifth and sixth chakras consciousness is expressed in creativity and spiritual vision. Finally, individual consciousness dissolves into Spirit or universal consciousness when it reaches the seventh chakra, at and beyond the crown of the head.

For practitioners of kundalini yoga, the rising of the kundalini is sometimes experienced as currents of electrical energy moving up the spine. These experiences may be induced by transmission from a guru, or they may occur spontaneously, particularly in association with intensive meditation. These dramatic experiences that are usually interpreted as signs of spiritual awakening can also be emotionally and physically disruptive. Guidance from an experienced teacher can be helpful for anyone who is disturbed by them. If such experiences are sought as ends in themselves rather than occurring in the context of an authentic spiritual path, they can become entangling golden chains. On the other hand, if they are discredited or invalidated, stress may be increased rather than alleviated.

In the Christian tradition, Saint Teresa of Avila used the metaphor of the butterfly to describe the process of transformation on the spiritual path. At first one is like a caterpillar, greedy for teachings, searching for spiritual nourishment from external sources. After a time, when one recognizes that turning inward is essential, one is drawn to silence and contemplation. One spins a cocoon of solitude and enters into the innermost chambers of what she called the interior castle. When stillness reigns and it appears that nothing is happening, God does the work, and transformation takes place. The soul emerges as a butterfly into the experience of light. In the final stage of mystical union, when the separate self disappears, the butterfly dies. Even this sacred marriage, however, is not the end of the journey. As the soul cannot hold on to these ecstatic, transcendent states, one returns to service in the everyday world. This stage is known as "the fruitfulness of the soul."

Another metaphoric mapping of stages is depicted in the ten ox-herding pictures of Zen Buddhism. Here the ox symbolizes our true nature. Again, the search begins in the external world. Here one follows the tracks by studying spiritual teachings, then catches a glimpse of the ox by recognizing that it can be found only in direct experience. In time, when one has quieted the mind and mastered the energies that are released, one makes friends with the limitations of ego and rides the ox home. At home in the universe, the sage remains alone until everything vanishes, only to be recreated moment by moment. The sage has become one with the Source. From there the sage returns to the marketplace of the world with helping hands, to awaken others. The sage who manifests enlightenment overflows with life-energy and compassionate love. He or she has gone beyond, not to move away from humanity but to return completely into the human world.[9] Here the sage follows no path and remains invisible to those who lack spiritual discernment.

I recognize parts of my own path reflected in all of these descriptions, and I have found the sequence of stages portrayed in the ox-herding pictures particularly meaningful. They have helped me to recognize illusions of progress in the early stages and remind me that I must always return to being here now.

THE HEALING JOURNEY

For many people in contemporary Western society the spiritual journey begins with inner work undertaken in psychotherapy. Although *psychology* originally meant the study of the soul, conventional psychology tried to divorce itself from religious terminology in order to gain respect as a science. Today, however, many psychotherapists are interested in spirituality and recognize its healing potential.[10]

Carl Jung, the Swiss psychiatrist whose pioneering work in depth psychology is widely respected, believed that psychological problems must be understood as the suffering of a soul that has not yet discovered its meaning, and that healing depends on a deep experience of Spirit.[11]

More recently, Abraham Maslow's study of self-actualizing people indicated that when basic needs for security, love and self-esteem are sufficiently satisfied, healthy people are motivated by altruism and service, and they aspire to self-transcendence and creative contribution.[12] Maslow found that the healthiest people in our society had a profound awareness of spirituality in their lives, although they were not necessarily religious.

Unfortunately, many people who fail to find a sense of meaning in conventional religion find themselves living in a wasteland of spiritual deprivation. Some of them discover a wealth of spiritual resources within the psyche in the process of psychotherapy. Sometimes this healing journey begins with a personal crisis, sometimes with a vague feeling of discontent. It may also be catalyzed by a transpersonal experience or any major turning point. For one woman the spiritual quest began when her child died. Another discovered it in a love relationship. One man remembered that he had started asking what God wanted him to do with his life when he was only thirteen.

John was a man whose spiritual journey began when he had a powerful psychedelic experience in college. The experience was both ecstatic and terrifying. He felt that he suddenly understood the significance of his choices in life as light and dark forces seemed to struggle for control of his mind. After that experience, John resolved that he would not take any more drugs, but from then on his spiritual life was of deep and central importance to him.

For me the spiritual quest began in earnest in the wake of a profound transpersonal experience in which I seemed to merge with the world around me. At a time when my life was primarily devoted to childcare and housekeeping, I often felt lonely, living in the country far away from friends and relatives. One day my heart opened to an experience of love that no words could describe. On a quiet afternoon, while gazing at a flowering tree, a sense of joy bubbled up inside me. As I watched a ladybug busily scrambling about in the grass, I had a new awareness of life feeding on life, and a clear insight into how truth makes us free. My awareness seemed to open to a reality I had intuited yet never known directly, in which boundaries dissolved and I was one with all of creation. I felt that opening to this experience meant saying yes to life with all of its pain and paradox.

Reflecting on this experience, my previous studies of comparative religion seemed superficial and limited concepts of God seemed to have little to do with reality. Terms such as being-consciousness-bliss suddenly made sense and took on new meaning. Although I could not communicate what this experience had meant to me, I wanted to understand it. I went back to graduate school to study psychology, but traditional psychology had very little to say about transpersonal experiences.

Whatever the precipitating factor, it seems that a path is revealed to those who seek for it wholeheartedly. Once a person is consciously on a spiritual path, everything becomes part of the journey. Psychotherapy, art, literature, myths, philosophy and other disciplines can all contribute to spiritual realization.

In psychotherapy the path is sometimes envisioned as a healing journey of growth toward wholeness. This process can include healing emotional wounds from childhood, uncovering unconscious conflicts and plumbing the depths of the psyche. Pursued in depth, this path can lead to archetypal dimensions of consciousness, where spiritual realities are encountered as powerful unconscious forces.

The journey to wholeness usually involves restoring balance and expanding awareness through reclaiming what has been denied, repressed or overlooked. In a patriarchal culture restoring this balance includes reclaiming feminine values such as relatedness, empathy, warmth and caring, particularly for men. For women the imbalance may be the opposite if they have been enculturated to believe that only their femininity is acceptable. I have seen many women regain a feeling of well-being when they claimed and accepted the active, dynamic side of themselves that is sometimes disparaged as too masculine.

Women and men may have different healing tasks to accomplish on the spiritual path, yet in reclaiming the soul both may go through the classic stages of the mythical heroic journeys. Many women find it difficult to relate to hero myths that are essentially masculine stories, although fairy-tale heroines, such as Dorothy in the Land of Oz, Alice in Wonderland or Snow White, can also mirror the process of spiritual awakening. No single metaphor will fit everyone, male or female. Some people resonate to fairy tales or Sufi stories, others to Celtic, Greek or Egyptian mythology, others to Indian, Chinese or Native American stories.

Whatever the metaphor or cultural context, recurring themes on the journey to freedom include hearing a call and undertaking a period of preparation. On the other hand, a person may sometimes be plunged into a spiritual crisis with no preparation at all. Spiritual emergencies have received increasing attention in the last decade,[13] although processes of gradual awakening that are less noticeable are probably more common. New beginnings are often marked by initiations, and illuminating, transformative experiences happen equally to men and women. Finally, the completion of healing often includes a return to the place of departure, seeing it with new eyes, as if for the first time.

The call:

A call to spiritual awakening may be heard at any time. Some people feel called to a spiritual life at an early age. Others do not heed the call until late in life. Some never hear it at all. It may come as a shock, as in a close call with death or as a time when life seems hard and pointless. Sometimes the call is heard first in a dream and possibilities may be intuited long before they are fully recognized. The call may also be felt as divine discontent or vague dissatisfaction when everything seems to be going well.

Sometimes a person feels impelled to seek psychological help in finding a more meaningful sense of existence. If one responds to the call by entering into a self-disclosing process of psychotherapy, a journey begins that is potentially life changing. Although the initial motivation for entering psychotherapy may be simply a desire to relieve pain, a spiritual wake-up call may include an urge to understand oneself and one's relationship to the cosmos more fully.

Katie, who had attained everything she thought she wanted in the outer world, came into my office complaining of a desperate longing for something more. She knew she did not want more of what she already had. She was ready to begin the spiritual quest that she had avoided for nearly forty years.

Answering the call often entails redefining priorities. Sometimes it means taking time out from busy activities to reflect on the life of the soul. Some people respond to the call by withdrawing for a time from their usual occupations, taking time in solitude for reflection, meditation or contemplation. Others find a supportive relationship with a therapist, teacher or friend indispensable. Some are called to service in the world, like Mother Teresa of Calcutta or Martin Luther King. Most people find that both solitude and service can deepen awareness of soul.

The golden chains that prevent answering the call are often the seductive aspects of the world of ego. Success, for example, is one that can be all-consuming. The virtues associated with service and codependency are also golden chains that may seem difficult to break. Any self-concept that keeps one tied to unsatisfying old habits is a hindrance to progress on the path.

Preparation:

Preparation for the spiritual journey usually begins with self-examination. Reflecting on personal history and letting go of resentments and regrets releases us from the past. When suffering is acknowledged and old secrets confessed, we are relieved of unnecessary burdens. Although this process is necessary, obsessive preoccupation with the past can be another golden chain that keeps us in bondage to the past, while we overlook the freedom of this moment.

Another aspect of preparation that easily becomes a golden chain is the confrontation with the shadow. Each person who confronts the personal shadow, the dark and despised aspects of oneself, can recognize the dangers of becoming obsessed with it. The shadow is endlessly fascinating and can engage our attention for a lifetime.

Preparation may take either a short or a long time, depending on how fearful we are about letting go of defensive patterns of resistance. Guilt, fear, anger, depression, dependency or any other psychological issues can make the journey seem slow and arduous at first. Letting go of resistance becomes easier when feelings can be explored in a safe environment with the help of a guide who can help one cut through self-deception and recognize when a particular process has served its purpose and is no longer useful.

Although we can find help along the way, each one of us travels this path alone, just as each of us is born alone and dies alone. In the legends of King Arthur's court, each knight who set out in search of the Holy Grail had to ride into the dark forest alone. Likewise, each person who seeks the wisdom of the grail must face the inner world alone. In time each one may learn to listen to inner guidance to determine where help can be found and when a particular method that was helpful at an earlier time has become an obstacle to further progress on the path.

Initiation:

Initiation usually designates a new beginning. On the spiritual path initiations may be formal, as in ordination, or informal, as in dreams or spontaneous experiences. Esoteric or secret initiations sometimes involve ecstatic experiences, in which one seems to be transported out of oneself. Such experiences can have a profoundly healing effect and provide a new perspective on being in the world. Psychotherapy that leads a person into the depths of the psyche tends to encourage *enstatic* experiences, in which one goes into the center of the self. Either the enstatic or the ecstatic experience can lead to a fundamental recognition of our spiritual nature.

Dramatic examples of initiation, such as the sudden conversion of Saul of Tarsus on the road to Damascus, or the contemporary Native American sun dance, can radically transform a person's life. Other initiations may not appear to have any effects at all. Furthermore, some initiations are gradual rather than sudden, as when a person slowly begins to explore transpersonal work in psychotherapy.

One person who was committed to deep work in psychotherapy told me that she thought of me, her therapist, as a midwife to her soul. Her descent into the darkest regions of the psyche was her initiation into inner work, and the subsequent stages of struggle to claim a new sense of identity could certainly be viewed as a slowly unfolding process of death and rebirth.

Another woman who had given up a high paying corporate job to study psychology, told me the following dream:

> I am in the family chapel of an old castle. A female corpse is wheeled in on a gurney. As I watch, the woman revives and assumes a priestess-like demeanor. She flies up to the altar and draws a map of an elaborate maze. She points to a remote area, and I now seem to be following the map. When I arrive at my destination, I see a dark figure washing his hands. When he turns toward me, I see he is an elegant black man with Rastafarian dreadlocks, wearing a long red cloak woven with gold. He rushes toward me, and I have no time to run away. As he touches me, my whole body is jolted with an electric shock. I wake up tingling all over.

This woman's inner work in psychotherapy and meditation helped her interpret this dream as an initiation. She recognized the corpse as a part of herself which had died and now seemed to be resurrected. Following a path which led to the encounter with the unfamiliar dark masculine figure was energizing and empowering for her. Some time later she told me that she realized the red-robed man reminded her of the Hermit in the Tarot cards, a figure she had identified as the image of her soul.

A person on a spiritual path may experience many different kinds of initiation. In addition to being depicted as a kind of death and rebirth, initiation may be portrayed as an inner marriage, a union of opposites or the joining of masculine and feminine elements in the psyche. Sometimes, when an initiation occurs in nature, as on a vision quest, nature is perceived as a mirror of the psyche, and one may notice correspondences that were overlooked before.

Dramatic initiations involving radically altered states of consciousness, such as those associated with shamanic vision quests, intensive meditation or psychoactive medicine journeys, may be either healing or disruptive, depending partly on the psychological state of the person going through them, and partly on how the experience is subsequently integrated.

I remember feeling energized and inspired after an initiation experience with Baba Muktananda, a Hindu teacher, at an intensive retreat in 1981. The effects were temporary, however, and I was not aware of any significant lasting impact. In the ensuing years I learned that not everyone found such experiences beneficial. I talked with some people who found similar experiences emotionally disturbing and sometimes severely disruptive. Unfortunately, people who are emotionally unstable tend to be attracted to rituals of initiation, sometimes hoping that their difficulties will be magically resolved. I have often worked with people suffering from psychological stress after initiations that uncover repressed material.

For example, one young woman who had received *shaktipat*, a transmission of energy from her guru, experienced recurring surges of what she described as electrical currents rushing up her spine that disturbed her sleep and made her extremely anxious. She understood this as an awakening of the kundalini energy which was not uncommon in this tradition, but she was not prepared for the intensity of what occurred. A combination of diet, exercise and psychotherapy helped her regain a sense of equilibrium, and she gained a new respect for the powers of the mind.

Although initiations do not necessarily resolve psychological difficulties, those that result in new perceptions of reality can help a person outgrow conditioned beliefs. Once a person has gained a different view of reality, it becomes difficult to pretend that there is only one way of seeing things. Sometimes an initiation can help one break out of habitual patterns of perception and see how thoughts, words and actions in the present shape the future, day by day. Such new ways of seeing offer both gifts and challenges on the path. Although not all initiations lead to spiritual freedom and responsibility, they can be a significant turning point in a person's life.

Steve, for example, was a man who managed his life well. He had a good job and a reasonably happy marriage. He came to see me because he was troubled by intrusive sadistic thoughts and occasional, uncontrolled fits of rage. He was not physically violent, although he had been severely beaten as a child. Steve decided to try meditation and found the practice helpful. In addition to initiating him into a way of witnessing his inner universe, meditation enabled him to quiet his mind and direct his attention voluntarily to the cultivation of positive emotions such as love and compassion. Gradually, as Steve worked through his own self-contempt and unearthed some of the painful, buried childhood memories, his anger diminished and he was no longer troubled by intrusive thoughts. When unwanted thoughts did arise, he could accept them without blame or indulgence and release them more easily.

Initiations that offer a glimpse of a different reality tend to loosen the bonds of some of the golden chains of illusion, and when a symbolic initiation is honored and integrated, it can be a great blessing on the path. Sometimes people abandon the quest as soon as they feel released from the past and free to love and work in the world in more fulfilling ways. Yet this new sense of freedom may be only the beginning of a journey to wholeness.

Some of the golden chains associated with powerful initiations include idolizing the initiator, becoming addicted to the intensity of the experience and thinking that one has achieved some special spiritual status as a result of the experience. Any of these can prevent further development and keep a person fixated at the beginning of the journey. In order to continue, the initiation experience, like all experiences, must be released.

Transformation:
The initiate who chooses to continue the quest rather than return prematurely to the distractions of the outer world will probably continue to feel the stirrings of divine discontent. After a powerful initiation, practices that were helpful before may seem flat and dull. Teachings that previously captured attention may not seem relevant, and what served a purpose earlier may become a burden. Beliefs that supported the journey at an earlier stage may now be perceived as binding golden chains. When methods that were useful at an earlier stage are relinquished, guidance must be sought once

again in order to find different approaches for the new phase. At this stage a person may need to ask for help in accessing inner resources.

Sometimes feelings of elation induced by initiations are followed by depression, since experiences, no matter how dramatic, are always temporary. Symbolically, entering the inner sanctum means passing between the opposites, represented by the guardians at the gate of the temple. In psychological terms, both inflation and deflation must be avoided. Ego inflation occurs when seekers think they have arrived at the end of the journey and know all the answers, when, in fact, they are just beginning. Ego deflation may be experienced as hopelessness or despair in the face of whatever seems overwhelming.

The guardians at the gate are sometimes interpreted as representing confusion and paradox. Those who are not deterred by confusion and paradox and continue the journey of transformation discover new dimensions of soul. For example, the inner sanctum may afford a glimpse of unitive consciousness, in which the soul recognizes its prior oneness with Spirit. This is the pinnacle, but not the end of the journey. It is sometimes described as becoming one with the Source, claiming the hidden treasure within or union with the deity. When the separation is healed, self and other disappear as separate entities. Such unitive mystical experiences, though ineffable, can be profoundly transformative.[14]

Transformative experiences that result in a fundamental reorientation of consciousness do not necessarily reach a unitive state. A near-death experience, for instance, can have a lasting impact on a person's beliefs, values and priorities while still leaving the separate self-sense intact. Other experiences that are less radical can still have a profound, far-reaching effect. A dream, for example, may reveal the possibility of transformation, although the power of the dream to bring about a lasting change in consciousness depends on whether or not it is consciously integrated with waking life. One successful young businessman who was deeply committed to the spiritual journey told me the following dream:

> I was walking on a road across the wilderness toward a beautiful, luxurious resort. I had been walking for a long time. There I met a friend, and we were enjoying ourselves in the company of other guests. My friend said we should continue to travel further out into the wilderness, as we had not reached the end of the road. I knew we would have to go on foot. It would be a long, difficult hike, and we probably would not get back before dark. I was not sure

if I wanted to go, but I agreed, and we set out across the desert. After walking for many miles, standing on a hillside overlooking a valley, I was surprised to see a whole forest of dogwood trees in bloom. Beyond the forest was the ocean. I was deeply moved, almost overwhelmed, by the beauty before me. We walked down through the woods to a stream and followed the stream to its source at a granite spring. We had reached the end of the road at last! I drank some water from the spring and was filled with joy and life energy. I had never tasted anything so sweet. I felt I was one with everything. Feeling thoroughly refreshed, we began the long journey back.

This dream could have been meaningful to anyone, but the dogwood trees had special significance for the dreamer who had grown up in an area where they bloomed every spring. The meaning of the dream was clear to him and needed no interpretation. He felt that the dream reflected his willingness to continue with his inner work and reclaim some of the positive aspects of childhood on the way to reconnecting with a deep inner source of inspiration and renewal. He knew he wanted to keep going and he did. The dream encouraged him to go deeper, and he was not disappointed. The dream also reassured him that he was on the right track.

Although certain dreams can be a doorway to mystical experience, a dream is not the same as a waking realization that leads to enduring transformation. Dreams can reflect a deep intuitive knowledge of states of consciousness that sometimes seem inaccessible from our ordinary, pre-occupied waking state. All too often, however, we tend to dismiss them as unreal.

Unlike initiation, which tends to be brief, transformation takes time. It is often a gradual process of reorientation rather than a sudden conversion experience. For example, if anger is to be transformed from destructive impulses into creative engagement, or pain and sorrow into compassionate action, one needs to cultivate patience and practice. Any lasting shift of motivation from fear to love and a change in behavior from egocentricity to altruism usually demands continuing effort and practice.

The people I know whose lives have been transformed by deep inner work have usually made persistent and sustained effort to live in accordance with what they have learned about themselves and the nature of consciousness. They are usually open to deep experiences, but do not seek them as ends in themselves. If a person becomes addicted to them, these powerful experiences can become the golden chains that prevent freedom of the soul.

Each of us must be willing to keep walking until we reach the end of the road and find the Source. When we have found it, we return to walk again on the way of everyday life. I do not know anyone on a spiritual path who has not struggled at times with doubt, disappointment and despair when the certainty of freedom seems to be lost. In the words of the Buddha,

> At the end of the way is freedom.
> Till then, patience.[15]

The return:

Fulfillment in time is not forever, and returning to the world one left behind to follow a call can be arduous and challenging. One may long to remain in an ecstatic, unitive state or be plagued by doubts and fear of loss. The task of the return is to carry the treasure or blessing back to the society one left to begin the quest. To me this means forgiving the past, accepting one's spiritual roots and sharing what has been discovered.

At this stage the challenge is one of integration. The self-scrutiny that was so essential earlier may now become a golden chain of self-indulgence. One's ego may want to make the most of what has been found and become inflated with self-importance, only to become deflated when others do not seem to appreciate the treasure. Learning to become invisible, to pass unnoticed by those who would hinder the return, can be helpful. I think this means that we have to know when not to talk about spiritual experiences if we want to honor what is most sacred. Expecting approval usually leads to disappointment.

When the awakened soul that pressed through to the culmination of the journey returns to the world with a new perception that renders it transparent to Spirit, there is nowhere to go and nothing to do but assist others along the way. As they say in Zen, before enlightenment, chop wood and carry water. After enlightenment, chop wood and carry water. To the physical eye the enlightened sage may be indistinguishable from other people, while radiating inner peace, joy and love.

The mythological journey that ends with return to everyday life does not address the final stage of old age in which senses begin to fade and physical powers diminish. The sage evidently surrenders to the inevitable and faces death without fear. In some traditions the body of an enlightened person is said to disappear into light. In her book *Old Age*, Helen Luke brings her insight to these final stages of the journey, reminding us of the necessity of forgiveness and surrender and the willingness to let go of everything.[16]

TRADITION AND THE PATH

The path that leads through psychological individuation as described here does not necessarily fit any formal system. It is, rather, a process of discovery that unfolds as a result of inner work and self-awareness. On the other hand, many traditional paths that are embedded in culture-bound religious forms have evolved over time and offer a wealth of collective wisdom. Wisdom and discernment are necessary on any path, although being on a spiritual path obviously does not require being religious in a conventional sense.

Tradition usually refers to a particular set of doctrines and rituals that have been practiced for generations among social groups, whereas spirituality is internal and experiential. Tradition tends to be associated with orthodoxy, authority and obedience rather than with autonomy and personal freedom. In time, as the original revelation of truth becomes codified and is continually reinterpreted, the pearls of wisdom tend to become encrusted with the mud of misperception and misunderstanding.

However, tradition is actually much more than custom and inherited patterns of thought, being inextricably linked with revelation and related to the transmission of knowledge and practices for spiritual development.[17] The founders of the world's great religions were human beings who taught what was revealed to them in their own transcendent experiences. Unfortunately, few conventional religions encourage such experiences in their followers, and the study of world religions tells us very little about the subjective experience of individuals who believe in them.

Among Eastern traditions familiar to Westerners are the four yogas of Indian philosophy: *karma yoga* (action), *bhakti yoga* (devotion), *jnana yoga* (knowledge) and *raja yoga* (perception or mental discipline). In Western Hermeticism the corresponding paths are symbolized by images of the pentacle, the cup, the sword and the wand, respectively. These are reflected in Carl Jung's psychological types as sensation, feeling, thinking and intuition. Wholeness presumably includes physical, emotional, mental and spiritual aspects of development. Seekers may therefore explore many paths and discover that each one enriches the others.

Those who defend tradition claim that without belonging to an established institution one may easily go astray and fall prey to self-deception.

Furthermore, a person who is not committed to a particular religious tradition is likely to be perceived as a dilettante by those who are. These are risks, but those who travel a path outside of traditional systems are not necessarily dilettantes, nor are those who follow traditional forms immune to self-deception. The wisest, like fools, are said to follow their own counsel. It seems that the further one goes along the way to spiritual maturity, the more one learns to trust inner guidance, and the more trustworthy the guidance becomes.

Religion provides spiritual nourishment for many people, and the great traditions offer indispensable teachings for anyone on a spiritual path. Religion may be compared to a basket that contains the fruit of spirituality. The earth then, may be compared to the garden in which the fruit ripens. However, fruit is not always contained in a basket.

The religions I find problematic are those that claim to offer the *only* way to spiritual awakening. Authentic spirituality manifesting as wisdom and compassion in action can be found in many traditions and outside them. Sometimes, however, truth is discovered only when systems have been transcended. I have found that acknowledging freedom and responsibility for spiritual choices is necessary for spiritual maturity regardless of affiliation to traditional forms of religion.

Sometimes people plagued by self-doubt and uncertainty may seek refuge in the golden chains of comforting collective illusions, even when they know they are false. Just as Dostoyevsky's Grand Inquisitor argued eloquently for giving people the security they seem to want instead of freedom, some people today shy away from the uncertainties of freedom and accept irrational beliefs in exchange for the reassurances. While some find it expedient to deny their autonomy and conform to collective norms, others find this intolerable.

In any tradition, dependency on golden chains of authority, though comforting at times, tends to undermine trust in one's own direct experience. To the extent that it fosters illusions, traditional authority becomes an obstacle to realization.

In a well-known teaching, the Buddha advised,

> Do not believe in what you have heard; do not believe in traditions because they have been handed down for many generations; do not believe anything because it is rumored and spoken of by many; do not believe merely because the written statement of some old sage is produced; do not believe in conjectures; do not believe merely

in the authority of your teachers and elders. After observation and analysis, when it agrees with reason and is conducive to the good and benefit of one and all, then accept it and live up to it.[18]

In the West, Ralph Waldo Emerson said it this way:

> Why should not we also enjoy an original relation to the universe? Why should not we have a poetry and philosophy of insight and not of tradition, and a religion by revelation to us, and not the history of theirs?[19]

The problem that many thoughtful people have with religion is that it seems to offer illusions in place of truth as a palliative to human suffering, and often fails to acknowledge and integrate the shadow. Yet truth can be discovered even among golden chains of illusion. Sri Aurobindo, the twentieth-century Indian sage, said that although illusions have no reality, they conceal our distortions of truth.[20] To be disillusioned, then, is to unmask wishful thinking and face the shadow. Following an authentic spiritual path, traditional or otherwise, requires a continuing commitment to discovering the truth that makes us free.

MAKING A SPIRITUAL CONNECTION

Whatever criticisms we may have of tradition, religion provides not only a creed, but also a code of ethics, a culture and community that can be essential to the spiritual life. Making a good connection with a spiritual community and a teacher can be a great help on any path. Teachers can help students reclaim their own souls and recognize golden chains. Wise teachers know that trust is often granted them by people who are anxious and confused and who want to turn over responsibility for their lives, as they would to a benevolent parent.[21] The resulting dependency, however, inevitably breeds resentment and conflict. A skillful teacher, therefore, respects and encourages self-determination. Teachers who would avoid the pitfalls of unacknowledged transference need to be aware of the corrupting influences of power and how it becomes a golden chain.

Stephen Mitchell, a well-known scholar and translator of spiritual texts, writes about his Zen Master who instructed him that his first job was to kill the Buddha. Mitchell knew that this meant he was to let go of any concept of a separate, superior, enlightened being outside of himself. The Master then said that his second job was to kill his parents. This meant accepting them as they were, not wanting anything from them. "Your third job," said the Master, "is to kill me."[22]

Killing seems to be a rather ruthless metaphor for letting go of attachment, yet killing the egocentric desire for others to respond in a particular way makes it possible to let go of needless personal pain. No matter how lofty, any idealization of idols, parents or teachers interferes with liberation.

Sometimes, when a person has finished with a particular phase of the journey, he or she may turn against a former teacher or community in anger. This is likely to happen when a person has stayed too long at a particular stage, or when the teacher has not encouraged the student's freedom of choice. Blaming the teacher does not help the student, but anger can achieve separation.

On the spiritual path everyone needs help at times. It therefore seems appropriate to honor the teachers and traditions that have helped us, without idealizing them. Eventually everyone may be perceived as a teacher and all of life as a process of learning.

We are all teachers insofar as we demonstrate what we value by how we live and relate to each other. Each of us lives our message, consciously or unconsciously, as the journey through time unfolds, and our choices determine what we become. Each of us must also determine the appropriate balance between solitude and community along the way. Both are necessary, both support the journey, and either one can become a golden chain.

The spiritual path is sometimes described as a journey of return to our original home. The process of awakening the soul to its original nature as Spirit is not a journey that takes place in geographical space or calendar time, although many have searched far and wide for teachers and teachings. The path begins and ends in our own backyard.

I once met a man at an airport who carried my bags and drove the van that took me to the city where I was attending a conference. Like most of his passengers, I was tired when we boarded the van. During the ride he told me that he had a profound epiphany while waiting to go through customs at Kennedy Airport in New York. He was returning from a long pilgrimage to India on a search for spiritual teachings. He had been disappointed by what he found. Here, in the place where he started, he realized that what he had been seeking was already here, and everywhere. His presence and attitude bespoke the authenticity of his story. Somehow everyone seemed to feel better after the ride. Years later, long after I had forgotten the conference, I remembered his story and understood something about the necessity of undertaking the search and the paradoxical nature of awakening.

When a person has had a spiritual awakening that affords a glimpse of states of mind in which a sense of ultimate belonging and awareness of love as the fundamental ground of being seems incontrovertibly real, other perceptions of reality seem narrow and limited. Those who have never had such experiences may think they are illusory, yet to dismiss them is to dismiss the wisdom of the saints and sages of all time.

The fact that many people cling to belief in the absence of experience and that some spiritual groups pander to the inner child that wants to be cared for by an omnipotent parent has led some people to see only the traps and psychological problems associated with the spiritual path. Yet the universal longing for living spirituality that heals the heart and nourishes the soul is ever present. For some, it becomes the only thing that matters. For others, spirituality is woven so unobtrusively into the fabric of their lives you might never notice it. The spiritual path does not require leaving the world, but it does mean shifting priorities and transforming our perception of reality.

In the early stages the spiritual path seemed to me to be a solitary journey which required letting go of previous self-concepts and relationships. I felt challenged to face my shadow and own my soul rather than transfer feelings of dependency from parents to spouse to spiritual teacher. I did not want to trade one conventional set of beliefs for another, so I pursued a path of spiritual inquiry, trying to learn from different traditions as well as from my personal experience. I soon discovered how valuable a community of fellow seekers can be. Although being a beginner, asking questions and trying different practices sometimes felt foolish, help seemed to be available when I asked for it. So I persisted in the journey, trusting an intuitive perception of something of infinite worth and unsurpassable truth, and I have not been disappointed.

The deeper we go into the depths of the individual psyche, the more we uncover universal themes. I like to think of each of the great traditions as a well that gives us access to the underground stream of living waters of spirituality. Although the soul in pursuit of spiritual goals can easily become entangled with golden chains, if we persist on the path the transformation of consciousness continues, increasing our awareness of love and freedom.

CHAPTER 2

Living in Two Worlds: The World of Ego and the World of Soul

Modern life is characterized by fundamental conflicts between religious worldviews that see humans as spiritual beings in a meaningful cosmos and a scientistic worldview that sees physical matter and physical energy as the only reality.[1]

—CHARLES TART

WE LIVE IN TWO WORLDS: THE OUTER world of ego and the inner world of soul. Many people suffer from being out of touch with the inner world of soul. Others suffer because they have tried to explore the world of soul without having come to terms with the world of ego. Freedom depends on acknowledging both worlds, harmonizing them and bringing them into balance.

The dualism of matter and spirit, body and soul that has pervaded Western thought for centuries usually fails to recognize the intimate interdependence and interpenetration of these apparent opposites. Although the illusion of separation between body and mind, and soul and Spirit, tends to perpetuate conflict and alienation, the distinction between ego and soul can serve a purpose on the path.

The world of ego and the world of soul correspond roughly to the exterior world and the interior world. Although the correspondence is not rigid, the ego is primarily oriented toward the visible world of objects, whereas the soul is oriented toward the inner world that is invisible to the senses. The invisible world of soul may be expressed in the outer world in the arts, in love relationships or in compassionate service. Conversely, the world of ego, concerned with accomplishments and appearances, may be internalized as aspiration or ambition.

Developing a healthy ego, capable of self-reliance and self-determination in the outer world, seems to be an essential step on the way to wholeness and self-fulfillment. For example, a healthy ego claims autonomy, sets boundaries and makes choices. Even the choice to practice a spiritual discipline leading to transcendence of ego is most effective when freely chosen. Although the ego is sometimes condemned by seekers who have recently discovered the joys of spiritual life, condemnation is not transcendence. To transcend is not to reject or eliminate something, but to include it in a larger view. Without a strong, healthy ego, a person can fall easily into illusion and self-deception. The ego becomes a problem only when it is alienated from the world of soul and ignorant of spiritual realities.

Conflict between the desires of the body-oriented ego and the longings of the soul sometimes becomes apparent in dreams and reveries. The inner and the outer world reflect each other, and conflict between them generates tension. Since the world of soul is usually neglected in a materialistic society, paying attention to inner experience and listening to the voice of the soul can bring relief to many stress-related conditions that result in physical, emotional and mental pain.

For example, Nancy, a woman suffering from depression, felt strongly that she wanted to make changes in her life, but she did not know what she wanted. When she tuned in to her inner experience, she had trouble deciding which of her many inner voices she should heed. Gradually she learned to give each one an opportunity to speak, whether or not she liked what it had to say. When she was able to articulate some of the conflicting messages she was given in childhood, she began to recognize her own authentic values. She had been taught never to discuss feelings and to believe that if you did not talk about feelings, they would go away. Of course, they did not go away, although they seemed unavailable when she wanted to express them. In time, as she was able to let go of these inhibiting beliefs, she began to hear the voice of her authentic self, which she called the voice of her soul. As she became more aware of what this voice was saying, the apparent conflict between her inner world and the demands of the outer world were resolved. Her self-esteem and her relationships improved, and she found a more satisfying job. Her healing clearly involved both listening to her soul and mobilizing her ego strength. Either one without the other would have been incomplete.

Although a strong, healthy ego has long been considered the hallmark of mental health, it is not enough. Enhancing one's image and achieving personal goals divorced from the depth dimension of soul can feel hollow, leading to deeper depression rather than happiness. In one case, a successful lawyer who had achieved an outstanding degree of success in her professional life, tried to overcome her depression by giving up her practice. Her attempt to create a more satisfying personal life for herself led her to explore new possibilities that awakened her interest in spirituality for the first time. On the other hand, a person who is totally immersed in the inner world, such as a man who had been a monk since he was nineteen, may have difficulty with relationships and work in the outer world. Awareness of both worlds is necessary for balance and wholeness, and differentiating them is an important step on the way to integration.

THE WORLD OF EGO

The world of ego, like Newtonian physics, offers a useful though incomplete picture of reality. Although egocentricity is essentially self-centered, a healthy ego is neither narcissistic nor codependent. As an organizing principle of consciousness, a healthy ego enables one to be both self-determining and related to others in a meaningful way. A mature ego is capable of empathically taking the place of others and reflecting on its own roles. Healthy individual ego identity is therefore a fundamental underpinning of a pluralistic democratic society that supports cultural diversity. A person with a strong ego can accept differences without feeling threatened, whereas a weak ego is more likely to be hostile and defensive.

From the perspective of ego, spirituality may serve a legitimate social function. It may also be regarded as an expedient way of encouraging ethical behavior. Many groups that claim to offer spiritual training use self-improvement techniques such as visualization and affirmations to enhance prosperity and well-being as measured by the standards of ego.

Living exclusively in the world of ego, however, people tend to feel isolated, alienated and deprived of love. Sometimes they settle for wealth and status as substitutes for love, hoping to find some sense of security in specialness. Sometimes they seek escape from alienation by identifying with a particular social group and dividing the world into *us* and *them*.

31

Disowned hostility and other shadow elements are then projected onto *them*, whoever the outsiders happen to be.

One couple I knew who became part of a cult were required to cut off all contact with their families and the people who had previously been their friends. They were instructed not communicate with anyone other than group members. Everyone else was suspected of being evil. When, after several years, they became disillusioned and left the group, they both felt deep sorrow about what they had done. The woman grieved for having cut off communication with her mother who had died before they disengaged from the cult.

Sometimes identifying with a powerful leader creates an illusion of security in an uncertain world, but this illusion is fragile and easily shattered by disappointment and betrayal. If the leader fails to live up to idealized expectations, the person who wanted protection is likely to become angry and resentful. Whenever we put people up on a pedestal, we risk wanting to knock them off.

There seems to be no escape from anxiety and depression for the ego that struggles with guilt and aggression. When a person feels guilty about something, the guilt is often expressed as anger or resentment. For example, one young man who borrowed his girlfriend's new car and damaged it, became irate with her when she was upset about it. The rage he felt was real enough, but he did not have enough self-awareness to recognize the connection to his own feelings of guilt. Later he felt sorry for his outburst, but it was too late. The relationship ended soon afterwards, not because of this one incident, but because he invariably reacted with hostility whenever he thought she was acting like his mother.

In working with adolescents, I find they rarely have any awareness of how guilt and dependency feeds the resentment they feel toward their parents. They may be rebellious or depressed, but until they can gain some sense of independence and self-sufficiency they have difficulty relating to their parents as people like themselves. If these difficulties are not resolved, similar dynamics tend to be re-enacted with teachers and leaders of any group they join. Spiritual teachers can easily become surrogate parents, and therefore any unresolved family problems tend to surface in spiritual communities. Furthermore, this type of adolescent behavior is not limited to teenagers. It can be observed in adults of all ages who are still hoping someone will relieve them of the responsibility of ego development.

Even a person who succeeds in fulfilling conscious goals in the world of ego, gaining a sense of relative independence, may feel alone in a hostile universe. Success in the world of ego is not synonymous with ego strength, and many individuals who appear to be strong may feel hollow inside. The weaker the ego, the more fearful and defensive one is likely to be. For example, both men and women who are afraid of aging may retreat into denial or become defensive when they are worried about losing their youth. They may try desperately to compensate for inevitable changes by having affairs or resorting to painful cosmetic processes that promise to preserve the illusion of youth.

One woman who came to see me when she was approaching fifty had already subjected herself to breast implants, liposuction and repeated collagen injections. She spent much of her time keeping her body in good shape and a good deal of money on her clothes. None of this seemed to have much effect on her self-esteem, however, and she was quite depressed. Her life had never been happy, and now she was afraid of losing what she considered her most valuable asset, her good looks. In the conventional world of appearances youth is supposed to be the best time of life, yet for many people, as for this woman, youth seems to be the most difficult time, and life gets better as they get older and develop more ego strength and improve their ability to cope with difficulties and enjoy themselves. After many months of therapy, she said she was glad to be as old as she was, because she didn't care as much about what other people thought and was much more in touch with her soul.

Unfortunately many highly successful people find themselves feeling emotionally and spiritually deprived without knowing how to change. Some spend most of their lives pursuing material or sensory gratifications, regardless of how little real satisfaction they find. Those who feel hounded by disappointment and driven by fear, greed and anger live in a world of conflict, competition and conspicuous consumption, afraid of change and assuming that there is nothing else. Trying to change may seem futile, and the force of habit may be hard to break.

This attitude seems particularly evident among successful people who make a lot of money early in life, such as those in show business. Those who lack ego strength and spiritual resources are highly vulnerable to addictions. One highly successful musician who came to see me because his wife was threatening to leave him did not succeed in overcoming his alcoholism, and his marriage did break up. He was devastated. His wife, on the other hand, discovered that she could create a more meaningful life for herself, although she had to give up the affluence to which she had become accustomed.

When individuals have the courage to claim their autonomy and think for themselves, they often seem to discover deeper sources of satisfaction.

Among the relatively successful people who know that material possessions do not provide enduring happiness, well-being, or peace of mind, many still believe that finding their soul mate would put an end to their feelings of dissatisfaction. Certainly a good partner can make a big difference in a person's life, but the perennial search for the perfect partner can also be a source of pain and distraction.

A strong ego is essential for healthy personal relationships between equals. When someone who has not yet developed a healthy ego identity expects the partner to take care of him or her, this can become a burden on the relationship. Believing that the right partner will answer existential questions inevitably leads to disappointment. Even if the search seems to be successful, disillusion sets in when one wakes up to discover that the idealized partner is either unreachable, or turns out to be an ordinary human being whose imperfections mirror one's own neuroses. Although any relationship can contribute to developing awareness of soul, particularly if an interest in spiritual growth is shared, a person needs a reasonably stable ego identity before cooperative, mutually supportive relationships can be sustained.

I remember Sharon, a self-sufficient woman who had spent years in a rather unfulfilling relationship with a man who was unwilling to make a long-term commitment. She cared for him deeply but saw that he would never fulfill her dreams of partnership, since he didn't seem to know what he wanted. When he was diagnosed with cancer, it was a wake-up call for both of them. In the last few months of his life, they were able to appreciate the positive aspects of their relationship more fully and acknowledge their deep soul connection. This connection did not depend on the form of their relationship or how much time they spent together. Although it was relatively short-lived and far from perfect, Sharon felt this relationship had been transformative. She said that, strangely, she felt less lonely being alone after he died than she had in the early years of their relationship.

Many of us who know that neither personal relationships nor material objects can fulfill our deepest longings still perpetuate the illusion that well-being can be found by pursuing them. In our culture, where the advertising industry is devoted to cultivating sensory desires, billions of dollars are spent in creating illusions and encouraging the rest of the world to be more like us. People everywhere now want to enjoy the fruits of industrialization that are idolized in the world of ego.

A Buddhist might characterize this world as a realm of hungry ghosts, inhabited by creatures with huge bellies and tiny throats who can never swallow enough to assuage the pain of craving. As Mahatma Gandhi said many years ago, the world has enough for everyone's need, but not enough for everyone's greed.

The earth cannot sustain insatiable human greed. Population explosion, resource depletion and pollution hang like the shadow of death over the collective world of the ego where individuals feel helpless and hopeless in the face of the magnitude of global problems. No amount of material abundance can obliterate the skull that grins at the banquet. As different factions of the human family become increasingly polarized, conflict looms on every horizon. No one feels secure in an insane world consumed by the mad pursuit of illusions that gratify egocentric desires while leaving the soul untouched.

Jim, for example, was a charming man who had succeeded in living in the fast lane for many years. As he approached middle age, the pleasures that were exciting in earlier years began to pall. He no longer wanted to have multiple liaisons with beautiful women who traded sex for money or glamorous vacations. He said he felt dead inside and alienated from everyone. He had depressive episodes that seemed to be getting worse. He acknowledged that he was at risk for drug addiction. He said he longed for a meaningful relationship with a woman but had not been able to find one. It was not until Jim had discovered his own experience of depth and meaning in therapy that he was able to connect with others in a more meaningful way.

As long as one identifies exclusively with the ego as a separate self, one is likely to be afraid of rejection, abandonment, pain, helplessness and death, to name a few of the fears that lurk in the shadows on the periphery of consciousness. Haunted by fear, one may try to numb the pain or cling to illusions that make one feel safe. The avoidance of fear can lead to many forms of addiction and a frantic pursuit of instant gratification. In the attempt to avoid facing inevitable death, the ego may cling to fantasies of more offspring, more fame or other symbols of immortality, or find solace in belief in reincarnation. But the cravings of a weak ego can never satisfy the gnawing hunger of the soul. On the contrary, these substitute gratifications become the chains that keep the soul in bondage to the world of ego. One can never get enough of what one does not really want.

A healthy ego, capable of taking responsibility for behavior and personal choice, can recognize its own limitations. For example, a person who becomes conscious of generating self-defeating patterns in personal relationships may choose to confront fear by facing the shadow and changing behaviors and attitudes, thereby becoming better able to relate to others. I have often been impressed by what a person with a strong ego can accomplish by the power of intention. A healthy person with a clear intention to accomplish something usually finds a way to carry it out. This is particularly apparent in the inner world of thought and perception. For example, when a person seriously intends to practice some form of concentration meditation, he or she will do it.

The effectiveness of clear intentions was demonstrated to me by a client who had overcome a difficult childhood, worked her way through college and had a successful career. She was accustomed to working hard and knew how to get what she wanted in the world. She came to see me because her marriage seemed to be falling apart. When she worked through her own ambivalence and clarified her intention to change the patterns at home, I was surprised by how quickly things improved. As soon as she turned her attention to what she really wanted, she changed her behavior and the marriage became more satisfying for both of them.

It seems clear that the quality of relationships can be changed unilaterally as long as the person desiring change does not expect other people to do the changing. I have also seen people let go of dysfunctional relationships quite easily once they work through their ambivalence and clarify their intention to move on. For example, when a person wants to let go of a dysfunctional relationship, two major obstacles seem to be fear of being alone and ambivalence about the relationship. When intentions are clear, action follows.

No amount of changing behavior or even changing partners, however, can satisfy the soul's yearning for a deeply meaningful connection. Sustaining a soulful connection with another person depends on finding an inner source of spiritual renewal which can then be shared.

How people use their ability to control and direct their thinking depends on where they are in their psychological and spiritual development. In the service of ego, powers of the mind can be used to enhance self-image or effectiveness in the world. Bent on satisfying personal desires, a person identified exclusively with ego may try to use spiritual practices for egocentric purposes, thereby reinforcing the prison of the soul. In the service of Spirit, on the other hand, the ability to direct one's thinking can be a doorway to liberation.

One problem with egocentric control is that some people who are successful in carrying out intentions and getting what they want become increasingly convinced that everyone should be more like them. They might assume that if only everyone would think positive thoughts, we would all be healthy, happy and free from suffering. They may then begin to blame others for how they think and for what happens to them. This is commonly called blaming the victim. What may be hidden from view is the tendency to blame themselves too, whenever they fail to get the results they want. This is part of the shadow side of positive thinking. Whenever people think they have the only right answer, blame and judgment tend to follow.

Positive thinking can certainly affect a person's life in a positive way. It is not true, however, that we are necessarily responsible for our suffering. Nor does it follow that we are guilty for whatever happens to us, or that if we fall ill we have voluntarily created the illness. When pain, anger or fear are denied in an effort to practice positive thinking, a backlash may occur, and whatever was denied may erupt uncontrollably. Sooner or later everyone encounters something that is beyond the control of egocentric thinking. This can become either a source of bitterness or a doorway to the world of soul.

For example, the eminent psychologist Rollo May, who always stressed the importance of being aware of the dark side of the psyche, told me that his life was totally changed by illness. As a young man he contracted tuberculosis, and his long recovery involved a process of deep soul searching that significantly influenced his life's work. However, when a person is in the midst of struggling with adversity, it is difficult to see what the final outcome will be, or how an ordeal can become an opportunity for spiritual awakening.

In addition to the physical limits to growth confronting humanity at the end of the twentieth century, the psychological consequences of an exclusively egocentric worldview can be devastating. Facing the human predicament from this perspective can plunge anyone into despair. At this point, being thoroughly disillusioned with the world of ego and giving up hope of finding relief from suffering in egocentric solutions, one may begin to search for another way of being in the world.

A CHANGE OF HEART

When we have passed beyond enjoyings, then we shall have Bliss. Desire was the helper; Desire is the bar.[2]

—SRI AUROBINDO

A change of mind is often preceded by a change of heart and a conscious desire for spiritual nourishment. This change does not imply a rejection of

tific knowledge, nor does it imply escape into a subjective
ial illusion. It does imply a worldview that incorporates a
spiritual values and qualities that enhance human life and
tious, co-creative relationship with nature.

for happiness where it can never be found, we are like the
for his key under a lamppost where the light seems better,
st the key inside the house where it is dark. The key to
meaning is never found in the outside world of appearances. By turning
attention inward, we may discover a new source of meaning in the universe
within. Here one is not the helpless victim of circumstances that one may
seem to be in the world of ego.

From the perspective of the inner world of soul, the world of ego is only
a tiny island on the surface of a vast ocean of experience. This awareness
dawns when the heart opens to embrace the poignancy of suffering in
the existence of all creatures that struggle for survival against all odds.
Pushing the rock up the mountain with Sisyphus, grieving with women
whose sons and lovers go off to war, feeling the pain of those who feel
deprived of love and the good things of life, facing personal frustrations and
disappointments, we begin a descent into the darker regions of the psyche.

A person who would face the reality of life, not sugar-coated by denial,
but stark as it is when men kill each other and children die and women
grieve and labor to survive, also recognizes the pain of living only in the
world of ego. Acknowledging how avoidance of pain and suffering leads
to hardening the heart and how fears constrict awareness, one may feel
compelled to change. Rather than clinging to a diminished existence, locked
away in isolation in the company of personal demons, one may risk facing
the shadow and entering the inner world of soul.

If we have the courage to face the truth of existence, we may discover
a whole new world in which no one is alone. If we ask for help, help is
given. "Seek and ye shall find." "Ask and ye shall receive." I had no way of
knowing if this were true until I began to seek and learned to ask. Once I
started seeking and asking inside, instead of outside under the proverbial
lamp post, I discovered a whole new world.

It is never too late to learn how to ask and where to look. For Bill, a
successful attorney, it was not until he was willing to let go of conditioned
patterns of competition and consumption that he discovered a world of
connection, cooperation and co-creation. He had burned out in a highly
stressful environment and had become severely depressed. After he joined
a twelve-step program for recovery from incipient alcoholism, he was able
to make new friends and find another professional position that was better

suited to his temperament. He had to surrender his desire for control before he could see new possibilities.

I have often heard people say, "I thought I should be able to handle my own problems. Then one day, in desperation, I asked for help, and everything began to change."

When we stop denying our own sorrow and open our hearts to the suffering of others, we can genuinely grieve the losses, disappointments and pain of the world. In the depths of sorrow, we may discover that personal pain reflects the suffering of all creatures. From this awareness compassion is born. One day, shortly after going through a difficult divorce, I was sitting in a silent meditation retreat and felt overwhelmed with sorrow. I felt at times that my tears were not my tears alone. I seemed to be crying for all people whose dreams had been shattered and who had faced painful losses in their lives. My tears, like all tears, signaled a letting go of defenses against deep feeling. Letting go and allowing the barriers I had built against the ocean of compassion to crumble, I sometimes felt frightened and dreamed of drowning in this ocean. As I stayed with it and dove deeper into it, in spite of fear, I found myself in a world of soul, experiencing a deep sense of connection to others, as if they were a part of me. Since that time I have often sat with people as they plumbed the depths of their personal sorrow, eventually coming to a place of inner peace and compassion for others. As an unknown rabbi said, "It is only when the heart breaks that God can enter."

Sorrow is not the only doorway into the world of soul, but it is one that opens for everyone at some time in life. Other familiar ways of accessing the world of soul include dreams, meditation, a variety of aesthetic experiences, creativity, falling in love, a close brush with death or any other transpersonal experience that shocks us out of complacency and denial. I now see dissatisfaction with the world of ego as divine discontent which, like the hound of heaven, will never let us rest.

THE WORLD OF SOUL

We live in a world of unreality, of illusion. The main point is not that the world or even our ultimate selves are illusory, however, but that our ideas about reality and our selves create illusions.[3]

—CHARLES TART

The world of soul affirms both our divinity and our humanity. The world of soul is therefore more encompassing of reality than the world of ego. The soul is our link to the infinite; it is neither a thing nor a process, but the inner witness of every experience. In an extroverted culture where the soul is neglected, we may yearn for the quality of soulfulness in life, without being certain about what is missing. Care for the soul offers a welcome antidote to the aridity of materialism. When a person becomes disillusioned with ego goals, identifying self as soul can provide a sense of renewal and inspiration. The soul is not something to have or possess; it is a spiritual identity to be awakened.

According to many traditions, the world of soul is a world of spiritual forms and qualities. Although it is invisible to the physical eye, it seems plainly visible to those who develop spiritual vision. It is a world inhabited by spiritual patterns of energy or beings that may be called by many names. They are called spirits in Shamanism, angels and demons in Christianity, gods and goddesses in Greek mythology and Hinduism, beatific and wrathful deities in Vajrayana Buddhism, inner guides or archetypal images in psychology. In the world of soul emotional states as well as beliefs, hopes and fears shape our experience.

The imaginal realms of this invisible world are more important to the soul than the visible world of ordinary reality. While inner realities are affected by events in the outer world, they are not determined by external circumstances. The world of soul may therefore be revealed in circumstances of adversity as well as in moments of spontaneous joy.

Different ways of regarding the world of soul can be found among adherents of different religions and among people who do not consider themselves religious at all. Some people assume that experiences of these realms are literally true. On the other hand, most academic psychologists and philosophers tend to dismiss them as subjective projections and may interpret them symbolically. Psychologists such as James Hillman and Kenneth Ring claim an independent ontological status for the mythological figures that inhabit these imaginal realms. Debates about the relative reality of inner experiences are not easily resolved. Recent controversies over false memories attributed to early childhood have highlighted the problem of differentiating inner and outer realities.

On Ken Wilber's map of the spectrum of consciousness,[4] the subtle inner world of soul lies midway between the ordinary world of egoic self-consciousness and the formless causal realms of transcendental super-consciousness. How we relate to this subtle realm can exert a powerful influence on our lives, even if it is perceived as a separate reality. It seems crucial, therefore, to be conscious of what we encounter in this domain.

I have personally been more interested in observing the effects of aware-ness of the world of soul on people's lives than in trying to define its ontological status. The subtle, imaginal realms are very real to those who have explored them, and for many people they provide a source of solace, empowerment and spiritual renewal. Experiences can be observed and validated without getting lost or indulging in omnipotent fantasies, yet the risk of becoming entangled with illusions in this area seems unavoidable.

In the world of soul we tend to find what we seek. If I seek comfort in suffering and sacrifice, I will find it. If I seek joy and freedom, that too may be found. The world of soul is like a labyrinth through which we wend our way until we find the center. Every step along the way is part of our reality. In the world of ego the self is identified with the body that dies and disappears. As I see it, in the world of soul the self identifies with an immortal soul that transcends the physical world. Both the world of ego and the world of soul can be perceived as existing within the Self that is one with Spirit, as the Source of all being.

If we choose to identify with soul rather than ego, a new adventure of consciousness begins. Exploring the world of soul is a fascinating, vital part of the spiritual path. However, one can also get lost or bogged down in it, since the difference between truth and illusion in the world of soul is not as easy to discern as it appears to be the world of ego.

As a soul I can easily identify with mythological figures. For example, I might identify with Odysseus as he makes his way home after the Trojan War, seeing the war as representing the world of ego and the journey home as the path of the soul, fraught with perils. Or I could identify with Allerleirauh,[5] the fairy-tale princess who leaves her father's house and runs away into the woods. While the story of Allerleirauh is sometimes understood as a metaphor for leaving one's family of origin, it can also be read as leaving the world of ego. Or the soul may appear as a divine child in my dreams. Whatever the story, beginning the journey means letting go of the familiar world and moving into the unknown. Odysseus is blown out of control, and Dante wakes up in a dark wood. Similarly, Dorothy is blown away into the Land of Oz, and Alice falls down a rabbit hole.

For Cynthia, a woman in her thirties, life seemed to go out of control when her husband left her for another woman and she was fired from her job. She did not know where to turn for help. By chance she happened to meet an acquaintance in a bookstore who told her about a meditation retreat and suggested she might go. Cynthia had never considered anything like this, but since she had a lot of free time she decided to try it. When she arrived she felt like running away, but decided to stay. She was not prepared for how deeply she would be stirred by the teacher, Vietnamese Zen Master Thich Nhat Hanh. Cynthia came to value that retreat experience as a threshold of awakening that opened a previously unsuspected depth dimension to her inner world and gave her the strength to begin her life over.

CREATING REALITY

Whether one identifies primarily with the ego or the soul, the belief that we create our reality can be either liberating or entrapping, depending on how it is viewed. Some people recognize that they affect the world around them by their attitudes as well as their behavior; others claim that they are fully responsible for creating their own reality. An ancient precedent for this can be found in the Buddha's teaching that we are what we think, and with our thoughts we make our world.[6] This encourages taking responsibility for thoughts as well as behavior, yet a superficial belief that we create our reality can be a heavy burden, entangling the mind in feelings of guilt and inadequacy.

A person who has not developed a healthy ego may be driven by compelling biological passions that contribute to many forms of pathology that plague contemporary society, including violence and addiction. For the person who seeks instant gratification, creating reality means getting more of whatever brings fleeting pleasure or numbs pain. Illusions of invulnerability eventually crash, sometimes with a great deal of pain. A person lacking a healthy ego is also likely to feel like a victim of circumstances, and blame does not ameliorate anything.

Likewise, a person identified exclusively with ego may also seek immediate sensory gratification and think of creating reality in terms of acquiring more possessions or symbols of pleasure. When this pattern is successful, belief is reinforced. If it is unsuccessful, whatever happens can be rationalized. Even when one knows that fulfillment of ego goals related to money, sex and power does not provide lasting satisfaction, one can easily become addicted to the intensity of the pursuit.

On the other hand, a person identified with the soul may interpret whatever happens as an opportunity for learning and direct attention to cultivating qualities such as peace and harmony. The soul that looks for meaning in existence may regard every experience, even adversity, as a challenge, a lesson or a blessing. In my experience, the belief that the universe is designed for awakening the soul casts a different light on seemingly random occurrences.

The person who is hurt or ill or unsuccessful in achieving ego goals may be justified in feeling like a victim from the point of view of the ego. However, from the point of view of the soul, taking responsibility for experience precludes blaming circumstances or other people, and feeling sorry for oneself becomes an unacceptable indulgence. While identifying with soul encourages taking personal responsibility instead of blaming the outside world, it can still lead to self-blame.

I remember working with a woman who was convinced that she must be a bad person because she had been injured in an automobile accident, although it was not her fault. She was convinced that she had created this experience; therefore she must be guilty. People who are ill may also feel guilty for creating their illness. One woman with cancer asked herself repeatedly, "What have I done to create this?" The question itself was asked from the point of view of the ego, seeking someone or something to blame.

Paul was a man in his fifties who came to see me when he was dying of cancer. All his life he had felt a conflict between his devotion to work and family and the desire to retreat into solitude. He blamed himself for resenting the demands of his family and never taking time to go to the woods alone. His fulfillment of duty had left no time for him to do what his soul had most wanted. In the last few weeks of his life he was able to forgive himself, release old resentments and acknowledge how much he loved his family. He only wished he could have done it sooner.

In both the world of ego and the world of soul, recognizing how we create our *experience* of reality is an expedient teaching that helps us recognize that we are free to choose values, attitudes and ways of seeing. However, the belief that we create reality is only relatively true and should not be mistaken for a final truth. As separate egos we have a very limited perception of reality; as individual souls we have a deeper insight into reality, yet it is still only partial. Difficulties with pride and inadequacy, or inflation and deflation, may be encountered in both worlds.

Since subjective experience is significantly affected by the goals we choose and by our response to circumstances we cannot control, I find it useful to differentiate the desires of the ego from the desires of the soul. Perception alters according to whether one identifies with the ego or the soul, and identifying with the soul can be deeply healing for anyone who has been exclusively identified with ego.

Genuine transcendence seems to depend on disidentifying from limited self-concepts.[7] When a person disidentifies from the ego, he or she might say, "I have an ego, but I am not my ego." The person who is identified with soul rather than ego may regard everything as an opportunity for spiritual growth. For example, when confronting pain or difficulty, he or she might ask, "What can I learn from this?" or, "What meaning does this have for me?"

Many religious traditions encourage people to sublimate egocentric passions in spirituality. However, identifying exclusively with soul can also be problematic. The problem is that it can lead to psychological denial and avoidance rather than transcendence. Historically, identifying with the soul usually meant denigrating the body, the feminine and the world of nature. Wholeness implies an identification with soul that includes and affirms all aspects of existence. To discover the divinity of all creation is to include more of reality, not to denigrate or deny either the physical or the spiritual aspects of human nature. A materialistic perspective that denies the reality of Spirit, or an idealistic perspective that denies the reality of the phenomenal world, are both limited views that devalue what is excluded.

Waking up to one's identity as an individual soul, or having a transcendent experience in which soul dissolves into formless Spirit, does not necessarily imply rejecting or abandoning the world of ego. Some people find it desirable to retreat for a time from the preoccupations of the ego world in order to cultivate the life of the soul, but this is seldom a permanent reorientation. Usually the person who retreats for a time to do spiritual practice returns to the world of everyday life, although changes in values, attitudes and motivation may be pervasive and enduring. A taste of the infinite can make ego gratifications pale by comparison, and the person who is aware of soul may want to devote more time to activities that nourish and heal the soul.

In time, when spiritual experiences fade into memory, the illusions that keep the soul in bondage to the world of ego can still be alluring. Both ego and soul are subject to fear and desire and, therefore, not immune to the promise of illusions. While shadows and illusions serve a purpose, they can still imprison the soul. Regarding the price of illusions, a wise Tibetan teacher says,

To hold as the truth what is merely illusion is needless exhaustion of body and mind.[8]

LIVING IN TWO WORLDS

Trust in God and tie your camel.

—Sufi PROVERB

Following a spiritual path toward wholeness demands that we live in both the world of ego and the world of soul. As we have seen, the desires of the soul are different from the desires of the ego. Whereas the world of ego is dominated by the pursuit of excitement, stimulation and dominance, the soul longs for peace, joy and self-expression. Contemporary society can be described as suffering from a sickness of the soul in which the well-being of the soul is often sacrificed to egoic ideals of progress and ambition. The soul in bondage to the world of ego may feel neglected or sick. For example, in a world·that rewards extroverted accomplishments, the soul may be bereft of the sweetness of silence and solitude. The soul that yearns for love, beauty, harmony and communion may be quickened by aesthetic experiences, a moment of truth or a taste of religious ecstasy, yet it must also function in the world as it is.

Neither the world of ego nor the world of soul can be ignored in contemporary life. To deny one and affirm the other is to fall into the illusion that we can live exclusively either in the outer world or the inner world, which is obviously impossible. Both are real, and both have value and relevance to the spiritual path. To believe that I can find fulfillment by retreating into the world of soul and avoid the world of ego is to imagine that by creating a separate reality I can escape the world of nature into which I have been born. This is what many young people who chose to leave the secular world and devote themselves to religious life have discovered. Painful though it may be, one way or another, many of them have returned to living in the world.

When spirituality is cultivated in order to escape from difficulties in the world of ego and a person engages in a "spiritual bypass," re-entry into the outer world can be difficult. One man who had been living in an ashram for nine years spoke of his life after leaving the ashram as being filled with shame, pain and struggle. Feeling like a spiritual failure, as if abandoned by God and cursed as a traitor by his guru, his task was to reclaim his identity in the outer world. This he characterized as "reawakening the real self instead of posturing as this fiercely transcendent spiritual being."[9]

Another young man who went to Asia to practice intensive meditation for several years told me he felt a persistent sense of deprivation while living as a monk. This eventually led him out of monastic isolation back to the world. He recognized that his own demands for perfection had sabotaged his sense of well-being, and his efforts had avoided some deep psychological issues. In retrospect he realized that his quest for liberation meant coming to terms with the totality of his personal life.

In my experience, it appears that neglecting either the world of ego or the world of soul leads to difficulties. Believing that I alone create reality in either world can be a trap that keeps the soul in bondage to the world of ego or in a prison of its own specialness. Grandiose illusions that try to exclude what I cannot control are difficult to sustain and fail in the end.

When I am willing to live in both worlds, recognizing that I am responsible for my attitudes and perceptions, my appreciation of both worlds begins to deepen. Much has been written about the world of ego and how we can change it. Very little has been said about the world of soul and how awareness of it changes our lives.

The ego that becomes inflated with the belief that it is in charge of creating reality rather than learning to live in harmony with it sooner or later learns the lessons of humility. The soul that becomes similarly inflated also falls into despair. Nevertheless, I am responsible for the consequences of my beliefs and my behavior in both the world of ego and the world of soul. Whether the consequences of behavior are seen in terms of karma and reincarnation, belief in an afterlife or the fate of the earth, both individual and collective behavior have predictable consequences. In the words of the Buddha,

> Speak or act with an impure mind
> And trouble will follow you . . .
> Speak or act with a pure mind
> And happiness will follow you
> As your shadow, unshakable.[10]

Although this may not appear to be the case when we see only the world of ego, it becomes increasingly evident when we become familiar with the world of soul. When we are aware of both worlds, we may sometimes experience conflict between the ambitions of the ego and the longings of the soul. At other times we may sense that when these two worlds are in harmony, they are not really separate.

The inner world of soul and the outer world of ego do reflect each other, and they are not as separate as they seem. Awakening the soul does not mean abandoning, destroying or negating the ego. It is quite possible to befriend the limitations of ego. The ego can melt or dissolve in the world of soul, surrendering to love rather than struggling to defend the illusions of separateness and self-importance.

We can claim the freedom to change our perceptions of both worlds. By increasing awareness of the world of soul, we not only enrich life with a sense of depth and meaning, we may also discover that identifying with the soul instead of the ego enables us to see both worlds in a new light.

I have repeatedly observed that when people begin paying attention to the life of the soul, their experience in the outer world of ego changes in a desired direction. They begin to feel more inspired, more creative and more empowered. This change process often begins by looking inward, since we seem to have more leverage in changing the inner world than the outer world. Eventually we see how the two are inextricably interconnected.

Wherever the journey may lead, the world of soul, like the world of ego, is permeated by a sense of divine discontent. There is no final resting place for the separated soul. The thirst for unity and wholeness is never satisfied by substitute gratifications, even those in the world of soul. No matter how wondrous and ecstatic the adventures on the path may be, divine discontent impels the soul to walk on.

SPIRIT, SOUL AND EGO

I discovered that it is necessary, absolutely necessary, to believe in nothing. That is, we have to believe in something which has no form and no color—something which exists before all forms and colors appear. . . . No matter what god or doctrine you believe in, if you become attached to it, your belief will be based more or less on a self-centered idea.[11]

—SUZUKI ROSHI

To speak of Spirit as the Absolute is to speak of no-thing. Anything that can be said about it, therefore, sounds paradoxical. Yet the world of soul cannot be separated from Spirit. Just as awareness of the world of soul brings depth and meaning and aliveness to the world of ego, so awareness of Spirit sacralizes the world of soul. Without acknowledging Spirit as the creative Source that transcends both ego and soul, I perceive reality only in terms of distinctions and boundaries, unaware of the divinity that permeates existence. A new perception of soul in relationship to Spirit replaces the anguish of the isolated, separate self with renewed inspiration and love.

Beyond space/time, in formless Spirit, there is no separate identity. Both the personal ego and the immortal soul exist in a world of shadows that is always changing, always in process. If either the ego or the soul believes its existence is divorced from Spirit, it falls into illusion and suffers the consequences of alienation and despair. The Self that knows its Source as Spirit, acts with compassion in both the world of ego and the world of soul, relinquishing attachment to shadows and illusions that bar the way to liberation.

CHAPTER 3

Sex and Death: Eros and Thanatos

Death is a mirror in which the entire meaning of life is reflected.[1]
—SOGYAL RINPOCHE

DEATH IS THE VALLEY OF THE SHADOW, and lust, we are told, is a deadly sin. We cannot know our shadows without coming face to face with sex and death. The deepest passions of human life are stirred by sex and death, and fear of death is deeply rooted in us all.

One day a man who had been celibate for many years said to me, "I have always equated sex with death. The day after I made love to a woman for the first time, I was almost killed. I felt I had lost my protection."

Few people attain the sacred knowledge that transforms sex and death into spiritual experiences that are free from fear. The spiritual path requires coming to terms with the personal pain and passion associated with sex and death before compassion, as caring for the suffering of others, can be awakened. Yet sometimes spiritual teachings that are meant to help us face and understand suffering and joy seem to focus only on suffering and fail to pierce the veils of illusion surrounding sex and death.

Although death is inevitable, many of us live in denial and avoidance of death, clinging to unexamined illusions of immortality. These attitudes toward death are reminiscent of Victorian attitudes toward sex that denied the universality of sexual desire. It seems strange that while individual and species survival are the most basic and compelling instincts, the denial of death and the repression of sex are still with us. At the same time, both are endowed with a compelling attraction. The entertainment industry, which thrives on sex and violence, continually reminds us of their endless fascination.

Sigmund Freud's characterization of Eros as the life instinct and Thanatos as the death instinct portrays sex and death as opposites that are inextricably intertwined. Sexual frustration can contribute to increased anger and aggression, and sexual repression can contribute to emotional numbing or psychic death that leaves a person feeling dead inside. Freud regarded the fear of death as analogous to the fear of castration. He argued that since we have no experience of death, it could have no representation in the unconscious. Not all analysts agreed with Freud on this point, and existential theorists claim that men and women have an innate, intuitive awareness of death, experienced as a primary source of anxiety. In his later years Freud postulated the death instinct, Thanatos, and admonished those who would endure life to prepare for death.

Freud's worldview was strictly materialistic, and his model of the psyche was essentially mechanistic. The mind was conceived to be subject to instinctual forces of attraction and repulsion, resulting in inevitable conflict. In the unconscious, then, Eros and Thanatos are forever locked in battle. In this view, Eros is essentially sexual and aims to establish unities and to bind together. Thanatos aims in the opposite direction, toward a regressive and destructive disintegration of ego. The conflict that every person experiences between the demands of society, or the superego, and the demands of the id, the natural instinctual self, can, at best, only be ameliorated by a strong rational ego. Based on the assumption that human beings are basically selfish and pleasure seeking, it is assumed that every civilized person must learn to control instinctual hunger and aggression. The task of the psychoanalytic endeavor was to extricate the individual, insofar as possible, from the collective neurosis through self-understanding and rational analysis.

For Freud and many of his followers, it was the sexual force, or libido, that was the primary motivation of thought, behavior, anxiety and pathology. Among those who did not accept his mechanistic dual-instinct view of human nature were well-known theorists such as Carl Jung, Alfred Adler and Otto Rank. Rank, in particular, stressed the importance of death anxiety and suggested that humans are inevitably caught between the fear of isolation inherent in individuation and the fear of death or annihilation. Modern theorists such as Rollo May, Ernest Becker and Irvin Yalom see the fear of death underlying all fears of separation, abandonment and castration.

Ken Wilber points out that Eros as the life force is not only sexually erotic. It operates in biology by uniting bodies, in the mental realms by uniting people and ideas in a community of discourse and in spirituality by seeking to unite the universe.[2]

Unconsciousness with regard to sex and death perpetuates suffering by relegating the passions they engender to the dark, shadow side of the psyche. It is no accident that Satanism, as a symbol of the collective shadow, is always associated with sex and death. This split in the psyche also contributes to ecological devastation resulting from failure to appreciate the preciousness of life and the intricate interdependence of all forms of life and death. Paradoxically, making peace with sex and death enables us to heal the imagined split between soul and body and open more fully to the joy of life, with full awareness of our mortality. Some contemplative traditions recommend meditation on death as a foundational spiritual practice. Such practices not only prepare us for physical death but also reduce the fear of ego death which lies at the root of much psychological suffering.

Since a path to wholeness demands that we bring to consciousness whatever we have denied, facing sex and death is a necessary part of the journey. Awakening to reality rather than living in illusion means acknowledging the power of sex and death and seeing them as they are.

DEATH ANXIETY

The fear of death plays a major role in our internal experience; it haunts as does nothing else; it rumbles continuously under the surface; it is a dark, unsettling presence at the rim of consciousness.[3]

—IRVIN YALOM

Although we may be conscious of numerous fears, such as fear of pain, loss, disease, isolation and old age, few people contemplate seriously the inevitability of their own death in the absence of some immediately perceived threat. The source of free-floating anxiety, the fear of nothingness or of nothing in particular, remains a mystery to the unreflective observer. I have often heard people who are dealing with life-threatening illness say they wish they could have appreciated the fleeting, temporary nature of life sooner, rather than waiting until it was almost over.

Psychological defenses against awareness of sex and death are familiar themes in psychotherapy. While the root of deep-seated anxiety can sometimes be attributed to intrapsychic conflicts about sexuality, death anxiety may still be regarded as *the* fundamental fear, underlying all other fears onto which it is displaced. Rather than reducing fear, this displacement tends to lead to a numbing constriction of awareness that results in pathological symptoms. Integrating sexuality into one's life and facing the terrors of nonexistence are basic developmental tasks for all of us, yet we employ a variety of psychological defense mechanisms to avoid them.

Fear of both sex and death is further reinforced by enculturation. Fear of sex may be related to the child's fear of the omnipotent parent or other adult. Survivors of child abuse carry deep wounds that sometimes lead to their own attempts to dominate, control and humiliate others. Through centuries of patriarchal domination men have been cast into the role of oppressors, while women, children and nature have been cast in the role of victims. Since victims of abuse tend to become abusers, women and children also abuse each other, making escape from the senseless cycle of cruelty and violence seem impossible. For example, a woman abused by her father may continue the cycle by abusing her children, and a man who has been victimized by an abused and abusive mother may have great difficulty overcoming his hatred of women.

Children wrestle with the fear of death and annihilation at an early age. By the time a child reaches the latency period of psychosexual development, he or she has usually suppressed this anxiety and has perhaps attempted mastery over fear by experimenting with killing insects or other small creatures. Adults may also resort to killing as a way of warding off death anxiety, not only in primitive sacrificial rites and rituals, but also in rationalizations for war, hunting and other forms of socially sanctioned killing. In many cultures manliness is associated with fearlessness in the face of death. Killing animals for food was once a matter of survival, and the warrior who could kill unflinchingly was greatly respected.

The one who deals out death wards off the fear of death by cultivating the illusion of mastery and invulnerability, even as he kills a part of himself in the process. Men trained for war learn to suppress any feelings of empathy or compassion for their victims. Women and children and other innocent victims may then be considered fair game as long as they are perceived as enemies.

Literal killing is not the only way of buying time in the battle with death. Other more subtle forms of aggression such as domination, exploitation and soul murder may serve the same purpose. The drive for power in any form, either in the world of ego or the world of soul, may be motivated by this aggressive defense against deep-seated death anxiety.

In the end, defenses against death anxiety seem to crumble in despair. When the realization of personal helplessness and mortality returns, the old anxiety resurfaces and brings with it terror and depression. Eventually, the heroic quest that attempts to challenge, deny or avoid the confrontation with death is doomed to its own undoing. Each of us must finally surrender whatever we have most valued about ourselves and meet death defenseless and alone.

Fear of life as a separate person mirrors the fear of death. Resistance to individuation and familiar fears of abandonment may therefore be perceived as masking death anxiety. Whereas one person may cultivate courage in the face of death through heroic exploits, another may attempt to avoid the challenge of mastery and seek solace from being in relationship to someone who is believed to be a strong and powerful protector. The first of these is typically a masculine defense, the second a more feminine defense, although at times men and women employ them both. Whereas the male ego tends to project the fear of death onto loss of autonomy, the female ego tends to feel more threatened by loss of relationship. One seeks to conquer fear; the other to avoid it.

I have known many women afraid of abandonment who choose to stay in dysfunctional relationships rather than face the challenges of individuation. Men, on the other hand, who fear engulfment by the feminine, may stay locked into loneliness and isolation.

Peter and Jeannette were a couple who struggled with this dynamic for many years. She felt dependent and afraid of being abandoned. He, on the other hand, felt suffocated by her needs and demands and would withdraw at times into long periods of moodiness. Once Jeannette started her own inner work that enabled her to face her fears of aloneness, Peter was able to be more emotionally vulnerable with her. Their relationship improved rapidly after Peter was involved in an accident that nearly cost him his life. The recognition that their time together was not unlimited helped them both appreciate how much they loved each other.

Unexamined beliefs about an afterlife or reincarnation can also be a way of avoiding or denying the terror of annihilation. Sometimes religious rituals are believed to provide insurance against imagined dangers awaiting the soul after death. Belief in a magic rescuer, a personal god or an omnipotent servant may all serve to avoid death anxiety.

Sometimes a guru or other authority figure takes on the role of protector from the stark and awesome realities of our finitude. While parents reassuring a child that everything will be all right may deny their own fears in the process, one might hope that spiritual teachers would have faced their own fears before telling others what to expect. Unfortunately that is not always true. Facing the fear of death seems to be something that each of us has to do for ourselves.

Other forms of avoiding death anxiety may include identification with a group whose continued existence becomes a symbolic form of immortality. Illusions of personal immortality may also be supported by having children, creating great works or doing great deeds that promise that one will at least be remembered and live on in the minds of others. However, none of these strategies seem to alleviate fear.

THE NEAR-DEATH EXPERIENCE

Every major culture of the world includes in its mythology archetypal figures representing death and rebirth or transformation.[4]

—STANISLAV GROF

Strange as it may seem, coming close to death and confronting our fears rather than repressing, denying or avoiding them can have a powerfully healing effect on the psyche. The person who is willing to be aware in the face of death may reap the reward of reduced death anxiety and a transformation of consciousness.

In recent years medical technology has, for the first time in history, enabled millions of human beings to come close to experiencing biological death and return to recount the event. Although skeptics have argued that these experiences are purely subjective and triggered by brain states associated with oxygen deprivation, those who have them find them transformative.

In their investigation of near-death experiences, researchers Dr. Raymond Moody[5] and Dr. Kenneth Ring[6] found that people who have had near-death experiences—being pronounced clinically dead and subsequently resuscitated—lose their fear of death. Most people who recall their experiences have reported profound experiences of awe, wonder and bliss. When they return, their view of life is profoundly altered, and their values tend to shift in the direction of increased love and compassion, appreciation of beauty and sensitivity to feelings. Upon resuming ordinary life, they tend to value love and learning more highly than any other interests.

In one case a man who had been living a life of crime landed in an emergency ward with seven bullets in him. When he recovered, he totally changed his life. He said he had seen God in a near-death experience and felt called to become a minister. He has been a prison chaplain for many years and is deeply committed to a life of service.

According to Ring, studies of the near-death experience show a common pattern of transcendental elements and transformative aftereffects, including positive changes in self-concept and personal values, a greater appreciation of others and an increased inclination toward spiritual growth.[7] Profound changes in religious or spiritual orientation tend to be experienced inwardly and are often mystical in nature. Belief in some sort of postmortem existence is endorsed, together with the conviction that "the Light" will be there for everyone at death. Ring regards the near-death experience as a catalyst for spiritual awakening and suggests that the increasingly widespread incidence of this and other transcendental experiences may represent an evolutionary thrust toward higher consciousness for humanity at large.

In one case, a man who had been an atheist all his life described his escape from hell in a near-death experience. Suffering from a ruptured intestine, he found himself traveling through a dark region, being taunted and physically dismembered by hostile beings. He heard a voice within him urging him to pray, but he resisted it. Eventually, in desperation, he cried out to Jesus, and his prayer caused the demonic creatures to disperse. Soon a speck of light appeared and grew until it engulfed him in an overwhelmingly intense sense of love and cosmic knowledge. The impact of this experience was so profound that he left his position as a professor and became a minister.

After talking directly with a number of people who have had a close brush with death, I have learned that fear of death can be greatly diminished by these experiences. I remember one man who suffered severe injuries in an automobile accident. He was involved in a head-on collision in which his car was totalled, and he went into a coma that lasted several days. When I spoke with him some months later, he told me that the moment he saw the collision coming, he seemed to leave his body and to be watching the accident from somewhere above. He had seen people gathering around him and the ambulance taking him to the hospital. Later he checked his perceptions with two witnesses, and they were apparently accurate. At the time of the accident he was perfectly calm and felt no pain. The pain came later, during recovery. He felt that the most significant and lasting impact of this experience was that it totally removed his fear of death.

SYMBOLIC RITUALS OF SEX AND DEATH

Half the art of living is a talent for dying.[8]

–HUSTON SMITH

By contemplating the truth about sex and death, we begin to appreciate the possibility of freedom from the terrors of living in illusion. There is no freedom from fear in a world of illusion, for the mind always projects the shadow onto something or someone perceived as other. Although repression of sexuality is not as prevalent today as it was in Freud's time, many psychological problems and a great deal of emotional pain is still associated with it. Death anxiety seems to be as prevalent as ever. Even when awareness of sex and death is not repressed, the relationship between them may be overlooked.

It is obvious that reproduction without death, or death without reproduction would mean an end to existence as we know it. In the history of evolution, sex and death arise together. Reproduction by cell division does not require death. In biological organisms, when reproduction occurs as the result of the joining of male and female, the parents die soon after reproducing. This observation has contributed to the recurring association of celibacy with the attainment of immortality.

The creatures of earth live by killing and eating. Humans have survived under circumstances of eat or be eaten, kill or be killed since the dawn of prehistory. The realization that death sustains life is therefore considered a fundamental motivation supporting rites and rituals of early agricultural societies that often involved both human and animal sacrifices. In some cultures ritual killing is viewed not as a crime, but as a sacred necessity.

In agricultural societies the cyclical nature of time is observed in the death and rebirth of plants, the cycle of the seasons and the cycles of the moon, which appear to die and be reborn each month. Survival, then, is believed to depend on the continuing process of death and rebirth, and killing and reproduction are both perceived as necessary.

In a discussion of rites demanding human sacrifice, Joseph Campbell says that such rituals cannot be attributed to economic necessity or social need.[9] It is supposedly the harmony and well-being of the community, its coordination with the ultimate nature of the cosmos and the integration of personal desires with this universal circumstance that is the fundamental aim and nature of these ceremonies.

Campbell has described in detail one tribal ceremony representing the beginning of the world in which many days and nights of drumming lead up to boys' puberty rites during which everyone engages in a sexual orgy. On the final night a beautiful young girl, ceremoniously costumed, is led out, and all of the initiates cohabit with her, one after another. When the youth chosen to be last is embracing her, both are killed, cut up, roasted and eaten.

Similar rites of human and animal sacrifice existed in many agricultural societies, where new life was observed to spring from the seeds of those who have died.[10] Such horrifying examples of ritual magic meant to ward off evil through death as sacrifice seem to have been part of the collective psyche for millennia. When we deplore the prevalence of violence today, we sometimes tend to romanticize the past, forgetting that the dark shadow side of human nature, ruled by fear, is an integral part of recorded history.

Today ritual abuse is widely condemned yet still fascinates the popular imagination. For example, ritual killing of animals is still socially sanctioned in some places as bullfights, which some spectators say are sexually arous- ing. In many places the slaughter of wildlife is still a popular sport, though shorn of religious significance. Popular preoccupation with Satanism also reflects this fascination.

From a psychological perspective, the association of sex and violence, repeatedly depicted in movies and television dramas, can be regarded as a manifestation of the collective unconscious that may erupt in psychotic experiences and aberrant behavior, as well as in dreams, fantasies and altered states of consciousness in normal adults. It may be assumed that guilt, often associated with sex and death, also lies at the root of the need for ceremonies and rituals of expiation. In many archaic societies and pagan religions, sex is imbued with religious significance. While positive attitudes toward sex may manifest as fertility rites or ritual orgies, negative religious attitudes toward sex tend to manifest as asceticism and the denigration of the body.

Stanislav Grof, a pioneering consciousness researcher and psychoanalyst who has done extensive mapping of realms of the human unconscious, says,

> The evidence suggests that the human body harbors a mechanism which translates extreme suffering, particularly if it is associated with suffocation, into a form of excitement that resembles sex- ual arousal. This mechanism has been reported by patients in sadomasochistic relationships, by prisoners of war tortured by the enemy, and by people who make unsuccessful attempts to hang themselves and live to tell the story. In all these situations,

agony can be intimately associated with ecstasy, even leading to an experience of transcendence, as it is the case with flagellants and religious martyrs.[11]

Grof associates this powerful unconscious material with the biological birth process. He has observed that deep experiential encounters with death and rebirth are typically associated with existential crises of extraordinary proportions. Grof maintains that birth trauma may account for a variety of psychosexual disorders and offer some insight into cult behavior, ritual abuse and the prevalence of violence against women.

After observing hundreds of regressed patients reliving the birth process, Grof concluded that aggressive and sadomasochistic elements are associated with the struggle of the infant pushing through the birth canal, where survival of the organism is threatened by suffocation. This basic aggression may be expressed in images of wars, massacres, tortures and abuses of various kinds, or it may assume a self-destructive quality. A person reliving this phase of birth may alternately identify with the victim and the victimizer.[12]

Grof claims that these traumatic experiences can be successfully resolved only by connecting with the spiritual dimension of the psyche. When this occurs, Grof notes that the resulting personality transformation can be compared to changes described in ancient mysteries of initiation and rites of passage. He also points out that in birth, sex and death, we are inextricably linked to nature.

The association of death with transcendence is familiar, not only in religion and near-death experiences, but in a variety of experiences of ego death, when a person feels a total loss of identity and then emerges into a new awareness of joy and love. Ecstatic experiences associated with mystical initiation rites, psychedelics and therapeutic techniques such as holotropic breathing can reenact the death/rebirth process involving struggle, surrender and awakening to a new sense of self.

When the extreme intensity of such experiences is expressed as wild, ecstatic rapture, it may be described as Dionysian. Dionysus was a Greek god of revelry, whose priestesses, the Maenads, celebrated his orgies with drunkenness, nakedness and sacramental feasting. At one time he was believed to be incarnated as a beautiful youth who was torn to pieces by a bull and reincarnated as a grapevine. The blood of men murdered by Dionysus' Maenads was used to fertilize the vines. Later an animal sacrifice was substituted for the man, and finally his flesh and blood were devoured in the form of bread and wine, the classical Dionysian sacrament at Eleusis.[13] Today Dionysius is widely regarded as a god of revelry and a symbol of death and rebirth.

The theme of human sacrifice also appears in other religions and is familiar to Christians who believe that Jesus died on the cross for the sins of the world. His death and resurrection are celebrated in churches around the world in the symbolic eating of flesh and drinking of blood in the ritual of holy communion. He is born again every Christmas, and his death and resurrection are reenacted every Easter.

Historically some Christians believed that death was punishment for sin, namely sex, while others regarded both sex and death as a natural, inevitable part of life. Today pluralism is more acceptable among many Christians who disagree on matters of doctrine. While some Christians take the symbolism of Christmas, Easter and other holy days quite literally, others read the stories as metaphors for psychological processes that occur each time we let go into an experience of ego death and reawaken the soul.

In the northern hemisphere, Christmas follows celebrations of the winter solstice, when pagan festivals celebrate the turning point of the year and the return of the light. Many people who participate in social rituals at this time of year have only a superficial understanding of the inner meaning of the Christ child, as the incarnation of divine love. When the deeper meaning of Christmas remains hidden beneath the tawdry commercialism of a materialistic culture, we are bereft of the solace of authentic, transformative ritual that rekindles the light of divine love in the soul. Christmas then seems meaningless and is often a painful time for people who feel a lack of love, regardless of whether they are alone or in the midst of family.

At dawn on Easter Sunday, in the springtime, when the renewal of life is most evident in nature, the resurrection of Christ is celebrated with the words, "Christ is the Light." While some Christians believe in the resurrection of the body, others interpret Easter as celebrating the resurrection of the soul, following crucifixion of the ego. Others interpret the story of the resurrection as a myth, not to be taken literally but as a teaching about love and forgiveness and the triumph of Spirit over physical suffering and humiliation. The mystery of the empty tomb is at the core of Christian mysticism. Whatever the interpretation, Easter is an annual celebration of death and rebirth throughout Christendom.

Teachings of death and rebirth and reincarnation can be found in many of the world's religions, but when we cling to any belief because of fear of death, we may overlook the possibility of release and the peace of letting go. Buddhism teaches that the root cause of suffering is craving, clinging and attachment in a world of impermanence, where everything is in flux. The self that seems to exist in the throes of fear and desire is only an ever-changing, illusory self-concept. Only when we can see through our illusions can we be free from suffering.

Spiritual freedom and transformations of consciousness seem to depend on an ego death that involves letting go of a particular structure or sense of identity in order that a more encompassing, more complex sense of unity may emerge. Wilber posits the aim of evolution as the realization of ultimate unity in Spirit, for which ego death is necessary.[14] He writes,

> The *release factor* in this case is indeed a type of *death*; it is a real dying to an exclusive identity with a lower structure in order to awaken, via love-expansion or transcendence, to a higher-order life and unity. In this sense, such death-and-transcendence occurs at every stage of growth, matter to body to mind to bodymind to spirit. One accepts the death and release of the lower stage in order to find the life and unity of the next higher stage, and so on until either growth arrests and preservation alone sets in, or actual spirit is resurrected in the Great Death of final transcendence and ultimate unity.[15]

Thus Thanatos, no less than Eros, promotes growth, unity and transcendence. And the death of the small, separated ego self that clings to illusions of permanence and fears annihilation at every turn becomes the doorway to life.

CHANGING IMAGES OF SEXUALITY

In Greek mythology Eros was an ageless, bisexual deity of erotic love, believed to be the god who gave souls the strength to ascend to heaven after death.[16] Eros was worshiped as a powerful deity who could grant virtue and blessing to humankind both in life and after death.

When Freud identified Eros with the life principle, other forms of love such as *agape*, love of God, or *philios*, brotherly love, were considered derivative of Eros. Consequently, Western psychology has given more attention to the role of sexuality in psychological health than to the role of love and spirituality.

With the advent of psychoanalysis, widespread cultural attitudes toward sex changed radically. The repression of sexuality was perceived as a root cause of mental illness, and the newly emerging science of psychology turned away from the religious teachings of Christianity which viewed sex as evil except when sanctioned by marriage.

Pagan rites that made sex a holy sacrament enacting the union of gods and goddesses had been attacked by the Church, and in the Middle Ages the Roman Inquisition attributed witchcraft and Satanism to women's carnal lust. Puritanical religions that favored asceticism tried to destroy the sensual feminine nature that was perceived as the root of corruption and sin.

Today feminine eroticism is commonly associated with affection, tenderness and sensitivity to emotional needs, whereas male eroticism is typically thought to be more impersonal, often tinged with lust for power and violence. Sexual aggression can be exacerbated by cultural conditioning that imbues sex with fear and guilt. When sexuality is suppressed, anxiety, guilt and anger become closely associated with it. On the other hand, aggressive acting-out can also perpetuate dysfunctional patterns of behavior. Preoccupation with sexual dominance by either men or women can also be a defense against unconscious feelings of powerlessness.

A more mystical view of sex in Hindu, Buddhist and Taoist tantra uses ritualized sex in the service of transcendence. In tantric practice sexuality is perceived as a means for spiritual development and the attainment of freedom and immortality. In Hinduism, the *lingam-yoni*, symbol of the conjunction of the male and female principles, is an object of adoration. It represents the union of the god Shiva and the goddess Shakti. In this view, Shakti, the feminine, is the activating principle, and union with the female is, therefore, considered essential for a man's spiritual progress. The man who seeks to achieve realization of divinity through controlled sexual intercourse withholds orgasm in order to conserve his vital fluids. These energies are then supposed to rise through the chakras, or psychic energy centers, to flower at the crown as divine wisdom.

Most historical accounts of tantric practice indicate that female practitioners were relatively rare and that female consorts were usually used for the benefit of male initiates. According to contemporary research by Miranda Shaw, author of *Passionate Enlightenment: Women in Tantric Buddhism*, this reflects the androcentric bias of male historians who overlooked women practitioners.[17] Tantra provides important teachings on the union and integration of masculine and feminine energies and women practitioners may be accorded equal status with men. However, despite the presence of female representations of the divine, women do not have social equality with men in Hindu and Buddhist countries where tantra is practiced.

Theoretically, spirituality has nothing to do with gender, and attainment is supposed to be a matter of desire and dedication. Yet in the Vedic tradition there was no provision for women to renounce the world and live a monastic life. A woman's spirituality was supposed to center around her husband. At the request of his chief disciple, Buddha allowed women to join the monasteries, but the acceptance of female monastics did not alter condescending attitudes. In Hindu society women are still treated as impure and are not allowed to take part in religious or spiritual activities during menstruation.[18]

On one occasion when I had the opportunity to talk with His Holiness the Dalai Lama, I asked him to comment on the status of women in Buddhism, since I had observed that monks and nuns were not treated equally. He responded that although it was true that they did not have equal social status, from a spiritual perspective they were equal. The spiritual ideal of balance has not yet translated into equality in the social, economic or political spheres in most of the world.

The ideal of a final reintegration of opposites is a common goal in tantra and it provides a framework for sexual energy to be expressed in the service of the sacred. Rather than being an obstacle to spiritual realization as it is commonly assumed to be in traditions that recommend celibacy, sexuality becomes the vehicle for the realization of unitive consciousness. The great bliss of absolute nonduality that transcends opposites cannot be known discursively. It can be apprehended only through direct experience. In Vajrayana Buddhism it is said to be obtained by the unification of *prajna* (wisdom) and *upaya* (the means to attain it), *sunyata* (emptiness) and *karuna* (compassion) and other pairs of opposites that designate "female" and "male." These terms are often represented by a couple in sexual embrace. Transcendence of sexuality is sometimes represented by the androgyne, or two deities in one body.[19] Men and women who participate in these tantric practices visualize both male and female deities within themselves.

Tantrism can be found in many parts of the world in different forms and under different names. Some early Christian sects practiced sexual adoration of the feminine life force as Sophia, the feminine Holy Spirit. Some Gnostics, however, believed that souls were entrapped in flesh by love and lust and could be reunited with God only through cessation of sexual activity. In the rite of spiritual marriage, men and women would prove their chastity by lying together naked without copulation. These sects were suppressed and destroyed by the end of the fifth century.

Sufi mystics who adored the feminine principle as the world-sustaining power were similarly suppressed by orthodox Islam. Tantric practices nevertheless endured underground and appeared again in the legends of courtly love. Tristan's name was said to be the reversed syllables of *Tantris*.[20] In China, Tantric Buddhism apparently flourished until Confucian patriarchs eliminated it. Tantric Taoism continues to the present time.

Another symbol of the union of opposites is the widespread archetypal motif of the sacred marriage, sometimes appearing as the death wedding. It occurs in many different cultures, particularly in those where the great goddess and the feminine principle predominate. Sometimes depicting the union of the soul with the universe or with the *anima mundi* or world soul in the womb of nature, and sometimes in connection with the image of the great mother, the death wedding reminds us of the intimate connection between sexual union and death.

Discussing the sacred marriage initiation ceremonies of the ancient Gnostics, Elaine Pagels points out that the Eucharist was also perceived as a marriage feast, in which the soul was reunited with Spirit. When the two are separated, they are diminished and fall into degradation.[21]

The sacred marriage can also be interpreted as liberation from ego-centricity and entrance into a state of divine wholeness. Analyst Marie Louise von Franz observed that the wedding motif appears not only in ecstatic experiences at the end of life but also in dreams which point to an impending death. Carl Jung described his own experience of this marriage when he was in a near-death state, saying, "I do not know exactly what part I played in it. At bottom it was I myself: I was the marriage. And my beatitude was that of a blissful wedding."[22]

DREAMS OF DEATH

The fear of [death] grieves man because of the ignorance of the soul.[23]
—THE NAG HAMMADI LIBRARY

In Greek mythology, Hypnos (sleep), Eros and Thanatos were brothers. Sleep not only restores body and soul, it also prepares us for death. The state of deep dreamless sleep is often compared to death. Tibetans claim that with sufficient training in dream yoga, a yogi learns to maintain lucid awareness not only in dreams and waking life but also in deep sleep and after death. According to Vedanta and Tibetan teachings, when a yogi has learned to remain conscious twenty-four hours a day, throughout the three states of waking, dreaming and dreamless sleep, awareness can be maintained in the even more subtle after-death state. This yoga is an important part of preparation for death. Sleep and dreams thus become much more than a doorway to the unconscious. An intuitive understanding of sleep and dreams illuminates the world of soul and helps us understand how the mind creates subjective experience.

Dreams of death are common, and unconscious fears often surface in dreams, sometimes as nightmares. In some cases the fear of death can be ameliorated by paying close attention to death as it appears in dreams. Some people think that if you die in your dreams, you will actually die. This is evidently not true, since I have heard many people recount dreams of dying. Dying in dreams can be traumatic, and the dreamer may awaken in a cold sweat, but death dreams do not have the finality of physical death. One may awaken from a death dream only to die again and again in subsequent dreams. Although an intense panic reaction often precipitates waking up, a dreamer can learn to become lucid in the dream and stay asleep to confront the fear and complete the experience. When a person is determined to do this, sooner or later an opportunity to carry it out seems to present itself. Most people find that lucid dreams of death tend to reduce fear of dying.

The usual automatic response to fear, whether in dreams or in waking life, is some form of fight or flight. Yet either of these responses tends to increase fear instead of diminishing it. In the dream world, running away seems to engender pursuit. On the other hand, fighting a battle may be all consuming. The possibility of remaining fully present without giving in to the impulse to attack or run away seems to be the most skillful way of dispelling the terrifying shadows and illusions of death that may be encountered in the dream world.

The acceptance of death in a dream can have a transformative effect on the dreamer. Acceptance may also complete a particular dream sequence, although a similar theme may appear in some other form if the message of the dream has not been fully understood. Death dreams may also herald a major life transition such as the death of a relationship or a loss of identity, as in ego death.

One middle-aged woman who dreamed frequently of dying was not consciously obsessed with a fear of death. She wrote,

> I have faced death in my dreams many times. I have died in airplane crashes, drowned, driven over cliffs, been shot, been run over by

trains and devoured by wild animals. No one way seems worse than another. Each dream has seemed absolutely real, although sometimes I have a flash of lucidity and wonder if I am dreaming. Sometimes I say to myself, "Perhaps this is a dream. Its alright to let go." Then comes the thought, "No, this time its real. This is it." After many years of remembering these dreams, it seems easier to let go, to surrender and accept my inevitable destiny. I have asked myself, "What the purpose of these dreams?" I used to think they might be preparing me for an early death. But they started when I was a child, and now I'm in my fifties, so that doesn't make sense. Maybe they were helping me come to terms with my fear of dying. I feel less afraid of whatever is in store for us after death than of the process of dying. As I have become more accepting of these dreams, I find that I am less fearful in waking life. I am not sure which came first, but a greater sense of peace now pervades both my waking and my dream life.

A more detailed account of a dream of dying is given by analyst June Singer in her book, *Seeing Through the Visible World*:

I am lying on a narrow hospital bed, perhaps a gurney such as they use to wheel a patient into an operating room. I was very comfortable. I noticed that I was hooked up to all sorts of wires and tubes. It struck me as strange that I could be in this place and in this condition and feeling very well, unusually well. I was relaxed and peaceful. But I felt weak, not in an unpleasant way, simply weak. I did not feel that I could get up, but then I had no inclination to do so. It was as if my strength were slowly ebbing away and the realization came to me that I must be dying. Oh well, I thought, if this is the way it is, just let it happen and observe it carefully. You may not have another opportunity. I paid close attention to the sense of everything slowing down, my body, my thoughts. Yet I kept a keen awareness of a growing calm and a very quiet pleasure, as it is to sleep in the arms of the Beloved. I felt my life slipping away from me and I felt myself slipping like a drop of water sliding into the sea. And then I was no more myself alone, but merged into the fullness.[24]

Since having this dream, Singer says she has not experienced any fear of dying. It left her with a pervasive sense of peace. She recommends practicing the art of dying by imagining that you are on your deathbed, leaving everything in your life as it is. The only thing to do is to let go. As you release your sense of self-importance and let your identity slip away, you begin to feel lighter and more peaceful. This practice can help you do everything more slowly, with care and love. Letting go more and more upon entering the invisible world beyond death, you leave everything behind, including sexual roles. When you have made the male and the female one and the same, you can enter the kingdom of God.[25]

In an extensive investigation of dreams and death, Marie Louise von Franz found that the theme most commonly appearing in dreams of people approaching death was not death itself, but marriage.[26] Images of light and descriptions of energy are also common. Von Franz proposes that at death a gradual liberation from the bonds of space-time occurs. She suggests that at a certain threshold of increased frequency, our perception of time and space ceases functioning. Jung also stressed the view that part of the psyche is not bound to space and time. He wrote,

> . . . our psyche reaches into a region held captive neither by change in time nor by limitation of place. In that form of being our birth is a death and our death a birth. The scales of the whole hang balanced.[27]

The death marriage motif appears in various forms in the dreams of both men and women. In one case, an elderly woman dreamed of preparing for her own wedding, which she anticipated with joy. Upon waking she felt that the dream was preparing her for death.

Other stories of beautiful women falling in love with death personified as a man suggest the seductive quality of death. When life is hard, death may seem to offer welcome relief from the burdensome trials of earthly life. Just as a woman may dream of being rescued from her struggles by a lover who will take care of her in this life, she may also come to regard death as an escape from the pain of loneliness and despair. Fear of death, like fear of sex, can be obliterated in the passionate longing for release.

Marriage itself is sometimes experienced as a kind of death by those young women who expect to relinquish individual identity in order to assume a new identity which is subservient to the husband. The virgin dies to become the matron when she takes the vows of matrimony and gives up her former name and identity, assuming a new one as a wife.

Although dreams can help us confront death, contemporary society offers little help in preparation for dying. Medieval literature on *the art of dying* stresses both the relevance of death for living and the importance of preparation for dying. The contemplation of death in life was directed toward impermanence, the meaninglessness of worldly pursuits and the omnipresence of death. It was believed that at the time of death diabolical forces attempt to divert the soul from its way to heaven. It was therefore essential to face death courageously and accept it. It was considered mandatory not to offer false hope of recovery or denial of imminent death in order to help a person create the best attitude toward dying. To die unprepared was considered a great misfortune.[28]

Tibetan meditative practices in preparation for death include contemplating the ways in which you might die in the next twenty-four hours and imagining your own death in great detail. Other guided imagery techniques for coming to terms with your own death in life include visualizing your own funeral and listening to what people say about you after you have died. Writing your own obituary or imagining what you would do if you only had six more months to live can also be useful practices to increase awareness of the inevitability of death.

A Zen master introduced me to the idea that it is possible to die before you die. At first I thought this simply meant giving up attachments; then I discovered it to be an ongoing challenge, part of living one's life ready to die at each moment. Although I have certainly not attained unwavering equanimity, this teaching has helped me be mindful of the transient nature of life. These practices of death awareness that increase appreciation of the preciousness of life can have a profound effect on the way we live.

Coming to terms with death is also a gateway to the world of soul. Conversely, as one becomes familiar with the world of soul and identifies with the soul instead of the ego, it is easier to make peace with death.

BEYOND DEATH

Of all mindfulness meditations,
That on death is supreme.[29]

—THE BUDDHA

Most religious traditions offer some instruction for dying, and some give detailed accounts of what the soul can expect to encounter after death. The *Tibetan Book of the Dead,* for example, offers specific instructions for the soul that is believed to separate from the body at death.[30] When a person dies, the family gathers, and the lama recites or reads the instructions for the departing soul. According to this tradition, at the moment of death the departed soul experiences the clear light of pure reality, also known as the universal mother light, and total disintegration of the separate self. At this moment there is no obstruction between the soul and the universal clear light. The lama reads,

> O nobly born, (name), listen. Now thou art experiencing the Radiance of the Clear Light of Pure Reality. Recognize it. Thine own consciousness, shining, void, and inseparable from the Great Body of Radiance, hath no birth, nor death, and is the Immutable Light.[31]

Here the boundaries of the soul dissolve into the radiant void. The supratemporality of the soul is asserted not as an individual separate entity, but in the recognition of its identity with the clear light of unmanifest Spirit.

If awareness of the clear light cannot be sustained, the soul is instructed to contemplate the deity in the area of the sixth chakra. If this concentration fails, the soul should open to the divine radiance of the four directions in the area of the fifth chakra.

If during this process the departing soul is afraid, it is holding on too tightly to identification with the separate self. Hell is being stuck in individual separateness because of fear, clinging and attachment. Whatever is most valued becomes a golden chain that prevents liberation. If, for example, one takes pride in one's intellect, beauty or achievements, these become the obstacles to illumination. One should not try to get rid of anything, but use everything in the service of higher learning. Everything, whether in life or after death, can teach one about transiency, fear of loss and the pain of attachment.

Instructions for the departing soul may continue for a period up to forty-nine days, to guide it through the changing phenomena of the Bardo realms through which it passes on the way to reincarnation. Throughout the journey, the primacy of the soul is asserted. The giver of all things is said to dwell within it. Since humans resist seeing themselves as authors of their circumstances, this esoteric teaching is given only to those who have died or been through secret initiations culminating in symbolic death and rebirth. At a certain level of insight the soul of the dead person knows that thought-forms all emanate from one's own mind and that the four light-paths of wisdom that appear before one are the play of one's own consciousness.

The dying person is instructed to adopt the following attitude:

> I have arrived at the time of death, so now, by means of this death,
> I will adopt only the attitude of the enlightened state of mind,

friendliness and compassion, and attain perfect enlightenment for the sake of all sentient beings as limitless as space . . .[32]

The full wisdom of this ancient text reveals itself only to vision acquired through training and experience. It is not readily comprehensible to the layperson. Hearing it, however, is said to provide healing for the soul even beyond death. Jung pointed out that the custom of reading it at the time of death also serves the psychological need of the living to do something for the dead.[33]

Myths pertaining to the survival of the soul after death are found in most religious traditions. Each one is unique, yet they share some features in common, such as the theme of death and rebirth or resurrection.

According to the ancient Egyptian *Book of the Dead*, at the time of death, the heart of the departing soul is weighed against the feather of truth. Those found to be unjust are devoured by a monster who waits below the scales. Those who pass the test are led by Horus to be presented to Osiris, Lord of the Underworld.

In Egypt the death and resurrection of Osiris conveys the promise of salvation and eternal life to his followers. His flesh was eaten in the form of cakes of wheat, the "plant of truth." Osiris was restored to life by his divine mother—who was also his bride, Isis. It was Isis who put his dismembered body back together and raised him from the dead. She married him and conceived his reincarnation, Horus, who became Osiris again. She also took him to heaven where he reigned as the father god, Ra. They were cyclically reincarnated as father-son, and son-father, dwelling in the Mother as fetus, lover and corpse. As Lord of Death, Osiris was sometimes identified with the Great Serpent of the underworld,[34] a symbol of regeneration. Osiris was originally an ancient corn deity, associated from earliest times with birth, death and renewal. His followers came to believe that he ruled as a just king in another world where they hoped they would find eternal happiness.[35]

A similar theme of death and resurrection is found in the Greek myth of Persephone and Demeter in which Persephone is abducted by Hades, Lord of the Underworld. Her mother, Demeter, in wrath and grief, curses the earth to bear no fruit until she is released. When Persephone returns, the earth becomes fruitful again. However, since she had eaten the seed of a pomegranate in the underworld, Persephone must return to spend one third of each year with Hades. This myth, and others like it, are usually interpreted as a symbolic allegory of the seasonal cycles of vegetation. For initiates in the Eleusinian mysteries, however, the myth was a metaphor for spiritual transformation. The Orphic cult, Dionysian rites and other mystery schools shared the theme of death and rebirth. Similar rituals can be found in many other traditions.[36]

Here, as in the Egyptian myth of Isis and Osiris and the Grail legends, the feminine plays a significant role in restoring the earth to fruitfulness and healing what has been broken. The power of the feminine, manifesting as love and compassion, restores what has been dismembered to wholeness and transforms the wasteland into a garden. Her presence, however, is cyclical, and her connection with the underworld endures. She attends the cycles of birth, death and rebirth.

Transcendence of sexuality beyond death is depicted literally in a Huichol Indian yarn painting that portrays the departing souls arriving at a wild fig tree and divesting themselves of their sexual attachments in the shape of the penises and vaginas of their former partners. In return the souls receive the fruits of immortality.[37]

Encounters with powerful beings beyond death is another common theme appearing in visions of death and in near-death experiences in many cultures. Meetings with gods, rulers and judges are depicted in numerous traditions. Although the judgments are, from a psychological perspective, projected onto authority figures, it appears that at the end of this earthly life, the soul reviews and evaluates its own evolution.

In medieval Christian myths of the Last Judgment, the good deeds of a Christian soul are weighed against the evil. Angels and devils are sometimes portrayed as competing for possession of the departing soul. The departing soul may have to cross many barriers. A safe crossing of the narrow bridge across the River Styx depends on inner equilibrium. Souls who succeed in crossing the bridge are directed to heaven by angels, while sinners who fall into the river are swept away into hell.[38] This theme of reward and punishment for the soul after death is not unique to Christianity.

In the *Zohar*, a book of Spanish Kabbalism that dates back to the end of the thirteenth century, the tree of knowledge is also the tree of death. Eating the fruit of the tree of knowledge is what brings death to Adam and Eve and all their progeny. Death is related to the world of good and evil, in which humans can use knowledge destructively. The tree of life, on the other hand, represents the power of the Holy Spirit, invisible and diffused throughout the world.[39] The soul, but not the ego, can taste the fruit of the tree of life.

In each of these traditions the soul may be awakened by its encounter with the interdependent, archetypal forces of Eros and Thanatos. Birth, sex

---

70

and death provide the crucible of experience that challenges every human being to contemplate the meaning of existence at the intersection of time and eternity. If death is an end to physical suffering, could it also bring peace to the suffering of the soul?

In contrast to other traditions, Buddhism calls the very concept of soul into question and regards realization of impermanence and death as a fundamental realization for awakening. Writing on Tibetan Buddhism, Alan Wallace says meditation on death is needed to counteract the illusion of immortality that is always accompanied by grasping onto reality as if it were unchanging.[40] This practice sweeps away trivial attachments, regrets and grievances.

In the Hindu sacred text, the *Bhagavad Gita* (Song of the Lord), the Lord Krishna teaches Arjuna, the warrior disciple, that the death of the physical body is inevitable. The individual soul does not die but is reincarnated. The Eternal Self, or Atman, the seed of divinity within the soul, is birthless and deathless and cannot be destroyed. At death it merges with Brahman. The yogi who knows the Self does not die. All over India the Shiva lingam, the phallus of Shiva, lord of creation and destruction, is worshiped as a symbol of divinity that fuses sex and death.[41]

MAKING PEACE WITH DEATH

For someone who has prepared and practiced, death comes not as a defeat but as a triumph, the crowning and most glorious moment of life.[42]

—SOGYAL RINPOCHE

Preparation for death, then, is soulwork *par excellence*. For while contemplating death is terrifying to the ego, it awakens the soul and can have a powerful impact on the way we live our lives. For the person identified with soul rather than ego, the face of death changes from a specter of annihilation to a challenge of accountability. The soul that is free of guilt, anger and attachments has nothing to fear. It follows that authentic, ethical behavior leads to peace and joy, while self-deception and unethical behavior leads to misery. To live life ready to die means leaving no unfinished business with respect to the past. Awakening the soul is more than nourishing it by indulging in soulful activities. It also calls for cleansing and unburdening the soul, thereby liberating the mind from terror.

It appears that dying to who we think we are by letting go of limiting self-concepts time and time again enables us to grow into a fullness of being that is also a peaceful emptiness. Death, then, is no longer perceived as an enemy. In the latter part of life, if one is no longer captivated by illusions, one may welcome death as a friend, accepting it as a transformation that puts an end to the suffering of this life.

In my work with clients facing the shadow of death because of illness, listening to their reflections on living and dying, I have learned that facing our fears and coming close to death helps us make peace with death. I often encourage people to tell me what they believe about death. Bringing these beliefs to consciousness seems to help us come to terms with death.

For example, you might ask yourself what *you* think is true about the after-death state. Is it really the end, or does something continue? Is there some kind of reckoning for a life lived well or badly? What beliefs are grounded in personal experience, such as a near-death experience, and what have you learned from others? What are your unquestioned assumptions? If you have had an experience of ego death in which the roles you used to play are no longer relevant and you feel stripped of your personal identity, what have you learned from this experience? What does it mean, to die before you die? How do you react to fear? Do you take flight in avoidance and denial, or do you respond in anger, fighting for your threatened position? Can you stop for a moment in quiet stillness and allow all concepts to drop away? What are you avoiding now?

The peace that can be experienced in a moment of witnessing death is not easily understood. When fear is absent and the angel of death is welcomed as friend in old age, it may be attended by love rather than sorrow. Love fills the opening of those moments when life is not taken for granted. Regret for love spurned or withheld and gratitude for love given and received often attends death. When my parents died I was thankful that I had done enough inner work to heal my relationship with each of them.

Elisabeth Kübler-Ross, noted author and researcher on death and dying, once remarked that most people on their deathbed regretted not having taken more time for relationship in life. No one ever regretted not spending more time at the office. Sogyal Rinpoche, a Tibetan lama, says that when people are dying, the main question is whether their life has been meaningful.[43]

To be prepared to die before you die is a practice recommended in many spiritual traditions. To complete all your relationships, to leave no loving thought uncommunicated, no gratitude unexpressed and no debt unpaid, is not only a way to die in peace, but also a way to live in peace. When you carry no unfinished business from the past, no unfulfilled obligations, you are free to be fully present at the moment of death, as in life.

Growth-oriented psychotherapy can often help us complete unfinished business from the past, releasing our creativity and changing our perceptions of death. Death seems tragic when it cuts short a life of unfulfilled promise. It seems like a blessing to one who has lived a full life and is ready to rest.

We do not have to wait for an accident or a diagnosis of illness to face the inevitability of death. We can make peace with death by acknowledging regrets and making reparations for mistakes at any time. In a discussion of various exercises that are helpful in confronting death, author John White calls meditation the world's best fear remover.[44] Fearful images tend to haunt us only as long as we are unwilling to face them. If we can look past fear, a different perception of death may be revealed.

For example, a poem by Tom Greening offers a different view:

AWARENESS

Although I'm aging,
my retinas still see
in living color
a few electromagnetic waves,
but just those
from .4 to .7 millimicrons—
that is, from what we call red
to what we call blue.
And, I'm happy to say,
my tympanic membranes
still hear a few waves
amidst the acoustical ocean.
Some we call Bach.
I can't explain how I taste
certain molecular structures,
but I do,
and so it is with touch and smell.
Thus I keep in contact
with what we call reality,
and I have a lot of opinions about it.
My problem is
I know I'm missing out

on most of the waves.
Why should bees see more,
dogs smell more,
bats hear more?
And even they are missing
most of the show.
Why plunk down
such a small receiver
in the midst of this symphony?
When I die
do I get to hear it all?[45]

Those who have been close to death often say that there is nothing to fear. Yet we tend to cling to traditional beliefs rather than face unknown shadows. Telling stories about heaven and hell, karma, reincarnation and life after death are some of the ways that we try to make sense out of the mystery of death. Esoteric wisdom teaches that death is not an end, but a transformation, and that death is followed by rebirth. A tendency to take things literally often leads to reification of these myths. For example, reincarnation is usually believed to be linear, and people speak of past lives and future incarnations. It is as if human imagination cannot conceive of existence except in terms of linear time and individual identity.

Death invites us to live in awareness of the miracle of life surrounded by mystery. We try to make sense of it, but we get into difficulty when we reify intuitions of soul into dogma. From a nondual perspective, time itself is an illusion. Although our limited perception cannot encompass the totality of time and space, we can at least avoid reducing the awesome nature of reality to simplistic concepts. Faced without preconceptions, the great mysteries of Eros and Thanatos can change our lives and awaken the soul.

For example, one day an eminently successful, achievement-oriented physician was out clipping the hedge in his yard on a weekend when he suddenly had an image of a long road ahead of him, bordered by trees on both sides which prevented him from getting off the road. At the end of the road he saw his tombstone. The vision had a tremendous emotional impact on him. It disturbed him deeply, and he understood that he could not ignore its significance. He began a spiritual quest that has lasted for over a decade. The quest led him to give up his prestigious position and take some time off. Later he took another less demanding position where he could be more involved in teaching medical students and emphasizing human values in medicine. Facing the inevitability of his own death brought greater clarity and a renewed sense of meaning and purpose to his life.

Sometimes an experience of ego death can take a person beyond conceptual constrictions. Surrendering to an ego death that involves letting go of the separate self-sense altogether, albeit briefly, can engender either panic or ecstasy, depending, at least in part, on adequate preparation. The radiant bliss of freedom is hidden by the veil of fear. The saints and sages who dared to surrender have tried to tell us about this process, yet until we have an experience of self-transcendence ourselves, we may not understand the meaning of their words. Sometimes we taste it in some of the little deaths we go through in the course of a lifetime. Sometimes the soul rises like a phoenix from the ashes of the ego. Whenever we give up an image of what we were for the sake of what we might become, we seem to die a little. New possibilities seem to present themselves only after we take a leap of faith into the unknown.

SUICIDE

How do I know that loving life is not a delusion? How do I know that in hating death I am not like a man who, having left home in his youth, has forgotten the way back?[46]

—Chuang Tsu

Although many religions teach that suicide is a sin, the desperate act of suicide speaks for the soul that already feels imprisoned in an eternal hell with no hope of change. The only hope is that nothingness will be an escape from the hell in which the soul feels helplessly, hopelessly trapped. In the play *No Exit*, Jean-Paul Sartre portrayed three such hopeless people in hell, who preferred to stay where they were rather than go through a door into the unknown. Hell is experienced as intense suffering, not in the future, but in the eternal present. Those who are in hell *have* abandoned hope.

Attitudes toward death by suicide are shaped by beliefs about the afterlife and the soul. If the afterlife is conceived to be a happy existence, and if suicide is perceived as neutral or worthy of reward, suicide rates tend to increase. In ancient Rome, for example, Seneca believed that the Divine had given humans a number of possible exits from this world and that the individual had the right to free choice in the matter. He himself chose suicide.

In ancient Greece suicide was tolerated and sometimes regarded as honorable. Socrates accepted it and even welcomed it as necessity. When he was encouraged by friends to attempt escape, he chose not to. He said human beings belonged to the gods, who reserved the right to bestow life or take it away; therefore a man should not take his own life. Socrates argued that a philosopher, however, should welcome death and not be afraid of it, for when the body died, the immortal soul was freed from its limitations.[47]

Suicide was considered honorable in cases of defeat or disgrace. For example, Jocasta's suicide in response to learning of her incestuous relationship with Oedipus was considered appropriate. Aristotle, on the other hand, regarded suicide as an offence against the state, and his view of suicide as a social outrage has dominated Western thought until the present time.

In Japanese culture, suicide could be an honorable and glorious death for a Samurai warrior. Ritual suicide by disembowelment was a legal institution in Japan from the beginning of the thirteenth century. It was important in the *bushido*, or warrior's code of ethics, because it showed that the warrior held certain values to be more important than life. The seat of the soul was believed to rest in the lower part of the abdomen, and by opening the abdomen the warrior would expose the purity of his soul for everyone to see.[48]

In medieval Europe suicide was also deemed an honorable exit from intolerable situations, such as defeat by an enemy or disappointment in love. In the case of defeat, death was considered preferable to the humiliation of capture. Romantic suicide, epitomized by Shakespeare's Romeo and Juliet, was popularly accepted, in spite of official Church doctrines that condemned suicide as an unforgivable sin.

Mainstream Christianity generally viewed suicide as a form of homicide. In fact, it was considered worse than homicide, since it precluded the possibility of repentance. St. Augustine argued that it was never justified, even in such dire circumstances as when a virgin had lost her honor. St. Thomas Aquinas supported this view and Dante placed suicides in the seventh circle of the inferno.

In the seventeenth century this belief was challenged by John Donne, dean of Saint Paul's Cathedral in London, who argued that this totally negative attitude was untenable since it implied a limitation on God's love and mercy. Nonetheless, corpses of suicides where buried at crossroads with stakes driven through their hearts to prevent their ghosts from causing harm, and their property was confiscated by the state until the nineteenth century.[49]

The distinction between martyrdom and suicide is blurred in religious history. It was considered saintly to die for one's faith, but not by killing oneself. Death was sometimes actively sought by deliberate provocation and ascetic practices resulting in death were also condoned. Some Christian heretical sects committed mass suicide in the face of persecution, both by burning themselves and by voluntary starvation. In the Bible several honorable suicides are mentioned in the Old Testament. In the New Testament the only case of suicide is the death of Judas Iscariot, who took his life after betraying Jesus, and this has been interpreted as a sign of repentance.

In Hinduism religiously motivated suicides by renunciates were acceptable if the person was sufficiently prepared. Favored methods included drowning in the Ganges, burning or starving oneself. The practice of *sati*, widow burning, was common. The woman facing the degradations of widowhood might choose to burn on her husband's funeral pyre rather than suffer continued existence without a husband; but she could also be subjected to social pressure, since her voluntary sacrifice was believed to purify her and her deceased husband.[50]

Buddhism legislates against suicide for the ordinary person, and for practitioners of deity yoga in Vajrayana Buddhism, suicide is believed to have dire karmic consequences. Killing anything is forbidden, and killing oneself, when one is identified with the deity is tantamount to killing a buddha. However, contemporary Buddhist monks have been known to immolate themselves as a form of protest against social injustice. Furthermore, the story of one of the lives of the Buddha in which he sacrificed himself to feed a hungry tigress portrays this as an act of compassion.

Contemporary Western society tends to condemn suicide if it is sought as an escape from the ordinary suffering of human life but takes a more compassionate view in cases of extreme suffering. It is also considered honorable to die for one's beliefs, religious or secular. For example, going to war could be considered a form of honorable suicide in defense of ideology. Slower forms of voluntary self-destruction caused by drug abuse, cigarette smoking or alcohol addiction are not considered suicide.

The distinction between suicide as avoidance and as self-sacrifice remains unclear. When does self-sacrifice become self-indulgence? Modern humanity as a whole condemns human sacrifice in religious rituals, yet self-sacrifice may be deemed worthy of respect. In some Islamic sects, a man is denied entrance to paradise if he takes his own life, while entrance to paradise is guaranteed for one who dies in battle. Conflicts of insurmountable odds may therefore be actively sought as a means of heroic suicide.

Suicide, however unacceptable, remains an option to anyone who chooses it. Many people see it as a rational choice in the face of terminal illness. The debate over the right to die, like the debate over euthanasia and abortion, will undoubtedly continue for the foreseeable future. When suicide is perceived as an escape, it reflects a materialistic worldview in which the self is exclusively identified with the body. Perceived as a sin, it reflects religious dogma.

Is suicide a final cop-out? If soulwork transcends death, is it a setback? Religious injunctions against killing may certainly be extended to suicide, yet I know many people who would never think of killing someone else seriously consider suicide. I often hear people say, "I would never do it, but I have been thinking a lot about suicide." I listen carefully because I know that talking about it reduces the risk of carrying it out.

These days, with a worldwide AIDS epidemic, drug abuse and sexual promiscuity might be considered a form of suicide. Yet the risk of disease and the stark connection between sex and death does not deter people from throwing caution to the winds in the heat of passion. The intimate connection between Eros, Thanatos and Hypnos is evident when unconsciousness is reinforced by fear and denial. Freedom to choose life or death is contingent on being awake.

Those who have attempted suicide and survived often say that they would never do it again. On the other hand, I have known people who voluntarily ended their lives in old age by stopping eating. They seemed to be choosing a peaceful and dignified exit from this world. I remember talking with a woman whose aging parents had agreed to suicide together. They had discussed their decision with her and her brother. She understood that they could not be persuaded to change their minds. Although she grieved their death, she also empathized with their conscious choice in the face of serious illness and debilitation.

Today, when medical technology can keep the body alive even when the soul seems ready to depart, many family members are faced with agonizing decisions about when to use or refuse heroic medical measures to keep someone alive. A person who has made peace with death and prepares for it by signing a living will that gives explicit instructions to doctors and family, relieves others of this burdensome responsibility.

Those who have had near-death experiences often say that they return with a new appreciation of the preciousness of life and are glad to be here, although they are no longer afraid of dying. They have walked through the valley of the shadow and it no longer terrifies them. Freedom from fear lets us say yes to life, sex and death. When we have seen past the shadow, everything can be perceived as grace.

A FINAL VISION

If you are capable of dying with presence and awareness, . . . you will have no difficulty recognizing the mother light.[51]

—NAMKHAI NORBU

From the point of view of ego, I may envision death as the grim reaper, a hooded skeleton that appears to take me away when I am not ready to leave. In the Tibetan tantric tradition, one aspect of Yama, Lord of Death, is depicted as a dancing skeleton, joined in sexual union with a female counterpart. For the person who identifies only with ego, death is an inevitable defeat; for those identified with soul, there is no death. From the point of view of the soul, I may envision beings of light and boundless compassion that are ready to greet me and guide me into the hereafter.

Although fear of death is partly a biological survival instinct, it appears to be predominantly an ego fear. When death is perceived to be uselessly destructive, it is fearful. When it is perceived as a necessary fact of life in which the old is relinquished to make room for the new, death becomes an instrument of transformation.

You do not have to believe in anything in particular to entertain the possibility of making friends with the angel of death. If angels are believed to be messengers of God, you have only to make peace with God, whatever that means to you. For many people that means forgiving oneself and others and God for whatever one has condemned. Experiences of self-transcendence often reduce fear of death, as does attending another person's death with awareness. I am grateful for the opportunities I have had to be with loved ones when they died. Each time I was surprised by a deep sense of peace.

If I am ready, will death come as a lover or a friend? Or, as Emmanuel suggests, is dying like taking off a tight shoe?[52] Could it be that letting go of the body is like letting go of some deep-rooted attachment that could be experienced as a release? Is the French expression for sexual orgasm, *la petite morte,* the little death, an intimation of something yet to be revealed? Is death the biggest orgasm of all, as Alan Watts expected it to be? Will dreams and shadows disappear or will consciousness cling to familiar realms of experience?

Each of us can benefit from asking ourselves what we believe about sex and death. The truth is no threat to reality, but our illusions may blind us to the inevitabilities of life. The shadows of sex and death exert a profound influence on the soul seeking liberation. Both engender fear and desire, and both can awaken the soul. No one can avoid encountering them. We can choose whether we will try to avoid thinking about them and pay the price of denial and psychic death, or whether we will wake up and face reality with awareness. When we are willing to face our fears we may discover that behind the shadows and illusions surrounding sex and death runs a deep and all-pervading undercurrent of love. This awareness can help us make peace with death and surrender to the creative energies of Eros.

Pointing beyond images to the mystical union of the awakened soul with the divine, Huston Smith writes:

> Body dies, but the soul and spirit that animate it live on. Revelation comes first as judgment. First the body drops away, then the mind drops away in forgiveness, and the soul is freed to pass into the beatific vision of its immortal center.[53]

CHAPTER 4

The Path of Love

Ecstatic love for God—heart and mind melted by passionate longing for Truth—is the one essential factor in the process of awakening.[1]

—LEX HIXON

LOVE IS STRONGER THAN DEATH. IT DOES not die when the body dies and cannot be limited by laws or logic. Love pervades existence, even in the midst of suffering, and opening the heart to love may be the best way to prepare for death. Shadows seem to disappear when we are in love. The perfect love that casts out fear transforms the experience of sex and death into ecstasy and joyous surrender. Love is a time-honored way of awakening the soul.

Although some men and women spend their entire lives searching for love, love as the creative Source of being is always already present. The path of love is fraught with illusions that seem to indicate that love is limited, and we only find it if we are lucky. When we mistake particular forms of limited love for its eternal essence, we tend to overlook the mysterious presence and power that transcends death and awakens the soul.

Thinking of love merely as an emotion, or devotion to a particular object, person or deity, limits our understanding of divine love as the ground of Being. Although any form of love can provide a glimpse of eternity, mistaking the form for the essence of love is to mistake shadows for reality. No specific form of love endures, and no object can satisfy the soul's longing for union with the Beloved. Yet love itself is like an eternal flame that can always be rekindled in the human heart that has the courage to open.

Sometimes the eternal nature of divine love is understood only after the heart seems to have been broken.

The challenges we encounter on a path of love reflect the illusions we have about the nature of love and how to find it. I have never met anyone who did not want to give and receive love. Yet who has not been disappointed in love? One of my Buddhist teachers used to say that disappointment is a great teacher. However, I think we probably learn more about our attachments from disappointments and disillusionments than we do about love itself. If someone I love does not meet my expectations, I may feel betrayed, angry and unloved. Love never seems to fulfill our egocentric expectations, but it often surpasses them.

One woman I know had several disappointing love affairs before she fell in love with a person she could truly love. Every one of the relationships she had explored had taught her something about sharing another person's life and remaining true to herself. Each time she let go of a relationship that was not what she really wanted, she struggled to understand what was not working, until she knew herself better and understood more clearly what she really wanted. When she finally met the person who was to become her husband, her expectations had changed. She expected less in some ways and more in others. As the relationship deepened over time, she said she had never imagined how fulfilling love could be.

To unveil the reality of love is to be released from illusions of limited love that lead to disappointment. Romantic illusions projected onto an attractive other tend to place impossible demands on the idealized person, and the shadow of romantic love can easily be seen in possessiveness, jealousy and rage. On the other hand, love as a universal experience that illuminates the spiritual path is a source of healing and guidance at every step along the way. By clearing away the blocks to our awareness of love's presence we reawaken to its original blessing.

Since love can only be experienced in the present, our preoccupations with past and future tend to diminish our capacity to give and receive love in the present, and our hopes and fears tend to interfere with its expression. Yet the deeper we go into our own suffering and sorrow, the more we discover that the seeds of love and healing lie hidden under the pain. When love is revealed, even when a person is close to death, suffering can turn to joy. This is one way that love redeems suffering and forgives even the illusions that prevent us from recognizing it.

At every stage of the journey, the soul seeks fulfillment in love, at first through romantic attachments, eventually in ecstatic love without an object.

Love nourishes the soul and draws the seeker deeper into the quest for the Beloved as the object of devotion on the spiritual quest. When the spark of divinity in the soul is ignited, it is expressed in love.

Eros, as the impulse to union, inspires the soul and draws it into mystery, in spite of fear. The yearning of the separated soul to rediscover its original identity as Spirit is often felt as a longing for love. St. John of the Cross says the soul needs nothing but simple, pure and loving awareness, for it is God who infuses into the soul loving knowledge and wisdom.[2] As we learn to open the heart and quiet the mind in spiritual practice, we prepare the way for unconditional love. When divine love illuminates the heart, it leaves an indelible impression on the soul.

There is a profound contrast between the emptiness of mind infused by the fullness of ecstatic love and the emptiness we associate with fear and lack. The love we discover when the mind is quiet and the heart is open is not fueled by desire. It is boundless, unconditional and ecstatic, independent of objects. From time to time we may intuit this state of being long before it is fully realized. In our usual, limited states of consciousness, however, we understand only relative truth, and our understanding of love changes with the seasons of our lives.

SPIRITUAL VISION

To those who, their hearts having been opened, can see with its eye (the Sufi's "eye of the heart," Plato's "eye of the soul"), spiritual objects will be discernible and a theistic metaphysics will emerge.[3]
—HUSTON SMITH

Seeing with spiritual vision means looking past appearances and perceiving what is ordinarily assumed to be invisible. Universal love is more easily recognized when one is not obsessed with a particular form, such as romantic love. The soul that welcomes love without fear and awakens spiritual vision sees love's reflection in all aspects of creation.

When the heart is closed and love seems to be absent, the world becomes a wasteland of alienated individualism. In religious life, feeling a lack of love indicates separation from God and signals a dark night of the soul. The classic dark night of the soul occurs only after the soul has had a vision of God that subsequently fades. When no such vision has been attained, feelings of alienation may be more aptly described as a dark night of the ego that clings to its separate reality, mistaking the shadows of love for its reality. This also characterizes the existential experience of hell as a place of no exit. While the despair of ego often precedes embarking on the spiritual path, the despair of the soul that feels separated from its Source seems to be an integral part of the soul's journey.

Sometimes the rediscovery of love occurs through a conversion experience or a personal relationship with a spiritual teacher. For Christians, Jesus offered teachings of love and forgiveness. The Buddha pointed to the possibility of escape from a life of inevitable suffering by way of the eightfold path, a prescription for ethical conduct and practice which supports the cultivation of wisdom and compassion. When the mind is perceived as the source of all pleasure and pain, quieting the mind can reveal a source of love at the core of our being. *Bhakti yoga*, the yoga of devotion, is usually perceived as a path of love, although devotion usually implies dependence on an object, whereas unconditional love does not *need* anything. For example, a devotee may at first feel bereft of love when he or she is not in the presence of the guru. In time, when the devotee has understood that the guru reflects the image of the Divine within, he or she will no longer need to be physically with the guru to experience divine love.

Spiritual vision that perceives the presence of love as something outside or disconnected from oneself is an illusion that can be valuable at first, but it can also be entrapping. Shadows are dispelled when we begin to see the world through the eyes of love and acceptance rather than judgment. Trusting an intuitive response to love seems to be a necessary though insufficient condition for developing spiritual vision.

A woman who came to see me recently told me about how she fell in love with a teacher with whom she spent seven years. She said that in his presence she had such overwhelming feelings of love that she gave up her relationship with her boyfriend and joined the community of devotees. At first everything was wonderful. The glow did not last, however, and she soon began to notice authoritarian practices on the part of the teacher that bothered her. She discovered that she could not question his authority. Doubts about the value of the group were not allowed. When she expressed doubts or difficulties, she was told that it was her problem because her ego mind had not fully surrendered. She began to feel that everyone around her was extremely judgmental, while paying lip service to universal love and compassion. Eventually she decided to leave the group and discovered that her capacity for love did not depend on being part of that particular community. At first her reentry into the outside world was difficult, but after claiming her freedom she said she began to see love in the world for the first time.

Spiritual insight depends on developing a nonjudgmental intuitive perception associated with the wisdom of the heart. Clarity of spiritual vision also needs to be cultivated in order to find the right teacher and recognize when it is time to seek a different way.

Spiritual traditions offer a variety of different methods for opening the eye of the soul and developing discernment. All suggest some form of purification and awareness training. Before the eye of the soul is opened, one can learn from any of the great traditions, listening to those teachers who seem trustworthy, possibly following those who demonstrate love and wisdom in their lives. After the eye of the soul has been opened, discernment is guided by love and inner wisdom. This may lead one deeper into a tradition or out into an unknown way.

TRADITIONAL TEACHINGS

Love is a cornerstone of the Judeo-Christian tradition. According to the New Testament, Jesus said,

"You shall love the Lord your God with all your heart, with all your soul and with all your mind." This is the greatest and first commandment. And a second is like it: "You shall love your neighbor as yourself." On these two commandments hang all the law and the prophets. (Matt. 22:37–40)[4]

Jesus also said,

This is my commandment, that you love one another as I have loved you (John 15:12).

Although the desire for love is universal, love does not seem to respond well to commands. It seems, rather, to be a spontaneous experience that happens to us when we are open to it. We can invite it, welcome it and remove the emotional blocks that prevent us from experiencing it, but love cannot be grasped, ordered or controlled. In Christianity love is considered the greatest of spiritual gifts. In the words of St. Paul,

I may speak in tongues of men or of angels, but if I am without love, I am a sounding gong or a clanging cymbal. I may have the gift of prophecy, and know every hidden truth; I may have faith strong enough to move mountains; but if I have no love, I am nothing. [. . .]Love is patient; love is kind and envies no one. [. . .]there are three things that last for ever: faith, hope, and love; but the greatest of them all is love. (1 Cor. 13:1–2,4,13)[5]

The unconditional love that extends to everyone and everything is impossible without forgiveness, and genuine forgiveness of others is only possible when we have forgiven ourselves. Only when we are willing to acknowledge our gifts, our mistakes and our limitations, can we forgive and accept ourselves and each other.

This was clearly demonstrated to me when I was working with Anne, a woman who was troubled by deep feelings of guilt after her mother's death. In the week preceding her mother's death, Anne, who had been angry with her mother for years, had refused to go to see her. Even after she died, Anne still held on to old resentments, feeling that her mother had neglected her when she was a child. As we worked through the painful feelings of aloneness, she began to feel some compassion for herself as a child who felt unloved. In time, as she began to see how much she was like her mother and how deeply they had both been caught in fear and defensiveness, Anne was able to forgive herself and then her mother for their failure to love each other better.

I was taught when I was young that God is love and that the message of the *Gospel,* meaning "good news," is that anything can be forgiven. It was only later, when I studied the history of Christianity in college, that I realized that not everyone understood the central message of Christianity as a teaching of love and forgiveness. Some who believed that Jesus died for their sins felt burdened by guilt and unworthiness and focused more on the crucifixion than the resurrection. Condemnation and punishment often seemed to take the place of love and forgiveness.

In a contemporary translation of the *Gospel According to Jesus,* Stephen Mitchell tried to sort out the teachings *of* Jesus from the teachings *about* Jesus, which are sometimes at odds with his essential message. He points out that there are no preconditions for God's love for everything earthly. He says,

> When we are ready to receive it, it is there. And the more we live in its presence, the more effortlessly it flows through us, until we find that we no longer need external rules or Bibles or Messiahs.[6]

The kingdom of heaven that can be found within is a state of *being in love,* and this state of mind can be discovered by anyone who truly wants it. The path of love leads through forgiveness to the realization that love is always, already present, even when the shadows of fear, guilt and anger block our awareness of it.

The Judeo-Christian tradition is not the only one that emphasizes love as an integral part of the spiritual path. Other examples of the centrality of love are also found in Eastern thought.

In *The Synthesis of Yoga*, Sri Aurobindo said,

> By knowledge we seek unity with the Divine in his conscious being; by works we seek also unity with the Divine in his conscious being, not statically but dynamically, through conscious union with the divine Will; but by love we seek unity with him in all the delight of his being. For that reason the way of love, however narrow it may seem in some of its first movements, is in the end more imperatively all embracing than any other motive of Yoga.[7]

The Hindu concept of love as *bhakti*, or devotion in its highest form, finds expression in the teachings of the great Indian saint Ramakrishna, who was certain that all seemingly contradictory philosophies were means to the same end, and that all paths to God lead to the same goal. For Ramakrishna love of the Divine Mother was experienced as a steady flow of undiluted bliss.[8] In this ecstatic, transcendental love, the subject finds union with all objects. In Ramakrishna's words,

> The sole purpose and goal for human life, the supreme ideal of which all other ideals are simply an expression, is to cultivate love. . . . There is no boundary whatsoever to pure love—it embraces humanity and Divinity equally. In this most intense love, no sense of duality can remain.[9]

The experience of love as union with the Divine is also described in the writings of St. John of the Cross. Here the path of the soul leads from initial stages of purgation through its meeting with Christ (illumination) to mystical union with the Beloved. On its way to God, the soul learns to love as God loves, with the pure disinterested love that Christians call *agape*.[10]

Although in English the same word refers to many different aspects of love, other languages have several different words for love. In Greek, for example, *Eros*, or erotic love, is associated with sex and passion as well as the creative cultural love toward the good, the true and the beautiful. *Eros* drives the soul in its aspiration to union with the Beloved. *Philia*, or brotherly love, is the love of friendship and the root of *philosophy* as love of wisdom. *Philia* is a personal expression of love in the world. *Agape* is the unconditional, benevolent love of God pouring into the world. The great theologian Paul Tillich said,

> [A]gape is the word used in the New Testament meaning the acceptance of the other one as a person, which includes the principle of justice. It is the power of reuniting with the other person as one standing on the same ultimate ground, and therefore he is the object of acceptance, forgiveness, and transformation.[11]

Today we might add that *agape* embraces not only humanity but the earth and all creatures as well, for this love transcends distinctions. According to Tillich, the Christian idea of love is not to be confused with sentimentality or reduced to compassion which can be exploited. It is, rather, the creative ground of everything that is, in which *agape* and *eros* are united.[12]

CONTEMPORARY PERSPECTIVES

There is a love like a small lamp, which goes out when the oil is consumed; or like a stream, which dries up when it doesn't rain. But there is a love that is like a mighty spring gushing up out of the earth; it keeps flowing forever, and is inexhaustible.[13]

—ISAAC OF NINEVEH

Interpretations of love are shaped by personal experience and spiritual vision. Some interpretations are shallow and restrictive; others are deep and spacious. While some people think of love as an illusion or a temporary emotion, others experience it as the creative source of all life. Ramana Maharshi, a twentieth-century Indian sage, said that love is caused by joy and that we can experience this joy every night when the mind is subdued in deep dreamless sleep. In order to realize this joy, however, it is essential to know oneself.[14]

In healthy spiritual development love does not depend on external reinforcement. For some, love is a gift of grace. Others believe that practicing altruism makes love accessible. Love expressed as altruism is found in all cultures, not only in social service and philanthropy, but among parents, teachers, healers, mentors, friends and lovers of all persuasions. When I have asked people to remember a time when they were significantly helped by someone, many of them remember someone who cared enough to listen and pay attention to them. The loving quality of their attention is remembered long after the content of their advice is forgotten.

When love is contingent on how another person behaves, it tends to be fragile and disappointments lead to resentments. We therefore see many examples of people falling in and out of love, sometimes ending in bitterness and cynicism. "I'll never love again" is an expression of anger that blocks the rekindling of love in the heart.

I remember Robert, who told me a few years ago that he had finally met the perfect woman. He had been married and divorced before, but this, he said, was different. He married his new friend within a few months, only to discover later that she was not perfect after all. A year later they were divorced, and he was bitter and angry. She had let him down, he felt, and he was determined not to get intimately involved with anyone again. In desperation he began psychotherapy and in time came to discover a deeper capacity for love in the depths of his own being.

Everyone seems to have some awareness of love, if only in lamenting its absence. A path of love can be painful, difficult and challenging at times, but when we trust it, love can heal the heart and awaken the soul. When the universal desire to love and be loved is expressed as the soul's longing for the Beloved, the Beloved may be perceived everywhere—in nature, in other people or in art—and the whole of creation becomes transparent to the bliss of Divine presence. I know one person who claims that her ability to help others through their healing process in her work as a nurse depends on her capacity to feel connected to the Beloved. In addition to her professional skills she brings the gift of a loving presence into the lives of all of her patients.

Love and death are often seen as belonging together. Love of honor, glory or country sometimes means dying for these ideals. Love of freedom may also be associated with willing self-sacrifice. Sometimes erotic love relationships also seem to demand sacrifice of the separate self, particularly for women. The desire for union with the beloved, albeit fleeting and elusive, can be so compelling that a lover may gladly sacrifice hard-won independence. In medieval Europe, the penalty for adultery was death, yet illicit love relationships were immortalized in poetry and song.

Passionate romantic love is among the oldest recorded experiences of humankind. It plays a prominent role in Greek mythology and was part of ancient history in the relationships of Samson and Delilah and of Anthony and Cleopatra. Prior to the eleventh century, the dominant form of romantic love was heroic, involving pursuit and capture of the woman by the man. The fulfillment of love was commonly sought outside of marriage. The appearance of courtly love in the eleventh century shifted the emphasis from conquest to courtship, or entreaty of the woman by the man.

The tragic aspect of romantic love in the West is portrayed in myths and stories such as Tristan and Isolde and Romeo and Juliet. Other classic examples of courtly love are Lancelot and Guinevere and Dante and Beatrice. This form of love was believed to be attainable only outside of marriage, often without sexual communion. Romantic love did not become associated with marriage until the late nineteenth century, and then only in the West. Only when individuals claimed the right to govern themselves, to personal freedom, choice and equality, did love become a criterion for marriage.[15]

The dissolution of ego boundaries involved in the experience of falling in love can be simultaneously joyous and painful. From an egocentric point of view, the pain sometimes seems more intense than the joy. Men and women build elaborate psychological defenses to protect themselves from abandonment and loss of love, but a strong experience of erotic love brings with it the shadow of possible loss and a keen awareness of the transitory nature of temporal existence.

Jungian analyst Aldo Carotenuto calls love a lightning flash of the eternal within the flow of time. He says,

> By its very nature love belongs to the realm of the inexpressible. Like everything that has to do with the soul, it is near to mystery and keeps company with silence.[16]

Jung considered the experience of falling in love as a powerful force for bringing the unconscious to light. Love activates self-knowledge and expands the inner world. On the other hand, erotic love can also lead to entanglements of secrecy, deceit, jealousy and betrayal. Suffering is inherent in separation from the beloved, and the emotional opposite of erotic love is hate. Nevertheless, erotic love can heal a broken heart, spark the imagination and inspire the soul.

The loss of a romantic love relationship, whether through betrayal, abandonment, death or disillusionment, brings us face to face with the inevitability of death. Not only is the despairing lover likely to feel suicidal, if not homicidal, but the loss of the relationship itself may be felt as a kind of death. Renewal comes from letting go and trusting in love's eternal rebirth rather than by clinging to an image of the lost object.

The person who is willing to give up denial and projection and accept the reality of death will recognize the transitory nature of partial, possessive love. The person who believes that love is possible only in the presence of a particular love object remains bound to illusions of limited love. Although reason may serve as a guide through peaks and valleys of emotional turmoil and attachment, it offers cold comfort in the face of grief and loneliness. Healing this pain requires rekindling the Source of love within.

Richard, a man in his mid-forties who came to see me to heal a broken heart, was an expert at rationalization. He could understand why his marriage had ended in divorce and why the woman he had been dating had ended the relationship. He said they were incompatible. His reasonableness had carried him through the interpersonal difficulties, seemingly unscathed. As we began to uncover more of his deeper feelings, Richard said he seemed to fall into a well of sadness that—as far as he could tell—was a bottomless pit. His commitment to a process of inquiry led him to explore several spiritual disciplines before he found one that suited him. Here, for the first time, he met a woman that he felt he could love without being afraid that she would leave.

Effort and surrender are both necessary for those who would move through progressive stages of awakening on a path of love. Each stage demands a willingness to love in the face of impermanence. To love truly without attachment may seem to be superhuman, yet in psychological and spiritual maturity, the capacity for love becomes increasingly independent of particular objects. The problem with thinking of love exclusively as an emotion or as erotic love, powerful though it can be, is that other equally inspiring experiences of love may be overlooked.

Describing love as a quality of essence, A. H. Almas points out that essence, which transcends both positive and negative emotions, is a felt experience, but not a feeling.[17] The feelings of joy and compassion associated with the opening of the heart center can produce ecstatic states, but are not yet essence. The opening of the heart can be an entrance to the universe of essence, but love as a purely emotional experience can also be addictive, in which case it becomes an obstacle to deeper spiritual realization. Some Sufi teachers, according to Almas, use the word *heart* to refer to the presence of true nature or essence, but it designates varying degrees of subtle meaning. In the absence of training in subtle perception, an emotional experience of love may be mistaken for the quality of essence. The latter, however, is described as a clear, peaceful, silent emptiness, pervaded by a very fine, subtle and exquisite compassion. There is no emotional discharge, and its intrinsic pleasurable quality is best described as loving kindness, although even this is inexact.

For me, discernment on the path of love means recognizing that love is much more than feeling or emotion. Love has feeling and emotion in it, but it is not an emotion. It can be likened, rather, to a reunion of separated entities that belong together. Following this path with integrity and commitment seems to ask that we face the dark passage through the hell realms of separation without running away into unconsciousness or projecting blame for negative experiences onto others. Although the path seems tortuous at times, I believe it leads, eventually, to the gates of paradise where the awakened soul is reunited with its Source as Spirit. Effort and reason, necessary along the way, become irrelevant in paradise. As Dante knew, here love is the only guide. Love, which transcends reason, may then be recognized as an all pervasive, essential quality of existence, a creative resource of inexhaustible abundance. It seems that the further we go on the spiritual path, the more we become aware of love's presence in our lives.

The choice to follow the call of love means abandoning previous assumptions about what is necessary for self-protection. The rational mind tells us that love and death are opposites and that heaven and hell cannot coexist. Yet the paradox of their coexistence is everpresent. Love may be revealed in the presence of death, and love without attachment becomes a *raison d'etre*. Surrendering to the joy of love in a world of death and suffering implies relinquishing beliefs that cannot encompass the mystery. On the path of love we are called to love as much as we can, trusting that God is love and perfect love casts out fear.[18]

The light of love is an inner light that is recognized by those who are receptive to it. We light the way for each other when we share and extend love, whatever form it takes. Love is not subject to birth or death; it is infinite, changeless and eternal, and it appears in many forms. In this sense, love is the bright, clear radiance of pure nondual awareness.[19]

DOORWAYS TO LOVE

Love is seen in the eyes of the beloved,
heard in the laughter of children,
touched in the hand of a friend.

Different aspects of love are like different doorways to a universal experience of love. Any of them can illuminate the spiritual path. Love in any form is recognized, not learned. Everyone has some sense of what love is, perhaps only in proclaiming an inability to love or by feeling that something is missing when it seems to be absent.

Whereas the pure reflection of love in mystical experience is without word or image, when it becomes conscious of itself and is transformed into knowledge, it is called *gnosis*. This sacred knowledge reveals the experience of love that lies at the heart of the great religions and represents humanity's highest spiritual aspirations. Gnosis can be understood as divine wisdom gained from an experience of divine love.

Mythologist Joseph Campbell said that in the twelfth century, the theme of romantic love emerged as a central, compelling motivation in the literature of diverse cultures. He identified the five types of relational love throughout the world as follows:

> The first order of love is that of servant for master.
> The second order of love is that of friend for friend.
> The third order of love is that of parent for child.
> The fourth order of love is that of spouse for spouse.
> The fifth order of love is romantic love.[20]

The first order of love may be consciously cultivated in traditions that emphasize the importance of the guru/disciple or teacher/student relationship. In these relationships unquestioning obedience tends to be regarded as a virtue. For example, a devotee may be expected to love the guru, regardless of how the guru behaves, interpreting everything the guru says or does as a teaching. Although the love of the master for the disciple is said to be manifested in every thought, word and action, this often does not appear to be the case to observers who are not disciples.

What may be overlooked is the fact that the discipline is meant to be a training in perception. It may not say anything about the ethics or appropriateness of the guru's behavior. It does say something about how the student is meant to see reality. In many religions God is revered as master; while humans are obedient, or disobedient, servants. Human beings are meant to love and obey God's laws. This type of relationship to authority seems equally prevalent in conventional and unconventional religious groups.

In the teachings of *A Course in Miracles*, a self-study course in Christian mysticism, the student is taught to see everyone as a teacher and every situation as an opportunity for learning.[21] This is a training in perception that is meant to awaken spiritual vision. Insofar as one looks for what can be learned from any encounter, judgments, anger and attack are less likely to be provoked. Seeing everything as a lesson means that mistakes are for correction, not for condemnation. Perceived through the eye of the soul, everything can help us wake up, and the practice of perceiving everything as a lesson in love opens the heart.

The second order of love, the love of friend for friend, is expressed as brotherly love in Christianity and among friends of all religious persuasions. The love of friendship grows out of mutual respect and acceptance. For example, a friend is someone with whom I can really be myself. I feel close to a good friend because I do not need to keep up any pretenses. I may care deeply about my friends and about their welfare, and yet fall short of accepting them unconditionally. *Philia*, the love of friendship or brotherly/sisterly love, though usually less exclusive than romantic love, is not always free from jealousy. Ideally it is inclusive, based on mutual appreciation among equals.

The love between parent and child is familiar to anyone who has loved a child with genuine devotion. It is also the first experience of love for any child who is held and loved by a parent. One need not be a biological parent to experience this type of love. The presence of love can be palpably strong in the presence of birth and often inspires love and awe in those who attend it. Love for a newborn infant is pure insofar as it does not make demands. We do not expect anything from a baby. Opening to this totally spontaneous, nondemanding love is one way of opening the heart. This is illustrated in the story of a woman who came to the great Indian saint, Ramakrishna, and said,

> "I find that I do not love God. The concept does not move me." Ramakrishna asked her, "Is there nothing in the world that you do love?" And she said, "Yes, I love my little nephew." He said, "There he is."[22]

It is in your service to the person you love that you are in service to the Divine.

At its best, parental love inspires selfless service. A healthy mother caring for her child does not hesitate to put the child's needs ahead of her own desires. Her devotion may not produce the results that she expects in the long run, but the experience of love may change her life in ways she could not have anticipated. A father, too, may be surprised by his experience of love for an infant.

Parental love may also be experienced in service to humanity by individuals who have come to regard all human beings as children of God. Mother Teresa of Calcutta acted on the basis of this love, caring for orphans and dying people of all ages as if they were her children. I also know a couple who chose not to have children of their own in order to devote their lives to caring for the earth as a whole. This kind of loving service does open the heart. Embraced with an open heart, sickness, old age, disease and death are not frightening or repulsive. They inspire compassion for suffering that can be alleviated by awareness of love.

Love of the newborn child is also expressed in the celebration of the nativity at Christmas. The story of Christmas reminds believers that Christ is born in the heart as an infant, a symbol of boundless compassion and unconditional love. The infant must be cherished if it is to grow and flourish. Dreams of giving birth or caring for infants and children can also herald the awakening of this form of love. In Jungian terminology the archetype of the divine child is a symbol of the Self.

Sometimes dreams of neglected children can awaken compassion for self and others. In one case a woman reported that a recurring dream of a dead child kept intruding into her meditation. She could not suppress it. As we discussed her associations to the image, it became clear that it represented a neglected part of herself that seemed to be dead inside. About a week later she had another dream in which the same child appeared, only this time it was not dead. It still looked ragged and unkempt, but was very much alive. When she continued the dream in active imagination and imagined herself caring for the child and making friends with it, she recognized what she needed in order to feel more alive herself. When the process was completed she found herself much better able to express her love for her own children in appropriate ways.

Just as physical birth is accompanied by physical pain, psychological pain may attend the birth of a transpersonal self identified with soul rather than ego. Resistance, holding on and fear of change all contribute to creating pain in times of transition that involve a new birth in the psyche. Even when we consciously want to let go of dysfunctional defenses and mental habits, the process can be difficult.

Kali, the fierce representation of the divine mother in Indian mythology, demands the sacrifice of all illusions. The world itself is perceived as a vast burning ground where the separate self-sense is utterly destroyed in order that we may awaken to the reality of divine love, at play in all forms of the universe.

I recently spoke with a woman who gave birth to a child for the first time. She had a very long and difficult labor. She was well prepared and aware that she wanted to let go and relax, but she found it impossible, despite strenuous effort. Although the pain of birth can be extremely intense, it can also be an initiation. In this case it was mystical experience for the mother, who said she experienced herself dissolving into an ocean of bliss, out of which she and the baby emerged as separate bodies sharing a single essence.

In psychotherapy as soulwork, the task of the therapist is analogous to that of a midwife, sometimes attending the birth of a new identity. The psychotherapist may also witness passages of psychological death and rebirth during this lifetime and attend the soul as it prepares for biological death. Any of these transitions can enhance the awareness of love in both therapist and client. Many therapists say they feel a caring, parental love for their clients. In Ken Wilber's words,

> Love is complete and sincere respect for another being . . .
> It is the ecstasy of the true self . . .
> Love extends beyond all planes and is limitless . . .
> After a million lives, and a million deaths it still lives . . .
> And it only dwells in the heart and soul . . .[23]

Sometimes pain, either physical or psychological, can teach us about love, depending on how we relate to it. Sooner or later everyone encounters pain that the conscious ego cannot prevent or control. Painful, involuntary spasms, physical, emotional or mental, can be difficult to release voluntarily. In opening to the pain and softening our attitudes toward it, we may also discover the healing power of love. Pain reminds us that we are usually not in control of our bodies, our minds or the world. Accepting pain with an open heart can provide a new awareness of the nature of love. I have witnessed deep changes in people with terminal illness who, in the midst of pain, felt a profound healing of the soul in opening to love, despite the approach of physical death.

In the willingness to experience the depths of personal pain and sorrow, compassion is born. It is the nature of compassion to respond with caring to the pain of others. If I can recognize my individual difficulty as a microcosm of the suffering of humanity, it becomes a means of connecting with others rather than contributing to isolation. The love that brings peace to the world is the unconditional compassion that empathizes with others. Every relationship then offers an opportunity for deepening love.

The fourth order of love, between spouses, is sometimes the most challenging, as indicated by the divorce rate. Yet the intimacy and loyalty between spouses who share a spiritual connection and a commitment to each other's well-being can be an ongoing process of opening to love. When two people are joined in marriage, their relationship can become a means of awakening and self-transcendence.

A man I spoke to recently told me he had not really understood love until he had to take care of his wife who was dying of cancer. They had many years of a relatively good marriage, but only in the last days of her life did their love blossom into the fullness of mystical union.

Traditional marriages were arranged by the family according to social custom, as they are in many cultures even today. Love between spouses was, therefore, related to social duty, to the family and the community. When a woman's social duty to her husband and children was a genuine expression of love, her heart could open. A husband could also feel inspired and nurtured by a loving family. Unfortunately, few marriages fulfilled the ideal.

The fifth order of love is romantic love. In contemporary Western culture we have attempted to combine the fourth and fifth orders of love, with mixed results. In contrast to the love between spouses that upholds the social order, romantic love upsets conventional rules by bringing together individuals of different backgrounds and different cultural expectations, as well as moving people to give up attachments to status and success in order to pursue the beloved. Romantic love is often passionate, illicit and irrational. A person who falls in love may willingly jeopardize financial and social standing. It is not uncommon for a woman to give up a career to devote herself to husband and family.

Falling in love can be a heart-wrenching experience. Regardless of whether the relationship endures or not, whether two people stay together or have only a fleeting encounter, plunging into romantic love can have a transformative effect. Each one is somehow changed when ego boundaries dissolve in their joining. The desires of the other can easily be placed above one's own. One wants the other to be happy; one wants to be in his or her presence; one yearns for intimacy, for contact, for communion. In the experience of falling in love, one longs to dissolve boundaries, to merge, to lose oneself, to surrender totally to the consuming fire that both includes and transcends sexual passion.

Romantic love may be sparked by sexual attraction, but it is more than that. Lovers often respond to each other in ways that are unconscious and irrational. Romantic love is spontaneous and often fueled by illusion and projection. It cannot be produced on demand. Romantic love tends to be passionate and conditional, shadowed by jealousy and possessiveness. Nonetheless, falling in love is a profound experience that awakens the soul to the power of love.

In addition to these five orders of personal love, other doorways to love take abstractions as their objects. For example, the love of truth, beauty and goodness were considered higher forms of love in Platonic philosophy.

In his recent book *Soulmates,* Thomas Moore says,

> Relationship to the divine, hardly discussed in these days of personalism and secularism, satisfies the soul in ways that no substitute can touch. We may well be preoccupied with the theme of interpersonal relationship precisely because we are stuck in a shallow pool of love, unable to arrive at the mystic's view in which the divine is the only satisfying lover, the only true soul mate.[24]

The more abstract forms of love may inspire creativity and art, a passion for social justice and many forms of personal commitment to lifelong service. As the eye of the trained artist perceives beauty where others overlook it and the ear of a trained musician perceives subtle qualities of sound to which others are oblivious, the spiritual vision that perceives love in the world is both a gift and a latent capacity that can be cultivated. Love of nature is often inspired by vision quests in the wilderness. The beauty of the earth itself had a transforming effect on the first astronauts. One of them remarked,

> That beautiful, warm, living object looked so fragile, so delicate, that if you touched it with a finger it would crumble and fall apart. Seeing this has to change a man, has to make a man appreciate the creation of God and the love of God.[25]

Upon returning to earth, another said,

> I was so happy to see the ground, already a little covered by the first fluffy snow. I wanted to fall into it, hug it, and press my cheek to it.[26]

Compassion is another form of love which can be cultivated. In Buddhism compassion is cultivated as an attitude that aims to remove suffering from all sentient beings, while love is understood as wishing happiness for others. Compassion is sometimes born out of an experience of self-transcendence, either through pain or joy. Opening fully to both joy and suffering, seeing what is possible and how we can be trapped by ignorance and illusion, we may be increasingly motivated to do what we can to alleviate suffering in the world. Unfortunately authentic compassion is sometimes confused with sentimentality that substitutes pity for caring and indulges in lamentations of "Isn't it awful?" without engaging fully with reality as it is.

Motivation born of authentic compassion is not a social duty so much as a desire to enable others to find a better way to live and love in the world. The Bodhisattva vow, to gain enlightenment for the benefit of all sentient beings, can be understood as a vow to devote oneself to dispelling illusions. The compassion expressed in the lives of mystics who were also active in the world, such as Jesus, the Buddha and Mohammed, or in this century, Sri Aurobindo, Albert Schweitzer and Mother Teresa of Calcutta, reminds us that compassion is a compelling and powerful source of social change.

Compassionate action in the world often takes the form of teaching and healing. A deepening commitment to love in everyday life is certainly not limited to formal spiritual practice. It can be found in the dedicated service of ordinary men and women of all creeds and no creed.[27] Love is described in different ways at different times and in different places, according to varying cultural assumptions, yet it can be found anywhere, wherever one sees with spiritual vision.

Clarity is a quality of spiritual vision that is necessary for discernment on a path of love. Since love is reflected everywhere, the source is not to be confused with the manifestation. If the source is perceived to be in the object, then one becomes attached to the object. When the source is discovered within, love is everywhere.

UNCONDITIONAL LOVE

If you achieve the faintest glimmering of what love means today, you have advanced in distance without measure and in time beyond the count of years to your release.[28]

–A COURSE IN MIRACLES

Love is the transforming power that heals the split mind and mends the broken heart. Love is also instrumental in healing the body. While healing remains a mystery even to physicians and healers, the capacity of the psyche for self-healing is demonstrated daily in the context of loving relationships.[29]

Psychotherapists have learned that providing an atmosphere of unconditional acceptance enables people to heal themselves. Whether they speak of unconditional positive regard, free-floating attention or love, they know people are affected by it. For a person struggling with pain and loneliness on a spiritual path, the healing power of love is a gift of grace.

Insofar as the forms of love described above are conditional, they are not free of illusion. Yet each form offers the possibility of opening to the unconditional, ecstatic love that depends on no-thing for its existence. Every form of love is a doorway to opening the heart and tapping into the well of inexhaustible abundance that sustains existence. The source of timeless unconditional love, like the Buddha nature, lies hidden within, awaiting only our willingness to see.

We recognize the presence of this eternal love in different ways, according to our particular needs or experiences. It does not depend on physical attributes or intellectual development. We become more sensitive to it with psychological health and maturity, but we do not create it. It is always, already present, awaiting our acknowledgment as we discover who and what we are. Although we all seem to want to give and receive love, our attempts to get it are often grossly distorted. Some people think they have to earn it, hoard it, hang on to it or reject it. They protect themselves against it, even while pursuing it. Yet love is available to everyone, and the path seems easier after an experience of ecstatic, unconditional love.

Rumi, the Sufi poet, says,

> Ecstatic love is an ocean. And the Milky Way
> is a flake of foam floating on that ocean.[30]

BARRIERS TO LOVE

Would you not go through fear to love?
For such the journey seems to be.[31]

—A COURSE IN MIRACLES

The transformative power of romantic love is a perennial theme in Western literature and mythology. One of the most famous examples of romantic love as divine inspiration was Dante's love for Beatrice. Although he had no social relationship with her at all, she led him to paradise. Today we might say that he was not in love with her, but with his projection or image of her. Dante and Beatrice did not have to deal with making a real relationship work. Yet she did awaken his soul and deepen his awareness of love.

Likewise, in Goethe's *Faust*, the romantic portrayal of love is predominantly love for an abstract image of the feminine. This idealized love leads Faust through a transformational journey, but the women in the story are not portrayed as whole persons. Unfortunately, in most romantic literature the feminine is admired only in this ideal capacity, rather than as an equal participant in the process.

Developing a capacity for love, even in an idealized fashion, can be a valuable part of the spiritual path. However, idealizing the feminine becomes a barrier to love when it perpetuates the split between madonna, as idealized love object, and whore, as sex object, in the psyche of both men and women. These projections obscure the recognition of the whole, authentic person that is both spiritual and sexual, and the deeper quest of the soul for love. In healthy sexual relationships love overcomes isolation and generates trust and responsibility. By fostering romantic illusion rather than enhancing the capacity for authentic love in personal relationships, the love of an ideal image becomes a trap.

In his book *When Nietzsche Wept,* psychiatrist Irvin Yalom portrayed the suffering inherent in this attitude as the protagonists struggle with their romantic obsessions.[32] As long as a man is obsessed with an ideal image of the feminine, he is likely to denigrate women and be incapable of real love relationships.

Major obstacles to love include the expectations one has about how others should be. When reality does not match the image, the person who chooses to ignore reality rather than give up the image pays a high price, since it implies giving up on life and choosing to live in illusion instead. On the other hand, in choosing to face things as they are, letting go of preconceptions, one may learn to love wholeheartedly.

I have been impressed by the courage of individuals willing to confront deep psychological issues and face reality in their struggle and desire for love. I am also inspired by those who are willing to change and grow and risk facing the unknown. It often seems easier to hang on to familiar patterns of behavior than to risk change that may disrupt relationships and plunge one into a whole new way of being in the world. Yet just as education can free the mind from the prison of certainty, deep psychological work can lead to the freedom required for a full experience of love.

For example, Patricia was a very successful, attractive young woman who came to see me for psychotherapy because she wanted to make her relationship with her boyfriend work better. She had been in the relationship for about two years, and she thought she wanted to marry this man. He seemed to be exactly what she had always wanted in terms of status, interests, background, education, looks, etc. Although the relationship was problematic, she was determined to make it work. First she tried very hard to change him, to make him be what she thought he should be. When this did not work, she tried making herself change to fit his ideas of what he wanted. She thought that if she could adapt, she could make it work. Finally, she gave up. The price for holding on to the relationship was too high. Her soul felt trapped when she could not express herself honestly. She found that she was withholding grievances and pretending to be happy in order to please him, trying to hold on to what she thought was security. She felt she could not really open her heart and be all of who she was in the relationship. When she finally summoned up enough courage to let go, she felt a great sense of relief. The strain of trying to make the relationship work when it was basically unsatisfying had taken its toll. Letting go of the relationship was not as difficult as giving up the dream of being happy together.

Letting go of the dream is often more painful than giving up the reality. For Patricia, giving up the dream meant confronting aloneness and a sense of failure. When she did, however, she began to feel much better. Before long she was ready to look to the future and to visualize the kind of man she wanted as a partner. Being fairly conventional in her tastes, she thought, in accordance with cultural stereotypes, that the man should be older, taller and make more money than she did. She soon found herself dating a man that, once again, met all her specifications. She was very pleased for a few weeks, until she realized that something was lacking. Everything appeared to be going smoothly, but the spiritual connection was missing. At this stage she was feeling stronger in herself and was unwilling to waste time in a relationship that seemed constricting. Once more she was willing to let go. This time it happened more easily and more quickly, and she felt better about being on her own again. As she began to give up her conventional ideas of what she thought she wanted and to be open to following her heart, she found herself being drawn to people that were different from those she had previously known. As she gained greater emotional independence from her parents and became more self-confident, she began opening up to new experiences and soon met someone whom she would not have noticed before. He was not what she would have imagined as an ideal partner for herself. Yet in time, as their love kept growing deeper and the relationship more fulfilling, it became clear that they were very well suited to one another. The last I heard was that they were married and considered their partnership an ongoing adventure.

This is a typical story. I have seen it happen over and over again as people become disillusioned by stereotyped images of romance and open to genuine love of a person rather than an abstract ideal. Yet even when we know this, the acceptance of things as they are is an ongoing challenge.

Romantic relationships are certainly more satisfying when both partners are willing to tell each other the truth about what they think and feel rather than trying to keep up appearances to conform to imagined role expectations. When each one is willing to see the other as an equal companion on the journey of unfolding consciousness, the awareness of love grows easily.

The path of love deepens our capacity for love in spite of pain and fear. Sometimes when love is blocked by fearful thoughts of abandonment or engulfment, it remains accessible through feeling and intuition. When love is blocked by anxiety and defensiveness, we tend to perceive only hatred and aggression in the world. Loving another human being without fear and without reservation is a freely given gift. It is also a challenge. Those who persist in traveling this path are rewarded with an expanded awareness of love in all its many forms.

Human tragedy is often rooted in an inability or an unwillingness to love. Some people close themselves off from love either because they are afraid, because they feel unloved or because they are clinging to an illusion of perfect love. To recognize an inner source of love is to access a source of self-healing without which therapeutic techniques and medicines are of limited value. Healing hearts and minds depends on opening to love in spite of fear and trusting its guidance on the spiritual path.

CHOOSING A PATH OF LOVE

Involuntary and immediate feeling reveals to us the meaning of love as the highest manifestation of individual life, which finds in union with another being its own proper infinity.[33]

—Vladimir Solovyov

Choosing a path of love means recognizing the essential quality of love that guides self-awareness as it unfolds on all levels, physical, emotional, mental and spiritual. It also means acknowledging the presence of love in personal, interpersonal and transpersonal dimensions of experience.

The historical roots of the path of love in Western philosophy can be traced to Plato. For Plato the highest good was discerned through feeling and intuition, and he recounts how Socrates, when he was condemned to death, chose to die rather than renounce his philosophy. Socrates was not afraid of dying and argued that death was desirable as liberation for the soul. In contrast, for Aristotle the supreme good was more practical, and happiness was sought through rational choices. He thought emotions should be controlled, suppressed and avoided in favor of autonomy and consistency.

A contemporary expression of these differences can be found in the work of Lawrence Kohlberg[34] and Carol Gilligan.[35] Both Kohlberg and Aristotle regard feeling as inferior to rationality. Kohlberg's stages of moral development emphasize individual rights and abstract principles of justice. Gilligan, on the other hand, places a greater value on love and relationship in moral development, reminiscent of Plato's emphasis on the capacity for emotional identification with the other in the development of character. For both Plato and Gilligan the rational, utilitarian calculation of effects breaks down when one loves.[36]

Psychological theories based on the assumption that human beings are basically selfish and pleasure seeking assume that well adjusted, mature individuals must balance instinctual drives against the demands of society. From a Freudian point of view, conflict between the desires of the id and the demands of the superego is inescapable, and a strong ego is required to mediate the conflict between them. Assuming that every civilized person must learn to control instinctual aggression, resolution is attempted through self-understanding and rational analysis. Psychological health is then perceived as the ability to love and work in spite of this inescapable condition.

Whether the primary cause of suffering is attributed to external oppression or internal repression, from this perspective human nature is not to be trusted. Such theories do not recognize the capacity for love and altruism as a primary motive or value. Ken Wilber and others identify different motivations at different stages of cognitive, affective and spiritual development.[37] Presumably the mature, healthy person does not settle for partial views, but integrates both rational and affective values in spiritual freedom.

Choosing a path of love does not mean neglecting other factors that contribute to wholeness. It does imply a fundamental belief in the power of love as a creative, healing force, and in the inherent capacity of every human being to experience it. Psychoanalyst Eric Fromm has said that to love God means to long for the attainment of the full capacity to love and the realization of that which God stands for in oneself.[38]

Another perspective on moral development is Rudolph Steiner's view that a good action is one which a free person intuitively loves. The ideal is not "out there," but is realized by the deliberate, loving effort of the individual. As the universal is realized in the particular, ethical individualism is considered a natural expression of a free spirit.[39]

STAGES OF LOVE

The circuit of love then becomes complete, as the soul of love returns to the Source of Love. Love pours into love, races into love, expands into love, and finds only love. Human love then realizes that it has always belonged completely to Divine Love.[40]

—LEX HIXON

Plato mapped stages of love from self-centeredness through erotic attachment and the competitive love of valor, to the love of absolutes, widening the sphere of altruism and ethical autonomy. The materialist who identifies exclusively with the body and seeks only self-satisfaction is susceptible to inner conflict and ethical inconsistency. In the erotic stage love expands beyond the self, but similar conflicts apply to the dyad. In the stage of honor, altruism expands beyond the individual to society as a whole. The love of honor may seek to promote the well-being of the whole community through politics or personal influence. One who aspires to honor and glory is not primarily concerned with comforts of the flesh. At the stage of philosophy, Plato's highest stage, the love of wisdom expands altruism to the edification of all humankind.

This expanding capacity for love is also reflected in the levels of consciousness associated with the chakras, or psychic energy centers, in Indian thought. The first chakra reflects self-love; the second, erotic love. The third is associated with love of power (honor); the fourth with universal love. At the level of the fifth chakra, love is more abstract, as in the love of beauty expressed in art and creativity. At the level of the sixth chakra, spiritual vision is associated with love of truth or love of God. Thus awareness of love progresses from being self-centered to being sociocentric, then theocentric and eventually cosmocentric, immanent in all things.

Similar stages of development on the path of love can be identified in Christianity. Despite St. Augustine's assertion that all you need to do is to love God and do as you will, few lovers of wisdom have been content to rest with that, and many have described stages on the path.

St. Teresa of Avila, for example, differentiates stages of love as different mansions of the Interior Castle, all of which are within the house of self-knowledge.[41] One progresses from the outer mansions to the innermost chambers. At first, engagement with worldly things and sense desires becomes a love of books, music and liturgy, and one turns to God in times of trial. At this stage one relies on external aids to contemplation and love is directed outward. As one goes deeper within, practice shifts away from discipline and the prayer of recollection which focuses on images of the divine, to the practice of effortless contemplation of the divine radiance and the prayer of quiet. When this deepens into the prayer of union, one is prepared for the mystical marriage where the illusion of separation disappears into a sense of deep abiding peace. Perfect love is found only in total dissolution of the separate self. The soul comes to rest only in its true home, the Source of love.

Progress on the path of love is often marked by a decrease in negative emotions such as fear, guilt and anger. The practice of forgiveness can also facilitate progress on the path. In contrast to the more abstract forms of love, forgiveness is grounded in the reality of personal relationships. In the absence of forgiveness, fear, guilt and resentment tend to block awareness of love at any level, whether it be love of self, love of other, love of humanity and the earth as a whole or the ecstatic love of the mystic. Letting go of the past through forgiveness can remove blocks to the awareness of love in the present.

In a classical study of mysticism, Evelyn Underhill describes stages on the path of love as leading from awakening through purification, illumination, recollection and contemplation, to the unitive experience and eventually to the unitive life. She said,

> The aim of the mystics . . . is to establish a conscious relation with the Absolute, in which they find the personal object of love. They desire to know, only that they may love, and their desire for union is founded neither on curiosity nor self-interest.[42]

In the words of Ramakrishna,

> The secret of the mystic way—including both path and goal, for they cannot be separated—is total passionate love for God alone, for sheer Divine Reality, however you may envision or experience it in the depth of your being.[43]

> Divine Reality alone is capable of transmitting Truth, and the timeless essence of the soul alone can receive this powerful transmission.[44]

GUIDELINES FOR THE PATH OF LOVE

If you choose to follow a path of love, I would suggest the following guidelines:

1. Remember your soul and follow your heart. It takes courage to act on motivations of love rather than fear. The stronger you feel, the softer and more vulnerable you can allow yourself to be. The more fearful you are, the more you think you have to defend yourself against potential dangers and scare people away in order to be safe. But no armor can keep fear out of your heart. Only a willingness to look deeper, to face the fear that lurks in the shadows can make illusions vanish like a dream.

2. Invite love into your life. Intend to be loving and accept being loved. Open to the abundance of mutual exchange available in loving relationships without self-sacrifice.

3. Notice how you resist or avoid love. Welcome the tears and laughter that express love.

4. Love yourself and others equally, not more or less. Love is kind. Be kind to yourself and to all beings. Ask yourself how you could love yourself and others better.

5. Learn to see love and beauty in the world. Love the beauty inside yourself and other people as much as the beauty of nature, light, color and sound perceived by the physical senses. Inner beauty is perceived with the eye of the soul.

6. Love the joy of being wherever you are as much as you can, growing into clear awareness.

7. Remember love is everpresent, here, now and always.
   Identify with love, and you are safe.
   Identify with love, and you are home.
   Identify with love, and find your Self.[45]

CHAPTER 5

Awakening Soul: Ancient Wisdom and Modern Science

You cannot sell your soul, but you can sell your awareness of it. You cannot perceive your soul, but you will not know it while you perceive something else as more valuable.[1]

—A COURSE IN MIRACLES

REMEMBERING THE SOUL

WHAT IS MEANT BY SOUL IS OFTEN VAGUE or half-forgotten. Nevertheless, we have been hearing a lot about soul in the Western world. Books are available on soul retrieval, recovering the soul and care of the soul, to name a few. I recently attended a conference in Europe where representatives from a dozen European countries were discussing the soul of Europe. America, we hear, is suffering from a loss of soul, or a sickness of the soul. I like to think of awakening the soul because the metaphor seems appropriate for most people who feel alienated, depressed or discouraged by a lack of meaning in their lives.

In English *soul* has become impoverished and discredited in the rational, scientific climate of Western culture. In psychology *mind*, which connotes rational, intellectual knowledge, devoid of emotional or moral overtones, has displaced *soul* in designating the invisible component of the person. Something is lost in translation when Teilhard de Chardin's use of the

French, *ame,* and Freud's use of the German, *seele,* are rendered in English as *mind* . Shorn of spiritual connotations, mind is disconnected from values and emotions and does not fully convey what is meant by *ame, seele* or *soul.*[2]

Despite the denial of the existence of soul by the prevailing materialistic ideology of the postmodern world, soul continues to be a meaningful concept for most people. In Shakespeare's time, the word *soul* referred to the deepest moral, emotional and intuitive currents of consciousness. Today both mind and soul are distinguished from body as the invisible, nonmaterial aspect of the person that is sometimes believed to exist independently of the body. Contemporary research in mind/body health blurs the dichotomy between mind and body but does not yet address soul as the spark of divinity that links body and mind to Spirit.

Since ancient times humans have been aware of the soul as a principle of life intimately connected with body and mind, yet not identical with either. Western concepts of soul tend to confuse elements that belong to the psyche, such as thoughts and emotions, with what lies beyond ego-consciousness as the indestructible, creative ground of existence that we call Spirit.[3]

According to the perennial philosophy,[4] the phenomenal world of things, people and ideas is the manifestation of this divine ground, within which all partial realities have their being. Human beings are capable of witnessing the nature of this ground by direct intuition. At the moment of such intuitive realization, the knower is united with that which is known. Humans have a double nature, a phenomenal ego that identifies with the body and an eternal Self that is identified with Spirit. The soul, as witness of both the phenomenal world of ego and the Self as Spirit, partakes of both personal reality and the transpersonal ground of being.

Spirit manifests as consciousness, soul, mind, life and matter through the process of involution, whereas evolution proceeds from matter to life to mind to soul to Spirit. In the process of evolution, consciousness may identify with the physical, subtle, causal and absolute realms of being at different stages of development. Being related both to the spiritual and the material world, the soul is primarily experienced as a self-sense in the intermediate, subtle realms of consciousness.

The soul yearns for an experience of Spirit as Source, but perceives only images of gods or archetypes, the first forms emerging from the formless in the process of involution. As patterns of creation, archetypal forms can also refer to those Platonic ideals such as truth, beauty and harmony. These objects of perception are neither soul nor Spirit. Spirit as the creative ground of manifestation may be experienced as consciousness without an object, in which the separate self-sense disappears. The soul, because it is the seer, can never be seen. As the eye cannot see itself, the soul as witness can never be observed. The subtle realms of the soul are characterized by multiplicity rather than unity, and the soul as witness is never fully satisfied by the shadows or phenomena that these worlds offer.

Awakening soul means living simultaneously in the eternal realm of Spirit and the temporal realm of earthly existence. The soul is nourished by direct experience of the sacred, and the awakened soul sees through the veils of illusion to the underlying reality they conceal. The soul may be awakened in spiritual practices such as contemplation, meditation and yoga, or in certain types of psychotherapy that include inner work. Symbols that point to transcendental realities seem to speak a language that is understood by the soul.

Symbols can either reveal or conceal the mystery of Spirit, depending on how we interpret them. For example, dreaming of giving birth to a baby can be interpreted as giving birth to the divine child as a symbol of the Self, or giving birth to a new creative potential, or as a portent of literal pregnancy and birth. It may also signal a new awareness of soul. Dreams of death, dismemberment and resurrection, such as those that are sometimes associated with shamanic initiations[5] can also signal the awakening of soul as an indestructible witness of experience. Only when we understand the dynamics of the invisible inner world and begin to experience the soul as witness can we untangle the illusions that seem to bind the soul to the suffering of the separate self.

Within the confines of a finite, personal life, the soul is a link to the invisible world of essential qualities and perceptions that endow human existence with a sense of meaning and purpose. To be soulful is to be filled with deep feeling; to be soulless is to be hard and callous. To be inspired is to be connected to Spirit; to be dispirited, depressed or anxious is to be out of touch with soul. Identifying with soul awakens spiritual vision and opens the way to awareness of the infinite and eternal Spirit. This awareness provides a wider perspective that helps us differentiate truth from illusion on the spiritual path.

A person identified with soul rather than ego tends to become increasingly inner-directed. This does not imply morbid introspection or being unresponsive to the needs of others. It does mean recognizing the essential freedom of the soul and taking responsibility for spiritual choices. Identifying with soul can lead to acknowledging the presence of the sacred in the innermost depths of the psyche and to seeing its clear reflection everywhere.

Theories on the physical seat of the soul have been many and varied. The fact that soul is intangible and nonmaterial has led many contemporary skeptics to argue that it does not exist. This is what psychologist James Hillman, who identifies soul with psyche, has called the mistake of literalism. He writes,

> Soul is distinct from body because soul may not be identified with any literal presentation or perspective. As the perspective that sees through, the psyche cannot itself be another visibility. As connecting link, or traditionally third position, between all opposites (mind and matter, spirit and nature, intellect and emotion), the soul differs from the terms which it connects.[6]

As the link between Spirit and nature, the soul partakes of both and is involved in a continuous process of change and transformation from gross to subtle to causal and the reverse, until dualism breaks down and Spirit and nature, form and formlessness are perceived as two aspects of one reality.

For Huston Smith, noted authority on world religions, different levels of selfhood correspond to different levels of reality.[7] In his view the body corresponds to the terrestrial realm, the mind to the intermediate realm and the soul to the celestial realm. Spirit, which corresponds to the infinite realm, underlies and illuminates all the others. The higher levels are not literally elsewhere, but they are invisible and inaccessible to ordinary consciousness. In the celestial realm, soul is the element that relates to God. In the infinite realm, it becomes one with God and all separate self-sense disappears. Smith writes,

> The soul is the final locus of our individuality. Situated as it were behind the senses, it sees through the eyes without being seen, hears with the ears without itself being heard. Similarly it lies deeper than mind. If we equate mind with the stream of consciousness, the soul is the source of this stream; it is also its witness while never itself appearing within the stream as datum to be observed. . . . We know it only indirectly, by its effects. The way it supplies us with life is completely invisible, as is the way it directs the trajectory of our ontogenetic development.[8]

The soul wanders through multiple levels of experience in the process of remembering its source as Spirit. It seeks fulfillment in love, at first through conditional love, eventually in the unconditional, universal love that encompasses all forms of love. Through love the divinity of the soul is discovered and expressed in the world. The soul has therefore been called the heart of the world, and its thirst for wholeness is quenched only in mystical union with the Divine Beloved.[9] In its essence, the soul is described as God's organ of perception. Love, lover and Beloved may then be perceived as one.

SOUL AND SPIRIT

There is a spirit in the soul, untouched by time and flesh, flowing from the Spirit, remaining in the Spirit, itself wholly spiritual.[10]
—MEISTER ECKHART

Mystics claim that the individual soul eventually becomes one with Spirit or Godhead, while orthodox Christian views emphasize the unalterable distinction between the two, maintaining that the soul can only enter into relationship with God. It can never become one with God. This seems reasonable to those who have not had a mystical experience that dissolves the separate self into the infinite. As long as a separate self-sense persists, the soul remains distinct from God.

To identify with soul is to expand the sense of identity from body/mind to include those elements of the psyche that are nonlocal in time and space, free of physical limitations and potentially at one with the Infinite. The soul as a separate self-sense is in relationship to God, the inner world of images and archetypes and the outer world of relationships and objects. In the inner world of imagination and mythology, the soul can embark on heroic adventures and experience death and resurrection. When the soul forgets its prior oneness with Spirit, it may seem to be imprisoned by the world of matter and illusion.

The belief that the soul is trapped by physical reality is illustrated by the myth of Sophia. Sophia was an incarnation of divine wisdom, a compassionate soul who fell in love with the world and was caught in its web of illusion. The task of liberation, then, was conceived as freeing the soul from its imprisonment in matter.

Anyone who has experienced burnout, a common occupational hazard among helping professionals, has probably had the feeling of being trapped in a web of necessity and impossible demands. Most recommended treatments for burnout consist of stress reduction and setting boundaries. They overlook the fact that burnout usually indicates a state of spiritual aridity, and that effective treatment may call for spiritual renewal or awakening soul.

Identifying with soul rather than ego, one is drawn first into relationship and ultimately into union with Spirit. When we think of soul as individualized Spirit, a separate entity that we imagine can be separated from its Source, we too have fallen into the illusion that soul is anything other than a manifestation of Spirit in action. The awakened soul recognizes its true nature as Spirit. When self as soul seems to be divorced from Spirit and becomes identified exclusively with the phenomenal world, it suffers the pain of separation, not realizing that this world of shadows reflects our projections.

Mystics of all traditions who have described the dissolution of the soul in Spirit agree on the supreme identity of Self as Spirit. The deep structures of consciousness that differentiate body, mind, soul and spirit are universal.[11] Human beings everywhere create concepts, rules and rituals that bring the individual into relationship with Spirit and connect the personal to the transpersonal realms of experience. While the mind generates ideas about soul and Spirit, the awakened soul directly intuits Spirit as its own essence.

Sri Aurobindo, the twentieth-century Indian sage, says it is difficult to distinguish soul from the mental and physical forms in which it appears, as long as its emergence is incomplete. When the soul has been differentiated from thoughts and feelings, it becomes aware of itself as the spirit supporting life in the body. Only when there is complete silence in the inner world can we become aware of a spiritual essence that extends into universality. Often a mixture of mental aspirations and emotional desires is mistaken for the soul, just as the ego can be mistaken for the Self.

This might occur, for example, if we mistake melancholy for soulfulness. Sadness may be indicative of unfulfilled expectations, a sense of loss or regret, all of which pertain to the world of ego rather than soul. From the perspective of soul as witness, any emotion, either positive or negative, is part of the passing melodrama of the world of ego. The soul may be deeply stirred by emotions, but is not an embodiment of emotion.

Aurobindo regards these confusions as a temporary stage of evolution. He says,

> Spirituality is not a high intellectuality, not idealism, not an ethical turn of mind or moral purity and austerity, not religiosity or an ardent and exalted emotional fervour. . . . Spirituality is in its

essence an awakening to the inner reality of our being, to a spirit, self, soul which is other than our mind, life and body.[12]

This differentiation of soul from body, emotions and mind can help us recognize soul as the witness of all experience. As witness it is neither separate from personal experience nor identical with it. It is the observing self that witnesses life and death, good and evil, matter, mind and spirit. As observer it inhabits the world of values and dualisms that preoccupy the ego, but is not identified with it.

Whereas the self as ego is identified primarily with the physical body, biological survival and social roles in the outer world, the self as soul is intimately involved with the more subtle perception of the multiple realities of inner experience. As we become more identified with soul as witness, greater acceptance and equanimity develop in relation to both sleeping and waking dreams. Events in both the inner and the outer world tend to seem less upsetting for the person who regards everything as a learning experience for the soul.

The inner world of soul includes the world of light and shadow, good and evil spirits, fear and desire. In this domain the reality of demons and angels, *devas* or *dakinis* is unquestioned. Inner experiences in dreams or other altered states of consciousness can seem as real, or even more real, than experiences of ordinary reality in the outer world. Sometimes the inner world seems to foretell what will happen in the outer world, as in precognitive dreaming. Many people have told me of precognitive dreams. One woman dreamed of an angel that warned her of impending danger. She said that by heeding the message she had avoided being in an airplane crash. The problem is that it is difficult to tell whether a dream is precognitive or not until after it surfaces in waking life. People have also told me of fighting with demons and witches in their dreams, even if they did not believe in them.

One woman who consulted me was frightened by a dream of being terminally ill. She was afraid it was a precognition. From the point of view of the soul as witness, this experience was very real. Whether it would be actualized in the outer world of physical reality might depend on whether the dreamer understood the message of the dream and what it meant for her. If someone can confront the fear of death after such a dream, it can be liberating. In this case she did feel more peaceful after we discussed it. Otherwise, if such experiences are not adequately understood, they can be deeply disturbing.

Not all spiritual disciplines address the subtle realities of the inner world of soul. Some attempt to bypass them, aiming instead for at-one-ment or emptiness. In Zen Buddhism, for example, dreams are dismissed as illusory. The Dharmakaya is the realm of no form, no self and no god. The soul dissolves into the infinite only when it transcends identifications altogether. According to Huston Smith,

> "Spirit" and "Infinite" are, like "Atman" and "Brahman," but two words for a single reality . . . Though it is possible to intuit it directly, we can think of it only by invoking a double negative. Peripherally Spirit is without boundaries; internally it is without barriers.[13]

When the ego that is subject to physical laws dissolves into an identification with soul, it enters the timeless imaginal realms that are perceived as other worlds or alternate realities. These may be accessed by a variety of consciousness-altering techniques such as meditation, shamanic journeys, holotorpic breathing, fasting, solitude and contemplation. We can all enter them effortlessly every night while dreaming, but are rarely conscious of what is possible in the dream state. Eventually, recognizing that all images and objects of consciousness are manifestations of Spirit, just as the colors of the spectrum are refractions of the one light, can facilitate the disidentification required for soul to dissolve into Spirit. To identify with soul is to find your true self; to identify with Spirit is to lose yourself, to transcend the separate self altogether. This self-transcendence sometimes happens when one has given up attachment to experiences in any form.

Rather than leading a person away from the world, experiences of self-transcendence can deepen a sense of identification with all beings and open the heart to boundless compassion. My own experience supports the research data that indicates that healthy people who have experiences of self-transcendence gain in wisdom and tend to become increasingly concerned with selfless service. Furthermore, the absence of such experience is often linked to pathology and suffering.[14]

I remember Doris, a woman who had been a social worker for many years and who felt burned out by her work in a hospital. She came to see me saying that she felt she was having a midlife crisis. She had lost interest in her work and was increasingly irritable with her co-workers. When she expressed interest in going on a vision quest which involved spending forty-eight hours alone in the wilderness, I encouraged her to try it, as she was planning to go with an experienced guide. Doris had a profound experience in which she saw herself going through multiple metamorphoses from identifying with rocks, to plants, to animals, earth and sky. Her consciousness seemed to encompass the totality of the universe. Seeing her personal problems in the light of this new vision made them seem less important and consequently less overwhelming. The predominant effect was a feeling of love for the beauty of the natural world and sorrow for the suffering of life. The tears she cried were tears of compassion as her heart seemed to be overflowing with love. She remembered what had motivated her desire to be a social worker in the first place—wanting to help those who were less fortunate. She did not abandon her profession, but found ways to use her interpersonal skills in other settings and soon began to feel more creative in her work. Her deep experience of self-transcendence transformed her crisis into an opening for spiritual renewal. She had awakened her soul and felt renewed and inspired. Doris continued to do inner work to integrate her new awareness with everyday life.

ANCIENT WISDOM: TRADITIONAL CONCEPTS OF SOUL

The nature of the soul has been a central issue of religious doctrine in virtually all spiritual traditions. The term is used in different ways both within and among different traditions. Since many Eastern concepts have found their way into popular Western psychology, I will briefly review some Eastern and Western beliefs about the soul that seem relevant to the contemporary spiritual quest. We find different versions of them among new religious movements, sometimes explicitly acknowledged, sometimes divorced from their roots.

Shamanic concepts

The popular resurgence of interest in shamanism has given many people an opportunity to see themselves in a new light, validating the spiritual dimension of experience and reconnecting them to nature in a meaningful way.

In shamanic traditions everything is believed to have one or many souls. Not only humans, but animals, plants, rocks and the forces of nature are the home of spirits, gods or *devas*. Power, soul and life are intimately linked. In shamanic societies spirit and matter are not separate, and the soul does not exist apart from nature. It is inextricably embedded in the fabric of earthly life.

The soul is believed to detach from the body in dreams, and shamans engage in voluntary soul flight or soul travel for the purpose of healing and helping others. The shaman who journeys to other worlds may feel that these alternate, nonordinary realities are more real than this so-called ordinary reality.[15] Whatever happens in these other realities seems to have profound and tangible effects on a person who asks for healing.

Shamanic journeys are soul journeys. When illness is attributed to soul loss, healing involves soul retrieval.[16] The shaman may journey to the lower world or the upper world in search of the lost soul. A person suffering from soul loss may feel dispirited, out of touch or weak and vulnerable. In the shamanic worldview, when the soul separates from the body, as it does in dreams and on shamanic journeys, and the separation becomes chronic, the soul is said to be lost and wander helplessly in other realms. Consequently healing is believed to require retrieving the lost soul and reuniting it with the body. The shamanic healer journeys to other realms for the purpose of bringing it back.

One woman who benefited from this type of healing felt that she had lost her soul as a teenager when she ran away from home to escape a dysfunctional family. She was able to support herself working as a waitress, but soon ended up in an abusive relationship. Later, after leaving the relationship and moving across the country, she found a better job and regained some measure of self-esteem, but still felt out of touch with her soul. She said the shamanic healer's journey had reconnected her to a part of herself that she felt was essential to her well-being.

Symbolic rituals, rhythm and sound are employed to assist the shaman in entering the altered states of consciousness required for the journey to other worlds. These worlds of nonordinary reality are inhabited by multiple spirits that may be either friendly or hostile. The shaman may interact with power animals and other spirits in the process of retrieving the lost soul. In contemporary adaptations of shamanism patients may also journey to other realities and encounter power animals that suggest what is needed for healing. A person may have an alliance with more than one power animal that imbues the soul with power.

In this cosmology the human being is inextricably linked with the earth, which is itself perceived as a sensate, conscious being suffused with spiritual power.[17] Shamans were probably the first explorers of the subtle realms of consciousness and are still masters of this domain.[18]

Many contemporary students of shamanism have deepened their appreciation of the life of the soul through participation in shamanic workshops, rituals and journeys. While the metaphysics often remain obscure, the exploration offers a revitalizing link with the world of soul and a sense of respite to those who have previously been confined to living in a constricted, materialistic world of ego.

Many people who seem to benefit from soul retrieval work do not necessarily accept the whole shamanic worldview. I have found shamanic journeys to be both instructive and revealing for those who participate with an open mind. Whether we believe the soul is lost and then retrieved, or that we are unconscious of it until it awakens, reclaiming soul can be deeply significant and beneficial.

Ancient mythology

The ancient civilizations of Egypt and Greece had multiple concepts of the soul. Some ancient societies believed that the soul was essentially feminine, derived from the mother goddess through the earthly mother. In Egyptian mythology, each person had seven souls, bestowed by feminine deities at birth.

On the other hand, the God of the Old Testament breathed life into a man. The soul as the breath of life that was bestowed by a patriarchal God was identified as male. In Greek the ideas of wind or breath are generally associated with *pneuma*, translated as "spirit." The verb *psuchein* means "to breathe," and the Latin *animus* is connected to *anemos*, the Greek word meaning "wind."

The ancients saw in breathing the evidence for life; and air, being present everywhere and supporting life as breath, became a symbol of Spirit and was later equated with soul. During sleep and at death the soul was believed to depart from the body through the nose or the mouth like the breath, and disembodied souls, like air, could be felt but not seen.

The Gnostic Christians, influenced by the Egyptian doctrine of seven souls, believed that the soul entered the body at birth, descending from the celestial realms through the seven planetary spheres, acquiring qualities from each one on the way. These were the seven deadly sins that could be shed again after death as the soul ascended to heaven in the opposite direction. A modern version of this process can be found in the Theosophical doctrine of the seven planes of existence and the seven rays.[19]

Ken Wilber has stressed the importance of recognizing both involution and evolution as Spirit in action.[20] He also points out that spirituality associated with the ascending path of evolution aspiring to transcendence is often ascetic and otherworldly and tends to devalue the world, the flesh and the senses. On the other hand, the descending path of involution that celebrates the earth, the body, sexuality and all earthly things as manifestations of Spirit tends to devalue transcendence and the ascending path. Each orientation tends to view the other as misguided and wrong.

The struggle between these opposing worldviews has been going on for centuries. Today we see it manifesting in the diverging views of deep ecologists, committed to the descending path that sees Spirit as immanent in nature, and yogic practitioners who strive to transcend the limitations of earthbound existence. Wilber argues that we need to integrate the two. The soul that is awake may be expected to recognize that ascending and descending paths are two aspects of one reality. Both are included in nondual traditions such as Tantra, that balance transcendence and immanence, the one and the many, emptiness and form. From this perspective the cyclical nature of involution and evolution is seen as the movement of Spirit infusing matter with life and returning through the evolution of consciousness to awareness of Spirit.

Whereas Egyptian culture was primarily concerned with the fate of the soul after death, ancient Greece developed different concepts of the soul of the living and the soul of the dead. At the time of Homer, the free soul, or *psuche*, was believed to be an unencumbered soul whose presence was the precondition for the continuation of life. It was inactive when the body was active and was manifest only during sleep, unconsciousness or death. In the underworld the *psuche* became a shade, a shadow or an image.

Psuche was differentiated from *thumos,* which was believed to be the seat of emotions, and *menes*, which was associated with mind. The term *nous* was used to emphasize intellect, thought or purpose. It was *psuche*, the free soul, that was capable of journeys, and stories were told of people whose souls were reputed to wander away during a trance, sometimes for years. It was also *psuche* that departed for the underworld at death. Gradually, *psuche* came to incorporate *thumos* and to represent the center of consciousness.[21]

In Plato's *Dialogues* Socrates explained that when the body dies, the soul continues to exist apart from the body. In life a person's most important task was to take care of the soul, and the objective of philosophy was to free the soul from identification with the body. Since the body and the senses were thought to hinder the soul from attaining truth and wisdom, Socrates argued that death is to be welcomed rather than feared by those who truly love wisdom.[22] This is a clear example of an ascending path or worldview.

Later Greek philosophers, such as Plotinus, connected the individual human soul to the world soul and believed it contained a higher faculty than the rational mind, namely intellectual intuition. Some believed that souls were newly created while others believed in their preexistence and transmigration until they gained sufficient wisdom to be reunited with their Source.

Reacting against Platonic idealism, contemporary commentators who embrace multiplicity and reject aspirations to oneness tend to divorce soul from Spirit altogether, interpreting mystical union as otherworldly and rejecting of soulful experiences. This perspective reflects the descending path or worldview that idealizes embodied existence and multiplicity. By romanticizing soul divorced from Spirit, we risk perpetuating the suffering and alienation that is so prevalent in the postmodern world. If we deny the potential of deeper, more evolved states of consciousness, we cut ourselves off from the most essential factor for positive, creative change in human behavior. Soul divorced from Spirit is doomed to suffering and separation. On the other hand, perceiving soul and world as manifestations of Spirit does not devalue the earth, soul or Spirit, the one or the many, but affirms their essential interdependence.

Contemporary seekers in search of a more soulful life may find it helpful to remember that the soul as self-concept or witness does not exist independently or in isolation. It is entirely dependent on its Source, just as our physical existence is dependent on the biosphere. As we become increasingly aware of our global interdependence as a species, we can also deepen awareness of our spiritual interconnectedness. We cannot live in total isolation. The crosscultural communion of awakened souls may be a key to cocreating a sustainable future and living in harmony with the earth.

Indian philosophies

The association of soul with breath also appears in ancient Indian philosophy. The word *Atman*, translated as "soul," is derived from the Greek *atmos*, or "air." Most Indian religious philosophies recognize an aspect to the human being that survives physical death and reincarnates according to actions performed in previous lives. At the same time, Atman is uncreated and unchanging, residing beyond the causal and normative realms. Different Indian traditions disagree on whether the soul is substantive or ephemeral, personal or impersonal. Here, again, the soul appears to have a dual nature: temporal and eternal, finite and infinite.

In Vedic philosophy the soul was believed to exist independently of the physical body and depart from the body at the time of death. The soul might also leave the body during times of unconsciousness, ecstasy or dream sleep. The possibility of getting lost in these other, noncorporeal worlds was feared, yet such moments of disembodied existence were prized for the knowledge that could be gained and brought back to ordinary waking consciousness.

Toward the end of the Vedic period in India, the principle of the subjective identity between microcosm and macrocosm, or soul and Spirit, was introduced, and the gods and all of nature were seen as reflections of inner realities. The teachings of the *Vedanta* (the end of the Vedas) held that beyond yet within the flux of personal existence there exists an eternal, unchanging, intelligent, incorporeal and joyful "Self" that is identical to Spirit, the creative ground of the universe. The mind and the intellect, which belong to the world of manifestation are not considered to be dimensions of the soul. Atman signifies the subtle, timeless, deathless microcosmic self; Brahman refers to the equivalent intelligent and blissful essence of the macrocosm.

The *Upanishads* portray the dual nature of the soul in this image:

> Two birds, inseparable companions, perch on the same tree. One eats the fruit, the other looks on. The first bird is our individual self, feeding on the pleasures and pains of this world; The other is the universal Self, silently witnessing all.[23]

The purpose of yoga is to "yoke" the individual soul, Atman, to the unmanifest, eternal godhead, Brahman, and thus attain liberation from the limitations of the physical world. Yoga demands discipline, intellectual knowledge and mental control in addition to love and devotion. This implies that the mind and the heart must be equally developed if the true nature of the soul is to be revealed.

Brahman, translated as "Spirit," is the final reality that exists independently of the phenomenal world. Without qualities, this reality is described as uncreated, nonexistent, formless, and imperishable. With qualities, it is the subtle and stable essence of all that is.[24] The *Upanishads* tell us that within the soul is infinity, and that Brahman, the seed of all, is hidden in all as the uninvolved witness, pure consciousness, free of all qualities.[25]

These ancient teachings appeal to many contemporary spiritual seekers who intuitively respond to this cosmology as expressing a reality that makes sense to them. Today the practitioners of transcendental meditation, based on Vedic philosophy as taught by the Maharishi Mahesh Yogi, describe the first stage of enlightenment as the capacity to maintain lucid awareness twenty-four hours each day in all three states of consciousness: waking, dreaming and deep sleep.[26] In his commentaries on the *Bhagavad Gita*, Maharishi says,

. . . when the fullness of Being overflows through the mind into the fields of perception, when spiritual Unity prevails even on the level of the senses, when the oneness of God overtakes life, then is that state attained where perception of anything whatsoever is perception of the Being made manifest.[27]

In a commentary on the Yoga-Sutra of Patanjali, Georg Feuerstein, a leading yogic scholar, says,

Rather like psychoanalysis or psychotherapy, the practice of Yoga involves the whole person, not only his waking consciousness but also the subconscious. The yogin's spiritual quest entails a complete reorientation of his entire life which, unsurprisingly, is also reflected in his dreams which become more vivid and charged with meaning. Moreover, his sleep acquires a remarkable lucidity and becomes the stepping-stone for spontaneous meditative experiences.[28]

Although the aim of self-transcendence as understood in classical yoga is often criticized for being oriented to escape from the world, it need not be interpreted as world-denying. It can, instead, provide a view of reality in which the apparent dichotomy between Spirit and matter, soul and body is itself perceived as a play of illusion. The awakened soul recognizes all things as projections of the imperishable Brahman.

Buddhism in America

The ancient teachings of Buddhism have recently taken root in American soil where Buddhist meditation practice is increasingly popular and widespread. Buddhist teachings have given many people a new appreciation of a nontheistic spirituality, since Buddhism does not subscribe to belief either in a personal God or an immortal soul.

A fundamental teaching of Theravada Buddhism is the doctrine of *anatta*, or "no-soul." To believe that anybody or anything has an unchanging self or soul is said to be incorrect because everything we know is impermanent. However, Buddhist teachings about the laws of *karma* (cause and effect, action and reaction) apply to what is experienced as a self. It is the functional, volitional, moral aspect of a person that is subject to cycles of death and rebirth. To cling to anything as unchanging is to misunderstand the nature of reality, and the concept of a permanent self is considered an artificial construction of an ignorant mind. Reality is *anatman* or *anatta*, meaning devoid of self.[29]

However, there is something within each of us that is called Buddha nature which might be characterized as awareness. Although some schools of Buddhism also speak of a true Self (*Mahatman*), in the final realization of enlightenment all ideas of a separate self disappear.

When the Buddha was asked if he was a god, he replied, "No, I am awake." Among the sayings of the Buddha are these words:

The person who is awake shines in the radiance of the spirit.[30]

All things arise and pass away. But the awakened awake forever.[31]

One may inquire, "Who is it that is awake?" As long as a separate self-sense persists, awakening soul as witness can be a helpful expedient teaching for nontheists as well as for theists. It seems to be problematic only if we think of soul as an object. Some practitioners of Buddhist meditation have told me that their practice has plunged them into meaningful soulful experiences such as visions of past lives, although they know intellectually that this too will pass and that the soul is only another self-concept that must eventually be transcended.

Buddhism in America today offers a variety of disciplines that can facilitate the process of awakening the soul as witness. Vipassana meditation, based on Theravada Buddhism of Southeast Asia, offers excellent training in awareness whereby the student learns to observe sensations, feelings and thoughts without reacting to them, simply witnessing them as they arise and pass away. Theravada Buddhism can be characterized as an ascending path since it emphasizes nonattachment and achieving liberation from the suffering of this world.

For those who are attracted to monastic discipline, Zen, as practiced in Japan, offers rigorous training. There are different forms of Zen available in the United States. Rinzai Zen engages the mind in a process of inquiry by concentration on a *koan*, a question that cannot be solved by the discursive intellect, such as "What is the sound of one hand clapping?" Soto Zen emphasizes just sitting, awake and alert in meditation posture, without *doing* anything. Zen is one form of Mahayana Buddhism that emphasizes the realization that you are already what you are seeking. You only have to wake up to realize your true Buddha nature. Enlightenment is a context for the practice, not something to be attained. The ideal is the Bodhisattva, who has renounced personal liberation for the benefit of all sentient beings.

For those who are drawn to exploration of the subtle realms of images and archetypes, Tibetan Buddhism offers a wealth of maps and instructions.

Tibetan descriptions of the nature of consciousness at this level are probably the most encompassing descriptions that I have heard. Tibetan maps of the inner world are detailed and elaborate. Tibetan tantric practices that work on balancing male and female energies encompass both ascending and descending paths, but the beginner is usually required to go through rigorous ascending path disciplines at first. The final teachings are usually kept secret. I can see the wisdom in this, as an aspirant who has not yet reached a comprehension of the importance of ethics and practice in freeing the mind from illusion may imagine that conceptual understanding is equivalent to practice, which it is not. Too much intellectual understanding without practice may lead a person to become complacent and preclude full awakening.

Conceptual knowledge offers one level of understanding and can pave the way for experiential practice in any tradition. Knowledge gained from direct experience, however, is altogether different. Those who have tasted various stages and states of consciousness may not realize that tasting is not the same as stabilizing a state. To awaken now and then is one thing; to stay awake is something else.

Chinese cosmology

The idea that the soul inhabits an intermediate realm that partakes of both finite, perishable existence and divine immortality is echoed in the ancient Chinese understanding of the soul as a refined vital force that mediates between heaven and earth. Soul enables a person to harmonize with nature and enter into a spiritual accord with the cosmos. For the Confucian, immortality for the individual soul is achieved by moral excellence and participation in collective political and cultural accomplishments. For the Taoist, on the other hand, immortality is attained through a process of inner transformation in which body and soul both became translucent, free from thoughts and worldly desires.[32]

Ch'i denotes the strength and power associated with blood and breath. Like the Greek *pneuma, ch'i* is the air-breath that binds the world together. Its expansion (*yang*) and contraction (*yin*) are the movements that generate the multiplicity of the universe. The cosmos, as an integration of time and space, is believed to have emerged out of the interaction of Heaven and Earth or the mutual interpenetration of *yin* and *yang. Ch'i* is the energy that animates the whole universe, and nothing is devoid of spirituality.

In Chinese thought a person is not an isolated individual, but a center of relationships, intimately connected with nature and heaven. Human beings are part of the cosmic flow, linked to an ever-expanding network of relationships, always open to the world beyond. For the Chinese, souls have a right to exist, along with stones, plants and animals, in the creative transformation of the cosmos.

Many of these concepts are familiar to Westerners who have studied the *I Ching*, the Chinese book of changes, that outlines the patterns of interaction between *yin* and *yang*, the receptive and dynamic energies of the universe, and cycles of change that are mirrored in human experience. Like Buddhism, it emphasizes the inevitability of change. For the contemporary seeker it offers wisdom and balance and an opportunity to ponder the ebb and flow of the opposites. For the soul that is awakened it provides insight into how a person can live in harmony with heaven and earth.

Other contemporary disciplines based on Chinese thought include martial arts such as *tai chi* or *aikido*. These disciplines combine movement with meditation and awareness of subtle energies. *Aikido* was imported to America from Japan, but is said to have originated in China where Bodhidharma taught Buddhist monks a physical discipline to enable them to defend themselves against bandits who attempted to rob the temples of their treasures in the sixth century. In these martial arts the goal of mastery is self-mastery and the integration of body, mind and spirit. The student meditates and relaxes to clear the mind for the purpose of developing concentration. Self-confidence and fearlessness enable the accomplished practitioner to walk away from a fight because he or she does not have to prove anything.[33] The martial arts do not speak of soul. Nevertheless, the soul as witness may be awakened by these practices, thanks to their emphasis on self-mastery and awareness.

Judaic concepts

Hebrew words for the concept of soul refer primarily to respiration, as the inner, animating element of life. When the first human (Adam) received the breath of life from God, he became a living soul (*nefesh*). The word *ruah* is often rendered as *spirit*, meaning "wind." It refers both to powers outside the body and to the mysterious vitality in the body which is considered a divine gift. Spirit, life and soul are attributed to God, but the soul is regarded as the active element that is responsible for sin.[34]

Judaism contains a range of beliefs, from no view of an afterlife to belief in the resurrection of the body and the immortality of the soul.[35] The Talmud presents the soul as a supernatural entity created and bestowed by God and joined to a terrestrial body. God takes back the soul at death.

According to one view, the soul ascends to heaven every night while the body sleeps, returning with renewed life for the body. The soul protests at birth and again at the death of the body.

Judaic scholars, like the Greeks, accepted the distinction between body and soul and believed that the body and its desires were the cause of pollution of the soul. The body was regarded as a prison from which the soul must escape in order to be reunited to the Divine. When the individual soul is united with divine intelligence, both the material world and the limits of the rational mind are transcended. According to the Kabbalah, the task of reintegrating the flawed material universe into the divine pattern of existence is entrusted to human souls.

From this perspective the world of the transcendent, preexistent, incorporeal Logos was the model for our world, in which all things, including individual souls, were reflections of ideas or images. Only some living souls were incarnate in human bodies. They were ranked according to their inherent level of likeness to the Divine, as a hierarchy of beings. The word *hierarchy* is derived from *hieros*, meaning "sacred," and *arch*, meaning "authority." Hence the hierarchy of beings was presumably established in accordance with how closely each being was attuned to divine guidance. To the Greeks the beings that offered divine guidance to humans were *daimons*, or "knowers." In Hebrew they are called "messengers," later translated as "angels" or "heralds." Without the support of God, souls would dissolve into their original, undifferentiated state.

Many seekers today, particularly Jewish men and women who are dissatisfied with conventional forms of Judaism and longing to find their spiritual roots, are attracted to studying Kabbalah, a path of Jewish mysticism. Sheldon Kramer, director of the San Diego Jewish Meditation Institute, explains that Jewish meditation comes from the classic Kabbalistic texts that date back to the first century. He says the goal of meditation is to elevate one's consciousness from *nefesh*, the seat of desires and distracting thoughts, to *ruah*, a state of inner calm that stands outside one's inner and outer turbulence.[36] Kramer believes we need a revival of Jewish meditation in order for Jewish spirituality to survive into the twenty-first century.[37]

Traditionally only Jewish men over forty years of age were allowed to study Kabbalah. Today, however, introductory teachings of Kabbalah are widely available to any interested student. One student said that after two years of study, she was required to convert to Judaism if she wanted to continue. More advanced students have said that it is difficult to find qualified teachers in America. In spite of these obstacles, it seems clear that

Kabbalistic studies can provide a deep and challenging path of awakening for the soul.

Christian perspectives

> *For what shall it profit a man, if he shall gain the whole world, and lose his own soul?*[38]

> —MARK 8:36

This biblical quotation implies that in Christianity the soul is believed to be of greater value than the whole of the material world. The soul is believed to have eternal value, in contrast to the physical body which does not.

The soul is symbolized sometimes as breath, sometimes as water and sometimes as fire. For example, the spirit of God is given to Jesus in baptism, and Jesus breathes on the apostles as a symbol of his bestowal of the Holy Spirit.[39] On the day of Pentecost the Holy Spirit is described as a descent of the Spirit in tongues of fire.

Christian concepts of the soul are by no means uniform. St. Paul identifies the soul of the Christian with the spiritual realm to which it is introduced through Christ. In this spiritual dimension the human participates in the Divine. When the emphasis is on the contrast between the carnal realm and the spiritual realm, the distinction between soul and Spirit tends to disappear. What matters to the spiritual person is the inner life, which has the capacity to become everlasting. It is to this that the soul is to be resurrected. When the soul is turned over to the care of Christ, it is anchored in God and may be aware of possessing eternal life.

Some Christians believe that God creates a new soul for each person at conception. Others believe that the soul preexists the body, its origins antedating humanity itself. The soul is then believed to pass through many embodiments in the process of development and spiritual growth and is judged according to ethical conduct. This was the dominant belief in Christian Platonism. Origen and the Christian school at Alexandria subscribed to this doctrine and taught that the soul was imprisoned in a physical body as a result of its former waywardness.

The destiny of the soul, thanks to the resurrection of Christ, includes the possibility of personal resurrection and immortality insofar as Christ's power and victory over death is accepted. The concept of hell in which an indestructible soul is tormented forever as a punishment for sin became popular in the Middle Ages.

In the thirteenth century, Thomas Aquinas taught that while body and soul together constitute a unity, the soul is an individual "spiritual substance" capable of a separate existence after the death of the body. The essence of the pain of hell was described as loss of the vision of God. The soul is sometimes envisioned as well rid of the burden of the body. In the end, however, body and soul are to be reunited in resurrection.

The idea of purgatory served to account for what happened to the soul in the interim. Purgatory provided purification, refreshment and growth for the soul. Souls in purgatory are thought to be disembodied but subject to the pain of waiting and longing. In 1336, Pope Benedict XII declared that each soul on its separation from the body is judged and then either admitted to heaven, consigned to hell or dispatched to purgatory to be cleansed and readied for heaven.[40]

In contrast to the orthodox Christians who attributed original sin to the human desire for knowledge, depicted as eating the fruit of the forbidden tree in the Garden of Eden, Gnostic Christians sought redemption though *gnosis*, or "knowledge," and encouraged people to explore inner experience, believing that each one could discover the Spirit within. Human psychodynamics were conceived in terms of the interaction of soul and Spirit, affirming the human potential for spiritual consciousness. Gnosticism teaches that when the soul is alienated from its spiritual nature, it falls into illusion and suffering. When it awakens to its true nature, it can attain internal harmony and wholeness.[41]

Many Christians today seem to be searching for ways to awaken the soul and few are aware of the diverse teachings about soul found in Christian history. Disagreements over theory and dogma have led to innumerable wars and persecutions over the centuries since the time of Christ. What seems to be missing in many conventional Christian churches is the transpersonal experience that awakens the soul as witness and rekindles awareness of Spirit.

As one devout Christian said to me, "My soul seems to have come alive ever since I left the church in which I was raised. The further away I get from organized religion, the more I see my whole life as a spiritual journey." Like many spiritual seekers, this man's soul awakened when he left the conventional observances of the church that had been important to him for many years and took some time for solitary retreat in the woods. Years later, when he had a family, he joined another church in order to provide his children with a religious education, but he no longer expected it to nourish his soul. He had awakened his soul by going into nature in solitude. Once awakened, he recognized that this awareness was something he could not expect to get from an institution. It could only come from inside, from his own direct intuitive knowing. Nevertheless, unlike other disaffected church-goers, he was grateful for the early instruction he had received.

Islamic thought

> *There is no limit to your light, except the dark shadows*
> *of the ego cast upon the sky which we call the self.*
> *Shake your soul! Awaken it from slumber!*
> *The time has come to awaken to your divine being.*
> —Pir Vilayat Inayat Khan

Islamic concepts of the soul vary, ranging from traditional to mystical. As in other traditions, the term *ruh* refers to the Spirit that proceeds from God to human and is related to the ideas of breath and wind. The term *nafs* refers to the human soul which relates to the divine Spirit.

The human body is thought to be created before the human soul. Once created, however, the soul is believed to be everlasting. Concern is primarily with the moral and religious orientation of the soul, with an emphasis on purification and the devotional course a soul must pursue. Identified with the flesh, the soul may incite to evil, may blame itself in the quest for goodness or, in the case of the virtuous believer, may rest in tranquility and return to God. The soul is believed to be an immaterial, immortal substance that leaves the body at death and rejoins it on the day of judgment. In the interim, souls may be punished or live in paradise. During sleep, souls leave their bodies temporarily and may communicate with other souls, of either the living or the dead. The body and soul interact, helping to shape each other's individual characteristics.[42]

The relation of the human soul to God is at the heart of Sufism, the esoteric mystical tradition of Islam. According to Al-Ghazali, Sufis subscribe to the doctrine of the soul's immateriality and reject the concept of physical reward and punishment after death. In the mystical experience the individual soul is annihilated in the divine essence. This experience, being ineffable, may be conveyed in symbolic language, but is always prone to being misunderstood. Sheikh Nur Al Jerrahi Lex Hixon says,

> Nomad who wanders the expanse of ecstasy,
> his beatific vision never obscured
> by limited conceptuality,

the Shaykh takes up the poetic word
to inspire members of his mystic Order.[43]

For Ibn al-Arabi, the great thirteenth-century mystic, perfect souls reflect the perfection of divine essence and the perfect soul is a microcosm of reality. Again in Lex Hixon's words,

> Creation is revealed as a reservoir of spiritual meaning to the soul who is aware of its own essence and is therefore consciously and constantly oriented toward the Source of Creation.[44]

Writing on the teachings of Najm Kobra, Henry Corbin says that all spiritual teaching depends on the soul. The soul either joins with a guide of light or succumbs to darkness. When the soul is healthy and pure, what flows from it is good. Three different words used in the Koran to qualify the soul refer to stages of metamorphosis that the soul undergoes in spiritual development. The first is the *nafs ammara*, the imperative soul, equated with the passionate, sensual ego. Feeding the fires of passion perpetuates the infernal fires of hell. The second is the *nafs lawwama*, the blaming soul, the self-conscious one who judges, criticizes and finds fault. This is comparable to the super-ego or the rational intelligence that is at home in philosophical arguments. Finally, the *nafs motma'yanna,* the pacified soul associated with the heart (*qalb*) returns to heaven, accepting and accepted. The pacified soul is compared to a perfectly polished mirror and visualized as an orb of light. Whatever heavens the soul may contemplate, there are always other heavens beyond; there is no limit.[45]

In psychological language these distinctions correspond to identification with feelings (passion), thoughts (rational mind) and soul (transpersonal witness). The awakened soul, then, as we are using the term here, would correspond to the pacified soul. Just as passion can obliterate reason, overemphasis on discursive thought can obliterate awareness of soul. Therefore quieting the fires of passion and the endless monologue of the discursive intellect favors the awakening of soul. When soul is exclusively identified with the emotional life it is said to be asleep, unaware of its Source and its true identity.

Seyyed Hossein Nasr, a contemporary Islamic scholar, emphasizes the doctrine of unity as the essence of Islam and as the truth that lies at the heart of all religion. According to Nasr, the unity of the Absolute can be known only through intellectual intuition.[46] The intelligence that can pierce the veils of illusion and know reality as such is itself a divine gift. It is described as light as well as vision and as the root and center of the soul. As long as we are cut off from the light of this intellectual intuition, the luminous source of reality and revelation remains a mystery.

These ancient wisdom traditions all point to a transcendent, infinite reality that we call Spirit. Each human being is linked to this reality by an indwelling soul, which exists both in the temporal finite physical reality of the body and in the infinite, eternal reality of Spirit. Whereas exoteric religion takes myths pertaining to the origin of the soul literally, whether Hindu, Christian, Jewish or Muslim, esoteric teachings, such as those of Sufism and mystical Christianity, regard them as metaphors of an inner reality. Paradoxically, Buddhism, which denies the existence of an individual soul as an entity, offers some of the most practical methods for awakening soul as transpersonal witness.

Some common elements of beliefs outlined above include the idea of the soul existing as a link between Spirit and matter, potentially partaking of divine wisdom. Immortality is often attributed to the soul, either in reincarnation or an afterlife. The soul that remembers its source as Spirit need not be polarized with nature or the body. These dualisms are products of partial perceptions that fall short of integrating ascending and descending paths and fail to encompass the unitive mystical experience. If we aspire to the spiritual life at the expense of embodied existence we split ourselves in two, rather than integrating body, mind and soul in harmony with the cosmos. Human beings are free to affirm *both* the value of earthly life *and* the value of spiritual life. To awaken the soul is to integrate them.

By becoming more conscious of soul as witness of both inner and outer experience, the awareness that registers sensations, emotions and thoughts but is not identical with any of these, we gradually become aware of self as soul. When we turn attention to inquiring into the nature of soul as witness, we may find that a self-concept is not a discrete, separate entity or substance that can be lost, but a way of seeing that, when awakened, is aware of its source as Spirit. Conflicting beliefs or assertions about the soul that are found both within and among the traditions need not interfere with the process of awakening. If we listen to their teachings as metaphors expressing different aspects of human experience, we can accept the cultural differences and find those that can be most helpful to our own awakening of soul.

Having reviewed what some ancient religious teachings have to say about the nature of soul, let us turn to contemporary psychological interpretations that describe the soul from another perspective. Some psychological language offers new terminology that draws on commonalities among traditions without resorting to religious dogma. That does not mean that psychology is not dogmatic, because it can be. However, I will try to present those psychological ideas that are particularly relevant for awakening the soul.

MODERN PSYCHOLOGY: A DEVELOPMENTAL PERSPECTIVE

Your body is the temple of your soul. Your soul is God's temple.[47]

—HARI DAS

Most behavioral scientists have denied or ignored the existence of soul altogether. However, some psychologists interested in human development beyond ego have recognized it as a meaningful self-concept for anyone on a spiritual path. Today an increasing number of psychotherapists are reclaiming the original meaning of *psychology* as "the science and study of the soul" and are rediscovering the healing value of awakening soul.

Following Wilber's map of the spectrum of consciousness and psychological development,[48] I see the soul awakening at the psychic level of consciousness and evolving as witness in the subtle and causal levels. Experience at these levels is primarily internal, although it is reflected in the outer world. Intuition is a key to exploring these levels of consciousness as knowledge gained may not make sense to the rational mind that is oriented primarily towards the external material world. Intuition as a way of knowing becomes more available and reliable when we attend to it and learn to quiet the discursive intellect.[49] However, it is a mistake to assume that intuition is opposed to reason. Intuition transcends and includes reason. It is transrational in that it goes beyond reason. Intellectual intuition is a term that is sometimes used to differentiate this deeper wisdom from hunches and extrasensory perception. Transrational intuitive understanding should not be confused with prerational or irrational ways of thinking that offer little or no insight into the soul. Those who assume that anything nonrational is prerational tend to be reductionistic in their views and dismiss soul as nothing but a figment of imagination. These are the materialists who have reacted against religion by denying spirituality altogether. On the other hand, those who glorify anything nonrational as transrational fall into the opposite error of romanticizing magical thinking about the soul and mistaking prerational thinking for transrational insight. Some advocates of descending paths and New Age enthusiasts fall into this error. Wilber has called this common misunderstanding the pre/trans fallacy.[50]

James Hillman refers to the soul as a perspective rather than a substance, a reflective viewpoint that makes meaning possible, is communicated in love, has a religious concern and a special relationship with death.[51] For June Singer the soul is the central guiding aspect of the unconscious that serves as a link between the conscious ego and the vast, unknowable unconscious. She quotes Heraclitus:

> You would not find out the boundaries of the soul, even by travel-
> ling along every path: so deep a measure does it have.[52]

In transpersonal psychology a distinction is made between the higher unconscious as a source of creative inspiration, wisdom and guidance that links us to our latent potentialities and the lower unconscious that acts as a repository for repressed memories and links us to earlier stages of evolution, both personal and collective.[53] Some conventional forms of psychotherapy tend to devalue awareness of the higher unconscious while exploring only the lower unconscious, and some spiritual teachings tend to focus on the higher, overlooking the need to come to terms with the lower. Wholeness seems to demand awareness of both.

The collective unconscious refers to those aspects of the unconscious that are present in all people. Collective structures of consciousness may be prepersonal, personal or transpersonal. For example, we all have the capacity for sensing, feeling, thinking and intuition. Recognizing these collective characteristics does not tell us anything qualitative about these functions. For example, one person might want to develop intuition to make money on the stock market (world of ego), while another might want to use it for awakening the soul. Extrasensory perception, then, is not necessarily transpersonal. We can only determine if a function is truly transpersonal when we know the context in which it is operating.

In Ken Wilber's maps of consciousness, ideas about the soul change according to the level of consciousness from which it is perceived. When exclusive identification with ego is transcended, existential self-concepts begin to shift into more subtle identifications. Wilber outlines the following distinctions:

> [At the psychic level] I begin to realize that there are *really* more
> things in heaven and earth than I have dreamt of. I begin to sense a
> single Divinity lying behind the surface appearances of manifesta-
> tion, and I commune with that Divinity. This is the general psychic

worldview. At the subtle level, I directly know that Divinity, and find a union with it. But I maintain that the soul and God are two distinct ontological entities. This is the subtle worldview—that there is a soul, there is a transpersonal God, but the two are subtly divorced. At the causal level that divorce breaks down, and the supreme identity is realized. This is the causal worldview, the worldview of *tat twam asi*, you are That. Pure nondual Spirit, which, being compatible with all, is nothing special.[54]

Elsewhere Wilber says,

A diamond will cut a piece of glass, no matter what words we use for "diamond," "cut," and "glass"—and a soul can experience God, no matter what words we use for "soul," "experience," and "God."[55]

In my view, Wilber's work offers the most comprehensive maps of consciousness within which we can investigate the nature of soul and its awakening from a psychological perspective. I think of the soul as the witness, which like the eye, cannot see itself because it is the seer. The soul can only witness that which is perceived to be other than self. The soul seems to be the final identity of the separate self-sense. As long as there is a knower and something that is known, a subject and an object, one remains identified with soul rather than Spirit.

Whatever we believe about the nature of soul, in daily life we have a choice of identifying either with ego or with soul. Those who identify exclusively with ego tend to be oriented toward the outer world and suffer the frustrations of life oblivious to the possibilities and joys of awakening the soul. When a person awakens the soul and discovers the intuitive wisdom and love that comes with such awakening, values and attitudes can be deeply affected.

When the soul awakens, the inner life becomes more important as a significant source of meaning, and the connection to Spirit is both healing and empowering. One man said his life totally changed when he learned of transpersonal psychology. He had been suffering from post-traumatic stress after the Vietnam War and was seriously depressed. Psychiatric treatment had not been much help until he learned that by going deeper within, he could let go of previous ideas and images of who and what he was and find a whole new sense of himself as a soul on a journey of awakening.

By recognizing that ideas of eternal damnation and separation from Spirit can be projections of guilt and anger inherent in the limitations of ego, the soul can be released from illusions that seem to imprison it. It is then free to rediscover its essential identity as Spirit. The soul that awakens to its true nature as Spirit becomes one with the Divine and rejoices in the luminosity of its inherent radiance. No longer is God conceived in the image of man or woman but experienced as the creative Source of all being, infinite and eternal.

In conclusion, some schools of contemporary psychology support the notion that the soul, invisible to the body's eyes and beyond the reach of ordinary perception, is a vital, essential part of our humanness. Soul is our connection to Spirit, the unconditioned ground of being-consciousness-bliss (*sat-chit-ananda*). When we remember who we are as souls on a journey of awakening and realize that we have been caught by illusions of separation, we discover a boundless source of peace and joy that is always already present in the innermost depths of the soul.

At times the soul yearns for the passionate intensity of living in the world, draining every drop of life's bittersweet elixir. At times the soul travels to other worlds in search of healing and wholeness. Sometimes the soul longs for stillness, silence and solitude. The soul wants it all: passionate immersion in the path of descent into darkness *and* absorption into light. The soul is Apollonian *and* Dionysian, creative *and* receptive, masculine *and* feminine. It partakes of manifestation and dissolution, joy and sorrow, life and death. The soul both eats the fruit of the tree *and* witnesses all.

Soul, like breath, is always present, but we may not be aware of it. We become conscious of it only when we attend to it. Sometimes attention is compelled by pain; sometimes it is voluntary. When we look for meaning behind physical or psychological symptoms, we may hear the voice of the soul crying for attention. If we listen to the soul as we attend to the breath in meditation without interference, we find that, like the breath, the soul's life is sometimes shallow, sometimes deep. The soul sometimes speaks through tears, expressing sadness and joy. Often, we can hear the soul's voice in creative expressions of love.

Sometimes the soul speaks in a dream, as in the case of a young woman who dreamed that an angel came to tell her that her destiny was to serve God by doing peace work. She subsequently decided to join the Peace Corps and felt certain that it was the right choice for her. Another women said that she had uncovered a well of sadness during a meditation retreat and cried for three days. She later felt this time had been a new beginning for her. After the flood of tears she felt a deep sense of peace and spiritual renewal. She no longer felt overwhelmed by the problems she faced in everyday life and found a renewed sense of love and courage for resolving difficulties in her relationships.

Listening to the soul is easier when we can silence the inner critic and the fears and desires of ego. These products of social conditioning that served a purpose in gaining mastery in the outer world can interfere with our ability to listen to the soul. When we can quiet the mind and practice loving kindness without resentment, our identity as soul unfolds in awareness and enhances the quality of each moment.

GUIDELINES FOR AWAKENING SOUL

In the East, the soul is sometimes symbolized by a lotus, rooted in the mud, nourished by the water and opening in the sunlight. In the West, the soul is sometimes symbolized by a rose. Before reading further, you may want to try one of the following visualizations:

1. Imagine that you are looking at a rose. Notice the color and the shape and the degree of openness. Notice whether it is attached to a vine or a bush that is rooted in the earth. Imagine that you are watching it open and mature until all the petals fall and return to the earth.

2. Imagine that you are a tiny seed of a lotus buried in mud. Imagine extending tentative new roots deeper into the mud and feeling an urge to push upwards. When the new sprout breaks through the surface of the mud into the water, you redouble your efforts, reaching up towards the light and simultaneously extending your roots deeper into the mud. Is the water warm or cool? Is there any movement in it? Feel it sustaining you. When you break through the surface into the sunlight, feel the warmth of the sun and the opening of the petals of the blossom of the lotus, offering its perfume to the air.

Afterwards, take a few minutes to draw the image on paper. If this exercise is done in a group, you will notice that everyone's drawing is unique.

Notice the relationship of the different parts of your drawing to each other. If you visualized a rose, notice whether it was connected to the rosebush or if it was cut off from its roots. How is it nourished? Have you placed it in water? Have you included any thorns or leaves in your picture? Was your rose a bud or a full blooming flower? One is not better than the other. Either one may reflect your awareness of soul at this time.

If you visualized a lotus, notice whether the water is clear or murky. How large is the blossom in relation to the stem and the roots? Sometimes each segment of the lotus is associated with a psychological function: the roots with sensation, the stem in the water with emotions, the blossom with the mind and the perfume with intuition.

The unfolding of the petals of the lotus or the rose are often associated with the development of qualities such as wisdom, compassion, beauty, harmony and inner peace. However, since awareness of soul is a deeply subjective experience, you need not accept any interpretations that do not seem relevant for you.

Another visualization that can enhance awareness of soul is as follows:

> Visualize someone you care about and imagine that you are seeing him or her as a soul instead of as a body or a personality. What do you notice about this person that you may not have noticed before? Would you relate to this person differently if you were more conscious of the soul?

This visualization can also be done with a partner, thereby enhancing the perception of each other as souls. If you work with a partner, notice first what you see with physical sight when you look at this person: what he or she is wearing, the color of hair and eyes and appearance in general. Next, remember what you know about this person's personality, or what you intuit about feelings and attitudes. Finally, in a receptive mode of consciousness, simply regard this person as a soul.

The soul may be perceived not only in imagination but also in creative endeavors. Inspiration comes through the soul. The voice of the soul may invite the daimon that compels creativity. If we listen for the voice of the soul in dreams, meditation, prayer or contemplation, inspiration and inner guidance become increasingly accessible. Although the soul may be overlooked, the infinite radiance of Spirit is never absent. The awakened soul is always aware of its presence.

CHAPTER 6

Soul and Gender

It is not female.
It is not male.
It is not neuter.
Yet, in assuming a body,
the soul takes on such forms.[1]

—THE UPANISHADS

LIGHT AND SHADOW, FORM AND EMPTI-
ness, time and space are perceived by way of contrast. Opposites exist
only in relationship to each other, and it is in this context of opposites
that consciousness of the soul unfolds. Matter and spirit, Shakti and Shiva,
yin and yang, feminine and masculine designate basic polarities of human
experience that are intimately connected to concepts of self as soul.

When the soul is believed to be separate from God, it is experienced as
receptive in relation to the dynamic, creative power of the deity. As this
quality of receptivity is equated with the feminine, the soul is sometimes
assumed to be feminine.

However, this is not always the case. Gnostic Christians, for example,
sometimes viewed the soul as male, sometimes as female. Some passages
assert that souls are neither male nor female. According to some Gnostic
teachings, God the Father is united with God the Mother (The Holy Spirit)
in the transcendental bride chamber. The bridal chamber exists in order to
reestablish the primordial unity that existed in the human being before the
separation of the sexes. The Gnostics believed this separation became the
origin of death, and Christ came to reunite the two.[2]

One Gnostic text tells how the soul, represented as Eve, became alienated from her spiritual nature and fell into self-destruction and suffering. Reconciliation was conceived as a process of self-integration represented by the marriage of Adam and Eve. Other Gnostic texts reverse the symbolism and depict Adam as representing the psyche, while Eve represents the higher spiritual intelligence. As such, she first emerged within Adam and awakened him to awareness of his spiritual nature. She was, however, badly misunderstood and resisted.[3] Orthodox Christians, like their Jewish forbearers, blamed her for Adam's fall into a state of sin and separation and hence justified the subjugation of women.

REPRESSION OF THE FEMININE

In most societies dominated by patriarchal religions, the feminine has been simultaneously idealized, neglected, oppressed and denigrated. Subjectively, as well as objectively, the feminine has been repressed, feared and despised. This is true not only for men, but also for women who have made a successful adaptation to patriarchal social values. In a patriarchal society well-adapted women tend to become either dutiful daughters of the patriarchy, excelling in the masculine virtues of competition, achievement and control, or anima women who conform to the culture's stereotypical images of femininity in order to please men. For most women survival depends on their relationship to father, husband, brother, son or other male protector. In many countries an independent woman cannot survive economically and is socially ostracized. Even in places that offer women some social freedom, many women feel they are at a disadvantage economically, politically and socially when they are single, widowed or divorced.

Social oppression of women, together with psychological repression of the feminine in both men and women, contributes to a romantic image of the passive, fragile feminine which then becomes another obstacle to the reclamation of authentic feminine values. Qualities such as nurturance, relatedness, cooperation and compassion, commonly attributed to the feminine, are necessary for both personal and planetary healing. Wholeness depends on restoring balance and reclaiming what has been overlooked. These qualities are by no means the exclusive property of women. They are qualities found in mature, healthy persons of either sex.

Our understanding of human nature depends on the language that describes it. Masculine dominance has had serious, destructive implications. Evelyn Fox Keller points out that sexism in language has shaped the way science is done.[4] The language itself reinforces the denigration of nature and the feminine. Embedded in traditional ways of thinking about masculine and feminine, the task of extricating language from patriarchal dominance is a compelling challenge. Although the ideals of equality for women and respect for nature have become more widely accepted in recent times, they are still strongly opposed by many factions of contemporary society that include both men and women.

Redressing the imbalance of male-dominated cultural values by affirming the value of nature and the feminine is essential, but reclaiming what has been repressed is only part of the journey. Persistent attribution of gender to what is essentially human experience perpetuates the tendency to anthropomorphize both spirituality and nature. In addition, it seems appropriate to make an effort to find a language that describes the experience of soul in terms that are trans-gender. Whereas ego development is personal and gender-related, transpersonal development of the soul transcends gender and eventually transcends the exclusive identification with physical form and space/time.

When the soul of a man is projected onto a woman, she becomes for him not a human person in her own right, but an idealized image that no woman who is a whole person can pretend to embody. Although she may indeed serve the man who falls in love with her by putting him in touch with his soul and the latent feminine qualities of his being, she may lose her own soul in the process.

Lisa, for example, was a woman who was exceptionally beautiful. She attracted attention wherever she went, and she had the social skills to handle herself well in almost any situation. In addition to the classic grace and beauty that could be admired from afar, she had a warm and engaging personality that appealed to men and women of all ages. She seemed to be someone who could have anything she wanted in the world. But when she came to see me she was thirty-six years old and seriously depressed. She had just broken up with her latest boyfriend, after a three-year relationship that went sour soon after they moved in together. He was jealous and possessive, and she felt suffocated by his demands. He seemed to worship her, yet when he had too much to drink, he would become abusive. She had been thinking of marriage and having a child, but it became apparent that marriage to this man would be a disaster. She said she was sick of the attention given to her for her looks. It was as if everyone was blind to her shadow, the part of her that felt miserable and angry, because she appeared to be so serene and cheerful. Everything the world had to offer her seemed hollow and meaningless. She felt lonely and afraid, and had started resenting the attention of men. She had no idea of who she was, except as a mirror for male projections.

During a brief exposure to Jungian analysis a few years earlier, she had learned that she was "an anima woman," a woman onto whom men tend to project their souls. Her role as an anima woman, she believed, was to serve men by helping awaken their souls. This left her feeling empty and worthless inside, as if she had no value in herself. After several months of intensive inner work she began to awaken her own soul and to find her own connection to the divine ground of being. When she began to paint she discovered a creative urge to express what could not be put into words. In time she was able to claim a life and joy of her own that did not depend on anyone else. It was two years before she was ready for another relationship. This time she was able to express all of who she was from the very beginning, without falling into the trap of playing the anima woman.

Being idolized by a man does not help a woman claim her own soul. It reinforces, rather, the tendency to conform to stereotypical madonna images of purity and goodness. The idealized woman then tends to feel guilty for not living up to the positive projections. This guilt is what Joan Borysenko has called a kind of autoimmune disease of the soul, in which the woman attacks her own substance as being unworthy.[5]

In the essay "The Unfolding Feminine Principle in Human Consciousness," psychotherapist Sukie Colegrave designates masculine and feminine as two arms of Divinity. She says, "The Feminine unfolds a path of becoming characterized by relaxing rather than striving."[6] She suggests that it is the patient, uncritical receptivity of the feminine that allows the repressed, denied, dissociated and unconscious parts of the soul to become conscious. Psychotherapy in this context offers a redemption of feminine values. To the extent that clients focus on being rather than doing, attend to feelings and listen to the heart, they gain access to their capacity for receptivity, nurturing and inner vision. While this is true for both men and women, wholeness requires a balance of dynamic and receptive modes of being.

Ken Wilber characterizes the feminine way as the path of descent, pouring love into the world as *agape,* or compassion, in contrast to the masculine path of ascent associated with *eros* and striving for enlightenment.

The soul may feel nurtured by reclaiming feminine qualities and developing the capacity for emotions such as love, reverence and serenity in a male-dominated society that rewards competition and egocentric willfulness. However, a deep experience of the one Source that gives birth to the polarities of masculine and feminine transcends the duality of male and female.

SOUL AS CONTRASEXUAL ELEMENT

If the soul is perceived as the contrasexual element in the psyche, it is presumably feminine in a man, and masculine in a woman. As long as the soul is associated with gender, when a man falls in love, he tends to project his soul onto a woman, and vice versa. This experience is at first intense and wonderful but is destined to burn out in the end. Two people caught in the dance of projection are likely to become disappointed and embittered when their human relationship does not fulfill the promise of eternity. One may catch a glimpse of the reflection of the soul, only to fall into despair when projections are withdrawn, and the other is perceived in human rather than mythical proportions. If we fail to attend to the inner life of the soul, we can easily become ensnared by romantic illusions, leading to an endless search for perfect love in another person.[7]

In analytical psychology the contrasexual element in the psyche of a man is called the *anima*; in a woman, the *animus*. Since feminine virtues are attributed to the soul and the animus is associated with logos rather than eros, the animus as understood in Jungian psychology does not serve women very well as an image of the soul. Whereas reclaiming feminine values in psychotherapy helps men get in touch with the anima, women are saddled with a masculine stereotype of the feminine they are supposed to embody. Sometimes they lose touch with the truth of their own innermost being as they seek to fulfill the image. Surrender to the dark side of their own nature implies authenticity through surrender, not to another, but to one's own truth, painful and terrifying as it may appear to be at first glance.

Anima is the Latin name given to Psyche. In Greek mythology Psyche was a young woman whose extraordinary beauty was envied by her sisters and by the goddess Aphrodite, mother of Eros. Aphrodite asked Eros to make Psyche fall in love with some despicable creature, but he fell in love with her himself. She lived for a time in blissful union with Eros, not knowing who he was. When her sisters tricked her into trying to see him, she disobeyed him and accidentally wounded him. He then abandoned her. Psyche's long search for Eros succeeded only after she had fulfilled a series of seemingly impossible tasks imposed by the jealous Aphrodite. In the end she was reunited with Eros and became immortal.

Eric Neumann's interpretation points to the love relationship that embraces both suffering and separation as the basis of individuation for women.[8] My own experience tells me that the myth is useful to some women at a certain stage of development, whereas others feel oppressed by the implied expectations and some find it irrelevant to their particular developmental challenges.

Any young woman in a patriarchal culture who does not fulfill the idealized male anima image of perfection tends to feel devalued and inadequate as a person. No wonder the beautiful young virgin is transformed into a witch when time runs its inevitable course, and the bloom of youth fades into the ravages of age. The bitterness, fear and rage of a woman who has counted her attractiveness to men as the sole measure of self-worth easily turns to hatred as she loses her power. If she has been sexually exploited by a mentor, which is not unusual, she only becomes more deeply entangled with idealized images, losing rather than gaining a sense of her own soul. Unless a woman can rescue herself, claiming her own authority in relationship and identifying with her own soul under the guidance of a wise and faithful teacher, she faces a bitter fate of disillusionment and despair.

Janet, for example, was a fashion designer who felt that her success in the business world was due to the fact that she had a sexual relationship with a senior associate who had been her mentor for several years, ever since she graduated from college. Janet was an attractive woman, with very poor self-esteem, despite her intelligence and relatively normal childhood. She had become disillusioned with professional success and was desperately seeking some deeper sense of meaning in her life. She felt that if she did not do something radical to change her direction she would become seriously ill. She thought her anger was under control, but it surfaced in the form of recurring nightmares in which she was alternately being pursued or plotting to kill someone. As she began to explore her inner world and trust her own judgment, she gradually withdrew from the relationship with her mentor and began to like herself better. Her relationships with other women improved. She found a new source of support in a women's group that helped her feel less isolated and better able to connect to the world of soul. She went on a pilgrimage to Israel to explore her spiritual roots, and when she returned, she decided that although she did not find what she was wanting in traditional religion, she would continue to pray and meditate, regardless of how busy her outer life might be. Her spiritual life became a priority, and she rediscovered the sense of wonder she remembered from childhood, but thought she had lost forever.

Janet was fortunate in finding support for inner work at a relatively early age, in her early thirties. I have worked with other successful women who do not question conventional cultural values until much later in life and find it difficult to change habits of mind that perpetuate a state of inner anxiety and anger toward men. One woman who came to see me when she was sixty-one, had been widowed after thirty years of a relatively good marriage. She had been a dutiful wife and raised one son. For years she had devoted most of her time to service as a social worker. She was angry that her husband seemed to have an easier time coping with the world than she did and angry toward God for all the failures and disappointments she had suffered in her life. She had been raised Catholic but had given up going to church long ago. Yet she was still plagued by feelings of guilt. It took a long time for her to work through the flood of repressed feelings before she could regain some sense of inner peace. Inner work was difficult for her, and she sometimes found it frightening and overwhelming. It took courage and perseverance on her part to come to terms with her life as it was and to reawaken her own soul.

In the literature of analytical psychology, the term *anima* usually refers to the contrasexual, less conscious aspect of the psyche of men. Analysis may then become a process of the development of the feminine, which means many things to many men. Hillman warns:

> In the guise of "anima development," there takes place a rich trade
> in smuggled hypotheses, pretty pieties about eros, and eschato-
> logical indulgences about saving one's soul through relationship,
> becoming more feminine, and the sacrifice of intellect.[9]

According to Hillman, descriptions of the anima as the contrasexual element in a man's consciousness in a rigidly patriarchal, puritanical and un-soulful period of history should not be confused with the anima archetype itself. Erotic contents are often associated with the anima. Anima is said to be moist, vegetative, receptive, indirect and ambiguous, while eros is fiery, phallic, spirited, directed, sporadic and unattached.[10] These masculine and feminine elements are present in the psyches of both men and women.

Although Jungian typology is theoretically genderless, thinking tends to be associated with masculinity and feeling with femininity. Jung regarded the animus as the carrier of logos, and it is commonly associated with the thinking function which is presumed to be an inferior function in women.[11] Jungian analyst Edward Whitmont has discussed the problem of identifying Eros, as the tendency to relatedness, with femininity, and Logos, as the creative ordering intelligence, with masculinity.[12] Eros is actually a male phallic deity, son of the Great Mother, who imposes his own order of connection and desire upon the void. Eros is closely associated with Ares, who expresses aggressive activity, erotic desire and sexuality. Whitmont reminds us that in Greek mythology, Ares is the lover and Eros the son of Aphrodite. As twin suitors of this erotic goddess, they are periodically put to death by one another.

Whitmont also argues that we cannot uphold the belief that consciousness in men and women is masculine and unconsciousness, feminine. Masculine values and patterns of perception have shaped the structure of consciousness because they have been given supreme value in patriarchal cultures. Feminine values, on the other hand, have been rejected and hence repressed. Today, as they are being reclaimed and are included in a larger view of consciousness, they need not remain unconscious. It is therefore inappropriate to equate masculinity with consciousness and femininity with unconsciousness. Whitmont recommends that the terms *anima* and *animus* be reserved to denote archetypal masculinity and femininity, respectively, regardless of whether they apply to women or men. Insofar as Jung defined anima as instinct or soul, Whitmont says it pertains equally to both sexes. He says,

> Men are not necessarily more oriented to the spirit than women. Neither do women have a monopoly on soul and instinct. Spirituality as a predominant male characteristic and woman as the embodiment of soul are heirlooms of nineteenth-century romanticism, still dominant in Jung's day but no longer valid in our generation. . . . We are discovering that many gender patterns which even 30 years ago were considered a priori genetically or archetypally prefigured have been the result of cultural repressive limitations.[13]

Men and women both have difficulty identifying with soul as long as it is gender-tied. When the feminine image of the anima in a man is glorified as the soul, and the animus in a woman is denigrated as an inferior function, both are estranged from self as soul. Cast in the role of an anima woman who wields power over men by inviting projection of their souls, a woman may not know how to experience her own soul independently of men's reflections. Men, on the other hand, tend to persist in perceiving the soul as other than self as long as it is believed to be feminine.

Paradoxically, classic tales of the journey of the soul depict the hero as masculine. It is not the anima that undertakes the quest, nor is the hero referred to as animus. Although the myth of the maiden rescued from the dragon may be interpreted as representing the anima rescued from the clutches of conformity to social constraints, it does not transcend the distinctions between traditional gender roles. Even when the symbolism of the inner marriage represents the joining of male and female, it may not transcend conditioned distinctions.

Both masculine and feminine archetypes are multifaceted. The yin/yang symbol portrays the interdependence of the two. The seed of one is always located within the other, and neither is held to be primary. The story of Eve being made from Adam's rib, like that of Athena being born from the head of Zeus, gives us only the patriarchal view of the feminine and says little about the possibilities of androgynous wholeness.

Negative animus images appearing in women's dreams tend to be dark, threatening figures; positive animus images tend to be heroic rescuers. Neither is adequate as an image of soul. When the positive animus is associated with success in a patriarchal culture, it is likely to be egoic rather than spiritual. The powerful woman who has a well-integrated animus and a strong ego can be threatening to men who unconsciously fear the feminine. As soon as she does not conform to patriarchal images of the well-adjusted female, she is likely to be perceived as deviant and discounted or pathologized.

Conventional, narrowly defined images of women that do not include a well-integrated masculine element keep them dependent on men, unable to function effectively and autonomously in the world. When a woman does achieve a healthy integration of masculine qualities, she does it in spite of the expectations of the patriarchy that a woman should find her fulfillment in stereotypically feminine roles. She has to cope with unflattering projections in addition to facing her own internal struggle to acknowledge both her dynamic and receptive capabilities.

A man may surrender to his soul; a woman must claim hers. In order to do so, she must surrender the desire to be the "beloved" and risk becoming herself. Whereas a man often becomes aware of his soul in relationship to a woman, a woman is more likely to lose hers in relationship to a man. Although women seem naturally more inclined toward paths of communion and surrender, while men are drawn to paths of effort, agency and attainment, every whole person must find a way to include both the ascending and descending dimensions of spirituality.

Contemporary research indicates that men in this culture are better able to master autonomy and have trouble with relatedness, whereas women are naturally more oriented to relationship and have trouble with autonomy.[14] Obviously this does not mean that relatedness is exclusively feminine or independence exclusively masculine. For each person, man or woman, wholeness calls for developing that part of the self that is undeveloped. Whereas the ego tends to be isolated and alienated from others, the soul is awakened in loving relationships that do not require sacrifice of autonomy for either the man or the woman. Authentic, healthy relationship is a product, not of dependency needs, but of free choice that is possible only when the capacity for both autonomy and relatedness is well developed. We are often attracted to the qualities of soul in another that are undeveloped in ourselves. Thus any relationship offers an opportunity for reclaiming aspects of soul that seem to have been lost.

According to both ancient Hebrew and Greek mythology, the soul was originally an androgynous creature that was split into two parts and incarnated as either male or female. The two halves longed to be reunited and spent their lives looking for each other. This myth finds expression in the search for the one and only soulmate. The belief that there is only one right person in a world of millions of potential partners can lead to a lifetime of restless searching. The problem with searching for the soulmate is not that one cannot benefit from sharing the spiritual journey with a partner. The problem is in making the partner a substitute for God or expecting the partner to fulfill the longing of the soul. If I think I have found someone who can relieve me of the task of reclaiming my own soul, I have probably entered into an idolatrous relationship that will only delay the process. The mystics say that the soul is always restless until it comes to rest in God. As long as one expects the partner to fulfill the soul's destiny, one is doomed to disappointment and despair.

I have known both men and women who unconsciously expected their partners to provide their connection to the world of soul and Spirit. Women who have been told that they must serve and obey their husbands who in turn will serve God, often find themselves experiencing inner conflict when their husbands do not live up to their expectations. On the other hand, men who think their wives can carry the spiritual life for the family and they need not concern themselves with it, find themselves feeling isolated, alienated and hollow, no matter how spiritual their partner may be.

Romantic ideals that perpetuate the search for soul in the other may also obscure the fact that a person driven by erotic libido may have little real connection to the soul. Furthermore, a woman may invite projections of soul purely as a trained response to cultural conditioning. Her soul as well as her partner's may remain unrecognized until they both engage in the task of reclaiming projections through genuine relational exchange.

Although the soul is usually portrayed as feminine in our patriarchal culture, transcendence of ego on the journey to wholeness means including more of what was previously presumed to be other. Transcendence implies incorporating contrasexual elements in the psyche that were formerly repressed, denied or projected. The awakened soul that transcends gender identifications, then, can no longer be defined by contrasexual elements.

TRANSCENDENCE OF GENDER

O thou soul, most beautiful of creatures, who longest to know where thy Beloved is, thou art thyself that very tabernacle where He dwells.
— St. John of the Cross

From a transpersonal perspective that encompasses the opposites, designating the soul as either masculine or feminine is inappropriate. Although most religious traditions are patriarchal, essential spirituality is *transgender* and soul is not limited by gender roles. Even St. Paul said, "In Christ there is neither male nor female." In other traditions, when the soul is believed to reincarnate, it is not limited to male or a female incarnations. In this life it may be expressed in both masculine *and* feminine attributes. It is receptive *and* dynamic, light *and* dark, temporal *and* eternal, human *and* divine. Perhaps the soul is therefore best portrayed as the androgyne, for as the soul transcends identification with the physical body, it also transcends gender.

In her book *Androgyny,* Jungian analyst June Singer says that in old age, when men and women no longer need to live by collective standards, they can become more of what they truly are, provided they have prepared themselves for this during a lifetime, completing the developmental tasks of each stage of the individuation process.[15] She describes a wise old woman who, living alone, carried the image of the Sophia-wisdom, the companion of the soul. She spoke of her willingness to be cognizant of the male and female elements of herself in their dancelike interactions, neither the one nor the other in dominance. Yet in the end, the willingness to surrender even the identification with the androgyne is required of the awakened soul.

When a woman undertakes the heroic quest to reclaim the dark feminine, the fierce dragon she encounters will not be slain or transformed into a well-behaved, accommodating feminine stereotype. Instead it may breathe fire into her soul and transform her life. Analyst Claire Douglas points out that the heroic woman must bring it all to consciousness: the captive, the hero, the treasure and the dragon.[16] The patriarchal male hero either slays the dragon or projects his fear of it onto women, who, if they do not fit the image of fair maidens, become dragon ladies. Douglas suggests that the tendency to unite rather than separate and slay is the biggest difference between women's way of initiation and that of the male hero. This characterizes the distinction between masculine agency and the feminine way of communion.

It appears to be a disservice to women and to men to characterize the soul as gender-related. Although such personification may be helpful at early stages of inner development, it perpetuates the tendency to attribute to both the mind and the soul the biological properties of the body and negates half of the whole for both sexes.

According to Rudolph Steiner, the founder of anthroposophy, the physical body is interpenetrated by a subtle etheric body which corresponds to the contrasexual element in the psyche.[17] In a man the etheric body is female; in a woman it is male. At death the physical body returns to the earth. After three days the etheric body is said to separate from the physical body and is reabsorbed into the ether. The astral body, or soul, is neither male nor female. After death the journey of the soul is determined by karma, the accumulated consequences of many lifetimes, leading to reincarnation. The immortal soul is believed to be on a path of development that participates in the collective evolution of consciousness. Help along the way may be provided by angels and archangels, perceived as beings of light.

The idea that the soul after death possesses a subtle body was also developed by Paracelsus, who believed that when the physical body died and was buried, ethereal bodies wandered about for a time and were gradually reabsorbed by the stars. Sometimes the astral body was considered transient, sometimes imperishable.[18]

The concept of the soul as a being of light is ancient and widespread. In Neoplatonism the pure soul was conceived to be a cloudless ray of light. Jacob Bohme said, "The Soul is like a ball of fire or a fiery Eye."[19] The soul was purified through discipline, and manifested in imagination.

The ancient *Upanishads* say,

> Linked with ego and desires, the soul appears as a light the size of a thumb. But when linked with the Self and discrimination it shines like the point of a pin.[20]

Hildegard von Bingen portrayed the soul as a fire-sphere descending in a stream of golden light energy from the Godhead with countless eyes whose all-pervasive seeing reaches out in the four directions to the ends of the earth.[21] Here the soul is perceived as descending from its home in light to animate the human body. In her mystical vision, Hildegard is told by the divine voice that this is the soul, burning in the fire of deepest knowing. Awakening to the realization that she is not corporeal or subject to decay, she is filled with strength and joy. The soul, then, is conceived as something etherial that nourishes the body, flowing through it as sap through a tree. The qualities of knowledge and will are also attributed to the soul. Understanding is regarded as the feminine aspect of the soul, whereas will is the masculine aspect that accomplishes action in the world. Hildegard's visions were reportedly heard and seen in a fully waking state of consciousness. She was not in a trance or mediumistic state.

In Gnosticism, as well as in Stoic philosophy, single human souls were thought to be sparks of the cosmic fiery ether or the world soul. When a person lived a spiritual life, these sparks would grow into an abiding light. Just as sparks of insight can gradually grow into the light of wisdom, flashes of spiritual inspiration, when cultivated, illuminate the mind.

THE SOUL'S RELATION TO THE ABSOLUTE

When the soul becomes trapped in a prison of gender identity, it may feel oppressed by demands of the body. The pursuit of special relationships as substitutes for the soul's relationship to the Absolute bind it to the suffering of egoic identification with transitory biological existence. These entanglements seem less seductive when the soul is illuminated by divine wisdom. As an androgynous subtle body existing in the imaginal realm, the soul mediates between formless Spirit and material substance.

Each night, when we sleep and dream, we enter the domain of the soul. Sometimes women dream of being male, and sometimes men dream of being female. Aeschylus said that while we sleep the soul is lighted up by eyes, and with these eyes it can see everything that was withheld from its sight during the day.[22] Thus the body's sleep produces illumination of the soul, and the truth of the soul is revealed when the body's eyes are closed.

Although images of eyes, fire or light transcend gender identity, no image can fully capture the essence of soul. Thus the same stories that first awaken it can also become the illusions that prevent further realization. Perceptions of soul are shadowy at best. The reality of soul is discovered only by direct experience. According to the Gospel of Thomas, Jesus said,

> When you make the two one, and when you make the inside like the outside and the outside like the inside, and the above like the below, and when you make the male and the female one and the same, . . . then you will enter the Kingdom.[23]

CHAPTER 7

_____

Healing and Empowerment

Love is a power which produces love;
impotence is the inability to produce love.[1]

—ERICH FROMM

SINCE ANCIENT TIMES HEALING PRACTICES
have been intimately connected with the soul. In our secular society, however, when people feel threatened by the shadow of illness, they usually turn to medicine in search of healing for both body and mind. In my experience, the soul is not responsive to conventional medical interventions. It is not a mechanism to be fixed or a biological organism that responds readily to biochemical alterations. From the point of view of the soul, a person may ask about the meaning of illness or discover spiritual healing in the face of death.

Sometimes the pain of the soul seems to be masked or numbed by drugs. Whereas cure for either physical or mental illness generally implies external intervention, I believe healing for the soul that comes from deep within the psyche depends on a subjective shift in consciousness that can occur either with or without drugs. Although some people think healing the soul takes a long time, to me the process seems more analogous to waking up than to physical recovery from illness. Staying awake may not be easy, yet once the soul is awakened, it is not easily forgotten again.

Spiritual healing is sometimes associated with curing physical illness or injury when conventional medical methods have failed or been unsatisfactory. Despite the wonders of modern medicine, people still suffer from a variety of ailments that do not respond to medical treatment. As one prominent physician remarked, "If it were not for Western medicine, I would be dead. If it were not for alternative methods of healing, I would be an invalid."

Innovative programs in behavioral medicine emphasize the importance of patient responsibility in maintaining health. Psychotherapy also encourages responsibility for emotional and mental well-being, but many people still suffer in silence with a wounded soul, although they would willingly seek help for physical or emotional difficulties. Furthermore, many who suffer from a sense of spiritual deprivation do not seek help because they do not know where to turn after they have become disillusioned with conventional religion.

I remember one man who came to see me because he was suffering from headaches for which doctors could find neither a cause nor a cure. He had been a spiritual seeker for years and had tried many alternative methods of healing, none of which gave him any relief. As we explored the deeper regions of the psyche, we discovered that his soul seemed to be stuck in a conflict between the opposites to which he was most strongly attached. They were difficult for him to discern at first, since he was convinced that his values were impeccable, that he liked his work and did not need to change. As he brought more of his deep, unconscious conflicts to consciousness, he was able to release some of his unexpressed rage and see the rigidity that lay hidden beneath a seemingly flexible and adaptable personality. He was reluctant to change the habits that were contributing to the excessive stress in his life, but when he was able to open his heart to loving himself and others more fully, he was able to do what was necessary. The pain gradually became less intense and eventually disappeared.

Psychotherapy can often contribute to the relief of stress-related physical symptoms, and most therapy focuses on alleviating emotional pain and resolving mental conflicts. Many growth-oriented therapies emphasize self-awareness as a means of enhancing well-being. Despite a growing recognition that health for the whole person necessarily includes mind/body interaction, attention to healing the soul is usually lacking.

Transpersonal therapies that are concerned with healing the whole person and liberating the soul from constricting illusions attempt to access the deepest inner resources of the psyche by encouraging introspection, self-inquiry, meditation, attention to dreams and other practices that enhance awareness of the longings of the soul. These activities facilitate a process of healing and empowerment leading from passive dependency to active co-creation. An important part of this process is acknowledging responsibility, freedom and choice. Healing is incomplete if the will is not free to claim autonomy and personal power.

Empowerment means claiming the capacity to be a co-creator rather than being a victim in shaping personal experience. To be socially empowered is to feel that one can make a difference to others in interpersonal relationships and become an effective participant in social change. To be spiritually empowered means feeling connected to Spirit, having access to spiritual resources for inspiration and renewal and replacing fear with love.

PERSONAL EMPOWERMENT

Personal authority is the ability to validate one's own thoughts and actions as good and true.[2]
—POLLY YOUNG-EISENDRATH AND FLORENCE WIEDEMANN

Personal power can be defined as the ability to choose and carry out intentions. Empowerment is, therefore, often associated with developing self-esteem and ego strength. However, I think it is empowerment of the soul rather than the ego that offers a key to healing hearts and minds. When a person is predominantly identified with body image and ego roles, the soul tends to be overlooked. When the impermanence of the body and inherent unsatisfactoriness of ego goals becomes apparent, we are more likely to aspire to healing the soul.

The ability to carry out intentions implies a capacity to exercise free will. Empowerment as a free, autonomous individual requires accepting responsibility for oneself in the world and acknowledging the capacity to change oneself and to influence others. Personal power may be experienced in relationships, in achievements and accomplishments, or as creativity in art, work or play. While personal empowerment is important groundwork for wholeness, it does not always involve the soul.

I have found that personal growth and empowerment takes place rapidly when a person is willing to confront fear and take responsibility, not only for behavior, but also for thoughts, feelings and perceptions. We are affected by our thoughts more than we realize. Every thought has power to affect the psyche and the body for better or for worse. Many spiritual teachings, Western and Eastern, tell us that we shape ourselves and our world with our thoughts. Developing self-awareness and self-mastery is, therefore, essential for anyone concerned with enhancing well-being, be it personal, social or spiritual.

Consistency and integrity are the foundations of personal power, whereas resistance to empowerment often manifests as inner conflict. When a person is in conflict—when what one says or does is not in alignment with what one thinks or feels—the split between inner experience and outer expression causes stress and reduces self-esteem. For example, the person who feels anxious or guilty about some real or imagined misdeed in the past is likely to react defensively in the face of conflict.

I remember Helen, a woman who was actively involved in women's rights who seemed excessively angry and defensive. She complained of anxiety and a variety of minor physical symptoms. She had no shortage of justifications for her anger. What was less evident was the pain and guilt she had repressed in connection with an abortion she had several years earlier. She had felt completely alone and unsupported at that time and had never fully grieved the deep loss she had felt. In addition to sorrow she also felt guilty about her action. When the foundation of personal power is undermined by a painful secret in this way, it crumbles easily in the face of any perceived threat.

Without some knowledge of the dynamics of the psyche, control of thoughts, feelings and perceptions can easily be misused. If, for example, powers of mind are used to suppress emotions, a backlash may occur, and emotions may erupt violently, in unexpected ways. On the other hand, when a person has made peace with the past and integrated different aspects of the personality in a coherent and harmonious whole, personal power is enhanced. When Helen uncovered the deeper emotions connected with the abortion and worked through some of her inner conflicts in psychotherapy, she was able to forgive herself. Her health improved, her anxiety diminished and she became much less belligerent and more effective in the world. Healthy personal empowerment, then, is not achieved simply by will power or self-control. It is, rather, a function of self-awareness, acceptance and integrity.

SOCIAL EMPOWERMENT

Giving is the highest expression of potency. In the very act of giving, I experience my strength, my wealth, my power. This experience of heightened vitality and potency fills me with joy.[3]

—ERICH FROMM

Social empowerment and healing relationships are closely related to freedom and interdependence. As living systems, humans are constantly engaged in communication, interaction and mutually conditioning exchanges with their environment. However, many people are afraid of taking responsibility for initiating change and sometimes feel overwhelmed by what they believe they cannot change.

Oppressive political regimes certainly limit personal freedom, but oppression does not necessarily destroy the soul. It springs to life again at the first opportunity. This seemed obvious to me when I visited Eastern Europe and China, where people lived under oppressive atheist regimes for more than a generation. At the International Transpersonal Conference in Prague in 1992, hundreds of people from Eastern European countries were eager to learn more about spiritual disciplines appearing in the West. Many of them had been reading and studying transpersonal ideas clandestinely, sometimes at the risk of their lives.

In China, an engineer in his forties, who attended one of my seminars, wept as he talked about how he had been cut off from his Buddhist ancestors and how much it meant to him to think of being able to reconnect his family to the spiritual wisdom of this ancient tradition. The new psychology that envisioned an integration of science and spirituality seemed to give many participants in the seminar permission to acknowledge the secret longings of the soul.

Another younger Chinese man told us that when he was a child he had always been frightened of "American ghosts." He was told that if he ever saw one, he should kill the ghost or run and hide. He said he was so glad to know that he didn't have to be afraid of American ghosts any more.

Everyone experiences social constraints in some form. Those who have the privilege of freedom of expression often do not realize that internal repression can sometimes be as crippling as external oppression. To the extent that one is unwilling to take responsibility for the quality of one's relationships and environment, one abdicates power. Social empowerment begins with the willingness to acknowledge the effects of one's behavior and beliefs on others.

Recognizing that barriers to change may be internal as well as external, effective social empowerment is a challenge for everyone, regardless of socioeconomic status. Paradoxically, many people who hold positions of power in society say that they do not feel powerful as individuals. They may see themselves as fulfilling a function, pursuing an ambition or trying to make a difference, but few feel empowered to make changes in the system from which they derive their positions of authority. In working with business executives and others in positions of leadership, I have learned that people perceived as powerful by others often feel stressed, overburdened and trapped by responsibility rather than free, creative and empowered.

Edward, for example, was a business executive who began therapy after the breakup of his third marriage. He felt like a failure, despite the success of the multimillion-dollar company he had founded. Going into therapy seemed like a shameful defeat, since he thought everyone should be able to solve their own problems. But he had finally realized that there were some things he could not control, including his ex-wives and the children who were now young adults. He was keenly aware of the effects of stress on his physical health but was impatient with anything that did not yield quick results. His main goal in life had been to attain financial independence, and he had achieved it. He had not been prepared for the emotional toll his ambition had taken, or for the sense of confinement and inner emptiness that he felt just when he thought he should be enjoying the fruits of his labor. His self-image was of someone who could dominate others and control his own destiny. Emotionally, however, he felt like a failure and a victim of his former wife.

Dominance and submission are two sides of one coin. The sadist who exploits, hurts and humiliates, and the masochist who is exploited, hurt and humiliated, have both failed to satisfy the desire for love and failed to respond to the problem of living by creative, productive activity. The dominators seek to escape the experience of aloneness by inflating and enhancing themselves by incorporating others who obey, while the submissive ones clutch the illusion of security by feeling part of something or someone else who seems great, powerful and certain. They mirror each other's shadows and neither of them has freedom or integrity. Their mutual dependency breeds resentment, leading to inevitable conflict. From the perspective of psychoanalysis, these are typical perversions of male and female sexuality which can result when a person feels incapable of giving and receiving love.

Susan was a woman who had married when she was she was eighteen, in order to escape a miserable home life. Her father was absent most of the time, and her mother was depressed. Susan tried to be a good girl, but never felt loved or appreciated. She married a handsome man who was considerably older than she was and did her best to please him. It was not long before he seemed to get bored with her and wanted her to participate in various sexual experiments, including group sex. She went along with his requests, thinking there must be something wrong with her because she felt so much conflict about it. He made her feel selfish and uptight whenever she objected to anything. After several years of submission, she finally gathered her courage to leave. It was the most difficult decision of her life. She had been totally dependent on her husband and had done her best to conform to his wishes, feeling ever more worthless as a person. When she ran away, she felt like a child in the world on her own, but she was able to get a job and go to school part time to get some skill training. It was a decade before she began to heal from what she described as years of devastating experience in which she had lost her soul. Susan thought she loved her husband when she married him, but she had to love and take responsibility for herself before she could really love another without sacrificing her soul in the process.

Psychoanalyst Erich Fromm said,

> Love is not primarily a relationship to a specific person; it is an attitude, an orientation of character which determines the relatedness of a person to the world as a whole, not toward one "object" of love.[4]

The many different ways in which people exert power over others impose limits on freedom and distort perceptions of love in both the victim and the victimizer. The person who identifies as victim usually feels deprived of love and powerless to change anything. On the other hand, the person who has a connection to the inner life of the soul can find a source of strength that does not give up hope of change.

Writing about life in a concentration camp, German author and psychiatrist Victor Frankl said,

> In spite of all the enforced physical and mental primitiveness of the life in a concentration camp, it was possible for spiritual life to deepen. Sensitive people who were used to a rich intellectual life may have suffered much pain (they were often of a delicate constitution), but the damage to their inner selves was less. They were able to retreat from their terrible surroundings to a life of inner riches and spiritual freedom.[5]

Carlos Castaneda, a champion of the warrior's way of empowerment, says dreaming is freedom to perceive worlds beyond the imagination. He writes,

> To seek freedom is the only driving force I know. Freedom to fly off into that infinity out there. Freedom to dissolve; to lift off; to be like the flame of a candle, which, in spite of being up against the light of a billion stars, remains intact, because it never pretended to be more than what it is: a mere candle.[6]

When the soul awakens to a larger view of reality and we realize that we can change ourselves, we begin to feel both personally and socially empowered. Although we may all feel helpless in the face of the overwhelming magnitude of global problems when individual efforts to make a difference seem so insignificant, we are not merely victims in this world. Social empowerment means responding creatively to whatever challenges we encounter and replacing fear with love wherever possible. The global problems that haunt us today are those that we humans, collectively, have caused. We have indeed become as gods, with the power to destroy the world. The wisdom to preserve it must also come through us. New perceptions of possibility for a sustainable society that envision a compassionate consciousness infusing the world, in which love is the unifying force that makes global reconciliation possible,[7] need to be adopted by those who aspire to freedom.

Although altruism in social action cannot be coerced, it is an option that has been demonstrated by spiritual teachers throughout the ages. Those who aspire to a level of psychological and spiritual maturity from which love and altruistic action flow naturally are already demonstrating that a change of mind is both possible and desirable. In the meantime we can teach and learn about ignorance as the root cause of unnecessary suffering and empower each other to shift motivation from fear to compassion and from domination to service.

SPIRITUAL EMPOWERMENT

Love is an action, the practice of a human power, which can be practiced only in freedom and never as the result of a compulsion.[8]

—ERICH FROMM

Sooner or later, I believe everyone must come to terms with power within themselves and in the world. Yet the power necessary for personal and social effectiveness is seductive and can be a trap for the soul that yearns for freedom. Claiming personal and social empowerment is only the beginning of coming to terms with power on the spiritual path.

Spiritual empowerment that frees the soul implies a shift in perception that invites awareness of love's presence and sees any situation as an opportunity for teaching and healing. Spiritual empowerment is evident in certain qualities and attitudes, such as a lack of defensiveness, a receptivity to learning, an open mind and an open heart. A person who is spiritually empowered is not resentful or vengeful and is fully present here and now. A good example is His Holiness the Dalai Lama, who seems to embody these qualities in his interactions with people from all walks of life. Even his attitude toward the invaders of his country is compassionate, and even in exile he is a world spiritual leader. I have heard him give brilliant lectures on consciousness and respond to even hostile questions with grace and humility. He seems curious to learn about everything, particularly Western science, and listens respectfully to the views of others.

I realize that to the extent that I am distracted from the present moment by reviewing the past or anticipating the future, I lose touch with the freedom of this moment. The soul that would be free and empowered in the present learns to let go of the past and future, for the past and future exist only in imagination. Although imagination is a creative function of the soul, the soul that is free is not limited to the realm of imagination nor does it cling to egocentric fantasies.

Scientific knowledge, which is often equated with power in the world, does not preclude using power unwisely, nor does it guarantee freedom and healing. Technological innovations do not always serve the purpose for which they were intended. For example, modern weapons of destruction do not make us feel safe, nor does contemporary communications technology help us to feel less isolated or more closely connected to each other. Despite the awesome advances of modern technology, individuals still feel powerless.

A conscious relationship to knowledge means recognizing its limitations as well as its power. As the humorist says, "It doesn't matter whether you think money is power or knowledge is power, as long as you have both." What you do with them determines whether they are entrapping or liberating.

When money is equated with power and is accumulated as a means to power, it can destroy freedom rather than enhancing it. Whether money is judged as good or evil, as long as it is given the mythical proportions of a god or a devil, it keeps the soul in bondage. Writing on *Money and the Meaning of Life,* contemporary philosopher Jacob Needleman suggests treating money as an instrument for self-study in the midst of ordinary life.[9] Living in contemporary society, we cannot ignore money, and we need to know what it can and cannot buy. Meaning is one thing it cannot buy. However, only by consciously experiencing our relationship to money, which represents the world of ego, can we aspire to freedom. This aspiration, says Needleman, requires an authentic spiritual path.

Every spiritual path offers some method of spiritual empowerment. In Tibetan Buddhism, ceremonies of empowerment sanction the student's participation in particular practices. In Christianity the transcendent power of the Holy Spirit comes through individuals who receive the gifts of the Spirit, such as the power of healing and prophecy. This power does not belong to anyone. It is a power that is *in* you, but is not *of* you. It is a gift of grace. All you can do is prepare to receive it by purification and prayer.

In contrast, practitioners of yoga are rigorously trained in concentration practices designed to stop the spontaneous, undisciplined activity of the mind and gain mastery of the subtle realms of consciousness. In yoga, as in other spiritual traditions, practitioners are warned against pursuing the *siddhis*, or psychic powers, as ends in themselves. The temptation to use these powers in the service of ego goals can be a major obstacle to spiritual development. The same powers that enable a person to master the subtle realms can become the obstacles that prevent spiritual freedom. Ethical purification is therefore a prerequisite for training.

In psychotherapy, when clients are willing to initiate change and critically examine beliefs and attitudes that shape experience, they become increasingly empowered, personally, socially and spiritually. They can then see that some change is voluntary and that a source of healing can be discovered within. Spiritual empowerment is incomplete, however, if the soul has not awakened to its intrinsic freedom.

HEALING THE SOUL

Today the resistance to reawakening to our inner divinity, of recovering our soul, comes not only from religion but from science as well.[10]

—LARRY DOSSEY

The sickness of the soul that manifests as emotional or mental illness often goes unrecognized by conventional medical models of mental health. There are no diagnostic categories for the soul. Yet the need for spiritual healing is widespread in contemporary society. By spiritual healing in this context, I do not mean affecting physical health by means of prayer or other forms of spiritual practice. I mean, rather, a form of healing that enables the soul to feel at peace and empowers the individual to be loving and effective in the world.

Healing the soul is a transformational process. This means that the process is not one of changing certain elements of the personality which can be compared to rearranging the furniture in a house. It is, rather, analogous to changing the context and thereby perceiving the contents differently. A significant shift in perception may be required for the psyche to be experienced as whole rather than fragmented and peaceful rather than conflicted.

Soul in psychology

Although psychology can be understood literally as the study of psyche or soul, psychology is commonly regarded as a behavioral science that studies human behavior, personality and the mind. Few contemporary psychologists take seriously the study of the soul. In a world of biological materialism, psyche is equated with mind, and its function is limited to regulating the organism's relation to the environment. The soul, then, is superfluous. In attempting to be scientifically rigorous, psychology has been inclined to avoid any language that has religious associations and has therefore shied away from dealing with the soul.

On the other hand, some contemporary psychotherapists are beginning to describe the form of healing they practice as soul work, and some attempts have been made to address the suffering of the soul in the postmodern world. In the 1960s Abraham Maslow's research on healthy, self-actualizing people included a concern for spiritual issues. Whereas behaviorism had been primarily concerned with prediction and control of behavior, humanistic psychology tried to deal with the whole person and to address issues of value, meaning and purpose in human life.

By the end of the decade, transpersonal psychology was differentiated from humanistic psychology, placing greater emphasis on the study of spiritual experiences, optimum psychological health and the full spectrum of human consciousness, including some states that had previously been mapped only by Eastern disciplines. Humanistic psychology then became primarily identified with feeling-oriented therapies and the process of self-actualization. Many humanistic approaches to psychological health focused on reintegrating repressed emotions for a fuller, more authentic life, particularly in interpersonal relationships. Transpersonal psychology, as it developed in the seventies and eighties, focused more on the relationship of psychological health to spiritual development and the investigation of inner experience.

Psychoanalysis had developed its own mythology of the inner life earlier in this century, devoid of soul and Spirit, explaining all human experiences in terms of past personal history, the unconscious, and the id, the ego and the superego. The study of soul in relation to Spirit found no place in its pantheon of pathology.

Although the soul has been called a healing fiction that may serve a useful purpose in the process of individuation, it is fictitious only insofar as any separate self-sense may be regarded as illusory. As long as we perceive ourselves to be existing in time, reclaiming the soul can have a powerful healing effect.

As an identity, the soul both transcends and contains our physical, emotional and mental egoic self-concepts. It does not depend on ego gratification for a sense of well-being. Its healing is related to, yet distinct from, physical, emotional and mental health. Just as physical health is affected by emotions and states of mind, hearts and minds are affected by the state of the soul.

Some practitioners of archetypal psychology maintain that the main task of psychology is soulmaking, and what matters most is how life is used to care for the soul.[11] The psychotherapist, in keeping with the original meaning of the Greek word *therapeutes*, is one who serves the gods and attends to the soul. Therapy can then be described as a process of individual soul-searching.

This is quite different from the more common perceptions of therapists as specialists in interpersonal relations or doctors who prescribe medication for mental illness. Yet many psychologists still shy away from using spiritual terminology for fear of being perceived as unscientific or of confusing psychology with religion.

Carl Jung regarded religions as therapies for the soul and pointed out that care of the soul was historically entrusted to priests. Today, however, when faith in dogma has been seriously undermined by science and people tend to question religious authority, many priests and ministers turn to psychology for guidance in pastoral counseling and spiritual direction. In a predominantly secular society psychotherapists have become priests by default. Many do their best to relieve the pain of spiritual deprivation, but few are qualified to care for the soul.

Soul work in psychotherapy

All healing involves replacing fear with love.[12]

–A COURSE IN MIRACLES

It is my experience that for many people psychological and spiritual well-being is intimately related to awareness of soul. Conventional psychological interventions that focus on interpersonal, cognitive or emotional work may be of little value in treating a condition of spiritual aridity or a dark night of the soul. Unless questions of meaning and purpose in life are addressed in soul work, therapy may do little more than provide temporary relief of symptoms. In addressing questions pertaining to meaning, freedom and the inevitable confrontation with death, aloneness and alienation, existential psychotherapy comes close to addressing the sickness of the soul. Unfortunately, it often stops short of exploring transpersonal realms where healing for the soul can be found.

Whether we believe that these realms are populated by spirits or regard the images that we encounter as autonomous complexes of the psyche, the process of healing requires that we relate to them and differentiate them. Wherever there is a sense of separate self there is other, and the unknown other engenders fear. Although every level of perception is influenced by projection, belief and expectation, regarding this whole realm as nothing but projection is reductionistic. Reductionism makes the mistake of attempting to explain the subtle levels of consciousness in terms of biological materialism which tells us nothing about subjectivity or such factors as intentionality and inspiration. Just as psychology cannot be reduced to biology, soul cannot be reduced to ego mind and its objects.

For example, when a young man dreamed of being killed by an overpowering, sinister automaton, he recognized intellectually that this image was a projection of his own shadow, but stopped short of exploring how he could relate to it. As we explored the feelings in the dream and he began to empathize with the blind rage of the automaton that could only do what it was programmed to do, he began to acknowledge the part of himself that felt like an automaton and the pain he felt inside. His own feelings of powerlessness surfaced when he continued the dream in active imagination and began to dialogue with this figure. In addition to the insights gained, he experienced an energetic shift that seemed both liberating and empowering.

Anyone who has explored the inner world of soul and worked with others in this process learns that the figures encountered here, whether threatening or benign, are experienced as autonomous and powerful and cannot be dismissed lightly. In recent years holotropic breathwork, as pioneered by Stanislav and Christina Grof,[13] has been established as an effective method of inducing altered states of consciousness that facilitate entering this world with remarkable healing results. This method combines prolonged deep breathing, based on the yogic practice of *pranayama*, with music and the presence of a skilled facilitator. This enables a person to access personal and collective levels of the unconscious and explore the inner world in a safe and supportive environment. Grof explains that the most important requirement for the therapist employing such nonordinary states of consciousness is not masterering specific techniques, but accepting and trusting the spontaneous unfolding of the process. He says,

> In Holotropic Breathwork, in the work with spiritual emergencies, and in thousands of psychedelic therapy sessions in my earliest research, I have seen many dramatic healings and positive personality changes, which have completely eluded all my efforts at rational understanding. . . . The wisdom for change and healing comes from the collective unconscious and surpasses by far the knowledge that is intellectually available to the therapist.[14]

Guided imagery and hypnosis can also access these realms for the purpose of healing, but experiences vary considerably in depth and may be used in the service of ego goals as well as in the service of deeper exploration. Those who use them need to be aware that a person in an altered state of consciousness is extremely suggestible and is therefore prone to find what he or she expects to find. For example, if a person believes that uncovering a the memory of a childhood trauma will result in relief of specific symptoms, it may do so, regardless of whether the memory is literally true or not. It is also important to remember that altered-state experiences sometimes seem even more real than those which are consciously remembered in an ordinary waking state.

Interpreting these experiences as literal memories can be problematic and sometimes detrimental to the healing process. This issue has come to the attention of the public in the debate over the veracity of recovered memories of sexual abuse. The fact that some memories are true while others are fabricated, adds to the difficulty of differentiating them. The same caution applies to interpreting hypnotic regression to past-life experiences, which some therapists believe to be therapeutic. Therapists who employ these techniques need to recognize both the value and the potential trap of elevating a healing fiction, i.e., a shared belief that produces therapeutic results, to the status of scientific fact. For instance, in the case of my client who had felt some relief when a hypnotic session with a previous therapist had interpreted her difficulty in assuming authority as a past-life residue, she was further empowered to fulfill her potential when we explored her relationship to her father. If she had not pursued further therapy, the hypnotic session would have been quite inadequate.

In contrast to the hypnotherapist or the guided-imagery practitioner who may use these techniques with a particular goal in mind, the breathwork facilitator who is trained to be open and nondirective does not attempt to interfere with the subjective experience of the person who is doing the breathing. The individual is encouraged to have his or her unique experience, allowing defenses to relax and bringing repressed emotions to the surface, trusting the wisdom of the unconscious to guide the healing process.

I have also had experience working for many months with people who subsequently felt the need to integrate their altered-state experiences. Although some resolution of trauma can occur in the breathing session itself, complete healing may require further integration. Any new revelation about a person's self or world can alter the course of life. Such people can benefit from guidance at these crucial times.

Conversely, when individuals who are already on a path of self-discovery feel stuck, they can benefit a lot from intensive breathwork. Furthermore, many people who would never go into psychotherapy can sometimes discover a whole new realm of experience in holotropic breathwork. I know may people whose lives have been changed by participating in this process.

In the inner world anything is possible. Experiences may be helpful, disturbing, instructive, surprising, exotic or mundane. Grof points out that human beings have a profound need for transpersonal experiences in which they transcend their individual identities to find their place in a larger whole that is timeless. He sees the spiritual craving as more basic and compelling than the sexual drive and notes that if it is not satisfied it can result in serious psychological disturbances.[15]

Effective use of these powerful therapeutic methods that access the inner world depends on adequate preparation and proper guidance. Given the appropriate context and attitude, it seems clear that exploring the inner world in this way can awaken the soul and promote healing and integration in the psyche.

Healing the soul in psychotherapy begins with a commitment to authenticity. When a person is willing to tell the truth about experience and let things be as they are, the process unfolds easily. On the other hand, when therapy is viewed as a means of manipulating reality for the purpose of fulfilling egocentric expectations, the process can be arduous. For example, if clients can tell me about their experience just as it is, without embellishment or apology, they begin to discover who they are and what is most important to them.

Barbara told me the first time we met that she was not here to please or impress me but to express her feelings and speak her truth. She had never revealed her deepest desires to anyone before and had spent most of her life doing what others expected of her. Now, in her forties, she began to be afraid of aging and thought that life was passing her by. She felt alienated from her family and fragmented by many conflicting demands on her time. She felt an unspecified sense of longing, as if there must be more to life, yet uncertain of what she wanted. By being willing to risk saying whatever came to mind as she listened inwardly for the voice of her soul, she made good use of our time together. I would remind her from time to time that she was here to speak her truth, not to report on other people and what they might think. Her truth included painful memories that seemed to bind her to the past, as well as inner conflicts, dreams, hopes and fears.

As we listened carefully to what she really wanted, what she really felt and what her intuition suggested, Barbara began to know herself better and to recognize self-deception and self-defeating patterns of behavior. Her inner world that seemed so chaotic and irrational began to make sense as we attended to it. Her dreams also became more lucid, reflecting the changes in perception that enabled her to see the world differently. When she began to feel whole rather than fragmented, she felt empowered to take responsibility for herself and face the challenges in her life rather than avoiding them. As she accepted herself and the choices she had made, she found that she did not need to resist the inevitable changes that life brings. Gradually she began to reclaim the freedom of her soul to enjoy music, the beauty of nature and the love of her children. She also recognized the importance of honoring the sacred in everyday life to help her stay connected to Spirit. She began a daily practice of meditation that for her was a way of coming home to God inside herself. Her spiritual practice continued long after her therapy was completed.

Confession, as in telling one's story, is an important part of healing for the soul. Some rituals and various forms of therapy can also facilitate the process. Understanding how the mind works and expressing emotions does facilitate healing, but healing is not caused by any particular method. Healing happens spontaneously from within. A skilled therapist or spiritual teacher who cares for the well-being of the soul and assists in transforming psychic pain into fertilizer for the field of awareness only sows the seeds of healing for the soul.

Soul loss

When parts of a soul split off and vanish into nonordinary reality, leaving a person in a weakened, dispirited condition, it is the job of the shaman to restore wholeness.[16]

—SANDRA INGERMAN

Contemporary shamanic practices that interpret illness as soul loss teach that healing occurs when the soul is recovered. Soul loss is a loss of power that can occur as a result of addiction, abuse, illness or any other adversity. Symbolic rituals of soul retrieval sometimes involve singing, dancing, storytelling and silence as well as journeying to other worlds. According to anthropologist Angeles Arrien, drumming symbolizes a heartbeat, and the sound of the rattle, reminiscent of rain, symbolizes cleansing and purification. Both may be used by a medicine man or woman in soul retrieval work to call home parts of the self that have been lost. On some occasions the patient may be empowered by being reconnected to a power animal. These rituals, symbols and ceremonies reinforce identification with soul and contribute to feelings of integration and empowerment.

Either physical illness or psychological stress may be interpreted as soul loss. It may be characterized by depression, anxiety, feelings of alienation, meaninglessness and a longing for something intangible, unnameable. In contemporary Western culture, this longing is often anesthetized by addiction to drugs, alcohol, food, compulsive spending, destructive relationships or even certain forms of spiritual practice. Many prevalent forms of addiction involve repetitive, destructive behavior that constricts awareness and deprives the addict of freedom and responsibility. Healing is facilitated when a person feels empowered to make free choices that contribute to harmony and wholeness.

When soul is recovered, staying connected to it is a function of awareness, not of will power. The power that heals the soul does not belong to the domain of the ego. It may be called higher power, as in addiction recovery programs, or transpersonal Self, or Holy Spirit, guru, inner guide or many other names. Many people suffering from wounds of emotional deprivation or childhood abuse need remedial ego work as well as recovery of soul. This work can be rigorous and challenging.

Family therapist John Bradshaw speaks of soul rupture in children who are shamed or abused.[17] In psychological terms, the parts of the psyche that are dissociated under circumstances of extreme stress need to be reintegrated to build a strong sense of identity. When soul rupture occurs at an early age, ego development is impaired, and the damage needs repair. When a person has felt victimized, claiming personal power and taking a stand against the abusive behavior seems to be necessary before pain and anger can be released in the authentic forgiveness that heals the soul.

Another type of soul loss is attributed to being obliged to forgo moral values. This happened to many Vietnam veterans who became disillusioned with a cruel war that made no sense to them. Left with a sense of self-betrayal and despair, some of them have been unable to reconnect with any faith after feeling wounded by the ideals they once believed in. Others have found solace in spiritual practices and have learned to see even this as a part of the soul's journey. The rage, however, may surface at unexpected moments. One vet confessed to punching a hole in the wall of his apartment in a fit of rage, although he had been meditating for several years and thought he had his anger under control.

Whatever the cause, anger must be acknowledged, communicated and released. Healing is obstructed whenever anger is suppressed or denied. Buried rage is a prison for the soul. It may surface in a variety of emotional and physical symptoms that make a person feel totally powerless. Although anger is a natural response to oppression, being stuck in anger is like being trapped in hell. Anyone who is enraged and does not feel understood just keeps on raging. Anger seldom dissipates by itself. It helps to be heard by someone who can empathize, contain and transform it. This process can reduce anxiety and provide a sense of mastery that liberates the soul as well as empowering the ego. Although the connection between repressed anger and anxiety is seldom apparent to the casual observer, it becomes obvious when we explore it.

Many individuals who have devoted themselves to a spiritual teacher for years and then become disillusioned report feeling both rage and anxiety in separating from the group. When a teacher or an institution fails to live up to an idealized image, people may feel wounded and betrayed, unable to trust themselves or anyone else. Nevertheless, many spiritual seekers who left an organization after becoming disillusioned considered the experience valuable, even when they suffered from it. Disappointed seekers who can accept their part of the responsibility for whatever occurred can gain a new level of personal empowerment when they reclaim their souls. In contrast, most of the disillusioned veterans found no redeeming qualities in the experience of war.

One man who came to see me after a particularly difficult disengagement from a spiritual group to which he had devoted nearly fourteen years of his life said he did not regret any of it. Through his suffering he had learned a lot about discipline and about trusting his own perceptions rather than what he was told. Leaving took great courage in the face of threats from the group. Although physical and emotional threats had been used against him before he left, the most difficult fear to face was the belief that his soul would be damned by breaking his vow of obedience. What had once seemed to be a noble commitment had become a prison, reinforced by threats of eternal damnation. When he did leave he felt he had reclaimed his soul. Just as the threat of excommunication from the Church in the Middle Ages was a powerful weapon in the hands of the clergy, similar threats are used today in cults that seek to coerce loyalty and obedience. The prison constructed by belief is a prison of the soul, not a physical prison. Breaking out requires courage, faith in oneself and faith in the reality of spiritual freedom.

Effective soul work deals with deep feelings as well as beliefs and attitudes about the soul and what it means to be spiritual. Since soul loss is not a recognized medical diagnosis, in some clinical settings soul work is called by other names. For example, treating depression, anxiety or post-traumatic stress disorders may include soul work. Unfortunately conventional treatment for these disorders usually does not address the deeper issues of healing for the soul.

While it is apparent that rage, fear and guilt need to be released in the process of healing, focusing only on negative emotions is not enough. For example, when anger is expressed in therapy, a person may feel better temporarily. The anger, however, tends to recur unless the seeds of love are sown in the garden of the soul and allowed to grow. Just as therapists must deal with their own anger before they can effectively help others release their anger, those therapists who facilitate soul work most effectively are those who are not afraid of shadows in the world of soul.

IMAGINAL WORLDS

Images in our mind's eye radiate like moonbeams or a comet's tail from the activity of the soul. To glimpse the images is to catch sight of the soul, whose movements are connected to but distinct from the experiences of the ego. We might say that as our deeds reveal the character of ego, imagination and its images tell the nature of the soul.[18]

—THOMAS MOORE

Since the soul inhabits imaginal worlds populated by archetypal symbols that may be personified as gods and demons, familiarity with these realms facilitates healing and empowerment. When the gods and goddesses that live in the psyche speak to the soul and we listen, we can often learn something of value. For example, a woman who feels bereft of love and recognizes how the symbolic meaning of the myth of Eros and Psyche pertains to her own journey of individuation may gain insight into the tasks that she needs to undertake before her soul can feel connected to the Beloved. Sometimes these imaginal realms of infinite possibility appear to be more real than ordinary waking consciousness.

I have noticed that empowerment in this domain seems different from empowerment in the world of ego. Skillful ways of dealing with threatening forces, for example, may not be applicable in the world of ego. Furthermore, encountering a demon or a monster in the imaginal world can be more terrifying than anything encountered in the outer world. If this is the case, it may be inappropriate to try to deal with the fear alone, and it is wise to ask for help.

In one case, when a woman who found herself doing battle with a witch called out desperately for help, an angel appeared and the witch disappeared. In another case, when a man who was wrestling with a black snake under water remembered he could ask for help, a dolphin appeared and carried him to safety. Another man dreamed he was being buried alive in a pit, and when he called for help, Jesus appeared in the dream and extended his hand, giving him what he needed to pull himself out of the hole.

To those who understand the power of imaginal worlds, the world of ego may appear flat and shallow, while the inner world takes on added significance and gives life a sense of depth and meaning. One man who was accustomed to listening to inner guidance was in a midlife transition, debating whether to accept a job offer in San Diego, when he was unexpectedly called away to Oregon. When he arrived there he recognized a landscape and a building he had seen twice before in a dream, and he said he felt certain that he should move there and not accept the offer in San Diego. Although he had no assurance of suitable employment in Oregon, he trusted his guidance and soon found a challenging job and a new love relationship that changed his life.

Some people who are not familiar with the inner world are frightened by it and deliberately choose to ignore it. Not long ago, even in this century, many people regarded mental illness as a form of possession.

A person who was possessed seemed to be a victim of external forces that he or she was powerless to escape or change. People struggling with addictions, whether to food, drugs or self-destructive patterns of behavior, often feel possessed. Consciously they want to change. Even when they have a reasonable understanding of what needs to change and why, they feel totally incapable of doing it.

One woman spoke about her food addiction in terms of being possessed by a dark entity that seemed to take over whenever she felt compelled to go on a binge. It seemed to be voraciously hungry, and never satisfied. Overeating made her feel sick and she slept a lot, preferring unconsciousness to feelings of depression and powerlessness. She could lose weight by fasting, but would gain it right back when she started to eat. She complained that unlike an alcoholic who could simply stop drinking, she could not stop eating altogether. As we explored some of the emotional issues that were crippling her life, it became clear that the weight problem was only the surface layer of much deeper issues. She came to describe herself as a lost soul, and this self-diagnosis seemed more accurate than anything that could be found in a medical textbook.

Although anecdotal data suggests evidence of possession in rare cases, belief in possession does not usually contribute to healing or empowerment. On the contrary, "The devil made me do it" is an abdication of responsibility that reinforces a sense of being a victim. In the past, accusations of possession led to witch hunts. From a psychological perspective we can be possessed by that with which we identify. Disidentification then becomes part of the healing process.

One young woman who was obsessed with a man after a brief, unhappy relationship felt psychically possessed by him until she learned to be more assertive in the inner world. After visualizing herself cutting the cord that seemed to connect her to him, she was able to let go of her obsession and felt free to take charge of her own life again.

I have worked with people who have suffered greatly by being accused of possession by cult members with whom they were associated. Belief in possession has powerful effects which often tend to reinforce pathology and victimization rather than healing or empowering the soul. It seems more skillful to reinforce the ability to reclaim and heal the soul than to reinforce beliefs that are debilitating and damaging.

The struggle with addiction and the beginning of recovery is often a time of reclaiming the soul. One who feels possessed is not free, and being in service to a god is significantly different from being possessed by a demon.

People in recovery often benefit from asking for help from a higher power in order to triumph over a personal demon. A man who was in recovery from alcoholism found that he was helpless not only with regard to alcohol, but also with regard to anger. Although he had stopped drinking, he would periodically feel possessed by rage. It was not until he had given vent to his feelings of rage in therapy and started practicing Tibetan Buddhism that he was able to gain some sense of inner freedom.

While some people believe that interpersonal support is the crucial element in successful recovery, recognition of the power of spiritual awakening is now increasingly widespread. Bill Wilson, the founder of Alcoholics Anonymous wrote,

> Is sobriety all that we are to expect of a spiritual awakening? No, sobriety is only a bare beginning; it is only the first gift of the first awakening. If more gifts are to be received, our awakening has to go on. [19]

Whenever dissatisfaction with the world of ego manifests as addiction, depression or anxiety, it can be denied, evaded by a variety of distractions, or masked by medication. On the other hand, it can also be an opportunity for turning attention to the deeper desires of the soul, what Christina Grof calls *The Thirst for Wholeness*. Writing about recovery as a spiritual path, she says,

> [Healing] is a process of remembering, of reconnecting with our wholeness. Recovery is really rediscovery. . . . In recovery we *get back* our wholeness. We bring our small self together with our deeper Self, and make a whole. [20]

When one seriously attends to the soul, ego desires tend to become much less compelling and the rediscovery of wholeness through healing and empowerment becomes a realistic possibility.

For example, one woman who suffered from depression and self-loathing because of her dependency on alcohol was able to stop drinking after she attended some AA meetings. When she started meditating, she acknowledged the longing of her soul for inner peace. She then began therapy which focused attention on inner listening and resolving inner conflicts. Just as a passionate love affair can serve as an antidote to preoccupation with food, a genuine awakening of soul can make the pursuit of worldly pleasures seem shallow and relatively unimportant.

Facing the fear of death in the imaginal world also contributes to healing and empowerment in both the world of ego and the world of soul. For example, grieving for a loved one can make the longing of the soul for love and connection more acute. By going deeper into experiences of loss or sadness rather than avoiding them, one may discover a sense of participation in the universal suffering inherent in living and dying that seems essential for spiritual awakening.

Two cases in particular brought this to my attention. The first was a thirty-five-year-old man who had lost the love of his life to another man; the second was an older woman whose teenaged child had died in an automobile accident. Each of these people had lived a life in which everything had been going well for them. Ego goals had been fulfilled, and they lacked nothing. Then something happened that was beyond their control. Their own pain and subsequent healing opened the world of soul to each of them for the first time. Circumstances had forced each to turn inward rather than relying on another person to give meaning to their lives. After periods of deep grieving, each came to a sense of acceptance and found a source of spiritual renewal within themselves.

A person who is plunged into suffering despite worldly success is brought face to face with the pain of the soul. If the pain is avoided or repressed, it may linger indefinitely as an aching heart or a sense of bitterness. On the other hand, when grief is experienced fully and communicated, a broken heart may open to love and compassion that is deeper and more real than before. In the psyche nothing is lost; everyone we have known becomes a part of our inner world. The realization of impermanence, that life is like a dream and nothing lasts forever, adds poignancy to every moment of awareness. Those who have made peace with loss and death have demonstrated that it is possible to find a deep serenity of soul even in the midst of suffering.

For example, Vietnamese Zen master Thich Nhat Hanh is a peace activist who has conducted special retreats for American Vietnam veterans since the end of the Vietnam War and helped many of them heal deep wounds of the war. When he recounts the story of a young girl raped by a pirate, he points out that if we look deeply, we will see that if we had been born in the village of the pirate and raised in the same conditions, there is great likelihood that we might also have become pirates.[21] He goes on to show the connection between personal inner peace and world peace. His Holiness the Dalai Lama says,

Although attempting to bring about world peace through the internal transformation of individuals is difficult, it is the only way.

The soul that empathetically identifies with both the pain and the joy of others begins to see that in the inner world we are not separate from each other. Peace and joy, no less than pain and sorrow, are shared, collective experiences. In the inner world it becomes clear that we can choose what we want to cultivate and that help is available.

The dangers of empathic identification for someone who has not explored the inner world of soul and who has not had sufficient training to be able to voluntarily direct attention in this domain was demonstrated to me recently by a colleague. She consulted me about physical symptoms that troubled her whenever she was with someone who was very angry or unconsciously blocking emotions. She said she sometimes felt overwhelmed by picking up other people's feelings, since she was very sensitive to them and could not close down her empathic identification. She had no meditation training and had done very little inner work as she had received traditional clinical training that did not encourage self-exploration. She recognized that her own unconscious was responding to the unacknowledged emotions of people around her. When she started some meditative mind training that focused on developing nonjudgmental attention to her own inner experience, she was better able to observe without merging or feeling overwhelmed, and her symptoms subsided. She also began asking for guidance from her inner teacher, who appeared to her in the form of an older woman whom she admired. This seemed to relieve her anxiety and helped her feel stronger.

Since imaginal realms are not subject to temporal laws of ordinary waking reality, exploring them can help us make peace with ourselves and glimpse the eternal aspects of soul. In these realms anything is possible and nothing ever dies. Experiences of death, dismemberment and resurrection are not uncommon. Killing an imaginal adversary, then, is not necessarily advantageous, since it tends to reappear in another form. However, anything can be transformed.

For example, Ralph was a man who had struggled with guilt and anxiety ever since returning from his time in Southeast Asia after the Vietnam War. He found himself reliving scenes of battle in his recurrent nightmares, and no matter how many times he killed the enemy, it would reappear in full force and seem to be more menacing than ever. He had one recurring image of being hacked to pieces. It was not until he became aware of the teaching of Thich Nhat Hanh that he was able to begin to see the erstwhile enemy as a human being with whom he could communicate. As we worked with active imagination to initiate a dialogue with some of the threatening dream figures, the nightmares subsided and he began to have dreams of adventure instead. The fear was still present, but after the terror subsided, it became easier to work through memories that had haunted him for years.

In Ralph's case the inner experiences of terror were directly linked to his waking life experiences. For Judy, on the other hand, a housewife in her mid-thirties, dreams of dismemberment seemed to have no relationship to anything in her past. She was a young woman who had done what was expected of her—married and had two children. Suddenly she seemed to be catapulted into a period of inner turmoil that led her to seek therapy. In her case, dreams of dismemberment became less terrifying when we explored what they meant to her. When she interpreted one of them as a shamanic initiation experience, she was inspired to learn how to be a guide for others on the inner journey. She felt these dreams marked a turning point in her life. She subsequently enrolled in a training program that enabled her to continue her exploration of the inner world in a safe and supportive context and in retrospect came to regard these dreams as important messages from her soul.

Exploring the inner world of soul calls for discernment and discrimination, knowing when to confront, when to avoid and how to transform whatever appears threatening. Western explorers of the imaginal inner worlds such as Rudolf Steiner and Emmanuel Swedenborg seem to have explored these realms in depth on their own, but everyone can benefit from the wisdom of good teachers. Many traditions warn people that it is dangerous to explore inner worlds without a guide. Shamans, for example, go through extensive training and initiation before journeying in the service of others.

In most shamanic cultures shamans regard the upper world and the lower world as independently existing realities to which they gain access. Since shamans experience the realms described in myth and cosmology, the question whether their experiences are shaped by their beliefs or whether the beliefs are created by experience is difficult to answer.[22] The same question can be asked of any spiritual experience. Does religious experience simply validate existing beliefs, or does the experience reveal a reality independent of cultural conditioning? My own experience leads me to believe that both are true. It seems that people do have inner experiences that are consistent with their expectations, whether they remain within the confines of their cultural conditioning or move out to explore others. A shamanic healer works effectively by traveling to other realities; a Christian may be healed by the laying on of hands; a Buddhist may dissolve illusions into emptiness. On the other hand, sometimes people are surprised, as when an atheist in holotropic breathwork session had a mystical experience that turned his worldview upside down. On another occasion a client of mine reported an extraordinary rush of energy and relief of physical pain after a Christian evangelical minister laid hands on her, even though she did not consider herself a believer.

Inner work is often constrained by fear and the implicit assumption that the subtle realities of inner worlds are identical to the physical universe. This seems unwarranted. Furthermore, behaviors that apparently contributed to biological survival and success in the world of ego, such as aggression, competition and strong defenses, appear to be counterproductive. In the inner world defenses appear to create what they defend against, and aggression generates conflict, whereas attitudes of friendliness and compassion tend to generate peace and freedom.

Symbols are the "vertical bridges" that establish a relationship between the inner and outer world by analogy or correspondence. They also mediate the relationship between different levels of inner reality. Their meaning is derived by inference from those levels that are experienced as more significant, meaningful and real than the material realm. Just as a book may be perceived as useless by an illiterate person, as a meaningless collection of words by an uneducated person and as a profound philosophical treatise by one who understands it, an appreciation of symbols depends on knowledge of various levels of perception. Although symbols can evoke intuitive responses in anyone, a deeper understanding of them depends on experience of the realms to which they refer. For example, a religious icon or talisman may signify superstitious beliefs to one person, while conveying a profound meaning to another. A symbolic object such as a sword might be perceived as a weapon of combat, a phallic symbol, or a symbol of mental clarity—the sword of discriminating wisdom that cuts through illusion. It could be employed to kill an enemy, as a tool for severing connection as in the visualization of cutting the cord of relationship to another person, or as a means of cutting through the delusions of ego. In each case it could be considered as a symbol of empowerment at different levels on the spectrum of development.

The effect of working with symbols and the imaginal realms is certainly not limited to the inner world. Carl Jung observed that the incidence of meaningful synchronicities increased as his patients became aware of archetypal symbols working in their lives. It is apparent to me that awareness of the symbolic dimension of experience can have a transformative effect on people's lives. One woman's life changed quite dramatically when she became aware of the evocative power of symbols depicted in the Tarot deck. Her life, which had seemed chaotic to her for some time, seemed to be given as sense of direction as she recognized certain patterns that were reflected to her by contemplation of the images that seemed to represent her inner process. For example, when she reflected on the *Strength* card depicting a feminine figure and a lion, she saw her need for taming the lion in herself and began to harness some of her own powerful creative energy. She also reflected that she could now witness her own process, like the sphinx sitting on top of the *Wheel of Fortune.*

Familiarity with the inner world of symbols and archetypes reveals and affects the soul in everyday life. Furthermore, skillful interpretation of symbols in a transpersonal context can have a profoundly healing effect. However, archetypes also have the power to captivate, fascinate and dominate. To become identified with any particular image to the exclusion of others is to limit, and therefore to forget, the true nature of the soul.

ARCHETYPAL EMPOWERMENT

The unseen region in question is not merely ideal, for it produces effects in this world. When we commune with it, work is actually done upon our finite personality.[23]

—WILLIAM JAMES

As universal patterns or templates of experience, certain archetypes emerge in all cultures. For example, in addition to personal experiences of mother, everyone has some idea of the archetypal mother. Although subjective experiences are unique, certain universal experiences such as birth, love and death, are encountered everywhere.

Archetypal psychology envisions archetypes as the deepest patterns of psychic functioning.[24] Since the possibility of transcendence of form in formlessness is not recognized, archetypal psychology embraces polytheism and radical relativism, implying that there is no reality independent of our perceptions and that one perception is not necessarily more or less true than another. In this view the collective dimension of the psyche encompasses the immense mythical universe and connects the individual soul to what happens to all people in all places at all times. We can therefore resonate to myths and stories from cultures other than our own when they deal with such universal themes as birth and death, joy and sorrow, hope and despair. Archetypal psychology stops short of self-transcendence and mystical union.

Wilber points out that Jung's use of the term *archetype* to apply to collective psychic structures of human experience, such as the Great Mother, the anima and animus, refers only to the mythic forms that are collectively inherited.[25] While these are important for psychological healing, they do not contribute to transcendent spiritual awareness. They are not transcendental in the sense that familiarity with them does not lead to liberation or union with Spirit. In fact, fascination with phenomena at this level of subtle perception can be an obstacle to deeper insight and illumination.

Wilber argues that the great mystics such as Shankara, Plato and Augustine used the term *archetype* to designate the first subtle forms that appear as the world manifests out of unmanifest Spirit. They are the fundamental patterns upon which all patterns of manifestation are based. The Greek term, *arche typon,* meant original pattern. These subtle, transcendental forms, then, are the first forms of manifestation. In most forms of mysticism, the archetypes are radiant patterns, points of light, audible illuminations, colored shapes and luminosities.

Specific images of archetypes are, of course, culturally determined. A Buddhist who expects to see Buddhas, a Christian who wants to meet Jesus and a shaman who encounters spirits and power animals all tend to have relatively predictable experiences, though each one is unique. Images appear to conform to beliefs and expectations of the subject, just as figures in a dream have particular relevance for the dreamer. Mythology, as the collective dreaming of the human species, offers teaching stories illustrating adventures of the soul according to cultural expectations of a particular time. While reading myths as metaphors can reveal a depth and richness of meaning that is missing from a purely rational or empirical worldview, mythology is an expedient rather than a final teaching. If cultural elements are mistaken for universal truth, this misunderstanding can hinder liberation instead of facilitating it.

Nevertheless, understanding the symbolic nature of myths and dreams is healing for the soul that has been trapped in the world of ego. Realizing that the inner world is not bound by physical laws may increase a feeling of freedom. For example, if I have a lucid dream in which I know I am dreaming, I may choose to wake up or initiate changes in the dream. On the other hand, I may let go of attempts to control my dream in favor of experiencing whatever unfolds, even if it means dying, flying or moving through solid objects in a dream. I have experienced all of these at various times, but one lucid dream that left a lasting impression was very simple.

I dreamed of having an interview with His Holiness the Dalai Lama. This was shortly after I had been with him at the University of California in Los Angeles, where I participated in a small group discussion with him. This time, however, we were in an unfamiliar place. When I realized that I was dreaming, I did not want to change anything. It was enough for me to enjoy his presence and the warmth and friendliness of his laughter. I knew this was a dream that could be attributed to memories of his recent visit. What seemed important to me was the intensity of the feeling of his presence, which seemed more penetrating and powerful than when I spoke to him in person. It was as if the dream were amplifying my waking experience so that I would not overlook the subtle qualities that his presence conveyed. When my surroundings in the dream dissolved, I seemed to dissolve with them. The joyful feelings of the dream persisted for several days.

A common, mistaken assumption about lucid dreaming is that lucidity means increasing control of dreams. Although this possibility enables one to be, do or have whatever is desired in the dreamworld, the potential for learning is limited when restricted to fulfillment of egocentric pleasure. On the other hand, the possibility of healing and empowering the soul in lucid dreams is extraordinary.

Many people believe that archetypal forces shape and influence human destiny whether we are aware of them or not.[26] Astrological readings, for example, are based on this assumption. As we become conscious of how various patterns operate in our own lives, we are better able to differentiate those tendencies that contribute to peace and harmony from those that create stress and conflict. When we understand how archetypes can affect us, we can view them as a source of transpersonal power that can heal and empower the soul. Their efficacy in our lives depends on our awareness of them as inner resources, and how we choose to relate to them.

FOUR ARCHETYPES

In the process of discovering an identity as soul, we can distinguish several stages in the development of self-concept, including physical, emotional, mental and spiritual levels of identification.[27] Four archetypes that represent these stages symbolically are the warrior, the healer, the teacher and the visionary.[28] We will consider them here from a psychological perspective that views each one as representing certain qualities, regardless of the cultural mythologies in which they appear. These qualities, when appropriately balanced, are characteristic of psychological health and spiritual maturity. Although exclusive identification with any single archetype is problematic, evoking their presence as inner resources can be a way of cultivating qualities for healing and empowerment.

The warrior

Ancient spiritual teachings say that wherever there is other, there is fear. Insofar as power is a function of the willingness to experience fear, the warrior archetype is a symbol of power. The warrior responds to the challenge of existence by confronting fear and is characteristically courageous. On the spiritual path courage is required, not only in times of conflict, but also in taking risks, making changes and facing the unknown. The major challenge for the spiritual warrior is self-mastery. Only when a person has the courage to confront fear, does he or she become capable of action rather than reaction. Carlos Castaneda, who has written several books on the warrior's path in the Native American tradition, says a warrior regards everything in life as a challenge.

Cultivating awareness of the inner warrior is a process of empowerment, associated with awareness of the third chakra, the power center in yoga psychology, located at the solar plexus. The warrior is not afraid to be powerful, to take a stand, to act and carry out intentions, and to fight, if necessary. The way of the warrior is a path of action, or karma yoga. The warrior takes charge of what needs to be done and knows how to make things happen. This power can be used either in service of the ego or in service of the spirit, hence Arjuna, the mythical spiritual warrior of the sacred Indian text of the *Bhagavad Gita*, is trained to carry out his social duty impeccably, free from passions such as anger and lust for power.

A warrior is not necessarily aggressive. In some martial arts training, for example, the goal is to harmonize oneself with the movement of the universe. Both *aikido* and *t'ai chi chuan* emphasize personal development, centering and the use of vital energy. According to the founder of *aikido*, true martial arts is a work of love. In *aikido* the mind leads the body and winning means overcoming discord in oneself. In practice the student learns to harmonize with the movements of a partner. The term *aikido* can be translated as a way of spiritual harmony.[29]

A story about a Zen master in Japan illustrates the difference between a spiritual warrior and a secular one:

> A warlord invaded a village and killed most of the inhabitants. The remaining villagers fled, except for the Zen master who continued to sit in the temple. The warlord stormed up to the temple brandishing his sword and cried, "Don't you know that you are looking at someone who could run you through with my sword without batting an eye?" The Zen master replied, "Don't you know that you are looking at someone who could be run through without batting an eye?" Thereupon the warlord bowed and withdrew.

A spiritual warrior recognizes that the inner power appearing as courage is not a personal possession. It is perceived as a power that is in us but does not belong to us. It is what enables us to change when personal efforts have proved ineffectual and to be fearless even in the face of death, as some early Christians appeared to be when they were tortured and thrown to the lions.[30]

Warrior Reflection:

The following instructions for personal reflection can enhance the recognition and integration of this archetype:

> Take a few minutes to relax, breathe and quiet your mind. Identify any fears that are particularly troublesome for you. Now put your fears aside for the moment and visualize a warrior standing before you in an open space. This warrior has nothing to fear and is therefore benign. Notice the posture, facial expression and clothing of this figure. Notice how it feels to be in the presence of someone who is strong and fearless. Imagine merging with this image as if in a dream. How does it feel to be strong, grounded, alert and totally present? Notice your body posture and any body sensations as your awareness of the warrior grows and becomes increasingly vivid. In this moment there is nothing to fear. When you are ready to separate yourself from the image, say goodbye to this warrior, remembering that he or she can be recalled at any time. If you wish, you can pick up your fears where you left them, or you can let them go.

Sometimes the image that appears will be an historical figure from a distant time or culture, such as a Viking or a Roman soldier or a figure from

Greek mythology such as Odysseus or Athena. Sometimes the image may have personal meaning, such as when a Native American warrior woman appeared to a woman who was interested in shamanism. Sometimes the warrior may appear as an ordinary person, such as the teacher who worked in a gas station in Dan Millman's account of *The Way of the Peaceful Warrior*.[31]

Whatever the form, the qualities conveyed by the image can be cultivated in oneself. These qualities usually include personal power based on the integration of body, mind and spirit and the absence of inner conflict. Strength, focused attention and good grounding are also characteristic of the warrior. In the absence of fear and conflict, the warrior may be transformed into the builder. Any qualities that appear to be troublesome in this image may be an indication of a need for healing.

The healer

Whereas the warrior confronts fear, the healer attempts to transform it. The healer includes and harmonizes the opposites and brings them into balance. This archetype is associated with the fourth chakra in yoga psychology, the heart center, where the opposites intersect. A healer embodies the quality of compassion. For the mystic, all healing comes from God. Whether the healer is male or female, witch doctor or physician, unless the source of healing is activated within the person in need, attempts at healing are likely to be ineffective.

The healers I have met have all been deeply compassionate human beings. The first healer I met was an orthopedic surgeon who was Alan Watts's personal physician. He had given up doing back surgery because he felt that most people with back problems were suffering from soul sickness, although he would not have used those words. He said that what most people who came to see him wanted was to talk about their pain and the stress in their lives. He counseled many people to explore alternative methods of healing and develop self-awareness in addition to getting whatever medical attention was indicated. Long after he retired from medical practice, people who sought him out seemed to feel better after consulting him.

Contemporary researchers who have written extensively on healing include psychologist Jean Achterberg who has studied the history of women as healers outside of the medical profession.[32] Within the medical profession, physician Larry Dossey has investigated the power of prayer in healing and, unlike many researchers, even used it for a time in his own practice. He says,

[T]he choice between science and spirituality appears increasingly artificial today, even from a scientific perspective. It is now possible to tell a new story; one that allows science and spirituality to stand side by side in a complementary way, neither trying to usurp or eliminate the other.[33]

Healing ourselves, our relationships, and the earth requires both scientific knowledge and skill and spiritual awakening. It also requires communication and listening, both inner and outer. This means listening inwardly to soul and outwardly to what others are saying, not only in words but also by their presence. Everything we know about conflict resolution is relevant for healing. The archetypal healer has a capacity for empathy, compassion and love. The healer as peacemaker does not take sides, but understands and forgives.

The human organism, like the earth, has an enduring yet finite capacity for self-healing. At times the need for spiritual healing and renewal may call for retreat from the world instead of active engagement as a warrior. Many people who have made significant contributions to human history have followed an alternating pattern of withdrawal and return in their lives, balancing periods of reflection or contemplation with service in the world.[34] Spiritual traditions also point to the need for discipline, meditation and prayer. The fruits of practice can then be expressed as compassionate service in the world.

The healer responds to human suffering with compassion in place of anger and attack, replacing fear with love and conflict with peace. The healer archetype sometimes appears as a wounded healer, sometimes as a healed healer. Our capacity for healing others and healing the earth depends on healing ourselves. The healed healer is believed to be more effective than the one who is not yet healed. Hence the empowerment of the inner healer may be essential in a time when personal, social and environmental healing are sorely needed. If we open our hearts to the suffering of the world, the healer in each of us is called forth to manifest the qualities of love and compassion and relieve suffering wherever we find it. In our effort to heal others, we also heal ourselves.

Healing Reflection:

Begin this personal reflection by closing your eyes and quieting your mind. Identify a source of pain that needs healing in your life. Any pain, sorrow or anger indicates a need for healing. Healing relationships means releasing any feelings of resentment, hostility, guilt or inadequacy you may feel in relation to others. Whenever someone has failed to live up to your expectations and left you feeling betrayed, rejected or disappointed, the relationship needs healing. Your own feelings of failure also need healing. Identify any sources of physical, emotional or mental pain in your life.

The following part of this process is best done with a partner. It can be either another person or the image of another person. Ask yourself if, for a few minutes, you are willing to give this person your full attention.

Looking at your partner, ask yourself silently if you are willing to experience the pain, sorrow and suffering that he or she may have felt in this life. Think of all of the rejections, failures, disappointments, losses and disillusionments that he or she may have experienced. By opening your heart to this person, you may begin to open to the pain of the world. Reflect for a moment on the fact that any personal pain is only a microcosm of the suffering of humanity and life on earth. Everyone is in need of healing. All creatures experiencing birth, impermanence, old age, disease and death, encounter pain in some form. Allow yourself to feel the unsatisfactoriness inherent in temporal existence. Be aware of your desire to extend love and relieve the suffering of your partner and the countless sentient beings in the world.

Close your eyes and imagine now that you are in the presence of a being of boundless compassion. Notice how it feels to be with someone who accepts you unconditionally, just as you are, right now. You do not have to do anything to earn love. You are already loved, just as you are. Notice the details of the image of the healer that appears in your mind's eye. Notice the posture, facial expression and attitude. Feel the radiance of benevolent compassion in the region of the heart. Imagine how you would feel as this being. Imagine that you are merging with the healer. What would change for you if you were not afraid to express your love and compassion wholeheartedly, without judging others?

From your heart allow the radiance of unconditional love to extend to your partner and to all beings. Allow yourself to feel loved and healed and whole. Looking at your partner again, reflect on all of the joy, love and caring that he or she has given to others in life. Imagine the joy of the parents at the birth of this child. Think of moments of joy in nature. Think of the love and caring given and received in many relationships. Reflect on all the love expressed by people everywhere who want to give and receive love. Feel the unconditional love of healers everywhere who want to relieve suffering wherever they find it. Remember that you are among them. You can find the source of infinite, healing compassion in the depths of your own heart.

When you have completed this part of the process, notice whatever still needs healing in you and tell your partner whatever you are willing to share, or write about this experience in a journal.

The teacher

The teacher relieves suffering by dispelling ignorance and illusion. The teacher archetype is associated with wisdom, manifested in discernment, communication, creativity and self-expression. These functions correspond to opening the fifth chakra in yoga psychology, in the region of the throat. The teacher may appear in the psyche as an image of a wise old man or wise old woman. For a person on a traditional spiritual path, the teacher is a spiritual master who gives instruction and guidance to the student. In Buddhism the mind of the teacher and the mind of the Buddha are not separate. The teacher may be regarded as an incarnation of the Buddha. In Sufism, finding the right teacher is considered essential for spiritual progress. The teacher may be a storyteller who perceives multiple levels of meaning. For a Christian, Jesus embodies the teacher archetype. People from any tradition may be attracted to those teachers who seem to have insight into the life of the soul.

For the seeker who does not espouse a particular religious tradition, every relationship can be an opportunity for teaching and learning. Life itself is a powerful teacher. When we are open to teaching and learning we can learn something from any situation, hence a wise person is said to learn more from a fool than a fool from a wise one.

We are all teachers insofar as we demonstrate wisdom by what we value and the way we live. Since we tend to learn what we teach, it behooves us to choose consciously what we want to teach and learn. We are continuously learning how to learn, how to think creatively and how to teach. As teachers, our creativity is challenged, and we are free to choose where we direct our efforts.

Teaching and learning enable us to change our minds about ourselves and the world. In this process our souls can be released from prisons of greed, anger and illusion. When we develop a capacity for compassion and learn to transform negative emotions into energy for creative change, we can also begin to teach others about change.

A story of a person seeking wisdom tells of someone asking the teacher for the secret of happiness. The teacher replied, "Good judgment." The student asked, "How do I get good judgment?" "By experience." "And how do I get experience?" "Bad judgment!"

When we are open to learning, any experience can contribute to developing wisdom. If we want to access the wisdom of the unconscious, we can begin by getting in touch with the inner teacher.

As we learn to communicate, to understand each other better and to live in harmony with nature, we become better teachers. In a healthy person the desire to teach what one has learned and contribute to the well-being of the whole supersedes self-indulgent fears and desires.

According to psychotherapist Robert Sardello, soul learning depends on seeing through the eyes of the heart and loving the subject matter. He says,

> True learning makes one vulnerable to the intoxication of love; when one is in love one is learning, the two conditions cannot be separated. The love between teacher and learner is directed not toward possessing each other, but toward caring for the world. It is precisely here that teaching becomes an art, the art of enlarging love to encompass the soul of the world.[35]

The wisdom of a good teacher is not identical with knowledge. Wisdom implies gnosis, or sacred knowledge that is intuitively perceived rather than being acquired through reason or the gathering of empirical data. Sacred knowledge is transmitted from teacher to student by being rather than content. The person who is positively related to the archetypal inner teacher tends to grow in wisdom as well as knowledge.

The image of the archetypal inner guide may or may not correspond to a teacher in the outer world. Socrates listened to the guidance of both his daimon and his female teacher Diotema. Dante followed Virgil, a symbol of reason, through hell and purgatory, but left him at the gates of paradise. From there on he was guided by Beatrice, his true love. For Jung, the figure of Philemon appeared as an inner guide who instructed him to write the Seven Sermons of the Dead.

Sometimes a teacher may appear in a dream and give specific instructions. Sometimes the teacher may not have a physical representation at all. He or she or it may be symbolized by an element, such as the Holy

Spirit appearing as tongues of fire at Pentecost. The teacher may also be perceived as a being of light such as an angel, or in shamanic traditions, as an animal. Whatever the form, the teacher represents one who transmits wisdom to those who ask for guidance on the path. When the student is ready, a teacher appears. A strong connection with a trusted teacher can be essential in facing the challenges and trials on the spiritual path, including the experience of ego death and rebirth. Feeling alone, without a teacher, can mean feeling cut off from power, wisdom and guidance.

Some spiritual seekers believe that a teacher should be obeyed at any cost. Others, who have paid a heavy price for unquestioning obedience, advise trusting only your own experience. The freedom to choose when to obey, when to question, when to follow and when to reject a teacher is often overlooked. When discernment is lacking and you do not trust yourself, you may not know whom to trust. Once you have made a commitment to be true to yourself and to eradicate self-deception insofar as possible, it is easier to recognize the truth that makes you free. False teachers always imitate and resemble true teachers. Discernment develops when we are willing to learn from experience.

Teacher Reflection:

> With eyes closed and a quiet mind, reflect for a few minutes on the people who have been spiritual teachers in your life. Some may have been formally designated as teachers, others not. Identify as many as possible. What are the qualities that you notice in those people who have been your teachers? How do you recognize wisdom?
>
> Imagine that you are going to meet someone who embodies the quality of wisdom. Ask this being to appear to you. Notice the features of this wise being, the presence, the expression and the attitude. How do you feel in his or her presence? Imagine that this is a being of infinite wisdom who can transmit wisdom directly to you, if you are receptive. If you want to ask a question, you may receive an answer that is significant for you.
>
> You may also imagine what it would feel like to be this teacher. If you are willing, imagine that you are merging with him or her. Finally, separate again to become yourself, and say goodbye for now. Thank your inner teacher for appearing, and, if you wish, say that you will call again, whenever you need guidance.

The visionary

The visionary perceives possibilities, envisions wholeness and embodies the quality of clarity. One who has attained stability of attention and experienced inner stillness may access a transformative vision of human possibility. Spiritual vision inspires and informs all activities of the spiritual warrior, the healer and the teacher and perceives the relationship of the archetypes to each other.

Vision is the faculty of perception that sees opposites in relationship to each other and infuses human life with a sense of meaning and purpose. It is associated with the sixth chakra in yoga psychology in the region of the third eye at the center of the forehead. Vision sees things as they are, by seeing through appearances and understanding the nature of illusion. If we refuse to see what is true, we perpetuate suffering, and the mind remains a prisoner of illusion.

The development of spiritual vision is not limited to perception of archetypal images. It is important to remember that we never see the archetypes, we see only representations or images of archetypes. Perceptions are always partial and always colored by projection. Perceptions are shaped by beliefs, expectations, cultural conditioning, emotional and mental states, and by everything else in personal experience.

In the cultivation of vision it is helpful to distinguish between observation, interpretation and communication. Whatever we observe is already shaped by selective perception. We see only fragments of reality, never the whole. How we interpret what we observe opens up another broad field of potential distortion. Whether we are aware of it or not, we are continually engaged in interpreting the world.

Working with the interpretation of dreams can give one a glimpse of how widely varied perceptions can be. Skillful perception can contribute to healing, whereas unskillful perception can increase fear and make healing more difficult. Interpretation can be either an obstacle or an asset in the healing process. However, when one is not aware of it, subjective interpretation becomes an unconscious distortion in which personal perceptions of reality are mistaken for reality as it is. Furthermore, in communicating a perception, one must be cognizant not only of subjective interpretations and projections, but of the other person's as well.

Discernment that enables us to distinguish truth from illusion and perception from projection is a faculty that can be cultivated by observing what vision reveals without interpretation. Clear vision is a function of intuitive discernment that sees through illusion and offers guidance on the spiritual path. It is closely related to spiritual empowerment and depends on training attention, quieting the mind and opening the heart.

Visionary Reflection:

> Sit facing a partner for this process. Take a moment to quiet the mind and attend to your breathing, letting go of the past and the future in order to give your partner your full attention in this moment. Look at your partner and notice the person you see before you. What do you notice about him or her? Make a mental note of any qualities you may attribute to your partner. After about two minutes, close your eyes and imagine that you are seeing the essence of your partner. What do you notice if you see him or her as a soul rather than as a body or personality? Notice any images or qualities that may appear. Once again look at your partner with your eyes open for a couple of minutes, and then close them again and visualize your partner's essence in your mind's eye. This part of the exercise should be done in silence. When you have completed it, communicate to your partner whatever you wish to say about what you have observed.

In the absence of a partner, this visualization may be done with an imaginary partner or a dream figure. If you experience any difficulty in any visualization, discontinue the exercise and do not force anything. It is best to find an experienced therapist or teacher to help you if it causes any discomfort.

INTEGRATING INNER RESOURCES

Effective healing and empowerment depends on bringing all of these archetypal qualities of the warrior, the healer, the teacher and the visionary into balance. In order to be an effective healer one must be strong as a warrior; to be an effective teacher one must understand the process of healing. The vision that manifests as mental, emotional and physical empowerment encompasses both the inner and the outer world. The ability to act with courage, to give and receive love, to teach and to learn and to see things as they are, are all necessary for healing and empowerment.

In summary, the power of these archetypes, like many others that inhabit the collective dimensions of the psyche, becomes more available to us when we are conscious of their presence. Each of these four, embodying courage, compassion, wisdom and clarity, are needed for spiritual development. Although we may feel more identified with one or another at various times, wholeness depends on both differentiation and integration of the qualities they represent.

Integrating Reflection:

> As a final reflection in this process, close your eyes and take a deep breath as a signal to your inner self that you are willing to see. Visualize yourself as you are now. Notice your body posture, your facial expression and your general attitude. Reflect on your life and notice which of these archetypes is well developed and which need more attention. Imagine yourself bringing them into balance, free to act with courage, heal with compassion, teach with wisdom and envision a better world. See yourself now in your mind's eye as you might appear when these qualities are fully developed. Once again, notice the details of your presence and remember the image as you see it now.

Conscious differentiation of these four archetypes supports a healthy balance of attention to physical, emotional, mental and spiritual well-being. Each of them contributes to healthy behavior motivated by creativity and compassion instead of the fear and confusion that characterize sickness of the soul.

INNER RESOURCES

Self concept	SOUL	MIND	HEART	BODY
Archetype	VISIONARY	TEACHER	HEALER	WARRIOR
Quality	CLARITY	WISDOM	COMPASSION	COURAGE
Path	PERCEPTION	KNOWLEDGE	LOVE	ACTION
Function	INTUITION	THINKING	FEELING	SENSATION
Training	DISCERNMENT	ATTENTION	MOTIVATION	BEHAVIOR
Process	WITNESS	INSIGHT	CATHARSIS	ETHICS

THE PARADOX OF POWER

Power corrupts and absolute power corrupts absolutely.

—LORD ACTON

Power is often perceived as unavoidably corrupting. Developing a skillful relationship to power can, therefore, be a major challenge on the spiritual path. Power is as much an integral part of human life as sex and death and love. Commonly identified sources of power include violence, money and knowledge. These are associated with physical and/or egocentric dominance. Spiritual power, on the other hand, does not belong to any one person. Nevertheless, problems of corruption and abuse of power are starkly evident in religious groups that claim to wield power not only over human life in this world, but over the immortal soul as well.

Those who search for a spiritual authority that will assume a parental role with regard to the soul's journey willingly surrender their power to another deemed wiser or more experienced. Although there is much to learn from spiritual teachers who have devoted themselves to spiritual mastery, avoiding personal responsibility by abdicating power contributes to a sense of dependency and imprisonment. The free spirit need not be subordinated to any human authority. However, the desire to find an omniscient parent figure who will tell us what to do and relieve us of the task of soul-searching is a seductive trap for many seekers on the path. Sooner or later, each one must be willing to come to terms with power and take responsibility for spiritual choices.[36]

One of the most insidious aspects of power as a shadow side of spirituality involves the worship of power, particularly in the form of a superhuman being. In a materialistic worldview, that which is powerful is often regarded as more real than that which is apparently powerless. The temptation of Jesus by Satan in the desert and the temptation of the Buddha by the Lord Mara under the bodhi tree both portray the seductive nature of the illusion of power. In both cases, freedom lies in the refusal of power rather than in its acceptance.

Recounting the legend of King Solomon the wise, Jacob Needleman tells us that through the power of magic, Solomon does not kill the demons, but turns them into servants.[37] When, at one stage, he is outwitted by the king of the demons, it is because his desire for knowledge and understanding is so compelling that King Solomon seeks to learn even from the devil himself. He takes the risk of freeing the devil in order to learn the secret of his power. What he learns is that the devil's power is his ability to take on the face and the function of the true ruler, the true self within. King Solomon suffers long years of exile and many trials and tribulations as a result of his thirst for knowledge. In the end he awakens to his true self and returns as a beggar to confront the devil who has taken on King Solomon's own face and function as king. Once confronted, the devil vanishes. Needleman says,

> The contest, the struggle has already taken place over the years. But now, with the true self fully awake, the false self instantly loses all its power. Our effort, the legend is telling us, must be to awaken that true self. It will triumph without any other struggle on our part.[38]

One must always be on guard against being taken over by one's chief weakness. King Solomon, it is said, had asked only for an understanding heart. Yet even this noble desire had a shadow side.

Goethe's *Faust* is another example of the thirst for knowledge leading to a pact with the devil. The temptation to sell one's soul in exchange for whatever is passionately desired is not only in the realm of legend. Everyone has probably made some trade-off in which the soul is abandoned in favor of worldly approval or success, or simply to get whatever the ego desires. The more powerful and successful the ego, the more seductive it becomes. Whether it is self-serving or couched in terms of service to others, power that is purchased or pursued at the expense of the soul becomes destructive.

Yet the demon resisted can become a servant or an ally. On the spiritual path the willingness to face fears and confront demons is both liberating and empowering. As long as one avoids confrontation with any part of oneself, one is pursued by fear, particularly fear of one's own weakness. Power, then, can be described as a function of our willingness to experience fear. When we avoid, deny or project it, we are disempowered. It is impossible to trust one's personal power when confronting the collective shadow. One must ask for help, and in asking for help, one must know whom to trust. The best protection against perceived threats lies in the cultivation of integrity, clarity and the voluntary control of attention. These attributes enable one to see more clearly and respond appropriately to perceived dangers.

POWERS OF THE MIND

Yoga is the settling of the mind into silence.[39]

—PATANJALI

Cultivation of powers of the mind in service of spiritual development is part of every spiritual discipline. The fulfillment of this possibility involves

---

rigorous training of the will. One who undertakes this training should bear in mind, however, that every tradition warns against seeking these powers as ends in themselves. These subtle powers can be even more entangling than worldly power. If power is idolized and used in the service of ego, no matter how virtuous the intention, it becomes a trap.

Training attention in concentration is one of the most effective methods of developing mental power and clarity. When attention is focused, like a laser light, it is far more powerful than when it is diffuse. William James believed that attention could not be sustained for more than three seconds, yet he also noted that the faculty of voluntarily bringing back a wandering attention was the very root of judgment, character and will.[40] Psychoanalyst Erich Fromm called concentrated meditation the highest activity there is—an activity of the soul which is possible only under the condition of inner freedom.[41]

Eastern meditative disciplines have demonstrated that attention can be trained effectively, given sufficient motivation and appropriate instruction. Attention is best trained in a quiet, supportive and safe environment. Contentment, freedom from desire and ethical discipline are recommended, since absence of inner conflict supports the voluntary control of attention. Quieting the mind and focusing attention are the foundations of meditation and contemplation. The object of attention may be visual (a candle flame), imaginal (the image of a deity), sensory (breathing), affective (the love of God), cognitive (a Zen koan), auditory (a mantra or sacred sound), or kinesthetic (the sensation of the breath). Whatever the object, attention can be trained to stay with a single object over an extended period of time. A good meditation teacher can help a person through any difficulties that may be encountered in this process, but the effort must be made by each one who undertakes the training. No one else can train your attention for you. When attention is stabilized, both inquiry and contemplation can be much more effective.

Concentration begins when discursive and logical thought is suspended. Concentration may also be described as the willed silence of the intellect and imagination. Interested concentration may be the result of a dominating passion, obsession or attachment. Disinterested concentration is possible only when the will is free of enslaving passions, obsessions and attachments. True concentration therefore presupposes a detached will. That is why spiritual disciplines such as yoga demand observance of rules of moral conduct as preparation for concentration practice. The concentration necessary for cultivating awareness of spiritual dimensions is therefore regarded as the fruit of moral purification of the will. The purified will can then achieve the silencing of thought and imagination in effortless concentration.

Concentration without effort is possible only where there is nothing to suppress. It is impossible when one is struggling with inner conflict, preoccupied by the past or obsessed with the future. It is possible only when one is content to rest in the present. Such contemplation becomes as natural as breathing and is accompanied by calm, relaxation and the silence of desires. With practice, the silence of effortless concentration becomes a fundamental element in the life of the soul. From this follows activity without effort and the knowledge that the soul is at rest and in contact with the spiritual world.[42]

In the absence of such experience, one is instructed to purify the will by making every effort to be guided by loving kindness as one follows the path of healing and empowerment on the way to freedom. The attainment of power in the service of the soul is thus fulfilled in its relinquishment. At this point one may understand the paradox of spiritual empowerment that requires consummate effort for the purpose of surrender.

CHAPTER 8

The Myth of Enlightenment

As our soul contemplates its Archetype, so that Archetype in turn contemplates the One, which is its Source.[1]

—PLOTINUS

UNMASKING THE GODS

AS LONG AS WE ARE DEALING WITH ARchetypes we are engaged only with the masks of God. Those who want to see beyond these appearances must be willing to unmask the gods and discover the reality they represent. When we inquire into the mystery of enlightenment, we leave the realm of archetypes behind.

Whereas archetypes are the original forms or patterns of manifestation, authentic mysticism is formless awareness. Awakening, healing and empowering the soul are all undertaken in the first part of the spiritual journey; the second part involves the dissolution of soul in Spirit. The inner light is then no longer separate from the divine light; the soul becomes one with God; Atman and Brahman are experienced as one.

Although enlightenment has different meanings in different contexts, it is always associated with a shift in perception that dispels the shadows of ignorance and delusion. A person who would reach enlightenment must therefore be willing to relinquish all attachments to symbols and illusions, both secular and religious.

In Western philosophy the Age of Enlightenment was associated with the rise of modern science and critical rationalism. The term *enlightenment* was used very differently in the West from the way it is used in Eastern philosophy. Enlightenment thinkers in the West rejected traditional beliefs and revelations of the Church, seeking to understand nature in terms of the organization and activity of matter. Reason was understood as the foundation of moral systems, determined by what was useful to society.[2] Tolerance of religious differences was encouraged, which resulted in the United States in the separation of church and state. People were to be given the opportunity to use their intellects to determine the faith they would live by. Emmanuel Kant associated enlightenment with the courage to think for oneself rather than having beliefs dictated by political, ecclesiastical or scriptural authorities. He claimed to be living in an age of enlightenment in which people were gaining the courage to free themselves from the spiritual oppression of tradition and authority.[3]

In the context of Eastern religions, on the other hand, *enlightenment* refers to a transformative experience that provides understanding and profound insight into the nature of reality. To attain enlightenment is to see through illusion to the truth that makes us free. It can, therefore, be equated with liberation. The experience of enlightenment is characteristically ineffable, and words can only point to it, as a finger points to the moon. The finger is not to be confused with the moon.

The word *enlightenment* is commonly used to translate the Sanskrit term *bodhi*, which is translated literally as "awakened." Although enlightenment affords insight into one reality, there are varying degrees of perceptual understanding. For example, a glimpse of enlightenment can be compared to seeing through a chink in a wall, whereas in a full experience of enlightenment, the wall disappears altogether. The world of enlightenment is not an object perceived by a subject. It is an experience in which the ego is said to be annihilated, and subject/object dualism is transcended.[4]

The Buddha taught that one must look into one's own mind in order to find out what is true. Stories of enlightenment, like other myths, are metaphors for human experience that can never be fully communicated in words. The meaning of the sacred myths and stories that tell of enlightenment cannot be fully understood in the absence of direct experience.

At the heart of every sacred tradition we find a roadmap to enlightenment. When those who have attained enlightenment, including the founders of the great religions, try to communicate to others what they have learned, they always resort to speaking in metaphors or giving instructions that lead to experience. Each culture has its own metaphors and prescribed practices, suited to a particular time and place.

For example, in the *Bhagavad Gita*, one of India's ancient spiritual texts, when Lord Krishna instructs Arjuna to carry out the duties of his caste, the timeless transcendental wisdom that calls for acting without attachment and doing one's duty is portrayed as a story of battle in the cultural context of its time.[5] According to the *Gita*, the root cause of suffering is ignorance, which in turn leads to fear and attachment.

By acting without attachment in accordance with the demands of the situation rather than the demands of ego, we grow in wisdom and compassion. Knowledge and devotion are often considered alternate routes to enlightenment, though one without the other is incomplete. Devotion implies an attitude of loyalty and dedication to the Beloved or object of worship. Based on a relationship to the sacred, devotion is a form of love that aspires to union and is related to eros. Compassion, on the other hand, implies empathy for the suffering of others and the desire to alleviate it. Compassion is therefore more closely associated with agape than eros. For the person aspiring to wholeness, knowledge and wisdom, devotion and compassion are inextricably interwoven. Sri Aurobindo says,

> Love of God, charity towards men is the first step towards perfect wisdom.[6]

With respect to the relationship of knowledge to wisdom Sri Aurobindo goes on to say,

> There are two allied powers in man: knowledge and Wisdom. Knowledge is so much of the truth, seen in a distorted medium, as the mind arrives at by groping; Wisdom is what the eye of divine vision sees in the spirit. . . . Wisdom looks behind the veil and sees. Reason divides, fixes details and contrasts them; Wisdom unifies, marries contrasts in a single harmony.[7]

THE BUDDHA'S STORY

Buddhahood is equally ever-present in the hearts of all sentient beings as their potential for the realization of liberation and enlightenment.[8]
—Namakai Norbu

The classic description of enlightenment in Eastern thought is the story of the Buddha. Siddhartha Gautama was an Indian prince, born in the sixth century B.C., who had grown up in a palace, protected from the outside world. One day he made his way outside the palace walls and encountered old age, disease and death. This prompted him to leave his home and wander in the world, trying to understand human existence. He explored the world, studied yoga, engaged in ascetic practices and finally sat down under the bo tree in Bodh Gaya in northern India, vowing to sit there until he attained enlightenment. While he was seated, Kama Mara, the Lord of Love and Death, sent his armies to attack him, his daughters to tempt him with lust and his demons to frighten him. The future Buddha remained immobile, resisted the temptations of greed, hatred and delusion, and touched the ground in a gesture of fearlessness, bidding the earth to bear witness. In the words of Joseph Campbell,

> With the sword of his mind he pierced the bubble of the universe—and it shattered into nought. The whole world of natural experience, as well as the continents, heavens, and hells of traditional religious belief, exploded—together with their gods and demons. But the miracle of miracles was that though all exploded, all was nevertheless thereby renewed, revivified and made glorious with the effulgence of true being.[9]

Gautama attained enlightenment at the age of thirty-five and spent the next forty-five years of his life teaching others the way to liberation. When asked if he was a god, he replied, "No. I am awake." He therefore became known as "Buddha," the Awakened One. When he died he said to his disciples, "Be ye a lamp unto yourselves."

Buddhism became known as the great middle way, which avoided the extremes of other religious disciplines of the time. A student of Buddhism aspiring to liberation must realize the four noble truths and practice the eightfold path. The four noble truths are:

1. All conditioned existence is characterized by suffering.
2. Suffering is caused by clinging and attachment.
3. There is a way out of suffering.
4. The way out of suffering lies in following the Noble Eightfold Path.

The eightfold path calls for practicing right view, (i.e., seeing things as they are), right thought, right speech, right action, right livelihood, right effort, right mindfulness, and right concentration.

The person who would attain enlightenment in this tradition must let go of desires and overcome the temptations of lust, greed, anger, laziness, doubt, pride and fear. One must also let go of any self-concept, recognizing that everything, including body and soul, is a process, not a substance. The idea of an immortal soul or personal god is only an illusion. Everything is impermanent, and there is no enduring, unchanging self. Enlightenment is the end of conditioned existence, *nirvana*, in which the separate self-sense disappears altogether.

Recognizing the link between ignorance and craving, Theravada Buddhism equates the experience of enlightenment with the extinction of craving. The Mahayana tradition associates enlightenment with seeing the emptiness of all things. D. T. Suzuki says,

> Knowing is impossible without seeing; all knowledge has its origin in seeing. Knowing and seeing are thus found generally united in Buddha's teaching. Buddhist philosophy therefore ultimately points to seeing reality as it is. Seeing is experienced enlightenment.[10]

However, he also points out that

> . . . seeing is not just an ordinary seeing by means of relative knowledge; it is the seeing by means of a *prajna*-eye which is a special kind of intuition enabling us to penetrate right into the bedrock of Reality itself.[11]

In this tradition experiences of light are not to be mistaken for enlightenment. Enlightenment is beyond all categories and remains ineffable.

In Buddhism the ideal of the Boddhisattva as one who renounces personal liberation in order to save all sentient beings inspires many students to take the Boddhisattva vow. Enlightenment, then, is sought not for personal liberation, but in order to relieve the inevitable suffering of conditioned existence and to show others the way to liberation.

Although Buddhist teachings are sometimes perceived as otherworldly and life denying, this is not true of all forms of Buddhism. It is true that some practitioners retire from the world to do their spiritual practice. However, many others do not, and those who do often return to the world wanting to be of service. Today many students of Buddhism in the West are committed to practicing in the midst of ordinary life, to seeing reality as it is and to following the eightfold path to awakening.

Buddhist meditation practices have also become widely available to anyone who wants to learn meditation without having to subscribe to any particular metaphysical beliefs. Since Buddhism offers a nontheistic spirituality together with psychological insight, it appeals to many Westerners who have rejected formal Judeo-Christian religious observances and feel the need for guidance on a path of awakening. I have found Buddhist meditation practice valuable in training awareness and have recommended it to both graduate students and clients. A better understanding of different perspectives on enlightenment can be particularly useful for those who are inclined to strive for enlightenment as if it were something to possess.

EXPERIENCE, BELIEF AND PERENNIAL WISDOM

Those who seek the light are merely covering their eyes. The light is in them now. Enlightenment is but a recognition, not a change at all.[12]

—A COURSE IN MIRACLES

Experience is shaped by beliefs, and beliefs, in turn, are reinforced by experience. In examining beliefs about enlightenment, what has been learned from hearsay must be distinguished from what has been inwardly observed about the nature of self and reality. As with any myth, some people are inclined to take stories of enlightenment literally; others read them as metaphors of awakening soul.

Experiences of illumination are sometimes described as a feeling that the mind and body are literally filled with light. One of my colleagues described a sudden experience of light this way:

I was walking home late one August afternoon after the rain showers had stopped. Everything was steamy and moist. I was at the edge of the park when the sun suddenly came out, lighting up the green in a golden glow. The light filtering through the leaves transformed what it touched. As I stepped into one golden pool, I became one with the light. Everything inside me became peaceful and still. I stood for a moment in the golden pool of light, transfixed. The obsessive thoughts which ordinarily preoccupied my mind evaporated. In that one moment, I had a certainty of knowing. I felt as though I were one with the wisdom of all life, through all time. All fear was gone. I left the circle of light at one with myself and the universe, feeling that I had arrived at a simple perfection, sure that my life was irrevocably changed. The peace dissolved gradually over time, but the memory has never faded.

Sometimes a sensation of light is accompanied by a profound realization that the essence of being is light, that we are beings of light. Sometimes the whole universe is perceived as a play of light and shadow. One man who was an experienced meditator described a meditative experience in which he had an intense sensation of his whole body and mind being suffused with light.

Pir Vilayat Inayat-Khan, a Sufi mystic, describes the transformation of the soul into a being of light as a process of purification, a passage from fire to light. He says,

> The fire of truth produces light and illumination. We are able to bring about illumination by burning more intensely in our lives . . . The fire is one's vibration to the truth, and it is that which transforms one into a being of light.[13]

Sometimes people who hear these descriptions create expectations which then interfere with direct experience. Others become intent on proving that such experiences are only an illusion. One story tells of God and the Devil having a conversation about truth. God says to the Devil, "Don't you get discouraged when the truth is so evident and plain to see?" The Devil replied, "Oh no. With a little help I can easily turn it into a belief."

Can enlightenment be characterized as a universal experience, regardless of belief, or is it contingent on belief? Philosophers argue about whether it is possible to have *any* experience that transcends cultural conditioning. Some postmodern thinkers argue that there is no such thing as an unconditioned universal experience. Others point to a common mystical experience underlying all religious theologies and doctrines and transcending cultural differences.

Writing on knowledge of the sacred, Islamic scholar Seyyed Hossein Nasr says,

> The Ultimate Reality is at once Absolute and Infinite. . . . It can only be known through the sun of the Divine Self residing at the center of the human soul.[14]

This revelation is not the result of mental faculties; it is being that reveals the nature of reality and enables one to distinguish between the real and the illusory and to know things as they are. Nasr goes on to say,

> Absoluteness is reflected in space as center, in time as the present moment . . . Infinitude is reflected in space as extension which theoretically knows no bound, in time as duration which logically has no end, in matter as the indefiniteness of material substantiality,

in form as the unlimited possibility of diversity, and in number as the limitlessness of quantity.[15]

The Absolute always remains beyond duality and relativity. According to the perennial philosophy, which embraces both philosophy and theology, a timeless wisdom of divine origin has been forgotten. This sacred knowledge may be revealed either through its historical expressions in various religious traditions or by direct intuition and contemplation.

Aldous Huxley's definition of the perennial philosophy pointed out four fundamental doctrines:

1. The phenomenal world of matter and individualized consciousness is the manifestation of a Divine Ground within which all creatures and partial realities have their being and apart from which they would not exist.

2. Human beings are capable not merely of knowing *about* the Divine Ground. They can realize its existence by direct intuition that unites the knower with what is known.

3. Humans possess a double nature: a phenomenal ego and an eternal Self, the spark of divinity within the soul. It is possible to identify with Spirit or the Divine Ground, which is of the same nature.

4. The purpose of life on earth is to come to unitive knowledge of the Divine Ground.[16]

This unitive knowledge of the Divine Ground is usually considered a fundamental quality of authentic mystical experience. Contemporary research suggests that mystical experiences are not uncommon and should be considered normal.[17] Furthermore, mystical experience is positively correlated with self-actualization[18] and psychological well-being.[19]

Following in the tradition of William James, psychologist Abraham Maslow undertook an extensive investigation of mystical experiences which he chose to call peak-experiences in order to distinguish them from those that occurred only in religious contexts. He found that the same experiential response which had previously been thought to be triggered only in religious contexts could also be triggered by other stimuli, such as love, aesthetics, creativity, etc. Maslow thought people could be taught that peak-experiences exist, what they are like, and how they are connected with a good life and psychological health. He also said that speaking positively about these experiences gave people permission to be conscious of them.[20]

Frequently reported triggers of peak-experiences include meditation, psychedelics, listening to music, prayer, observing nature and quiet reflection. Other doorways to such experiences include childbirth, being present at the death of a loved one, near-death experiences, fasting, vision quests, ceremonies and rituals, holotropic breathing, extreme physical exertion and space travel.

Commenting on the effects of his experience in space, one Soviet astronaut said the psyche of each astronaut was reshaped. After seeing the sun, the stars and the planets from outer space, he found himself being kinder and more patient with people. Rusty Schweickart, who flew on the Apollo 9 orbital flight around the earth, became a founder of the Association of Space Explorers, dedicated to exploring the implications of their experiences in terms of unity and cooperation on earth and in space. He says,

> When you go around the Earth in an hour and a half, you begin to recognize that your identity is with that whole thing. That makes a change. . . . From where you see it, the thing is a whole, and it's so beautiful.[21]

He compares seeing the earth from this perspective to seeing your mother from a new perspective after birth.

Edgar Mitchell, who flew on the Apollo 14 mission and was the sixth man on the moon, said he came to realize that the universe is made up of Spirit and matter but that they are not separate. He says,

> Spaceflight is one of the more powerful experiences that humans can have . . . getting outside of Earth and seeing it from a different perspective, having this sort of explosive awareness that some of us had, this abiding concern and passion for the well-being of Earth . . . will have a direct impact on philosophy and value systems.[22]

When Mitchell returned, he founded the Institute of Noetic Sciences, another institution aimed at changing human consciousness and social awareness.

Most of us do not have the opportunity to go into outer space, but we can all increase our sensitivity to the beauty of the earth and sky. A woman describing her solo sojourn in the wilderness on a vision quest said,

> On the second day I felt as though I did not exist separately from the mountains and the sky and everything that I could see. It was as if all boundaries dissolved and my soul opened up to infinity. I was forever one with all of it. The night sky reminded me of the vastness of Being and I saw how mistaken I was when I thought I

was separate from the universe. I felt a sense of intimate connection with the divine spirit that permeated everything. Moments of ecstasy were followed by tears of gratitude. In that experience my relationship to my family and all the people in my life whom I love was transformed. Each one of them seemed to live inside me and I was part of them.

Writing about sports as transformative practice, author Michael Murphy says,

> Many sportspeople testify to both the pains and joys of self-surpassing, to the freedom that emerges in the midst of discomfort, to the second energy that comes with transcendence of ordinary patterns. By enduring the naysaying voices inside them, athletes discover new capacities. Breakdown for buildup—whether physical, emotional, or cognitive—is the rule in sport as it is in all transformative practice.[23]

Murphy describes the more profound mystical experiences of Sri Ramakrishna, the nineteenth-century Indian ecstatic as follows:

> He practiced several Tantric disciplines, realizing the different ecstasies they were intended to promote, and entered *nirvikalpa samadhi* upon meeting the Vedantic teacher Totapuri, remaining in trance for a full six months. In the course of his spiritual realizations, he had visions of Krishna, Christ, and Mohammed that led him to declare that the contemplative paths of every religion were fulfilled in a single Divinity. No other modern mystic has dramatized so many kinds of religious experience.[24]

Even atheists have been known to have mystical experiences in holotropic breathwork sessions. One staunch Marxist remarked afterwards, "I had an experience of God, even though I have always denied the existence of God. I did not know God before."

Some therapeutic techniques such as hypnosis can access profoundly meaningful experiences that may be described as peak-experiences, yet do not reach full realization of the unity and love that defines authentic mysticism. Trance induction techniques do produce altered states of consciousness, but altered states are many and varied and should not be confused with mystical states of unitive consciousness or enlightenment. Altered states include any experiences that are not ordinary waking consciousness, including states of reduced awareness, such as hypnosis, intoxication or psychosis. Higher states are those that include all the capacities of the normal waking state plus additional ones, such as heightened perceptual sensitivity and feelings of euphoria. As a subset of altered states, mystical states are higher states since awareness is expanded rather than contracted, regardless of whether attention is focused inwardly or outwardly.

Sometimes certain altered states that are valuable for focusing attention and gaining insight are described as mystical or enlightening, particularly if they result in emotional catharsis. However, most would be more appropriately described as transpersonal or peak-experiences that release psychological blocks and contribute to spiritual development without reaching either a unitive state or enlightenment. Transpersonal experiences are not all alike, and cannot be equated with experiences of enlightenment as understood in spiritual traditions.

Although transpersonal experiences do not necessarily lead to enlightenment, they can afford glimpses of a state in which the mind is free of judgments and attachments. Freedom from fear and desire and the blissful awareness of truth, beauty and love attributed to mystical experience bestow supreme happiness, if only for a fleeting moment. Feelings of gratitude then tend to arise spontaneously, as in response to a gift of grace. This illumination is usually associated with a profound sense of surrender or letting go. Preparation for surrender involves effort, but ultimately every effort must be relinquished.

In summary, mystical experience surpasses ordinary experience through union with a transcendent reality.[25] Those who have had mystical experiences do not doubt their transformative value. Those who have not had them are rarely convinced of their validity by rational argument.

William James concluded that from a psychological perspective mystical experiences are characterized by an identification of our real being with the best part of ourselves, or "something higher." A person can become conscious that this higher part is continuous with a *more* of the same quality, operative in the universe outside ourselves. Although such experiences may have powerful effects on our lives, James poses the question of their objective truth. He points to the theoretical work of the various theologies that agree on certain issues and disagree on others. He says,

> They all agree that the 'more' really exists; though some of them hold it to exist in the shape of a personal god or gods, while others are satisfied to conceive it as a stream of ideal tendency embedded

in the eternal structure of the world. They all agree, moreover, that it acts as well as exists, and that something really is affected for the better when you throw your life into its hands. It is when they treat of the experience of 'union' with it that their speculative differences appear most clearly. Over this point pantheism and theism, nature and second birth, works and grace and karma, immortality and reincarnation, rationalism and mysticism, carry on inveterate disputes.[26]

James goes on to suggest that we must begin by using less particularized terms in describing the 'more' which psychologists may also recognize as real. He says,

Apart from all religious considerations, there is actually and literally more life in our total soul than we are at any time aware of. . . . The whole drift of my education goes to persuade me that the world of our present consciousness is only one out of many worlds of consciousness that exist, and that those other worlds must contain experiences which have a meaning for our life also; and that although in the main their experiences and those of this world keep discrete, yet the two become continuous at certain points, and higher energies filter in.[27]

The seeker of enlightenment who aspires to knowledge of these higher worlds can benefit from a better understanding of mystical experiences and their common characteristics.

CHARACTERISTICS OF MYSTICISM

The secret of the mystic way—including both path and goal, for they cannot be separated—is total, passionate love for God alone, for sheer Divine Reality, however you may envision or experience it in the depth of your being.[28]

—Ramakrishna

Mysticism belongs to the core of all the great religions, yet no definition of mysticism can be broad enough to encompass all experiences and practices described as mystical. Classical descriptions of mystical experience as noted by William James and W. T. Stace include the following:

• Ecstatic unity, with no separation between subject and object, self and other, inner and outer. Awareness is suffused in bliss, love and joy.

• Transcendence of time and space: Time disappears into the eternity of the present instant, and one is nowhere and everywhere, simultaneously.

• Paradoxicality: Awareness of the unity of opposites is not incompatible with a world of perception determined by the distinctions of dualism.

• Sense of sacredness: The world is rendered transparent to transcendence and the inherent radiance and luminosity of all phenomena is perceived as pervading all existence.

• Noetic quality: Mystical states afford insight into depths of truth unplumbed by the discursive intellect. These revelations carry a sense of intrinsic authority.

• Ineffability: Words cannot convey the full meaning and subjective impact of the experience.[29,30]

Ken Wilber distinguishes four types of mysticism as follows:

1. Nature mysticism: A temporary dissolution of the separate self-sense that results in an identification with the entire natural world, mountains, trees, rivers, the earth itself and all its creatures.

2. Deity mysticism: Characterized by union with God or Goddess, the yogic state of *savikalpa samadhi* (absorption). This aspect of reality is experienced as much deeper or higher than the gross natural world, or as transcendent to it. The words of Ramakrishna and the poetry of Rumi are expressions of deity mysticism.

3. Formless mysticism: The witness disappears in the yogic state of *nirvikalpa samadhi* (cessation). All objects vanish. This state of consciousness without an object is pure unqualified Emptiness.

4. Nondual mysticism: The union of Emptiness and all form.[31]

In her classic, comprehensive study of Christian mysticism, Evelyn Underhill defines *mysticism* as follows:

• Mysticism is the art and science of establishing conscious relation with the Absolute. The mystic is the person who attains to union with the Absolute, not the person who talks about it.

• The mystic has surrendered to the embrace of reality and sees a different world through transformed vision. The mystic lives the spiritual life.

• Mysticism can be viewed as the art of arts, their source as well as their end. Symbol and image are the means by which the mystic attempts to communicate a vision of reality, although the full meaning of the mystical experience can never be contained in any representation.

• True mysticism is an active, practical life process. It is not passive or theoretical. It is not a philosophy and has nothing to do with occult knowledge. It is not concerned with manipulation of the visible universe. Its aims are wholly transcendental and spiritual.

• Union with the One is obtained neither from intellectual investigation nor from emotional longings. These must be present, but they are not enough. The mystic way entails an arduous psychological and spiritual process and the liberation of a latent state of consciousness, sometimes called ecstasy or the unitive state.

• In mysticism the will is united with emotions in the desire to be joined by love to the one eternal and ultimate object of love perceived by the soul.

• The one reality is, for the mystic, an object of love that draws us homeward under the guidance of the heart. The business and method of mysticism is generous love in all aspects of life. This passion is never self-seeking, but pursued only for the sake of love.[32]

Reflecting on what I have learned about the characteristics of mysticism from reading and from opening to direct experience in a variety of contexts, I find myself wondering why some people discount it or dismiss it as purely illusion. I can only attribute this attitude to ignorance or lack of adequate understanding. While it is true that we can easily fail to distinguish between reality and illusion in our subjectivity, the validity of mystical experience has been consensually validated by saints and sages of all time.

Christian theologian Matthew Fox says,

> The mystic is neither neutral nor bitter or cynical toward the world. The mystic has taken in enough of the blessing of the world to be radically amazed by it and, therefore to *affirm* it. To embrace the "world as a whole" is to embrace a cosmology. What the mystic affirms is not the world laid waste by human neglect, sin, and greed, but the world *as a whole*. This affirmation enables us to receive sustenance, challenge, and power from the whole.[33]

While mystics are perhaps tolerated better in the postmodern world than they have been in more repressive societies, religious intolerance is also on the rise. Without awareness of the love and wisdom inherent in authentic mystical experience, there would seem to be no hope for reversing the self-destructive tendencies that are so prevalent among humans today. I have seen so many people's lives changed for the better as a result of opening to mystical experiences that I can only hope more people will learn to respect and understand authentic mysticism and learn to distinguish it from the myriad forms of false mysticism that constitute its shadow.

MYSTICISM AND MAGIC

When ignorance is destroyed, the Self is liberated from its identification with the world. This liberation is Enlightenment.[34]

—PATANJALI

Subtle powers sought for the purpose of manipulating reality are traditionally called *magic*. Magic can be understood as the exercise of the power of the invisible over the visible world. It can be differentiated into sacred magic, in which the magician becomes an instrument of divine will; personal magic, in which the magician uses psychic powers for personal ends; and sorcery, in which the magician is possessed by elemental or unconscious forces that are not freely chosen. All forms of magic assert that the subtle rules the dense, or consciousness determines the shape of matter.[35]

Underhill makes a crucial distinction between magic and mysticism. According to Underhill, magic always involves the use of will, whereas mysticism is the surrender of the soul to God in love.[36] Magic is concerned with power and using powers of the mind for manipulation, whether for good or ill; it presupposes a separate self acting on reality. Mysticism, on the other hand, is a science of pure Being. It is not about doing anything to extend the will. In genuine mysticism there is a willing surrender of selfhood to the advance of love; a stilling of the "I, Me and Mine," which is linked by sense desires to the world of visible things. Although some paths to enlightenment emphasize the importance of effort, the objective is liberation rather than power. The effort is made to change perception rather than attempting to change the world.

Underhill considers magic and occultism to be a perversion of spirituality which is both dangerous and confusing to the student or seeker. Instead of transcending the phenomenal world and attaining to the reality behind phenomena, magic extends rather than escapes the boundaries of the phenomenal world. Training the will through discipline and concentration to support the quest for power and knowledge risks feeding intellectual arrogance and neglecting love. The work of love requires union of the divine and the human will, distinct and free.

It is love that gives worth to being, and the mystical revelation that God is love is the sacred knowledge that can be transformed into wisdom. This transformation takes place in stages. The first is a pure reflection or repetition of the experience, without image or word. Then the experience becomes part of memory and is assimilated in thought and feeling, where it becomes a message or inner word. Finally it is formulated into communicable, symbolic language.[37] Underhill writes:

> The true mystic sees Reality in its infinite aspect; and tries, as other artists, to reveal it within the finite world. He not only ascends, but descends the ladder of contemplation; having heard "the uninterrupted music of the inner life," he tries to weave it into melodies that other men can understand.[38]

Brother David Steindl-Rast, a Christian contemplative, suggests that the great religions are rooted in a universal mystical experience of ultimate belonging. Inevitably, the verbal communication of this experience tends to become reified as dogma, and the emotional reenactment, originally intended to rekindle the feeling, tends to become empty ritual. Teachings and rituals can never be a satisfactory substitute for direct experience.

The path of Western mysticism leads through stages of purification and illumination to union with God. This describes the ascending path that finds its roots in Platonism. Socrates said,

> In order that the mind should see light instead of darkness, so the entire soul must be turned away from this changing world, until its eye can bear to contemplate reality and that supreme splendour which we have called the Good.[39]

Once attained, mystical realization is expressed in the unitive life of service in the world. The path then becomes a path of descent, or the pouring of divine love into the world as *agape*. The will of God is the guide and, in contrast to the magician who seeks to manipulate reality, the mystic is not attached to the fruits of the labor.

DUALITY AND NONDUALITY

Intelligence is a divine gift which pierces through the veil of maya *and is able to know reality as such.*[40]

—SEYYED HOSSEIN NASR

The language of metaphor is sometimes used to point to the experience of nonduality, as, for example, when the deity is described as fire and the soul is likened to a spark. When the deity is experienced as light, all phenomena are said to disappear in the one light of infinite love.

Among the sayings of Jesus in the Gospel of Thomas, discovered at Nag Hammadi, is the following:

> If they say to you: "From where are your origins?" say to them, "We have come from the Light, where the Light has begun through itself."[41]

According to these scriptures, cultivating the inner light contributes to enlightening the world, and gnosis is knowledge that illuminates the world. The cause of suffering is ignorance, and knowledge of transcendental being is the goal of life. The human soul does not require an external institution for redemption. It contains within itself the capacity for spiritual direction.

A Gnostic myth tells of a supreme light that sent its emissaries into the lower worlds of manifestation for the purpose of facilitating the enlightenment and liberation of all creatures from the realms of darkness. Although some Gnostics taught that this world was an entrapment to be escaped, Gnostic wisdom holds that the light will emerge from darkness, and the notion of the union of opposites is at the core of the teachings that say the kingdom of God lies in making the inner and the outer, the above and below and the male and female into a single unity.[42]

Ken Wilber points out that a radical change in spiritual understanding was introduced in the East by Nagarjuna and in the West by Plotinus in nondual systems that had one basic tenet: The manifest world of phenomenal reality is not an impediment to Spirit. It is, rather the perfect expression of Spirit.

> *Wisdom* knows that behind the Many is the One. Wisdom sees through the confusion of shifting shapes and passing forms to the groundless Ground of all being. Wisdom sees beyond the shadows to the timeless and formless light . . .
>
> But if wisdom sees that the Many is One, *compassion* knows that the One is the Many; that the One is expressed *equally* in each and every being, and so each is to be treated with compassion and care . . . because each being, exactly as it is, is a perfect manifestation of Spirit. Thus compassion sees that the One is the Many.[43]

The path of ascent is the path of wisdom which sees that all form is empty, and the path of descent is the path of compassion which sees that emptiness manifests as all form.

To try to separate these is to fall into the illusion that it is possible to have one without the other, a mistake that leads to a distorted sense of value that denigrates that which is denied. To deny the value of either the path of ascent—the aspiration to wisdom and enlightenment—or the path of descent which recognizes the eternal omnipresence of Spirit in all of manifest reality, can be a dangerous imbalance. Self-transcendence, then, is not the end of the path.

The great mystics have all tried to tell us what they learned from *seeing* through illusion to a larger reality, some more eloquently than others. One of the most articulate sages in the Indian tradition was Shankara. He was born in southern India at the end of the seventh century A.D. As a young boy, he was already aware that book learning was not enough and received instruction in meditation and yoga. He attained mystical realization as a young man and set out to teach. He died at the age of thirty-two, after establishing many monasteries and founding ten monastic orders. He was a sage whose work revitalized the spiritual life of his time and his teachings continue to inspire spiritual seekers to this day.[44]

Shankara's philosophy of nondualism may be summarized as follows: Brahman—the absolute existence, knowledge and bliss—is real. The universe is not real. Brahman and Atman are one.[45] This philosophy accepts as real only that which does not change or cease to exist. Behind all experience is Atman, the deep unchanging consciousness that witnesses all experience, whether waking, dreaming or in dreamless sleep. Whereas Western realism and idealism both make a distinction between mind and matter, claiming that only one of them is ultimately real, Vedanta philosophy regards both mind and matter as objects of knowledge and, therefore, equally unreal. This fundamental unreality can only be understood in the light of mystical experience in which the illumined soul passes into transcendental consciousness. The world is and is not. It is neither real nor nonexistent.

This paradox of world appearance is called *maya*, which weaves the world of names and forms to which the ego clings in its desperate attempts to maintain a sense of order in the world. Maya is not nonexistent, and yet it is not real, since it disappears in the light of knowledge. From a nondualistic point of view, maya is illusion; only Brahman is real. But maya is also creativity, the divine play of Brahman, the eternal, imperishable absolute, sometimes called the dance of life, or *lila*. Maya is also relativity, the source of separateness and multiplicity. Thus maya both veils and reveals the divine reality. In the words of Ramakrishna,

> Reality is beyond *Maya*, beyond any appearance of duality or multiplicity. What conventional consciousness habitually regards

as real—including both the complex social world and the religious world of creeds and visionary experiences—is simply the surface play of knowledge and ignorance.[46]

Brahman alone is real *and* Brahman is the world.

The claim that the true nature of reality is nondual appears in several philosophical systems, such as Advaita Vedanta, Mahayana Buddhism, Taoism and Neoplatonism. According to these traditions, the sense of separation and alienation between self and world is the root delusion that needs to be overcome. They all refer to awareness that does not employ dualistic concepts. This negation of dualistic thinking is a practice leading to an experience of the world as unity, that may be called Brahman, Dharmakaya, Tao or the One Mind. Since the whole cannot be whole if the subject is separate from it, denial that subject and object are separate follows from this experience.

In yoga the practitioner who attains *samadhi,* or one-pointed concentration in communion with the Divine, discovers that the nature of being is *sat-chit-ananda*, or being-consciousness-bliss. *Sat* is that which never changes; *chit* is consciousness; *ananda* is bliss. According to contemporary interpretations of Vedic psychology, consciousness in its pure state knows itself to be the knower, the known and the process of knowing. In this experience, the divided state of the ego and the soul is transcended, and the one unified transcendental Self is experienced as Being.[47] The term *samadhi* is translated as *enstasy*, which means "standing within the transcendental Self." This blissful, ecstatic state in classical yoga is a disembodied liberation in which attention is withdrawn from the world.

On the other hand, nondualist traditions such as Advaita Vedanta and Mahayana Buddhism aim for liberation in life, founded not on the introversion of attention, but on the transcendence of attention itself. This is known as *sahajasamadhi*, a spontaneous state in which everything is perceived as divine being. *Sahajasamadhi* is defined as spontaneous ecstasy, or the realization of unbroken transconceptual ecstasy (*nirvikalpa samadhi*) while engaged in external activities.[48] In other words, *sahajasamadhi* does not depend on any external support such as sitting in meditation. It seems to be analogous to lucid dreaming, only this implies being aware of waking reality as a dream in the midst of ordinary activity. In *sahajasamadhi* everything is perceived as a projection of consciousness or the play of Brahman. In Tibetan Buddhism this state is known as pure perception. In Vedanta it is called seeing Brahman with open eyes.

I find it helpful to remember that according to Tibetan teachings, there are four stages of realization. The first is conceptual understanding, which may be attained by reading descriptions of these states; the second is experiential understanding which may be attained from time to time as a result of practice; the third is stabilization, which may be attained by advanced practitioners and become a stable state or background of awareness in all circumstances. Finally, the fourth stage is liberation. Reflecting on these stages can help us remember that we are only beginners when we are still engaged in the first two stages and avoid the inflation that sometimes occurs after initial experiences at stage two.

When awareness no longer alternates between identification with the ego or the soul and becomes established in pure consciousness, liberation or freedom from suffering is attained. According to Vedic psychology, the unity of subjective and objective existence experienced in mature unity consciousness constitutes the endpoint of development and the ultimate nature of reality. Thus the source and goal of human development are said to be ultimately the same.[49]

In Mahayana Buddhism the teaching of nonduality extends to the equation of samsara and nirvana, or the negation of difference between duality and nonduality.[50] There is neither self nor nonself, neither birth nor death, neither beginning nor ending. Anything that can be said about ultimate reality is negated.[51] My Zen teacher used to say, "In Reality there are no theories or holders of theories. Zazen (sitting meditation) is meaning-free."

Of the three major schools of Buddhism, Theravada, Mahayana and Vajrayana, the Mahayana school of Zen is called the straight and narrow way, since it does not engage the subtle realms of the soul, but aims directly for the realization of nonduality. In contrast, Vajrayana Buddhism, best known as Tibetan Buddhism, has a wide variety of techniques that utilize visualization for attaining mastery of the subtle realms of consciousness. Yet these teachings also lead eventually to nonduality.

For example, Ken Wilber has outlined three stages in deity yoga as practiced in Vajrayana Buddhism: In the first stage the deity is visualized in front or above you, conferring blessings and wisdom. In the second stage you visualize yourself as the deity, thus establishing union with the Divine. In the third and final stage one dissolves both self and deity in pure unmanifest emptiness. Wilber says,

> At this point, the practice no longer involves visualization or mantra recitation or concentration, but rather the realization that your

own awareness, just as it is, is always already enlightened. . . . The unmanifest and the manifest, or emptiness and form, unite in the pure nondual play of your own awareness—generally regarded as the ultimate state that is no state in particular.[52]

The mystical experience of nonduality is accessible only to the mind that does not cling to self-concepts that keep boundaries between self and other intact. Fear of loss of self is the final barrier to transcending dualism between subject and object, self and other, soul and body, Spirit and world. One who seeks enlightenment must give up seeking pleasure and avoiding pain and relinquish all attachments, even this.

WISDOM AND INTUITION

Enlightenment is the secret essence of our consciousness, and the gradual revelation of this essence is the process of spiritual growth in which everyone is involved.[53]

–LEX HIXON

If we think we must strive for enlightenment and make ourselves different, we are already caught by the golden chains that obscure the reality of what can only be discovered through direct, nonvolitional experience. Paradoxically, however, on a spiritual path we find that in order to overcome ignorance, we need to train awareness, practice ethicality and remove psychological barriers to prepare the way for enlightenment. This seems to be a necessary stage of voluntary transformation. By quieting the mind and letting go of attachments, by lightening up, as it were, we can more easily remove obstacles to the awareness of our true nature.

Enlightenment is not attained by an effort of will. We cannot make it happen, but we can be receptive and prepare for it. Some people seek enlightenment through self-deprivation, others through indulgence in practices or substances that promise to induce it, yet every effort to grasp it is futile. Finally the soul can only wait in silence until it surrenders to the luminosity of Being as a wave surrenders to the ocean.

In the Sufi story *The Tale of the Sands*, a stream that traversed many different kinds of terrain eventually ran into a desert which seemed impossible to cross. A faint voice from the sands whispered that in order to cross, the stream must surrender into the arms of the wind. After some deliberation, the stream, which had never been absorbed before, surrendered to the wind and was carried to the faraway mountains where it fell gently as rain and became a stream again. Afterwards the stream reflected that it had learned its true identity.

The details of this story, as told by Idries Shah in *Tales of the Dervishes*,[54] evokes many different levels of meaning. In this context, however, it is enough for us to see the impossibility of thinking that we can remain in our customary modes of thinking and grasp what it is like to surrender what we think we are to the unmanifest, formless realm of Spirit.

One may approach an experience of enlightenment through self-transcendence, yet even this experience does not guarantee living in an enlightened state. Recent decades have seen many so-called enlightened teachers fall from grace, being accused of a variety of unenlightened behaviors regarding abuses of money, sex and power. Only when those fleeting moments of insight become an abiding awareness of being and nonbeing, life and death, love and emptiness, can one begin to express the gnosis or wisdom of enlightenment in everyday life.

D. T. Suzuki said that the wisdom of *prajna*-intuition can be experienced, but it cannot be told.[55] *Prajna* is the insight into emptiness that enables one to see reality as it is. Since language belongs to this world of relativity, words can never express the inner experiences that transcend linguistics. The fact that rational thought can never attain enlightenment leaves many modern thinkers subject to the powers of *maya* (the play of illusion), who exercises her spell most upon those who would deny her reality.[56]

The sacred, intuitive vision that sees through appearances and perceives the impermanent nature of existence, the emptiness of the phenomenal world and the egolessness of all things cannot be explained. Anyone interested in the investigation of this mystery must, therefore, be willing to follow the instructions that have led others to the threshold before any assessment of such experiences can be attempted. The eyes of the senses and the eye of the mind can never apprehend the wisdom that is revealed in contemplation to the intuitive eye of the soul. As long as one identifies with any separate self-sense, be it body, ego or soul, one inhabits a world of ignorance, fear and attachment, which is inevitably subject to suffering.

Identified with Spirit as the one infinite, eternal and all pervasive reality, the soul is free from suffering, fear and attachment. Identified with illusion it becomes entrapped in a world of objects and ideas that obscure recognition of its source and unsubstantial nature. Any image that becomes an idol binds the soul to a body/mind possessed by illusion. Objects of worship are objects of mind that appear illusory to the soul that worships only that which is not an object. For example, when a person becomes fascinated by a particular archetype, such as the magician, and forms an image in the mind that evokes qualities associated with this archetype, the image of the magician can become an idol that commands exclusive attention. The soul as witness observes all objects of mind with awareness and without entanglement. As one Buddhist teacher said,

> For those who do not understand Buddha, there is Buddha.
> For those who understand Buddha, there is no Buddha.

One way of understanding this is to see that when we feel the need for a specific image to address in our inner life, we can choose the image of Buddha or Jesus to relate to, without forgetting that this too is an image that both reveals and conceals the naked truth of reality as emptiness.

When the constrictions of ordinary consciousness have been released and a person has been afforded even a glimpse of enlightenment, the limitations of an exclusively materialistic worldview can never again be taken too seriously. In the absence of such experience, it may be impossible to believe that there is a state of unbounded awareness that transcends anything the rational mind can grasp. However, intuition may provide a link between the ordinary waking state and the world of mystical experience.

A glimpse of enlightenment, no matter how fleeting, can be the seed of a spiritual life. The noetic quality of authentic mystical experience gives rise to spiritual knowledge that bestows freedom, whereas ignorance keeps the soul in bondage. This sacred knowledge may be expressed in religious or philosophical language, as in Vedanta or Buddhist philosophy, or in the arts, as in the ecstatic poetry of Rumi. Any inspired creative expression can be informed by sacred vision that sees through illusion to the sacred source of all vision.

For the soul that has experienced mystical union, God is no longer an abstract concept. Arguments about the nature of God may then be perceived as no more than disagreements about various concepts of God, none of which are relevant to the mystical experience, except insofar as they obstruct enlightenment.

The soul that has attained mystical union is freed from illusion and the effects of limiting beliefs. Knowledge attained through such revelation affects thinking, which in turn affects the flow of energy and attention, and this in turn affects action and the world around us. Anyone who has been deeply moved by such experience may want to understand it, communicate it and put it into practice. The enlightened sage does not withdraw from the world, but he wants nothing from it. The sage rejoices in creation and acts without attachment, guided by wisdom and intuition. He or she looks deeply into things and sees their true nature.

The tenth ox-herding picture, the last in the series that portrays stages of enlightenment in the Zen Buddhist tradition, is called "Entering the marketplace with helping hands." Here the sage is depicted as a bodhisattva, one who renounces personal liberation and returns to the world to help others. Open hands represent perfect emptiness, and the enlightened one cheerfully manifests enlightenment and follows no path. He or she has gone beyond the end of the way and returned completely to the human world.[57]

TRANSMISSIONS AND SPONTANEOUS EXPERIENCES

When the world dissolves
Everything becomes clear.[58]

—THE DHAMMAPADA

A Zen student described her experience of a meeting with her teacher, saying that in the moment when their eyes met, she saw the whole universe in his gaze. Many years later she told me that this had left an indelible impression on her. In that moment everything had dropped away and she herself was not there. There was no time, no body, no thing. She called it a glimpse of enlightenment, a split second of eternity, of seeing through the veils of illusion. She felt it was a direct transmission of a state of consciousness. It was as though she were seeing through his eyes for an instant instead of her own. There was no separation between them at that moment. They were of one mind. The experience of that instant left a lasting, though ineffable impression on her. She had never discussed it with anyone, though she remembered it vividly.

I heard a similar description of a meeting with Sri Aurobindo from a man who went to see him in Pondicherry, India, shortly before he died. Gazing into the eyes of the guru, who at that time was maintaining total silence and speaking to no one, was a life-changing experience for this man. He felt that he had received a transmission of inestimable value which he never forgot. Although he was an eloquent professor of philosophy, he could not find words to describe what had happened to him in that moment.

Some practitioners of Siddha yoga described similar effects when the guru transmitted *shaktipat,* the spiritual energy that was meant to set in motion the spiritual unfolding of the Self. This could be done by a look or by touch. As one young woman said, "When the guru touched me, my whole body exploded into light."

219

It seems evident that some of the spiritual teachers who have gained widespread popularity in the West can induce significant transpersonal experiences in certain people. This, however, does not necessarily mean they are enlightened masters. From a psychological perspective the power of suggestion must be taken into account, in addition to transference and projections that add weight to the guru's every word and gesture. Nevertheless, a person receiving transmission may experience a profoundly altered state of consciousness that makes the ordinary waking state seem pale by comparison. In these situations the initiate can easily mistake the guru for the source rather than the conduit of the experience. As a gate-opener to the Self, the guru renders the seeker a valuable service. When the guru is idolized, however, the resulting diminishment of the devotee can be psychologically crippling. Enlightenment does not belong to anyone; it is potentially available to all. An opening to universal consciousness can be facilitated and mediated by a teacher but is not created by him or her. When the teacher is genuinely *transpersonal*, and functioning as an opening or a clearing through which the absolute can manifest, the transmission will be free of interference from the ego needs of the teacher.

Ram Dass tells of a sincere man who came to see him, saying that he had been doing spiritual practice for years, and yet he had never had any significant experiences. They did nothing special together, simply meditating and talking together for about an hour. Later that day, after the seeker left Ram Dass, he began to have some extraordinarily powerful experiences of kundalini energy and entered into radically altered states of consciousness. This lasted for several days. Ram Dass did not claim any credit, but something in the seeker had been released, and thus the obstacles to the experience he longed for were removed. The student must be open, receptive and willing to surrender defenses in order to allow such experience to happen.

Accounts of enlightenment experience in the Zen tradition frequently point to its occurrence after long periods of discipline and meditative practice, in a moment of nondoing. Thus a monk who practiced for twenty years might have such an experience after giving up hope of attaining it, upon leaving the monastery or when sweeping the floor.

One Zen story tells of a young monk climbing a mountain trail with a pack on his back. About halfway up he meets an old monk coming down the trail. He asks the old monk to tell him about enlightenment. The old monk takes the pack off his back and drops it. Without saying a word, he picks it up again and continues on his way. In a flash of illumination, the young monk understands.

Sometimes people report experiences of enlightenment in the midst of pain and suffering and death. A young doctor who had been on a spiritual path for about two years reported such an experience when he was in the hospital, attending someone who was dying. He had done everything possible to relieve the pain. The patient was lucid and in a moment of eye contact the doctor said both of them seemed to dissolve into a deep ocean of peace. The experience did not last long, but it seemed to erase all fear of death.

Some near-death experiences are also potentially enlightening. Those who have them often say their fear of death disappears and their feelings about life are profoundly affected. When, in the wake of these experiences, people are less concerned with worldly ambition and more concerned with spirituality, the deep feelings of gratitude for life and loved ones that are kindled tend to be pervasive and long lasting. Most people find it difficult to talk about what it is like to lift the veil that shrouds the mystery of death. A few have tried, but many important aspects of this experience remain ineffable.

For some people an experience of enlightenment is deeply desired and becomes the goal of the spiritual quest. For others it may occur spontaneously with little or no preparation. I have worked with people for whom such experiences were profoundly disturbing, and yet, when they were able to discuss them in depth, integrate them into a coherent cosmology and accept their significance, they came to regard these experiences as tremendously valuable and frequently life changing. In each case a shift in perception leading from ignorance to understanding and from fear to love replaces the bondage of illusions with spiritual freedom.

Acting as a magnet, mystical experiences can draw the seeker deeper into practice, purification and service. Just as inspiration favors the prepared mind, moments of enlightenment or mystical illumination become more accessible to those who devote time to contemplation. Reflection that cultivates awareness prepares us for the realization that the person we think we are when we set out on the spiritual quest never becomes enlightened. Enlightenment happens, rather, when the separate self-sense disappears and there is no one to become enlightened.

Some teachings say that enlightenment waits for everyone at the threshold of death and also every night at the threshold of sleep. We miss it when we go unconscious and fail to notice it. Conscious letting go requires unfaltering attention and the willingness to surrender any attachment to experience whatsoever.

The seeker who aspires to enlightenment, then, can only fail in the end. Self-transcendence is not something to be grasped by a separate self that tries to possess and hold a particular state of consciousness. Enlightenment, as our true nature, is always present, awaiting our recognition. The transient states that we mistake for enlightenment along the way can be either stepping stones or hindrances to awakening the soul to its identification with Spirit or no-self. Ken Wilber points out that any enlightenment that can be attained is not real enlightenment. Enlightenment is not a change of state, but the recognition of the true nature of *any* present state.[59] He writes,

> Unity consciousness is not a future state which results from some practice . . . for unity consciousness is present eternally.[60]

In Buddhism the student is warned against becoming attached to pseudo-nirvana, or the illusion of enlightenment. "Even to be attached to the idea of enlightenment is to go astray."[61] It is part of the teacher's task to help the student let go of any preconceptions about enlightenment. One who is lazy may be encouraged to make more effort; one who strives too hard may be told to relax. No single teaching is right for everyone. Therefore, we need teachers who can see our strengths and weaknesses and offer guidance in accordance with our particular needs. The illusion of fulfillment is but another obstacle that can be as encumbering as the illusion of deprivation. As an ideal, then, the myth of enlightenment can be either liberating or entrapping, depending on how one relates to it.

RELEVANCE OF ENLIGHTENMENT

You cannot realize the Absolute without participating in the dance of the relative. You cannot understand the play of relativity without being immersed in the radiant stillness of the Absolute.[62]

—RAMAKRISHNA

The universal teachings about enlightenment that can be found at the heart of the great religions express a unique perception of reality that is shared by many who have had authentic mystical experiences. When mystical experience is not repressed and is well integrated into ordinary waking consciousness, it seems to result in a sense of healing, renewal, inner peace and an outpouring of love and compassion for the suffering of the world. Insights gained from this experience can have a profound effect on behavior and relationships. Residual positive aftereffects of deep mystical experiences include feelings of gratitude, peace, generosity, loving kindness and reduced fear of death. In short, glimpses of enlightenment and experiences of unitive consciousness tend to have a lasting impact on psychological well-being.

In contrast, visionary experiences in which egocentric self-preoccupation persists may leave a residue of pain, separation and longing. Visionary experiences that fall short of unitive consciousness can be life changing, as when a person feels called to embark on a new life path, but even visions of light cannot be equated with enlightenment.

Those who have tasted enlightenment seem to have little or nothing to say about it. At times their lives seem pervaded by a sense of the peace that passes understanding. At other times they may still get caught in illusions of ego and soul, and most of the time they do not seem to be different from anybody else. We have no way of measuring the effects, but those who have spoken to me about such experience tend to regard it as the most significant experience of their lives.

Writing on the experience of enlightenment in sacred traditions, Lex Hixon says,

> From Enlightenment radiate the insight, compassion, and power needed to resolve individual and collective human problems as they continue to arise endlessly. Enlightenment is not a magical transcendence of the human condition but the full flowering of humanity, disclosing unity and equilibrium at the heart of the love and suffering we call life . . .[63]

Enlightenment experiences may be expected to manifest as compassionate, ethical behavior in ordinary life. Enlightenment is not an isolated attainment of legendary sages but a process in which our consciousness gradually becomes transparent to its own intrinsic nature. The first part of this process involves the awakening of the soul, the recognition of the Self that is one with the Divine, the little light that is part of the great light. The second part involves the dissolution of the separate self altogether, and with it the freeing of consciousness to be as it always has been, infinite, eternal and in perfect peace. The final challenge is to realize this truth in the midst of ordinary life. This enlightenment is called "living liberation."[64] In this state,

> All that is left of the personal soul is a hymn of peace and freedom and bliss vibrating somewhere in the eternal.[65]

CHAPTER 9

Spiritual Freedom

As one goes further and further on the path of truth, the freedom becomes greater at every step.[1]

—HAZRAT INAYAT KHAN

SPIRITUAL CHOICES

FOR MOST PEOPLE, FREEDOM IS EXPRESSED as personal choice. External freedom from oppression, however, does not guarantee internal freedom from repression, nor does the recognition of existential freedom guarantee spiritual freedom. Existential freedom is expressed in choosing goals, values and attitudes in response to the circumstances of life, and this personal freedom enables us to change ourselves and our environment.

Claiming spiritual freedom is far more challenging. What is at stake in spiritual choices is not only a transitory life goal, but the fate of the soul. Fear of making the wrong choice keeps many people from breaking the limitations of their beliefs, no matter how irrational or constricting they are.

Recognizing the existential freedom that empowers an individual to designate the meaning of events seems to be a necessary though insufficient condition for transcending tradition and claiming spiritual freedom. Transcending tradition does not imply devaluing tradition; it does imply recognizing the relative nature of spiritual teachings as they have been handed down across generations in every culture since the beginning of recorded history. Every tradition offers comforting illusions for those who would escape from freedom and roadmaps to liberation for those who choose to follow them.

Today many people leave the tradition in which they were raised, rejecting the teachings along with the dogma and the form. Some reject spirituality altogether. Others find new traditions more palatable and opt for a new set of constricting beliefs.

One woman I know, who was born into a conservative Jewish family, converted to Islam when a visiting sheik came to California. She had felt confined and restricted by her family and had moved to California to go to graduate school. When she attended a prayer meeting with the Sufi dervishes, she was deeply moved by the music, dancing and chanting. She felt she had found a new spiritual home that was inspiring and uplifting. She became a sincere devotee, only to discover later that the sect she had joined demanded strict obedience and was even more constricting for women than the religion she had rejected.

The fact that a wide range of spiritual choices[2] are readily available today does not necessarily contribute to spiritual freedom. The search for spirituality can sometimes lead people to join spiritual groups that have all the characteristics of a dysfunctional family: authoritarian parent figures that demand unquestioning obedience and the abdication of responsibility for personal choices, as well as various forms of addiction and codependency.

Ever since Nietzsche announced the death of God in the late nineteenth century, scientific psychology implicitly associated spirituality with psychological immaturity, if not pathology. Most spirituality was presumed to be dysfunctional, characterized by an avoidance of reality and the problems of living in the world.

For centuries choosing a religious life meant retiring from the world to a monastery or a cloister. Life in the world was presumed to be unsuitable for those who wanted to devote themselves to the cultivation of spirituality and the well-being of the soul. The belief that one can be spiritual only if one removes oneself from the world of ordinary life has long been an assumption of religious seekers, both in the East and the West. But life in the cloister or the monastery, ostensibly protected from the demands of money, sex and power, has not been immune to corruption. Whatever we are unwilling to face in the world tends to surface in consciousness, sometimes in unexpected and distorted ways. Hence resentment festers among those who would be obedient, envy among those who choose poverty and sexual obsessions among those who choose celibacy.

The choice to retire from the world is still available, but many people are aware that joining a religious order does not free them from the preoccupations of ego. The search for personal salvation divorced from the larger community tends to perpetuate a sense of isolation and reinforce illusions of a separated ego. A living spirituality for our time, based on awareness of our interdependence, cannot be cut off from the world, but also needs to honor the contemplative foundations of spiritual insight.

Today in the West few Christian monks and nuns live a contemplative life. Most are working in the world in the helping professions, such as teaching, nursing, administration or related ministries. One young woman was very disillusioned to discover that life in the convent offered very little time for the solitude and silence that she craved. She ended up leaving the convent, and it took her many years to forgive herself for breaking her vows. I have worked with several nuns, priests, ex-nuns and ex-priests who have sought psychotherapy in an effort to resolve inner conflicts about their vows. One former nun said to me, "I felt much closer to God after I left the Church."

Another nun struggled for a long time deciding whether or not to leave the community to which she had devoted twenty-five years of her life. She had joined the convent when she was eighteen, partly in response to a spontaneous mystical experience and partly to get away from her authoritarian father. She felt she had burned out in her teaching career and longed for a more relaxed life. After considerable soul-searching, she decided not to abandon her calling and to stay in the religious community. Her feelings about the community and her work changed considerably after she began a meditation practice and did some inner work that provided a renewed sense of meaning and purpose to her religious commitment.

In the second half of the twentieth century, following the psychedelic revolution of the sixties, many people dropped out of mainstream society in search of utopian communities. Spiritual seekers of various persuasions embarked on a search for inner peace and personal salvation away from the demands of ordinary life. The journey brought many of them back to the place where they started, some of them disappointed and embittered, others renewed and inspired to change the world. The integration of spiritual practice with being in the world can be equally challenging for those who remain outside of formal religion as it is for those who have made a commitment to religious life.

For those whose concept of God is still confined to childhood images of a patriarchal authority figure, and who have felt liberated by the scientific worldview that perceives no need for such a god, a nontheistic spirituality is more appealing. Many Westerners are therefore attracted to Buddhism, which denies the existence of a personal god and an immortal soul. However, those who have taken long retreats, sometimes for three years or more, either in Asia or in Western settings devoted to Eastern practices, often find it difficult to return to the secular world and integrate their practice with a more engaged life in society. One man who had difficulty making the transition from a few months of monastic retreat back to family life decided to leave his family in order to deepen his practice. He later regretted the decision, but it was too late to repair the emotional damage the family had suffered.

HEALTHY SPIRITUALITY

The fundamental choices for most people are the choices to be free, to be healthy, and to be true to oneself.[3]

—ROBERT FRITZ

As a subjective experience of the sacred, authentic, healthy spirituality does not hinge on a particular concept of God or religious observances. It depends, rather, on how we relate to ourselves, to each other, to the earth and to the cosmos. When we remember that we are only a tiny part of the whole, we can see ourselves embedded in an intricate web of relationships. Healthy spirituality is free from addiction and avoidance and is characterized by a willingness to face reality. Healthy spirituality acknowledges both our humanity and our divinity, inspires a reverence for life and enhances our capacity for love, peace and joy. It affects experience in both the inner and the outer world and has far reaching personal, social and cultural implications.

According to Father Leo Booth, an Episcopal priest who is an authority on spirituality and addiction, healthy spirituality is an inner attitude that emphasizes energy, creative choice and a powerful force for living.[4] He says spirituality is a co-creatorship with God that allows us to be guided by God *and* take responsibility for our lives.

Healthy spirituality can be found equally among the dedicated souls who have made the choice to live a traditional religious life and among those who do not think of themselves as religious at all. The fruits of spirituality may be evident in the good works of saints and sages and also in the work of such statesmen as His Holiness the Dalai Lama or Robert Muller, Chancellor of University for Peace in Costa Rica. Authentic spirituality can also be found in those who are invisible in the eyes of the world, such as ordinary citizens, or in people whose service is known to only a few. For example, Laurance Rockefeller's philanthropic fund for the enhancement of the human spirit has helped numerous people to carry on their spiritually inspired work in the world. When I met Arne Naess, the founder of deep ecology, whose work has been an inspiration to many people in the environmental movement, my impression was that his spiritual vision illuminated his presence as well as his work.

Authentic spirituality may be perceived as a quality of being rather than doing and described as presence rather than appearance. Perhaps it is visible only to those who can see with spiritual vision. Sri Aurobindo characterizes spirituality as follows:

> Spirituality is not a high intellectuality, not idealism, not an ethical turn of mind or moral purity and austerity, not religiosity or an ardent and exalted emotional fervour, not even a compound of all these excellent things; a mental belief, creed or faith, an emotional aspiration, a regulation of conduct according to a religious or ethical formula are not spiritual achievement and experience. . . . Spirituality is in its essence, an awakening to the inner reality of our being, to a spirit, self, soul which is other than our mind, life and body, an inner aspiration to know, to feel, to be that, to enter into contact with the greater Reality beyond and pervading the universe which inhabits also our own being.[5]

Spirituality presupposes certain qualities, including awareness of a transcendent dimension, a sense of wonder, love and gratitude, as well as compassion and kindness. Healthy spirituality supports freedom, autonomy, self-esteem and social responsibility. It does not deny our humanity or depend on suppression or denial of emotions. On the contrary, it encourages listening to the heart and trusting the wisdom of intuition.[6]

As an innate capacity that exists in every human being, then, spirituality cannot be limited to any set of doctrines or practices. From a psychological perspective, spirituality is a universal experience, not a universal theology. Spirituality may be theistic, atheistic or polytheistic. It can also be humanistic, as expressed in the work of Abraham Maslow. Spirituality can be found everywhere, not only in temples, churches and synagogues, not only in the stars, not only in music and song and dance, not only in the beauty of nature or the intimacy of a love relationship, but in every moment of every day of ordinary life. Authentic, healthy spiritual freedom can be found at the heart of the great religions and in no religion.

Spirituality is often awakened in the presence of death and whenever the heart opens fully to love without fear. Those who have found a source of peace, truth and love within themselves become the teachers who show us the way. As Mahatma Gandhi said, "My life is my message." And so it is with every one of us.

Healthy spirituality is based on experience rather than dogma, respecting individual rights and different forms of worship. It is associated with psychological health, creativity and compassion, and rests on *insight* or seeing through illusion. Characteristics of healthy spirituality are also characteristic of psychological maturity. For example:

Authenticity: A commitment to being responsible and true to oneself. This means living in accordance with professed beliefs and being consistent in thoughts, words, feelings and actions.

Letting go of the past: Living fully in the present means letting go of guilt, shame and resentment associated with the past. Identifying and releasing negative emotions is necessary groundwork for both psychological health and spiritual freedom.

Facing our fears: Healthy spirituality contributes to reducing anxiety and releasing fear. When we are willing to face the truth about ourselves, deepening spiritual awareness leads to an increasing sense of inner peace and equanimity.

Insight and forgiveness: When we see through illusions and understand ourselves better we can accept forgiveness and extend it to others. Psychotherapy often focuses on self-forgiveness, while spiritual teachings usually emphasize forgiving others. Both are necessary for spiritual freedom.

Love and compassion: Giving and receiving love in personal relationships is a measure of both psychological and spiritual health. When a source of love is discovered within, as it is in spiritual experience, it can be extended to others without demands for repayment. Relationships can then be based on mutual respect and sufficiency rather than on deficiency needs.

Awareness: The cultivation of noninterfering attention to the inner and the outer world of perception helps us recognize the power of the mind and the distortions of self-deception. Witnessing reality—temporal and eternal, finite and infinite—includes cultivating awareness of body, mind, psyche, soul and spirit.

Peace: Making peace with ourselves means accessing inner peace that can be cultivated and extended to others. Authentic inner peace does not mean living in isolation, but in discovering our own true nature and living in harmony with other people and the environment.

Freedom: Healthy psychological and spiritual growth is liberating. By releasing us from limiting, egocentric self-concepts it promises freedom from the shackles of fear and ignorance and awakens our creative potential.

Community: Since our lives are embedded in an intricate network of relationships, spirituality cannot be isolated from community. Those who are spiritually and psychologically mature are both realistic and altruistic, valuing themselves and others not only for what they are, but also for what they can become.[7]

Underlying both personal impulses to growth and all creative cultural enterprises is the fundamental impulse that seeks unitive consciousness. Ken Wilber points out that all motivational drives are subsets of the fundamental spiritual drive to attain unity with the Absolute.[8] Each successive stage of psychospiritual development achieves a higher order of unity. At each stage the self seeks unity in accordance with the constraints of the particular self-concept with which it identifies. The gratifications of each stage are the illusions that prevent liberation if we mistake them for the end of the path.

SPIRITUALITY AND ADDICTION

His craving for alcohol was the equivalent, on a low level, of the spiritual thirst of our being for wholeness, expressed in medieval language: the union with God.[9]

–C. G. JUNG

The shadow of addiction inflicts intense suffering on everyone who struggles with craving for chemical substances or other ego gratifications. Imprisoned in a private hell of fear, rage and desire, the addict attempts to ameliorate the pain of existence by avoiding reality. The search for temporary respite in transient altered states that reduce awareness is sustained only at tremendous cost to oneself and to society at large.

A former client came up to me one day at a conference, about two years after we had worked together on her addictive patterns of behavior. She said, "Thank you for setting me on the path to freedom." I could see that she was much healthier and happier than when I had last seen her, and I knew she had continued the work we started in the consulting room on her own. She had faced her demons and had the courage to claim her freedom.

Addiction can be physical, emotional, mental or spiritual, and since all addictions involve escape from self-awareness, they block psychological growth and spiritual development. As a compulsive, repetitive pattern of behavior, addiction is characterized by clinging to what is familiar and fear of letting go. Those who suffer from addiction often feel they have no control over their dysfunctional behavior. In this state of mind free choice seems to be an illusion.

The road to recovery from addiction, which demands courage, commitment and ruthless honesty, is sometimes precipitated by an involuntary death-rebirth experience or the desperation of hitting bottom. In many cases the challenge is a choice between self-destruction and self-transcendence.

A woman recovering from alcoholism described her experience of hitting bottom as falling into a bottomless pit of despair. For her there was no hope, no possibility of help or redemption. Her faith in God had been shattered. She no longer believed in fairy tales of the supernatural. She had experienced nothing but pain, shame and degradation in her life, falling into destructive relationships that always left her feeling worse about herself and her inability to be close to another human being. Flooded with memories of childhood abuse, she had sought oblivion in alcohol, only to find herself sinking deeper and deeper into despair. Even her rage had deserted her. She no longer cared whether she lived or died. If she had the courage, she would have ended her life, hoping that death was the end of it all. But she felt incapable of willing anything, even her own death.

She had experienced blackouts before. Her recent episode did not seem different; she could not remember what had happened. But when she awakened in the hospital, she remembered what she thought was a dream. In the dream she was moving through a tunnel in which she saw several of her deceased relatives. At the end of the tunnel was an intense but gentle and loving white light that seemed to be drawing her closer. As she approached she heard herself talking to a being of light. She said she did not want to go back to the world. The being asked her to look back, to see what she could see now. A scene of a family unfolded before her, ordinary people going about their lives on an ordinary day. Each one longed to be close to one or more of the others. They wanted to be together, but when they were together, they did not know how to communicate and usually found fault with each other. She wanted to tell them what they really wanted, but she could not make herself heard. She felt the emotional pain of their isolation and useless suffering, and she wanted to help.

When she awakened in her exhausted body, she felt, for the first time, that she was thankful to be alive. In time, the spark of life within her which had not been totally extinguished slowly began to reassert itself. As she began the long, slow journey of recovery she often reexperienced times of helplessness and hopelessness. But something had changed. Now she was able to reclaim her freedom to choose life, to ask for help and to reach for the possibility of healing. She had come so close to death, it was no longer something she wanted to avoid; neither did she long for it, as she had before.

Every addiction has an element of self-deception and escape from freedom. Anyone can get caught by addiction to food, drugs, religion, romantic love or whatever seems to offer an escape from loneliness and anxiety. Addiction is essentially an involuntary, passive state, sometimes described as possession, in which the addict feels helpless, the will seemingly taken over by something alien to the self. Addicts think there is nothing they can change and may resign themselves to living with despair. Whatever the addiction, the addict does not even dream of freedom.

Whether one becomes addicted to drugs, sex or spiritual experiences, the outcome is similar: one suffers when one is not in the desired state of oblivion to the pain of existence, and the desired state is always temporary. Even in the moments one might wish could last forever, extension leads to boredom, fatigue, disappointment and disillusion. When transient gratifications are no longer sufficient—and every one of them palls in time— the impulse to reach for a state of consciousness that is more genuinely satisfying can be awakened and encouraged.

Many people who are recovering from addictions describe themselves as being on a spiritual path, although few claim formal affiliation with religion. As spirituality becomes more widely accepted as essential to well-being and wholeness, it becomes increasingly important to distinguish healthy spirituality from forms of spirituality that are potentially addictive.

ADDICTIVE SPIRITUALITY

Nothing is everything. In order to grow strong you must first sink your roots deep into nothingness and learn to face your loneliest loneliness.[10]
—IRVIN YALOM

Like other addictions, addiction to spirituality can begin because it helps alleviate pain and may be sought as compensation for loneliness and lack of love. However, addiction to certain forms of spirituality, like addiction to pleasure in any form, can become the opposite of what it was intended to be. For example, if a person becomes addicted to the emotional highs resulting from practices that induce altered states, the consequences of the addiction can be destructive.

One young woman who broke off her engagement to a man she loved to join a spiritual group that offered emotional highs later felt she had made a mistake. Once having made the commitment, however, her loyalty to the group was unflagging, and she became one of the teachers, all of whom worked very hard. After about seven years she became disillusioned with her guru and the politics of the organization and left the group. She mourned the loss of the strong bonds of community which the group had offered and the deep feelings of love which her guru had kindled. She went through several months of depression, feeling cut off from any spirituality as she made the effort to adjust to living alone and supporting herself. The possibility of finding a source of spiritual renewal within herself seemed hopeless. She knew that she needed to meditate and take time for spiritual practice but found it very difficult without the support of the group. When she felt sad and lonely, she remembered the good things and forgot the emotional abuse she had suffered. When we spoke she kept reiterating that her former life had not been all bad. In time, as she learned to trust herself more and felt stronger about her ability to be on her own, she began to discover that her spiritual life could indeed be renewed and did not depend on anyone else. The soul did not die in the fire that had consumed her ego, but it needed a long period of healing before it could rise like a phoenix out of the ashes of despair.

A variety of refined states of consciousness and subtle phenomena such as sound and light can be extremely pleasurable. In Buddhism these might be identified as experiences of pseudo-nirvana. At any stage these altered states may offer seductive escapes from painful existential realities.

Instead of opening the heart and mind to a larger reality, unrestrained indulgence in addictive patterns of behavior can become a source of separation, pain and suffering. Although they may offer a taste of bliss and a temporary antidote to loneliness, whenever practices are bolstered by denial, inspired by guilt or pursued as an avoidance of relationship, they can become addictive. This risk may not be recognized until specific practices stop working, or until the desire for more intensity becomes a problem.

Spirituality can also be addictive when it breeds dependency. If it leads to avoidance of developmental tasks such as intimacy and autonomy, it can be detrimental to psychological health. Health, maturity and freedom demand coming to terms with the totality of existence. However, in a culture that devalues the sacred quest, people who are hungry for a taste of spirituality may willingly submit to almost anyone claiming to be a spiritual teacher. The desire to be as a child, free from the anxiety of not having answers to existential questions, trusting in a powerful, wise parent figure who offers guidance and protection can be very compelling. The decision to abdicate personal freedom is reinforced by projecting intuitive discernment onto the teacher and interpreting everything as a teaching. Potentially addictive forms of spirituality often appeal to people who have difficulty coping with the world on their own.

On the other hand, spiritual experiences and practices can be profoundly nourishing and healing when they are appropriately integrated into the fabric of life. Healthy contemplative practice requires a foundation of personal integrity as well as a competent teacher. It also calls for a commitment to be true to oneself. Transcendence of egocentricity does not imply abandoning oneself or neglecting relationships. Attention to every aspect of life with love, compassion and open-mindedness is a natural result of psychologically mature spirituality. Spirituality takes many forms in response to questions of ultimate meaning. Claiming spiritual freedom means finding the form best suited to our particular needs at a given time.

Reflecting on wholeness and balance as represented by symbols of integration such as the cross and the circle can sometimes help us bring our spiritual life into balance. Delving into the depths of the inner world and reaching for the infinite can be balanced by awareness of our spiritual connection with others and our dependence on the whole biospheric web of life. Nothing is excluded from the circle of wholeness. Even the preoccupations of ego can be viewed as stepping stones that contribute to healing by enabling us to reclaim what has been overlooked and restoring a sense of balance in our lives.

OBSTACLES TO SPIRITUAL FREEDOM

We kill gods but we sanctify their replacements—teachers, artists, beautiful women.[11]

—IRVIN YALOM

Psychotherapists often encounter people who have used spirituality as a means of repressing, denying and avoiding psychological problems. For example, a dysfunctional family may be very religious and attend church regularly, yet refuse to acknowledge the psychological pain of its members because of an unspoken rule that feelings are not to be discussed. Others may think that as long as they perform some formal ritual they are entitled to indulge egocentricities or exploit others with impunity. On the other hand, spirituality that is not connected to tradition runs the risk of deteriorating into magical thinking and superstition. Although the seeds of authentic spirituality can be found in both traditional and innovative forms of worship, it is sometimes difficult to distinguish between genuine and counterfeit spirituality.

Anyone can become intoxicated with status and success. Power is potentially corrupting, and even those who have attained some degree of realization may discover that when others are eager to listen, admire and believe every word, a spiritual teacher can also become inflated. Furthermore, charlatans tend to resemble genuine spiritual teachers quite closely. They themselves may be convinced that their teaching is authentic. In some cases, clear teaching does come through individuals who still have work to do on their own egos to resolve problems related to money, sex and power. It is often difficult for the untrained observer to distinguish the genuine from the counterfeit, or to separate true teachings from the imperfections of the teacher.

The philosophy of Taoism tells us that leadership is problematic when people are afraid of the leader. It is better when people love the leader, and best of all when the people say, "We have done this ourselves." Recognizing that power over others is a developmental stage that is outgrown when a person matures into awareness of interdependence and shared responsibility may enable a person to evaluate types of leadership more clearly. In healthy psychological development when a child outgrows dependency, he or she may go through a period of rebellion or counterdependency. As the young person matures, he or she establishes a sense of independence and later may realize that we are all interdependent. With the recognition of interdependence comes the desire to share power and make a contribution to the world.

When a person is rigorously ascetic and aversion to power predominates, judgmental attitudes may indicate a strong defensive reaction against unconscious impulses to dominance and control. It is often easier to criticize and find fault with others than to make a creative contribution to constructive change. The middle way that passes between the opposites, that leads beyond conflicts of greed and aversion to a reconciliation of opposites, neither condemns nor pursues illusions of power and control. Discernment of the middle way between denial and indulgence seems necessary for those who aspire to spiritual freedom.

Finding the midpoint between denial and indulgence is easy for most people to recognize with regard to sexual drives. Some people believe that sexuality must be repressed in order to preserve the social order. Others believe that uninhibited sexuality reduces conflict and violence. Whatever the cultural beliefs, a person has to make personal decisions about when to act on sexual impulses and when to suppress them. Many people think that these are the only options. It can be a revelation to discover that one can allow the feelings to be as they are without either acting them out or turning them off. Sexual feelings are not bad. What we do with them, either repressing them or acting out, can cause trouble. For example, St. Augustine's repressive attitudes toward sexuality that prescribed total abstinence have been interpreted as a reaction against his strong sexual drives which were acted out early in his life.

Finding the middle way also implies dealing with emotions such as anger in a similar way. Anger cannot be denied or repressed. Nor can it be acted out with impunity. As we become more empowered, we can learn to accept anger and communicate it without attack. If we indulge it whenever we feel angry, we run the risk of reinforcing the habit rather than freeing ourselves from it. When we see that anger is often associated with fear and unmet expectations—we get angry when someone does not live up to our expectations or when we are afraid—we have the option of revising our expectations and facing our fears, and anger is less likely to arise.

If freedom is the goal, the seeker needs to recognize how it can be subverted in the name of progress toward any unattainable ideal, such as never having negative emotions. However, spiritual bondage is a state of mind that can change, and spiritual development has predictable stages on the way to freedom. Teachings that say there is nowhere to go and nothing to do are rarely appreciated by the beginner. Devotion to a path is helpful until one awakens from dreams of bondage into a reality where the soul is free.

Teachings that free the mind from the shadow of constricting concepts point beyond illusions altogether to the ineffable reality they represent. While illusions may be stepping stones to liberation along the way, they can also prevent recognition of freedom. For example, recognizing family patterns that tend to be repeated unconsciously in our lives can help us overcome dysfunctional behaviors at a certain stage in our personal development. When a person becomes overly analytical, however, he or she can begin to view everything through this perceptual filter, assuming that the present is determined by the past and failing to appreciate the freedom inherent in the present moment. Progress on the path of freedom is evident when a person is no longer haunted by the shadows of the past, and fear, anger and constriction are replaced by love, wisdom and ethical responsibility.

Freedom is often obscured for the beginner by self-deception and self-doubt. Self-betrayal and lack of discernment can preclude the possibility of freedom. The seeker who has made a commitment to effort and practice may be constrained by either spiritual pride or unworthiness. I remember Margaret, a well-educated, competent young woman who lacked both self-esteem and self-trust. She seemed willing to believe whatever anyone else said, while distrusting her own experience. It was difficult for her to believe in her own abilities. She had spent several years in a relationship that was detrimental to her self-esteem. Her boyfriend discouraged any sign of independence in her, while making her feel guilty about the financial support that she had accepted from him. He also reminded her of all the ways she was not "spiritual." Whenever she was with him, Margaret felt consistently inadequate and dependent and thought she should be grateful that he wanted to be with her. When she finally stopped trying to live up to his expectations and meet his demands, Margaret began to discover that she did have a deep spiritual sensitivity, but she did not see that she was free to leave and become self-supporting. When she finally gathered the courage to leave the relationship, she said, "I wish I hadn't waited so long to claim my freedom and my life."

When suffering is idealized and regarded as more desirable than happiness, rigorous spiritual practices may be fueled by aversion to life. I know more than one person who has sought sanctuary in one meditation retreat after another, avoiding the challenges of relationship and being in the world. On the other hand, sometimes a genuine desire for deepening inner experience seems to be in conflict with the demands of the outer world. In such cases a person may feel torn between commitments to family and the urge to spend time in contemplation. Such conflicts need to be resolved rather that denied. The challenge of integrating spirituality with living in the world cannot be avoided.

In the following section we will consider how spiritual ambition, spiritual specialness, confrontation with the personal shadow and purification rituals can be both obstacles and stepping stones to liberation. We will also see how symbols and idols that draw us deeper into the spiritual quest can be both illuminating and entangling. When we understand the relative value of these devices and develop discernment and discrimination, we may discover the unexpected joy of spiritual freedom.

Spiritual experiences

> *Truth waits for eyes unclouded by longing.*
>
> —RAM DASS

Spiritual experiences that seem to reveal truth often have a liberating effect. They can stimulate psychological growth and radically alter perceptions of reality. At times, however, it is necessary to distinguish experiences that provide insight and contribute to psychological health from those that are regressive and potentially damaging. Furthermore, experiences that are beneficial at one stage of development may not be beneficial at another stage. In the context of psychotherapy, any experience, regressive or visionary, can be grist for the mill of the therapeutic process, provided that the therapist does not make inappropriate interpretations or confuse genuine experiences of self-transcendence with regression to undifferentiated prepersonal states in which distinctions are obliterated. *To transcend* means to go beyond, to outgrow, differentiating and including the earlier stages in a larger view or sense of self. For example, transcending the ego does not mean obliterating the ego and becoming dysfunctional. It means expanding the sense of identity to include more than what is designated by ego. One might say, "I have a strong, healthy ego, but I am not my ego."

The first glimpse of states of consciousness that transcend ordinary reality can be both fascinating and seductive. A taste of bliss or a sense of being at home in the universe can be more compelling than other desires. Such transpersonal experiences can help people wean themselves from chemical addictions and can be a valuable tool for recovery.[12] Transpersonal experiences can also be frightening to those who are unprepared for them. Problems may develop when the person does not have a healthy psychological foundation that permits recognizing the value of the experience without idolizing the person or the method that induced it.

In a letter to Bill Wilson, the founder of Alcoholics Anonymous, Carl Jung made the following comment regarding spiritual experience as an antidote to the craving for alcohol:

> The only right and legitimate way to such an experience is that it happens to you in reality, and it can only happen to you when you walk on a path which leads you to higher understanding . . . beyond the confines of mere rationalism.[13]

When the longing for spiritual experience is no longer satisfied by conventional religion, all kinds of false mysticism may emerge. Substitute gratifications take many forms, including codependent relationships and fanatical patriotism. Sharing transpersonal experiences with a group can lead to a feeling of belonging that is a welcome alternative to feelings of isolation and alienation. However, whenever critical intelligence is discarded in favor of emotional experiences or blind devotion to a person or cause, addiction and idolatry become a risk.

Reactions that sometimes follow initiation into this realm of experiences can be detrimental both in terms of generating dependency and in leading a person to believe that the source of the experience is outside in a substance, a person or a group rather than within oneself. For example, unconscious projections of power and wisdom onto the initiator can contribute to feelings of helplessness and dependency.

I remember one former cult member saying how impressed he was with the leader's psychic powers and how much he liked the feeling of belonging to a group ostensibly devoted to spiritual work. The leader was purported to be able to see a person's soul and to know if someone was possessed or controlled by alien entities. If he said they were, his followers believed him, and the person would then be subjected to intensive purification processes, sometimes involving long periods of isolation. Group members also learned how to control others by playing on their weaknesses. Individuals would be subjected to verbal abuse in the name of "ego reduction," presumably to help them disidentify from ego. Group pressure can be difficult to resist in any circumstances. When couched in terms of spiritual purification, it can be even more damaging.

Abuses of power in the name of spiritual purification are not new. Emphasis on sin and guilt is also used in more traditional settings for the purpose of keeping people in line. The question is, how are intelligent people drawn into practices that seem so irrational to the outsider? There seems to be no easy answer. Part of it may be a misguided idealism coupled with the belief that suffering is good for you. Another part of it seems to be the intensity of experience afforded by group rituals.

The hazards of dependency on a group must be acknowledged if one is to benefit from the profound changes that can occur when a person is given the opportunity to participate in practices that facilitate a genuine opening to Spirit. Whereas true mysticism, found at the core of the perennial philosophy and the world's wisdom teachings, heals the craving for substitute gratifications, false mysticism reinforces it.

Denial of the shadow

The flame of belief is fueled inexhaustibly by the fears of death, oblivion and meaninglessness.[14]

—IRVIN YALOM

Projection of the dark, negative shadow onto others is evident in spiritual groups that see themselves as unique in their dedication to truth and righteousness and devalue outsiders. Those who tend to divide the world into believers and nonbelievers are likely to project their own unresolved fears onto the other, whoever it happens to be. The dichotomies that reinforce the position that what *we* believe is right and what *others* believe is wrong leads to defensiveness and attack. Religious wars are not over. We have witnessed them recently on several continents, and Jews are still subjected to anti-Semitism in some places. Wars and persecution can happen anywhere, whenever a group believes it has a monopoly on truth. Obviously, these hallmarks of cult behavior can be found not only in religious groups, but also in secular society.[15]

Respect for other people's beliefs is essential to spiritual freedom. Respect does not imply agreement. It does mean that others are entitled to different points of view. Healthy spirituality does not presume that there is only one way to find the truth. Sometimes people who call themselves spiritual are in fact bigoted, judgmental and condemning of anyone who does not accept their dogma or belief system. At the same time, the opposite position that says all beliefs are equal is untenable. Some are obviously more bigoted and intolerant than others. The challenge for the seeker is to find those authentic teachers that embody wisdom and compassion and practice what they preach.

The psychological mechanisms of projection, whereby we accuse others of what we have not acknowledged in ourselves, and denial, whereby we pretend to ourselves as well as others not to know what is true, operate unconsciously. Those who see themselves as perfectly good while regarding others as evil are generally not aware of projecting their unacceptable impulses onto their enemies. It takes a certain degree of psychological maturity to acknowledge that the shadow, symbolizing what we most fear and dislike, must also be uncovered in ourselves.

Since nobody is perfect and we can learn from others' mistakes as well as our own, it can be useful to regard those who disagree with us as potential teachers from whom we can learn about different perceptions of reality. This seems to be a more rational, democratic and compassionate attitude than one which assumes others are wrong. Furthermore, it enables us to empathize and communicate with a wide variety of human beings who have different views of reality and nevertheless share the same longings for love and meaning in their lives.

Idealistic new converts to religious groups are particularly susceptible to projection of the shadow and to belief in their own infallibility. New converts are often used as recruiters, because they are usually fervent in their enthusiasm for the newly discovered joys of belonging to a group that has access to special knowledge. They have yet to be disillusioned or disappointed when newly accepted beliefs fail to provide anticipated rewards. A new convert is like a person who has fallen in love, blind to even obvious faults and unwilling to subject the object of adoration to critical examination. Sometimes swept away by an exhilarating taste of ecstasy, a new convert genuinely wants others to share in this wonderful experience and fails, as we all do within our own belief system, to recognize proverbial blind spots. New converts rarely seek therapy, hence integration of the shadow is unlikely until a dark night of the soul leads to the necessity of inner work.

Guilt and purification

> *Release from guilt as you would be released. There is no other way to look within and see the light of love . . .*[16]
>
> –A Course in Miracles

When spirituality is motivated by guilt and fear, it becomes psychologically crippling. A person suffering from low self-esteem can exacerbate his or her psychological problems by irrational feelings of guilt for perfectly natural human impulses such as anger and sexuality. Fear of punishment by some external authority, either human or supernatural, tends to keep a person locked into ritualized behavior designed to avoid punishment either in this world or in the hereafter. Fear may be related to the belief that if one is happy then something bad will happen or to fear of hellfire or an unfavorable reincarnation. This fear may contribute to a desire for self-mortification and sacrifice. It also makes one susceptible to manipulation by spiritual authorities who claim to know what one must do to ensure protection or a favorable afterlife. Sacrifices meant to propitiate the gods are only one form of ritualized behavior designed to ward off evil when one is bedeviled by guilt.

Fear of punishment is commonly associated with feelings of unworthiness and contributes to the widespread practice of purification rituals. These rituals can be beneficial or damaging, depending on how they are conducted and interpreted. Confession, for example, can have a healing effect on a person who feels unburdened, absolved from guilt and encouraged to start over with strengthened resolve to avoid past mistakes and find a better way. Psychotherapy often serves this purpose. On the other hand, if confession is simply a formality, it is useless, at best. At worst, if a person feels judged, confession can exacerbate feelings of guilt and unworthiness.

Group rituals of purification can also be powerful. Revealing long-kept secrets, discussing taboo topics and participating in nonverbal group activities such as chanting, dancing or playing music, all contribute to a feeling of bonding and belonging. Some spiritual groups tend to repress emotions; others encourage emotional sharing. Group meetings devoted to public confession of personal history that encourage everyone to reveal their darkest secrets serve the purpose of group bonding, while undermining individual pair bonding. These rituals also contribute to building a sense of loyalty and specialness in group members. Those who have been through initiation or purification rituals are the insiders, privy to secret knowledge and experiences that others presumably could not understand. When these practices exacerbate the dichotomy between *us* and *them*, however, they can become egocentric investments in self-righteousness.

Ram Dass speaks of the time in his spiritual journey when he realized that he was willing to embrace suffering and perceived suffering as grace. Then he realized that he was more willing to embrace suffering than to embrace joy, because it allowed him to hold on to his righteousness. One of the risks of purification, then, is the investment in self-righteousness that can ensue if the rituals have the desired effect of relieving the burdens of guilt. Whether the investment is in seeing oneself as especially pure or especially guilty, the ideal of purity can be an obstacle to recognizing our common humanity as the ground of authentic spirituality.

Spiritual ambition

The Bodhisattva's mind is like the void, for he relinquishes everything and does not even desire to accumulate merits.[17]

–HUANG PO

Beginning students of spirituality are likely to replace worldly ambition with spiritual ambition. Here the hazards of entrapment are similar to those in the secular world. The passionate pursuit that assumes grace is contingent on effort often precludes the experience of surrender and awakening.

The seeker who has made a commitment to effort in the pursuit of spiritual development can easily become inflated by a sense of personal achievement. Although such feelings of elation are often followed by deflation or depression, the problem is exacerbated when a person believes he or she must only try harder to attain the goal. The failure to temper spiritual ambition with ordinary existence can exacerbate the pain.

The question of the relative merits of effort and surrender reflects a perennial religious debate about whether people are saved through grace or effort. Some religions, such as Buddhism and Christianity, for example, are divided on this question along sectarian lines.

From a psychological perspective, both grace and effort are necessary. Relative emphasis on one or the other depends on the circumstances and personality of each individual. The person who follows a path of effort achieves liberation; the one who follows a path of surrender receives a gift of grace. Since both ways assume a subject/object dualism, both are instrumental, and both serve a purpose. Usually those who are overly ambitious need to learn something about trust, surrender and grace, whereas those who tend to be passive can benefit from making more effort and learning about the power of intention.

For instance, if you think you have arrived at this point in your life because of your own effort, notice the events that have made a difference that you did not arrange. If you feel that you have arrived at this point not owing to any effort on your part, but because of grace, karma, luck or other external circumstances, you may need to exercise intention and your own creative capacity. Conscious construction of reality in a postmodern world depends on intention and creative imagination. The danger lies in overlooking the fact that you do not do it alone.

Effort and surrender are both necessary for illumination and enlightenment. The hubris that results from exclusive attention to effort, or from false humility in surrender, can be devastating. Sooner or later both have to be given up. Until then, however, one is free to choose.

Appropriate psychotherapy can contribute to reducing anxiety and alleviating depression associated with spiritual ambition and false humility. For example, a clinician familiar with meditation, can assess the appropriateness of different types of meditation for a particular person and make relevant recommendations, while avoiding the pitfalls of a dogmatic or narrow approach.[18] In some cases, if a client is in the habit of praying, I have found it useful to ask how he or she prays and sometimes suggest variations. Since few people discuss their prayer habits with anyone other than a priest or a minister, they may not be aware of the psychological effects of different types of prayer.

In one case a man who was making every effort to pray and meditate each day complained that he could not concentrate, being obsessed by aggressive fantasies of uncontrolled rage, no matter how hard he tried to shut them out. After he had communicated this difficulty to me and we explored what meaning the intrusive thoughts had for him, working with them as if they were dreams, he was able to relax more easily, and the inner peace he had been praying for became increasingly accessible.

It seems evident that there is no one way that works for everyone. Furthermore, the same person may need to try different approaches at different stages of life. Each person must be willing to face the challenges and search for the way that is best suited to him or her at a particular time.

Spiritual specialness

The arising and the elimination of illusion are both illusory. Illusion is not something rooted in Reality; it exists because of your dualistic thinking. If you will only cease to indulge in opposed concepts such as 'ordinary' and 'Enlightened,' illusion will cease of itself.[19]

–HUANG PO

The desire for spiritual specialness, which is often related to spiritual ambition, lends itself easily to manipulation and control. Those who have special status in religious communities may be granted special privileges, and unquestioning compliance is often encouraged and reinforced. The more elaborate the spiritual hierarchy, the more entangling it can be. Particularly when the hierarchies are esoteric, secret and hidden, the implicit promise of power and status to be bestowed on the faithful leads many well-intentioned seekers down sidetracks that end in despair.

The assumption that spirituality is the privilege of an elect few rather that being available to everyone turns out to be another shadow that inhibits freedom. The real secrets of esoteric teachings protect themselves because the subtle meaning of words that refer to spiritual realities cannot be understood intellectually by those who have no contemplative training or other direct experience of what they are meant to convey. For example, a person who has no experience of transpersonal states of consciousness may argue that they do not exist or that they are purely wish-fulfilling fantasies. To one who is familiar with transpersonal states, on the other hand, they can be clearly differentiated and are just as real as the world of objects or ideas.

Those who are unwilling to explore a path for fear of being duped may miss an opportunity for valuable learning. Hence, being specially skeptical is no better than being specially gullible. The task is to develop discernment without judging what one does not understand. This can be done when we are open to doing a practice or undertaking a discipline that facilitates a larger view or a new perspective rather than reinforcing our existing prejudices. For example, it is difficult to explain what happens in meditation to someone who has never tried it. When we are willing to try it, we may discover for ourselves the subtle benefits that we could not otherwise appreciate.

Healthy spirituality makes no claim to specialness. Yet anyone on the path can fall prey to pride and spiritual specialness. Spirituality is a precious gift; at the same time, it is nothing special, since everyone has an innate capacity for it. Counting oneself as equal to others, no more important and no less important than anyone else, can help one avoid the trap of regarding oneself as either specially blessed or specially unworthy.

I believe that claims to specialness in any form obscure the possibility of spiritual freedom. Even the desire to be nobody can become a distortion of this task. Zen Master Thich Nhat Hanh has said that attachment to the idea of no-self is just as detrimental as attachment to any self-concept.[20]

Jack Kornfield tells the following story of two rabbis to illustrate this point:

> One day a rabbi entered the temple and began to pray. He said, "O Lord, I am nobody. O Lord, I am nobody." Soon his assistant came in and hearing the rabbi praying thus, he was moved to join him and also began to pray. "O Lord, I am nobody." Soon the janitor came along and he too was inspired to pray and knelt down and said, "O Lord, I am nobody." Thereupon the rabbi's assistant remarked, "Look who thinks he's nobody!"

Transpersonal psychologists have emphasized the importance of becoming somebody before you can be nobody.[21] In other words, ego identity must be claimed before it can be released. Transcendence of egocentricity in generativity and altruism appears to be a natural expression of psychological maturity and spiritual freedom.

A person lacking ego strength tends to be defensive, to resist change and to be motivated primarily by fear. A weak ego also implies low self-esteem and a negative self-image, both of which are associated with attachment to specialness. Transcendence of ego in spiritual freedom does not mean self-abnegation. Ego becomes relatively less important, while still necessary. From a transpersonal perspective, ego, like the rational mind, is a good servant and a poor master. The ego is typically concerned with survival and security. However, if it is discarded or ignored, a person can fall easily into pathological patterns of codependency, which means making other peoples' needs and desires more important than one's own. The ego has its tasks to perform in carrying out personal responsibilities, but tends to obstruct the awakening of soul when it is predominantly motivated by fear. The relationship of the ego to the soul can be compared to that of a driver to the owner of a carriage. The driver is in charge of carrying out directions given by the owner. If we carry the analogy one step further, the carriage can be compared to the body, which must be maintained in good condition if it is to be a reliable vehicle for carrying out the soul's purpose. As development progresses and these differentiated parts become increasingly well integrated, they function more smoothly and effectively.

Giving up unworthiness, or identification with being a victim, can be just as difficult as giving up self-importance in other disguises. Heroic fantasies of self-sacrifice take many forms. Anyone prone to codependency will be susceptible to them, and all of them are obstacles to spiritual freedom.

Growing up in a sexist patriarchal culture women are particularly susceptible to attachment to a negative self-image. Others, particularly men, are perceived to be more intelligent, competent and wise. They may be specially attracted to spiritual teachers on whom they can project the good father image of a wise and powerful protector. Patriarchal religions reinforce women's sense of inferiority whenever they are denied equal rights.

For example, I have often heard Catholic women express feelings of frustration and unworthiness about being denied the right to be priests. Furthermore, they resent being denied free choice about contraception and reproduction by men who are committed to celibacy. I also remember a woman expressing her dismay after traveling with her husband on a pilgrimage to Asia in the 1980s. Wherever they went, she discovered that men and women were not given the same teachings and nuns were always expected to defer to monks.

The search for the wise father is obviously not limited to women. Men who have grown up in this culture may also seek a substitute parent. To the extent that a spiritual teacher provides this, dependency is cultivated. Unless such transference (the projection of parental expectations onto the teacher) is handled impeccably, it can be detrimental to both teacher and student. The burden of freedom can weigh heavily on the shoulders of one who feels incompetent to judge or evaluate spiritual teachings, yet each one must choose whom to trust, whom to obey and whom to follow. If you do not trust your own experience, how can you possibly know whom to trust?

Perhaps a democratic approach that trusts the human capacity for intuitive discernment of truth and encourages peer relationships, while acknowledging that teachers know more than students, is better than traditional authoritarian models. Theologian Rhinehold Niebuhr pointed out that pessimism regarding human nature leads to tyrannical political strategies. He said that the human capacity for justice makes democracy possible, while the inclination to injustice makes democracy necessary.[22]

Spiritual discernment is both a gift and a skill that comes from practice and the willingness to see things as they are, giving up wishful thinking and eradicating self-deception insofar as possible, regardless of how difficult it may be. It is not easy to do this alone. It can be accomplished much more easily when we can reflect on the process with others.

Just as a discipline of truth telling can be useful in dispelling the shadows of addiction, a discipline of ordinariness can release the soul from the illusion of specialness. Practicing ordinariness can be a big relief to anyone given to excessive effort and striving. It can also undermine the rationalizations of those who are excessively self-indulgent. This practice is therefore recommended as an effective antidote to any form of spiritual specialness.

Idolatry

If you seek the Buddha outside of the mind, the Buddha changes into a devil.[23]

—DOGEN

Spirituality that focuses on idols or symbols of divinity believed to be the exclusive purveyors of spiritual blessing can be problematic from a psychological perspective since such focus may encourage dependency, avoidance, escapism and denial. Once trapped in a world of illusion, the possibility of transcending concepts and images may be overlooked or dismissed as wishful thinking. Idols that are either conceptual or imaginary can never be argued out of existence. The possibility of seeing through them, as through a veil of illusion, remains the prerogative of those who are willing to see reality rather than clinging to familiar symbols.

Fascination with idols and symbols of spirituality can reinforce illusion. Although such images encourage spiritual awakening at one stage, particularly when identification is shifting from ego to soul, they can become a trap if one becomes attached to them. Likewise, practices that are liberating at one stage can become imprisoning at another time. In guru yoga, for example, idealization of the guru is superseded by identification with the guru and finally with transcendence of form altogether. Getting stuck in the idealization of the guru as a person can interfere with the inner realization of what he or she represents.

The merits of a particular practice, then, can only be evaluated within the context of an individual's experience and stage of development. Letting go of previously cherished representations of the sacred is a challenge everyone encounters sooner or later on the path to spiritual freedom.

Devotion to a person as an idol can also mask death anxiety. Although abdicating decisions about life to a teacher may be comforting when obedience leads to a feeling of being protected, each person on a path of freedom eventually confronts aloneness. Sometimes disobedience is necessary for psychological health and spiritual freedom. Leaving a teacher can be just as important as finding a teacher at the appropriate time. We might say that when the student is ready, the teacher disappears.

Eventually authentic spiritual development leads to becoming one's own authority. It is not necessary to go through orthodox religious channels to experience love or attain illumination, although we have much to learn from religious traditions. Taking responsibility for choosing beliefs, values and attitudes calls for examining spiritual assumptions in the light of reason and experience. Healthy spirituality does not call for faith in idols, but for a willing acceptance of life itself as a meaningful encounter with truth.

THE FREE SPIRIT

Journeying from the relative toward the Absolute means at once losing the freedom of living in error and gaining freedom from the tyranny of all the psycho-material determinations which imprison and stifle the soul.[24]

—Seyyed Hossein Nasr

The mysteries of secret rites designed to awaken the soul have been a part of esoteric religion since antiquity. Unfortunately, when these rites and rituals become codified, they can inhibit the natural impulse toward spiritual freedom and become a prison for the soul.

In the evolution of consciousness, increasing degrees of spiritual freedom are attained with each level of consciousness— the gross (physical), subtle, causal (formless) and nondual. In each case, transcending the limitations of one level offers freedom in the expanse of the next. For example, the psychic/subtle domains offer freedom from physical laws, so that in dreams and imagination we can fly, go through solid objects and be free of the limitations of space and time. At this level, however, there is still a distinction between the observer and the observed, between subject and object. The soul may be experienced as a being of light, but it is still a discrete, separate entity. At the causal level dualities disappear in the formlessness of vast, unmanifest emptiness. The sense of separate self dissolves. Whereas in the subtle level the soul may swim in an ocean of bliss, at the causal level there is only pure awareness. There is no separate entity to do the swimming. The nondual, in turn, is the level where even the distinction between form and formlessness disappears. Hence it is referred to as "not two."

The surrender of illusions that constitute a prison for the soul at any level of consciousness requires faith, not in a specific form of divinity, but in the nature of reality. In the absence of experience, a person may take the promise of freedom on faith. On the basis of faith a person may be able to relax the defensive constraints of ordinary consciousness sufficiently to experience some release.

In dreaming, for example, faith can make it easier for someone to become lucid and transform fear of falling into flying or fear of death into transcendence. When faith is strong a person may endure incredible hardships, as some prisoners of war have done. Faith can enable a person to receive divine guidance and continue spiritual practice in the face of all kinds of difficulties. Faith is a key to overcoming fear whenever we feel separate and out of touch with the deeper levels of our own being. Faith receives and love gives. When we are not feeling capable of giving love we may benefit from reflecting on where we have placed our faith. Faith helps us open up to receiving love.

Strong faith, in my experience, rests on freedom to doubt. If we are not allowed to doubt and question our faith, it does not get stronger. On the contrary, faith that cannot be questioned becomes increasingly fragile and vulnerable. The loss of faith that is associated with depression and despair is a psychological and spiritual crisis that requires not a new faith that can be lost, but a deeper commitment to witnessing truth, allowing things to be as they are. Spiritual freedom based on faith in one's own experience of truth seems to be manifested naturally in the world as love.

Writing on *The Two Faces of Religion,* psychiatrist N. S. Xavier defines mature spirituality as being based on the dynamic factors of courage, love and wisdom.[25] Wisdom is defined as a healthy balance of reason and intuition. These three factors are intimately connected. It takes courage to act on the basis of love and wisdom, and love means nurturing oneself and others with courage and wisdom.

Among the people I have met who seem to demonstrate mature spirituality are His Holiness the Dalai Lama, Ram Dass, Mother Tessa Bielecki, Sonja Margulies, Brother David Steindl-Rast and Huston Smith. All of them combine a discerning intellect with a compassionate heart and a great sense of humor. All of them also regard themselves as nothing special. The Dalai Lama, who is both the spiritual and political leader of the Tibetan people, describes himself as a simple Buddhist monk.

Ram Dass, who has been the quintessential spiritual seeker ever since he left Harvard in the sixties, has courageously shared his personal journey in a way that has led many others to a spiritual path. Now he devotes himself to service, caring for the dying and raising money for the good works he calls compassionate action.

Ram Dass describes his process in these words:

> I listen from moment to moment, and what I hear changes, and I find that I can't be afraid of being inconsistent if I'm going to listen to truth and allow my uniqueness to manifest. Now I listen, and do what intuitively I must do. . . . The rule book isn't going to be good enough—no matter how fancy its covers and how august its authors.[26]

Mother Tessa is a modern-day contemplative hermit and spiritual mother in the Carmelite tradition, cofounder of The Spiritual Life Institute of America, a monastic community of both men and women. She is the author of *Teresa of Avila,* in which she says,

> The spiritual life is not an abstract, rarified affair relegated to periods of meditation and prayer, rituals and ceremonies, spiritual reading and guidance, our service and acts of charity. The spiritual life is our whole life.[27]

When I first met Sonja Margulies more than twenty years ago, she was a senior editor for the *Journal of Transpersonal Psychology* where I began working as an associate. I regarded her as an older sister whom I admired. She was ordained as a Zen lay practitioner at the time and later became a fully transmitted teacher. During the years that we were colleagues I learned a lot about Zen and started my own daily sitting practice which has lasted ever since. I have witnessed how Sonja has handled many difficult experiences in her life, including the death of her husband, her own battle with cancer and the serious illness of her daughter. Although I seldom see her now, her wisdom, clarity and equanimity continue to be an inspiration to me.

Brother David is a Benedictine monk and Huston Smith is a well-known author and philosopher of religion. What they have in common is that they demonstrate the integrity, kindness, humility and generosity of spirit that I trust and admire.

Many other teachers and friends who have taught me about spiritual maturity have also demonstrated wisdom, compassion, friendliness, courage and reverence for life. Although intellectual brilliance is not necessary for wisdom and spiritual maturity, it certainly does not preclude it. On the contrary, clarity is a great help to those of us who have inquisitive minds. Others, both famous and unknown, whose lives are guided by wisdom and compassion and who have the courage to act in the world, have taught me that mature spirituality is often inconspicuous. Many free spirits prefer to remain invisible.

Spiritual maturity is not about outward, visible signs of spirituality, although these may be present in some cases. More importantly, it is about a certain presence that is perhaps best described as grace. Spiritual maturity may be invisible to those who have not developed sufficient spiritual discernment to be able to see it. At first, a student looking for a teacher in the outer world may expect to find a person that can fill the role as imagined. In time, by turning inward, the student may discover an inner teacher. Eventually, he or she may regard everyone as a teacher.

Just as the world of soul remains invisible to one who does not believe it exists, spiritual maturity cannot be perceived by anyone who is not ready to see it. Spiritual maturity is recognized intuitively. Depth cannot be quantified, and we cannot see clearly beyond our own levels of development. Mature spirituality reflects our latent potentials and when we recognize it we can begin to cultivate it. Interestingly, the more I claim my own potential for spiritual vision and stop projecting it onto others, the more clearly I see it. It is not possible for us to see what is real unless we become real ourselves. The Gnostics say that what you see you shall become.[28]

Indications of spiritual freedom that I have learned to trust include an increased sense of inner peace, a reduction of fear and anxiety, an openness of heart and mind, an increase of kindness and compassion, a willingness to risk loving without attachment, a commitment to truth, authenticity and responsibility, and an acceptance of human frailties. My uniqueness does not separate me from nature. I am in the world and the world is in me. I am only an infinitely small, though not insignificant, part of the whole.

As I proceed along the way of spiritual freedom, I can appreciate both the reality of existential freedom and the value of choosing a particular path. The choices I make determine how I live and how I practice day by day. When what I have achieved seems insignificant and I imagine that climbing the next mountain will change everything, perhaps I will remember that necessary though this may be at a certain stage along the way, satisfaction gained from achievement alone is short lived. The freedom to co-create, to be and do what is deemed most valuable in any given time is a possibility to be realized.

Along the way, when I am attracted to illusions and forget they never satisfy the longings of the soul, my commitment to being true to myself reminds me of my essential freedom. The truth does make me free. Truth can only be discerned if I want it and trust it. It is difficult to follow, easy to be. It reveals the healing power of love and the reality of joy. The glamour of illusions perceived from a distance vanishes like a mirage in the desert when examined closely. Only the living waters of authentic spiritual freedom can quench the thirst of the soul that longs for the unitive life.

The way of spiritual freedom requires that I make every effort to attain whatever I believe will bring me happiness and to surrender it all in the end. Wilber has said that wisdom is recognizing and becoming the fundamental awareness of the universe. Compassion sees the One in the many. Wisdom sees the many as One.

When I can take responsibility for the quality of my life and learn from mistakes rather than judging them, the path becomes increasingly clear and easy to follow. The leap of faith required at the beginning to gain freedom from conditioned beliefs is no longer necessary when I have glimpsed the truth of spiritual freedom. Since every relative truth is necessarily paradoxical, I am left with the responsibility of choice and the necessity of freedom. And so the path that led from the bondage of illusions to spiritual freedom disappears at last in the great mystery of nonduality.

> Your mind can be possessed by illusions,
> but spirit is eternally free.[29]

_____

CHAPTER 10

Spiritual Practice in Daily Life

There is an art of conducting oneself in the lower regions by the memory of what one saw higher up. When one can no longer see, one can at least still know.[1]

—RENÉ DAUMAL

SPIRITUAL PRACTICE IN DAILY LIFE IS A WAY of liberating the soul and remembering what we really are. Practice takes many different forms. Some people practice within the context of traditional religion; others find their connection to Spirit in nontraditional ways. Here we will review methods that focus on inner work, cultivating wisdom and compassion, while engaging in ordinary life in the world. These practices may be done either alone or in the context of a group that shares similar values.

Some of the ways in which spirituality can be honored and deepened in daily life include spending time alone in nature, keeping a journal and engaging in artistic endeavors such as music, painting, singing and dancing. Dreamwork, meditation and other forms of inner work can also be oriented toward developing spiritual awareness. However, these activities can serve either the ego or the soul, depending on the intention with which they are pursued. Here our purpose will be to suggest ways of enriching the life of the soul by listening to the heart and training the mind to be a fair witness.

INTENTIONS AND ATTITUDES

Before beginning specific practices, you may want to ask yourself, "What is this for?" Clarifying intentions can uncover resistances and help you

_____

remember the purpose of the work. Be honest with yourself. If life seems unmanageable or overwhelming, you may just want some help. Perhaps you want happiness, love, inner peace or a deeper understanding of the meaning of life. Or maybe your soul is longing for freedom. Whatever the motive, clarifying intentions can make practice easier and more rewarding.

Reflecting on intentions may bring to light certain attitudes that affect anything we undertake. If, for example, you tend to be judgmental and feel inadequate, you will probably feel judgmental and inadequate in spiritual practice. Likewise, if you think nothing you do will make any difference, whatever you try to do will probably not make much difference. If, on the other hand, you are open-minded and interested in learning from experience, you may learn a lot. Becoming aware of habitual attitudes at the beginning of any new endeavor can free you from unconscious resistance. There is no need to be afraid of the discipline of practice. It can be a great help along the way, as long as we do not try to hold on to old habits after they have fulfilled their purpose.

INTUITION AND IMAGINATION

Intuition is a faculty of perception that can directly apprehend spiritual realities. Intuition, like thinking, feeling and sensing, can be developed. It becomes available when the mind is quiet.[2] Most of the time our minds are not under voluntary control. Many people who are willing to take responsibility for their behavior feel incapable of taking responsibility for their thoughts and feelings. Our minds and emotions have been programmed in certain ways by parents, peers and the culture at large. When you know this, you can change the program. Intuition perceives possibilities and helps to guide us when we explore the unknown.

If you are not satisfied with the quality of your life at present, you may want to begin consciously cultivating qualities such as intuition and love, instead of indulging in automatic responses of guilt, fear and anger. Cultivating intuition means trusting yourself and learning to distinguish truth from illusion.

In order to break through the consensus trance of cultural conditioning, we must be willing to shift attention away from familiar distractions to what is not yet known. By turning to the source of intuitive wisdom that can be found in the depths of the soul, we can discover a universal source of inspiration and renewal.

Affirmations

Some of the benefits of spiritual affirmations include increasing feelings of freedom and inner peace, an expanded capacity for compassion and sympathetic joy and a reduction of fear, anxiety and depression. Any quality can be consciously cultivated by consistent use of affirmations. Spiritual values suggest that the methods for cultivating qualities and training attention are best directed to goals that transcend ego desires.

When affirmations are used in the service of ego goals, such as attaining worldly possessions, they may have a backlash. "Be careful what you want. You may get it!" is a caution worth heeding. Getting what the ego wants can sometimes imprison the soul. Sometimes an unexpected side effect sparks fear and anger. The power of positive thinking is familiar to many people, and the shadow side of it, the unconscious backlash, has become familiar to psychotherapists. The consistent use of affirmations can be powerful, but any powerful tool can be abused. The misuse of affirmations in the service of ego defenses such as denial or repression can have troublesome repercussions.

For example, when Kathy, a woman in her mid-thirties, came to see me, she was struggling to balance her retail business and her relationship with her lover. She would sometimes fly into a rage and felt that her relationship would soon end if she did not control it. She had used affirmations successfully to expand her business which had grown considerably in the last year. But she had not been prepared for the added stress in her life that her success had generated. She had tried to use affirmations to suppress the anger, but then she developed a stomach ulcer. As we worked through the anger, she was able to reevaluate her priorities and give her relationship the attention it deserved. We also uncovered feelings of guilt about both her success and her relationship. After exploring these feelings, Kathy was able to balance and manage her life with much greater ease and confidence. She found that she did not need to sacrifice the relationship or the business or herself in the process.

Even affirmations for cultivating spiritual qualities can be problematic if they are used to avoid or suppress unwanted thoughts or emotions. Sooner or later whatever is repressed reclaims attention, sometimes erupting out of control in unexpected ways.

One man who was troubled by pervasive anger and sexual fantasies said he had worked with affirmations in combination with meditation and was quite proficient at concentration. He could direct attention to the affirmation and sustain the focus remarkably well. As soon as he stopped practicing, however, the troubling feelings and fantasies would return. There seemed to be little improvement in how he felt about himself or his wife. When we spoke it seemed evident to me that he had some unresolved psychodynamic issues stemming from childhood experiences that no amount of affirmation practice could resolve, but would probably respond well to psychotherapy. I therefore suggested that he find a good therapist in the city where he lived.

As long as we are prepared to work through reactions and do not expect affirmations to be a substitute for other forms of inner work, affirmations can be very helpful. A subtle but important difference between affirmations employed in the service of ego goals and the cultivation of spiritual qualities is that in spiritual practice, one voluntarily surrenders the will to a higher authority such as truth, Spirit or God, and ideally one is not attached to the outcome.

Affirmations are most effective when they are short and succinct. They should always be stated in positive terms; for instance, *I am calm and confident* is a positive statement, whereas, *I am not afraid* is a negative statement. The subconscious mind tends to be quite literal, and what is remembered is the word *afraid,* while *not* is forgotten. Fritz Perls, the founder of Gestalt therapy said, "To deny is to affirm." For example, saying, "I wouldn't think of leaving you," means I have already thought of it. Since the mind cannot deny anything without first thinking of it, affirmations should simply state what one wants to affirm.

An effective affirmation for psychological healing that I have sometimes recommended is the simple statement, *I'm enough.* It tends to counteract feelings of inadequacy and anxiety without encouraging ego inflation or striving for an illusory ideal.

Affirmations should be repeated subvocally as often as possible, ideally from the moment of waking throughout the day and continuing as one falls asleep at night. It is best to work with only one phrase for a period of days or weeks, until it is thoroughly ingrained in the subconscious.

Affirmations can address any level of the spectrum of consciousness. For example, if you want to affirm your spiritual identity, you might say, *I am spirit.*[3] If you want to feel more inner peace, you could say to yourself, *The peace of God is shining in me now.*[4]

You can make up affirmations to cultivate qualities such as kindness, generosity, compassion, peace, happiness, harmony, joy and love. For instance, you might start with, *I am happy and loving.* You could try this as an experiment for a couple of weeks to see what effects it has. Notice how often you remember to say it and whether it generates fear, anger or peace of mind. Whatever you experience, you can probably learn something about yourself by observing it.

Sometimes affirmations derived from dreams can be particularly helpful, since they relate to whatever is being processed in the psyche below the threshold of waking consciousness. For example, if you have a dream of confronting fearful images, you may want to affirm the quality of courage. If you dream of stage fright, you may want to affirm calmness and confidence. You probably know better that anyone else what qualities you need.

Creative decision making

Any decision can be an opportunity to ask for spiritual guidance. Creative decision making is an intuitive process that calls for accessing levels of awareness that are not available to habitual ways of thinking. Its effectiveness depends on quieting the mind and focusing attention.

Creative decision making depends on trusting intuition and exercising freedom and choice. You are not likely to be creative when you are angry or fearful or when you feel like a victim. Creativity means activating intuition *and* imagination, not as a substitute for information, but *in addition* to being well informed by relevant data. Whether one is making decisions about work, interpersonal relationships or spiritual practice, asking for inner guidance can help. On the spiritual path, making choices only after asking for inner guidance is a way of transcending the ego.

Clearing the field of awareness is a useful skill for creative decision making. Whatever thoughts and doubts intrude on inner stillness can be acknowledged, noted and released. The attempt sometimes reveals a variety of resistances and inner conflicts. Communicating them to another person can accelerate the process of letting them go. A person obsessed with worry will not be open to inspiration. Brainstorming, for example, whether alone or in a group, requires that we allow the creative flow of ideas to be expressed, temporarily suspending judgment. If we are unwilling to let go of our fears (emotions) and judgments (thoughts), we may feel blocked. When fears and judgments are discussed with someone who does not reinforce them, they usually diminish and sometimes disappear altogether. Co-creation implies joining with others to arrive at solutions that take more than one point of view into account.

Imagination

Imagination is a talent that often remains underdeveloped. Yet it can be tremendously valuable in creativity, healing and spiritual growth. The following exercises can help you use your imagination.

1. Imagine that you are having a conversation with one of your deceased ancestors who has something important to communicate to you.

2. Tell a story about a significant turning point in your life.

3. Imagine that you have received an important spiritual initiation and describe it in symbolic terms.

The next exercises can be done by talking with a partner who is willing to listen without interference:

1. What is your worst fear? Name it, describe it, then imagine that you are no longer afraid, and it disappears.

2. What is your favorite daydream? Tell this as a story in present tense, as if it were happening now.

Music, painting, mask-making, sculpting, writing fiction or any other creative activity that engages the imagination can become a means of expression for the soul. Imagine that you can creatively design the rest of your life.

Smiling

Buddhist meditation teacher Thich Nhat Hanh reminds us that although life is filled with suffering, it is also filled with many wonders. To suffer is not enough. If we want to share peace and happiness with others, we must learn to be happy and peaceful and to smile in our daily life. He calls this the most basic kind of peace work. He says,

> Breathing in, I calm body and mind.
> Breathing out, I smile.
> Dwelling in the present moment
> I know this is the only moment.[5]

Some Buddhist teachers suggest imitating the half-smile portrayed on the face of the Buddha. This brings awareness to the unconscious facial expressions that reflect tension, anxiety and anger. Smiling inwardly is a subtle form of body awareness and relaxation that is easy to practice anywhere, any time. You may also imagine that other parts of your body are smiling. For example, if you feel happy your eyes may be smiling, or your heart or all of you.

Smiles that cover pain do not heal. A fake or superficial smile deceives no one, least of all oneself. It is therefore suggested that smiling be practiced inwardly. If you can smile to yourself when you sit in meditation, when you are walking or doing daily chores, it may become a mental habit. This can be a way of learning to be gentle with yourself and others. Imagine that you have something to smile about.

Thich Nhat Hanh says, "Smiling is very important. If we are not able to smile, then the world will not have peace . . . It is with our capacity of smiling, breathing, and being peace that we can make peace."

DREAMWORK

Our dreams are the voice of the psychic center within us that enables us to strive for wholeness.

The close connection that exists between dreams and our central religious problems seems to justify our calling dreams "God's forgotten language."[6]

–JOHN SANFORD

Each night our waking life is interrupted, and we enter the nonphysical, imaginal world of the soul in which we are both creature and creator. Shadows and illusions become visible, and we discover all the secret wishes, fears, aspirations and idols that are hidden from view during waking hours. The soul as dreamer is free to choose its response to whatever picture the mind creates. At first the dreambody, like the ego, is presumed to be identical with the physical body. When this self-concept is transcended, the dreamer is not subject to physical laws. Experiences of flight, soul travel, dismemberment, death and rebirth are not uncommon in the dreamworld.

Dreaming is a universal experience. Yet although everyone enters this realm each night, few people avail themselves of it for the purpose of spiritual practice. Among those that do, some see dreams as a source of healing. Others regard dreams as a source of insight into psychological dynamics. Many instructions for working with dreams tend to use dreams in the service of the ego rather than the soul. Yet dreams also reveal the world of soul. If the purpose of dreamwork is to awaken the soul, dreams can be a source of spiritual renewal.

In sleep we withdraw from the action of waking life, only to return to it the next day. Since this is analogous to what is believed to occur in reincarnation, sleep is called the younger brother of death. Rudolph Steiner believed that during sleep we relive our waking life in summary form and these summaries are then relived on the astral plane after death.[7] The activity of the soul after death is said to parallel the activity of the soul during sleep, when the astral body leaves the physical body and returns to the spiritual world. Sleep is also the time when beings such as angels, Buddhas or avatars can influence our unconscious life. If we want to understand the soul's destiny, we should take into account the interaction between sleeping and waking life.

Seeing through illusions that imprison the soul can begin with turning attention to dreams. For example, dreams do not lie about our feelings. When the soul feels restless, dreams may be troubled and call attention to the inner pain that may be masked by success in the world of ego. While the ego may be attached to weaving illusions of change by manipulating the outer world, the soul is never satisfied by these changes.

An old Chinese saying goes, "If you want to be happy for a day, kill a pig. If your want to be happy for a year, get married. If you want to be happy for the rest of your life, plant a garden."

Tending a garden is an appropriate metaphor for cultivating awareness of dreams and the world of soul. There is much that can be done to provide a favorable environment for growth, but plants grow by themselves. We cannot force them to grow. Similarly, liberation of the soul is not achieved through manipulation. We can however, listen, understand and respond to it. Attention to both waking and sleeping dreams deepens awareness of soul.

Since ancient times dreams have been revered as revelation or messages from God[8] or the spiritual world. Today we are more likely to regard dreams as revealing the unconscious, either personal or collective. Sometimes the collective unconscious is equated with the world of soul, but not all contents of the collective are spiritual and not all dreams give voice to the soul.

Both sleeping dreams and waking dreams can be fraught with tension and conflicting wishes. From dreamwork we discover that dreams of terror change when we ask for help in the dream and when we relate to dream images as projected parts of ourselves. This role playing begins to break down the rigid barriers between self and other. As we see that dreams often reveal disowned parts of the psyche, we can begin to reclaim them. Conscious reintegration of these rejected parts of ourselves can be both healing and liberating. This process also demonstrates how connected we actually are to what appears to be separate, and how the split between subject and object is not as real as we might imagine.

The nature of the dream

The objects of dream are subtle objects, self-radiant, changing form rapidly—dream, vision, god. The gods and heavens and hells are what might be called the cosmic aspect of dream. The dream is the personal aspect of myth. . . . You and your god are one, just as you and your dream are.[9]

—JOSEPH CAMPBELL

The dreamworld offers direct access to heaven and hell and everything in between. In a spiritual context the meaning of a dream is often relevant to the soul's journey, and interpretation can be developed in the service of the soul. This type of interpretation benefits from dialogue with someone who is familiar with the meaning of sacred symbols. Although dreams may have a salutary effect on psychological well-being regardless of whether or not we try to unravel their spiritual meaning, they can be richly rewarding if we are willing to delve into them by using various techniques such as free association, amplification, active imagination and symbolic interpretation.

Free association means exploring whatever memories, images or ideas the dream brings to mind. Amplification focuses on the dream images themselves and what they evoke. Active imagination can be used to review the dream and give it a different ending, or to continue the dream in imagination. Symbolic interpretation involves learning to read the language of symbols. A symbol always points beyond itself to a reality it both conceals and reveals. It derives meaning from the context in which it occurs. For example, universal symbols such as fire, wind and water mean different things in different dreams.

Lucid dreaming

Dreams show you that you have the power to make a world as you would have it be, and that because you want it you see it. And while you see it you do not doubt that it is real. Yet here is a world, clearly within your mind, that seems to be outside . . . what you seem to waken to is but another form of this same world you see in dreams. All your time is spent in dreaming.[10]

—A COURSE IN MIRACLES

In a real sense, all the visions that we see in our lifetime are like a big dream. If we examine them well, the big dream of life and the smaller dreams of one night are not very different. If we truly see the essential nature of both, we will see that there is really no difference between them. If we can finally liberate ourselves from the chains of emotions, attachments, and ego by this realization we have the possibility of ultimately becoming enlightened.[11]

—NAMKHAI NORBU

One of the differences between being awake and being asleep is that when we are asleep, we usually do not know that we are dreaming. We may think that what is happening in our dreams has nothing to do with our own psyche. When we are awake or lucid in a dream, we know we are dreaming. Then we know we can change the dream and create a different experience by choice.

In the practice of lucid dreaming, which means continuing to dream while aware of dreaming, we are free to act without fear of physical harm. For example, in dreams we may go through solid objects, fly or breathe underwater. This type of experience has been portrayed in Hollywood style in movies such as *Ghost*, when the hero discovers he has died and can no longer act on the physical world until he learns psychokinesis, the ability to move objects by a mental effort of will.

In some dreams the body may appear to be transformed into other shapes, assuming the guise of a bird, an animal or any other creature. I once dreamed that I was a fledgling eagle, perched in a nest high on a mountain ledge overlooking a valley. I was amazed at how far I could see. Then I realized that I was dreaming.

In his discussion of dreams as God's forgotten language, Jungian analyst John Sanford reminds us that in the Bible dreams were regarded as manifestations of divine intention. God spoke to the prophets through dreams, and the revelations given by angels are equated with the revelations by dreams and visions.[12]

In Tibetan dream yoga, an effort is made to become lucid first in sleeping dreams, then in waking life as well. This means remembering that every perception is a dream. The monks are trained to maintain lucidity continuously, even in the state of dreamless sleep. When the yogi has learned to be lucid, or mindful of dreaming, for twenty-four hours each day, then this awareness is said to continue into the even more subtle state after death.[13]

When a person first becomes aware of the possibility of lucid dreaming, he or she is likely to fulfill whatever desires have captured attention in the dream. Fantasies of pleasure, sex, adventure can all be fulfilled. In time, however, the dreamer may begin to tire of repetitions of the same old themes and begin to explore higher aspirations. Dream control is no longer the objective. Learning about what is possible in this state replaces the more mundane desires for ego gratification. For example, in the course of his research on lucid dreaming, Stephen LaBerge learned that surrendering to the higher self, or what he called "The Highest," was far more satisfying than simply reenacting ego desires. He writes,

> I found myself driving in my sportscar down the dream road, per-
> fectly aware that I was dreaming. I was delighted by the vibrantly
> beautiful scenery my lucid dream was presenting. After driving
> a short distance farther, I was confronted with a very attractive,
> I might say a *dream* of a hitchhiker beside me on the road just
> ahead. I need hardly say that I felt strongly inclined to stop and
> pick her up. But I said to myself, "I've had *that* dream before. How
> about something new?" So I passed her by, resolving to seek "The
> Highest" instead. As soon as I opened myself to guidance, my car
> took off into the air, flying rapidly upward, until it fell behind me
> like the first stage of a rocket. I continued to fly higher into the
> clouds, where I passed a cross on a steeple, a star of David, and
> other religious symbols. As I rose still higher, beyond the clouds, I
> entered a space that seemed a vast mystical realm: A vast emptiness
> that was yet full of love; an unbounded space that somehow felt
> like home. My mood had lifted to corresponding heights, and I
> began to sing with ecstatic inspiration . . .[14]

LaBerge goes on to say that this lucid dream was deeply significant for him.

LaBerge outlines several stages of Tibetan dream yoga, beginning with lucidity, then controlling reactivity to dream content, realizing that dream content is maya or illusion, and transforming dream content into its opposite. Finally, when thoroughly proficient in these methods, one may reach the realization that all appearances are "merely playthings of mind."[15]

Each of us is free to choose the dreams that we aspire to realize. We seldom acknowledge this inner freedom that we already have, thinking of liberation as something to be attained in the future rather than something to be claimed right now. When the fulfillment of sensory pleasures in dreams is no longer satisfying, the dreamer may seek something more meaningful by invoking a transpersonal or spiritual experience, as LaBerge did in his dream. Alternatively, a person might seek for a symbol, a teacher or a deity. Another way of using dreams for spiritual awakening involves turning the dream over to a higher power, intending to witness whatever is revealed. A third possibility involves praying or meditating in the dream. Any of these methods can be illuminating. When the soul of a dreamer is aware of light in the dream, it is free to dissolve into emptiness.

Whenever we are lucid in a dream, we are free to be creative and initiate change in accordance with inner wisdom and our heart's desire. When we are uncertain of what we want, we can ask for help or guidance. Guidance seems to be equally available in sleeping and waking states if we remember to ask for it. One psychotherapist said he often silently asked for guidance from the Holy Spirit when dealing with a difficult patient. Each time he felt a sense of reassurance that helped him deal more confidently with the situation. A shift of perception enabled him to see things differently. Remembering to ask for guidance can increase lucidity and enable the dreamer to deepen dreamwork as spiritual practice.

The following exercise, originally developed by LaBerge, is recommended for practice when lying in bed before going to sleep or during wakeful hours in the night when you would like to be sleeping:

> Counting each breath, say "one" on the inhale; repeat "I'm dreaming" on the exhale: One, I'm dreaming. Two, I'm dreaming. Three, I'm dreaming . . . etc.

Keep going until you become aware of dreaming as you watch images arise and disappear of their own accord. By focusing attention on counting and on the sensation of the breath as you inhale and exhale, the mind may become increasingly calm and the body more relaxed.

Regular practice can improve concentration, deepen relaxation and increase lucidity in the dream state. If you try it, you must evaluate it for yourself. Do not force yourself to do any exercise or practice if you do not feel comfortable with it.

Some people have experimented with using this affirmation during waking hours to increase awareness of how much our minds are caught in dreaming of the past and future instead of being fully present here and now. Another way of applying dreamwork in waking life consists of reflecting on a particular event or situation as if it were a dream. One of my clients often spoke to me about her life experiences as her waking dream. One that I remember was her experience of being in an airplane in which the passengers and crew were prepared to make an emergency crash landing. The confrontation with terror and the helplessness she felt in that situation was more intense than anything she could remember. Fortunately, the airplane managed to make it to an airport and no one was hurt. She was able to work with this experience as if it were a dream and to interpret it as a call to wake up to the fragility and impermanence of the life she had previously taken for granted.

The dream of past and future knows no bounds. Even belief in reincarnation can be interpreted as a collective dream that extends our dreaming in linear time. The soul that reincarnates does not transcend time and space or the separate self-sense. It is therefore not yet fully awake to its identity as Spirit. Attachment to the dream of temporal existence, whether by fear or desire, perpetuates the dreaming of the world. If, on the other hand, one identifies with Spirit as the creative ground of being, time itself can be perceived as an illusion that limits awareness of eternity. Reincarnation may be perceived as a perpetuation of the illusion of linear time in which we currently exist. Eternity is not a very long time, but a point of awareness unbounded by space and time. If temporal existence is perceived as a dance of *maya* or illusion, the soul itself is but a figment of the dream.

Years ago, when I was experimenting with asking for guidance in dreams, I had the following dream:

> I descended through a curving tunnel, riding on an apparently self-powered small flatcar, spiraling down into a different reality. I emerged from a narrow passage into a dark, steamy jungle where unknown creatures lurked, peering at me from their hidden habitats. I was an intruder in this strange world, and I did not know where to turn. As I began walking cautiously through the mire, I felt I was being followed and I wanted to run. But which way would I run? I had no clue. I was scared as I sensed the presence of snakes and crocodiles. I felt that if I tried to run I would be overtaken and probably eaten alive, so I asked for guidance and tried to see more clearly.
>
> The snake that slithered across my shoulders was alive, but it seemed sensuous and velvety. I recognized it from a previous dream and realized I was dreaming. Then I saw a clearing and in the distance I could see the ocean. As I made my way toward it, I felt I had found my way home. The sunlight sparkled on the water, and I was filled with a sense of well-being. Somehow the brilliant light reminded me of another reality that seemed more real than the one I was in at the moment. As I gazed at the light on the water, I felt a profound release and the dream dissolved into light.

Dreams of other realities are not equivalent to waking up. We can change nightmares into happier dreams of peace and joy by facing our fears and making a commitment to self-awareness, yet any dream is still within the realm of illusion. Advanced meditators who claim to be able to maintain awareness not only in dreams but in deep sleep as well, describe witnessing dreams and dreamless sleep as "bliss."[16]

To one who is awake, the dream is of less importance than the reality of being awake. Yet as long as we exist in this world of physical space and time, witnessing dreaming can be both healing and liberating. Carlos Castaneda, writing on the art of dreaming, says dreaming is freedom to perceive worlds beyond imagination.[17]

The wisdom of spiritual guidance that dreams offer can be accessed in many different ways. Anyone can learn to listen to the dream voice of the soul instead of the ego and increase lucidity in any state of consciousness.

INTERPRETATION OF SYMBOLS

Symbols are sometimes called vertical bridges that enable us to appreciate different levels of consciousness. We all use symbols to interpret and understand our world. Our common everyday symbols, such as language, create the social world and influence our attitudes toward the natural world. Contemporary cognitive science uses mathematical symbols to construct logical models of reality. Religious symbols mediate our relationship to the sacred and shape our spiritual experience.

The meaningful interpretation of symbols is an art that can reveal processes and possibilities emerging in consciousness. Symbols can always be interpreted in more than one way. Discovering the spiritual significance of symbols can satisfy the thirst for meaning that is often missing from a life concerned only with the world of ego.

Awareness of symbols can be enhanced by meditating on specific symbols or images. These may be either simple or complex. For example, the practice of Vajrayana Buddhism involves visualization of deities and elaborate mandalas. Others may use visual images such as those that have been preserved from antiquity as Tarot cards.[18] Simple geometric forms can also convey symbolic meaning to the soul.

Five shapes

Five symbols that occur in the religious art of all cultures are the circle, the square, the triangle, the cross and the spiral. Anthropologist Angeles Arrien points out that these basic forms can be found in nature as well as in human art and architecture, and appear spontaneously in children's drawings in every society.[19] Although these simple geometric forms may be assigned different meanings in different contexts, Arrien says that the following interpretations are widely accepted.

1. *Circle:* The circle is a symbol of wholeness, totality and individuation.

2. *Square:* The square suggests the four elements, the four directions, the four corners, the four functions. It reflects stability, security and practicality, and the achievement of tangible results.

3. *Cross:* The cross represents the intersection of opposites. It is associated with relatedness, synthesis and meeting. As a religious symbol, the vertical axis is associated with spiritual depth and aspiration. The horizontal axis represents relationship and connection to the world.

4. *Triangle:* The triangle represents the visionary quest for meaning and spiritual sight. Mountains are natural triangles; pyramids and arrows are constructed triangles.

5. *Spiral:* The spiral is a symbol of growth, change and evolution. It appears in nature in the way plants grow and in rituals involving the spiral path and spiral dances.

Each of these symbols has a place in our lives. Emotional responses evoked by meditating on the symbols may indicate what aspect of the soul's journey needs attention. Sometimes these shapes appear in dreams. Relevant interpretation must always take the context into account.

If you wish to deepen your appreciation of what each of these symbols means for you, you can spend some time meditating on them as follows:

> Sitting perfectly still in an erect posture, close your eyes and visualize a circle (or a cross, square, triangle or spiral) in your mind's eye. Try to hold it still for approximately three minutes. Imagine that you are looking at it at a distance of about two feet in front of you at the level of your eyebrows, or third eye. Notice whether the image appears to move and change of its own accord or if you are able to hold the image clear and still for a few minutes. Without opening your eyes, replace the first image with the next one. Try to hold it firmly in your mind's eye without moving. After three minutes, let it go. Repeat the three minute concentration as described above with each of these symbols.

If you have difficulty visualizing the shapes clearly, simply think of them, one at a time, attempting to focus your attention on each one for two or three minutes each, even if you do not "see" the image with your inner eye.

If you find it difficult, simply notice what arises in your mind as distraction and what appears to be interfering with carrying out these instructions.

If you have never done any concentration meditation practice, you may find it impossible to follow the directions at first. It can be worth trying, however, if only to see how our thoughts are not under voluntary control. Be gentle, and do what you can. Concentration improves with practice.

Notice any feeling response evoked by each of these symbols. Rank them for yourself in order of preference, with number one indicating the one you like the best, and number five indicating the one you like the least. Number each one, from one to five before reading the meanings that have been attributed to the shapes and to the relative placement on your list.

According to Arrien the relative placement of these shapes can be interpreted as follows:

1. The symbol in the first place is the one that has your conscious attention.

2. The symbol in the second place is represents your hidden strength.

3. The symbol in the third place is a bridging symbol that can integrate the polarities in your life. It may be a tool for healing that you have overlooked.

4. The symbol in the fourth place is your current challenge.

5. The symbol in the fifth place represents something you dislike or something that does not interest you at this time.

The relative placement of these five shapes may change from time to time. I have found it useful to reflect on whatever emerges in consciousness when I do this process.[20]

Each of these five geometric symbols can also be associated with specific archetypes. For example, the hero may be associated with the circle, the warrior with the square, the healer with the cross, the visionary with the triangle and the teacher with the spiral. Each of these has its place in the inner world along with all the other images that emerge in myths, dreams and fantasies.

Familiarity with the meaning that is commonly attributed to symbols can be useful in deciphering the meaning of dreams, provided the interpretations are not taken literally. For example, one woman felt a strong response to an image of a coiled spring, similar to the inner springs of a mattress. There was no story to her dream, only this image. She associated strength and flexibility and connectedness with the spring. When she imagined herself as the spring, she felt connected at both ends, to her aging mother and to her children. She also felt resilient. She saw herself as a strong connector. The spring was clearly an image of a spiral, conveying a sense of vitality, growth and change. For her it also represented a connection between her spiritual life and her work in the world. Images of coiled snakes sometimes evoke similar associations.

Here is case a of a circle appearing in a dream:

> I was standing alone on a high plateau, beside a big fire in a circular fire pit. People of many different races and cultures were gathered around the fire. It seemed to be a council of earth stewards from many parts of the world. The feeling was friendly and warm, yet solemn. Joining the circle gave me a deep sense of wholeness and belonging. I felt honored to be included in the circle.

For the dreamer, joining the circle meant that she had arrived where she wanted to be. The sense of belonging she felt within the circle reassured her about the validity of the work she was doing in conflict resolution and citizen diplomacy. The dream made her feel less isolated and more connected to others doing similar work. She felt whole and accepted as part of a larger whole. She said the dream helped her feel at home in the world.

Five elements

The elements of air, fire, water, earth and wood are often associated with the triangle, the cross, the circle, the square and the spiral, respectively. As symbols these elements have been given multiple interpretations and also suggest some common associations. Air is traditionally associated with spirit, since it is invisible yet necessary for life. Fire is widely considered a symbol of purification and transformation. Fire may also represent either destructive rage or the creative flame of consciousness, among other things. Water is commonly associated with life, as the womb of life on earth. It also evokes feelings and emotions and the life of the soul. The ocean is often perceived as the collective unconscious. Underground tunnels and caves are also associated with the unconscious. Earth is the great mother, the ground of being that gives birth and receives the dead. The element of wood, symbolized as the tree of life, can represent growth, strength and transformation. In Gnostic teachings,

> The earth is faith, in which we take root. Water is hope, by which we are nourished. The air is love, by which we grow, and the light is Gnosis, by which we ripen.[21]

Each of these elements can evoke many more associations. Interpretations are always partial, both revealing and concealing what may be intuited nonverbally from an image. Ultimately the mystic seeks to go beyond all symbols and images. These comments are intended only to stimulate your interest in further reading and a deepening understanding of how symbolic perception can contribute to enriching your spiritual practice.

Some people find it useful to use symbols as visual aids to meditation. Others prefer to draw them or to use them as mirrors that help us see what we have overlooked. When a particular symbol appears repeatedly in a dream it may have special significance and may call for exploration of various interpretations. Dreaming of fire, for example, may be a signal of transformation under way, creative inspirations, or anger and destruction.

How we relate to symbols may also mirror the state of the soul. When I dream of water, for example, I may be swimming in clear or murky water; I may feel threatened by a tidal wave; I may be drowning, drinking from a clear spring, swimming upstream or floating in a quiet pool. Recently I dreamed that I was standing by a clear pool just above a waterfall. I was struck by being able to see far down into the pool and overawed by the power of the waterfall. In the dream I remembered Suzuki Roshi's analogy of the self as a drop of water in a waterfall, thinking it has a separate existence for a little while.[22] One woman in therapy dreamed that she was being washed down the drain. Our response to such dreams can reveal hidden feelings, hopes and fears.

Reflecting on symbols in dreams or in waking life reminds us that witnessing the inner life can help us be more aware of the life of the soul and the limitations of ego.

MEDITATION

Zazen practice is the direct expression of our true nature.[23]

—SUZUKI ROSHI

Zazen is one form of Buddhist meditation among many that are available in the West today. It is sometimes called just sitting. A student is not expected to do anything but sit still in meditation posture for a period of time, usually about forty minutes. In general, meditation consists of a variety of techniques for cultivating awareness through training attention or, in the case of zazen, transcending attention. Formal meditation usually has an inward focus and is practiced in silence, in a sitting posture, with the spine erect. In many Eastern disciplines one sits cross-legged on the floor or on a cushion, in a relaxed yet stable position which allows the mind to be simultaneously quiet and alert.

In his research on meditation, Harvard cardiologist Herbert Benson discovered that even short periods of meditation on a repeated sound resulted in lower metabolic rate, slower heart rate, lower blood pressure and slower breathing.[24] He first studied meditators who used Hindu mantras, or sounds endowed with ritualistic meaning. He then experimented with subjects using the word *one* and found results equally effective. However, boredom led most subjects to give up the practice. He then became interested in studying the effects of simple, short prayers such as "Shalom" or "The Lord is my shepherd" and found that they not only had similar effects, but that the people who used them instead of meaningless phrases were more likely to stay with the practice. The repetitive prayer was thought to inhibit the automatic stress reactions of fight or flight and create a relaxation response.

Benson then became interested in investigating what he called the faith factor. He began training hospital chaplains and other religious workers in this method to see if the relaxation response would influence their spirituality as well as their physiology. The study indicated that people who feel in touch with God are less likely to get sick and better able to cope when they do. The researchers developed a scale to test levels of spirituality, defined as a feeling that there is more than just material reality. Those who scored high in spirituality also scored high in psychological health and had fewer stress-related symptoms. Those scoring high in spirituality also gained the most from meditation training, including the sharpest drop in pain. Benson concluded that meditative prayer evidently strengthens the spirit as it heals the body and its effects are being carefully documented.[25]

The work of Jon Kabat-Zinn, founder and director of the Stress Reduction Clinic at the University of Massachusetts Medical Center, has demonstrated the efficacy of mindfulness meditation in helping patients suffering from chronic pain and stress-related disorders.[26] The form of meditation that Kabat-Zinn teaches is based on an ancient Buddhist practice, and it opens the gate of awareness to the inner world.

There have been many other experimental studies that provide evidence for the benefits of meditation.[27,28] While a very broad range of experiences may emerge during meditation, research indicates that meditation can enhance creativity, empathy, moral and cognitive development and self-actualization. Familiar meditation practices include visualization, concentration, insight and contemplation. Recent polls indicate that twenty-one percent of Californians, or 6.2 million Americans in California alone, practice meditation.[29]

Visualization

The ability to visualize possibilities and concentrate on desired outcomes can go a long way to manifesting a particular vision. Visualization is often used in an effort to fulfill desires or attain goals such as improved athletic performance. In spiritual practice visualization may be used to envision desirable states of consciousness such as peace, loving kindness, generosity or a particular deity that embodies such qualities.

Visualization is commonly used to envision a deity or inner teacher in the context of a specific tradition. For example, a Christian may visualize Jesus at the stations of the Cross, while a student of Tibetan Buddhism is trained to visualize buddhas and mandalas in intricate detail.

Concentration

Visualization is most effective when one has developed concentration. Concentration involves training attention so that the mind can hold any object of attention in focus for a prolonged period of time. The undisciplined mind generally has a very short attention span. Anyone who has tried to concentrate on an image for a few minutes will soon discover that the mind has a mind of its own. It does not necessarily do what we want it to do. Trying to hold a clear image of a symbol in the mind's eye for a few minutes can be surprisingly difficult. However, concentration improves with practice. When well developed, the power of the concentrated mind is compared to a powerful laser light, in contrast to the soft, scattered light of diffuse attention.

Insight

Insight develops naturally when we learn to quiet the mind. Quieting the mind is similar but not identical to developing concentration. Whereas concentration means focusing attention on a particular object, suppressing any tendencies to wandering attention, quieting the mind may also be achieved by allowing thoughts, feelings, sensations and all experiences to be present in awareness, without trying to change or interfere with them in any way, simply noticing whatever is there. This training of attention is called choiceless awareness. The development of insight is enhanced by allowing things to be as they are and noticing how emotional reactivity shapes perception and distorts awareness. Mindfulness training is the basis for the experience of insight.[30]

Contemplation

Contemplation may invite the presence of God or simply rest in a state of inner stillness. In contrast to discursive meditation on words or the visualization of images, methods leading to contemplation aim at bypassing the thinking process and disidentifying from the contents of consciousness. The process is one of emptying, in preparation for the experience of divine union. Solitude and silence provide a favorable context for contemplation. When silence deepens to include a quiet mind and open heart, the practice of contemplation is accompanied by a deep and abiding sense of inner peace.

Beginning meditation

Setting aside time for meditation or contemplation on a regular basis can be very rewarding. One person chose to set aside two hours each day and two days each month for silent practice. Another practiced daily for thirty minutes each morning and made a point of going on a silent retreat each year. Whatever your level of participation, a regular schedule and the support of a teacher can be very helpful. Meditating alone is usually more difficult that meditating with a group. Beginners are therefore advised to find an experienced teacher who can help them through difficult periods of doubt and frustration at the outset. In the absence of a teacher, books and tapes providing instruction can help.

Anyone can get started by sitting quietly, preferably with eyes closed. Either sitting on a pillow or on a straight chair is acceptable as long as the spine is straight. Attention may be directed to the breath, noticing the sensation in the nostrils or the movement of the abdomen with each inhalation and exhalation. The mind will wander of its own accord. You can simply notice what comes into your mind that distracts you from awareness of the breath. You can start with five or ten minutes of sitting at first, gradually working up to thirty or forty minutes. When you can sit comfortably, wide awake and without moving at all for thirty minutes or more, you will probably feel some of the benefits of the practice. Effort and discipline are required at first. It helps if you can set aside a specific time each day, preferably early in the morning. Meditation gets easier as it becomes increasingly rewarding with practice.

One teacher recommends sitting in meditation at least half an hour every day, except for those days when you are in a hurry or exceptionally busy. On those days you should mediate for at least an hour!

PRAYER

The aim of prayer is to release the present from its chains of past illusions.[31]

—THE SONG OF PRAYER

Any form of prayer can be a meaningful part of daily practice. Prayer is sometimes characterized as talking to God, while silent meditation is said to be listening to God. Prayer is not always verbal. The prayer of the heart is often a silent prayer without words. Learning to verbalize the heart's desire, however, can be a valuable practice.

In his book *Healing Words,* physician Larry Dossey has collected remarkable evidence for the power of prayer in healing. In addition to the immmediate relief that prayer can offer a person in distress, his data emphasizes the nonlocal effects of prayer, such as when an individual prays that a distant person may be healed. He suggests that the scientific and medical community is slowly opening to the cumulative scientific evidence that prayer promotes physical health. Dossey reminds us of the Biblical injunction to pray without ceasing.[32]

Petitionary prayer is perhaps the form that is most commonly associated with the word *prayer*. However, prayers of gratitude, blessing, worship, intention and surrender can be expressions of love rather than petitions. Other forms of prayer include the prayer of recollection, the prayer of silence and the prayer of union described by St. Teresa of Avila. In prayers of recollection we are instructed to remember the presence of God, and in prayers of silence we are to quiet the mind. The prayer of union is that which occurs in a state of mystical union with God or dissolution of the separate self in Spirit. Prayer can sometimes be an expression of fullness, sometimes of emptiness. Either way, prayer nourishes the soul by focusing attention on spiritual reality.

Petitionary prayer

A simple petitionary prayer is a single word: "Help!" This is often effective, particularly for those whose faith is strong. Even for those who feel very tentative about it, the request for help, when sincerely uttered, can bring astonishing results.

Judith Skutch Whitson, president of The Foundation for Inner Peace, tells of her experience, more than twenty years ago, when her life was very full and she had everything she thought she wanted. She was, nonetheless, feeling miserable. She later characterized this period as a time of spiritual deprivation. She finally uttered a desperate call for help, not really expecting anything. Within a few days she found herself meeting people and following a chain of events that changed her life and started her on a spiritual path that still provides help whenever she remembers to ask for it.

Many people use petitionary prayer to ask for healing, forgiveness, love, relationship or anything else they want. Prayer seems to have a salutary effect whenever we feel helpless or hopeless. Many popular twelve-step programs for recovery from addictions make good use of prayer. The first step is essentially a prayer of surrender, recognizing that life has become unmanageable and must be turned over to a higher power.

A daily petitionary prayer that some people find helpful consists of asking for the kind of day you want. Perhaps one day you might ask for stillness and serenity; another day you might ask for energy and enthusiasm. Notice what you request and, at the end of the day, if you received what you wanted. This encourages an evening review of the day's events, which in turn increases self-awareness and deepens the commitment to continuing practice.

The Indian mystical poet Rabindranath Tagore asks this:

> Oh, grant me my prayer that I may never lose the bliss of the touch
> of the one in the play of the many.[33]

Intention

> *O Lord make me an instrument of thy peace.*
> *Where there is hatred, let me sow love;*
> *Where there is injury, pardon;*
> *Where there is doubt, faith;*
> *Where there is despair, hope;*
> *Where there is darkness, light;*
> *And where there is sadness, joy.*

—St. Francis of Assisi

Prayers of intention involve an inner resolve or commitment to a particular path of action. It may be a commitment to telling the truth to oneself and others, or a commitment to practice loving kindness in all relationships. Like New Year's resolutions, such intentions may be empty words in the absence of heartfelt prayer. Only you can know the depth of your commitment.

Father Thomas Keating, a Cistercian monk, describes centering prayer as a means of connecting with the divine life within us and deepening spiritual awareness.[34] Centering prayer cultivates receptivity to the sacred and enables us to listen more deeply within. Initially, one may begin by inviting the presence of God by simply repeating a word such as "Welcome." Father Keating says that intentionality distinguishes centering prayer from other forms of prayer. Centering prayer is a training of intention that prepares us for contemplation. The goal of contemplative prayer is emptiness of self, which means that awareness of God's presence supplants reflection on ourselves. Consenting to God's presence involves self-surrender and trust, bypassing concepts, images, thoughts, feelings and sensations. Eventually one simply rests in God.

Forgiveness

> *Forgiveness, truly given, is the way in which your only hope of freedom lies.*[35]

—THE SONG OF PRAYER

Prayers for forgiveness sometimes assume guilt. However, it is not necessary to be guilty in order to feel guilty. Many relatively healthy people feel guilty about something they have or have not done, even when they know rationally that they are actually confronting their own judgments. Spiritual freedom is intimately connected with learning to forgive ourselves as well as those against whom we hold grievances. In practice, giving and receiving forgiveness turn out to be the same. A lot of mental and emotional anguish stems from lack of forgiveness. When a person holds on to anger or guilt about something that happened in the past, attention is locked into reviewing past hurts, and healing is impeded. Spiritual teachers often encourage us to forgive others. In psychotherapy we learn that we cannot forgive others unless we forgive ourselves. Forgiveness can be understood as letting go of the past. In reality, the past is gone. It continues to exist only in the mind that clings to it. When we resist letting go of the past, we experience pain and suffering. When we learn to let go more easily, our lives become more harmonious and peaceful.

The following process can be helpful for letting go:

> Pair up with someone who is willing to listen quietly for the duration of this process, about ten minutes. Ask him or her to listen with eyes closed, in order to avoid the distraction of looking at you and expressing any feelings that might inhibit your process. Take a few minutes of silence to reflect on anything in your life for which you have not forgiven yourself. There may be several things that come to mind about which you feel some guilt or remorse. Pick one incident that you are willing to talk about at this time. When you are ready, recount the incident and your feelings about it in as much detail as possible.
>
> The person listening should remain silent throughout. If there is a long silence, he or she may ask, "Is there anything else you want to say about this?" When you have shared everything you want to say, close your eyes for a minute and reflect on what you have shared. Open your eyes and make eye contact with your partner. Reflecting on what you have shared and looking into your eyes, your partner who has been listening says, "You are forgiven." He or she should make every effort to speak from the heart and mean it, in order to make sure that you accept the words. "You are forgiven" may be repeated several times. Nothing else should be added.
>
> When you have heard the words and accepted the message, close your eyes once more and remain in silence for a few minutes, paying close attention to how you feel when you accept being forgiven. Finally you and your partner can discuss your feelings about this experience. When this has been completed, you can reverse roles.

For best results these directions should be carefully followed. A person doing the exercise for the first time may be tempted to add something, comment or interfere in some way. You will do yourself and your partner a favor if you follow the directions precisely, including saying the words, "You are forgiven" rather than some variation, such as "I forgive you."

If I have not condemned, I have nothing to forgive. When I can forgive the past and let it go, I am free to be fully who I am in the present.

Gratitude

Prayers of gratitude may involve not only thankfulness for blessings that are apparent in our lives, but also for the learning that happens on a daily basis. Perceived with spiritual vision, every day offers many opportunities for gratitude. I have found that irrational feelings of guilt can often be assuaged by prayers of gratitude. When a person prone to guilt and self-blame is able to replace guilt with gratitude, a different way of perceiving the world ensues.

For example, one mother of grown children was continually concerned that she had not done as much as she should have done for her children while they were growing up. In time, as she learned to be grateful for their presence in her life and felt better about herself, her relationship with all three of her children improved noticeably. Another woman told me that one day, when she was feeling depressed and guilty for having a life of relative plenty while so many people in the world were suffering from deprivation, she suddenly realized as she sat in meditation that she could feel grateful instead of guilty. At that moment she experienced a release of tension and a surge of energy that inspired her to embark on a new creative project that was service oriented.

Different forms of gratitude might include gratitude for being alive, gratitude for love, gratitude for peace and gratitude for beauty, as well as gratitude for learning from adversity.

Brother David Steindl-Rast, a Benedictine monk, says gratitude is the heart of prayer.[36] He writes,

> Year by year i try to learn a little better how to treasure each days' blessings, above all the blessings i am apt to take for granted: the air i breathe, clean water, the blessing of sleep. But i'm exploring also the other side of blessing: our power to bless. I've come to think of blessing as the force that fills the universe with joy.[37]

The art of blessing

Since we tend to experience whatever we desire for others, when we bless others, we also bless ourselves. Furthermore, when we bless ourselves, it is easier and more natural to extend blessings for others. It is therefore good practice to bless the world by sending peace, love and joy to all beings.

The following Buddhist blessing begins by blessing oneself and then expanding the circle of compassion to include others:

> May I be happy. May I be peaceful.
> May I be loving. May I be joyful.

Thinking of a particular person, holding a clear image of him or her in your mind's eye, repeat:

> May you be happy. May you be peaceful.
> May you be loving. May you be joyful.

Visualizing the whole earth, repeat:

> May all beings be happy. May all beings be peaceful.
> May all beings be loving. May all beings be joyful.

Repetition of these phrases can blur the distinction between self and others. Since we cannot share qualities of consciousness that we do not have, accepting love, peace and joy for oneself is necessary for extending them to others. Intending them for others heals the sense of separation. These phrases can be coordinated with the breath and the qualities associated with the chakras. Love, for example, is usually associated with the heart.

POSTMODERN YOGAS

Yoga means "yoke," or "discipline," and traditional yogas are designed to bring the separated person into union with the Divine. I have called these practices postmodern yogas because they serve a dual function: They are a form of mind training that awakens the soul and brings us closer to the recognition of our essential nature. At the same time, they are compatible with the postmodern view of multiple realities and the relativity of perception. Yogas require commitment and discipline, and each of these is a challenge. None of them require a particular metaphysical belief or theology. In what follows, I discuss four postmodern yogas:

1. The yoga of truth telling.
2. The yoga of ordinariness.
3. The yoga of eye-level relationships.
4. Healing relationships.

Truth telling

The yoga of truth telling requires a commitment not to lie to oneself or anyone else. The devil, we are told in the Bible, is the prince of lies. Lies contribute to keeping us in the dark, afraid of our own shadows. Truth telling does not mean saying anything, any time, or spilling your guts inappropriately. It does mean making every effort to recognize and give up self-deception and being deceitful in interpersonal relationships. A commitment to truth is a powerful tool for eradicating self-deception, clarifying intuition and waking up.

Anyone can practice this yoga, although it is more difficult to do it alone, since we cannot see our own unconscious denial. A mutual commitment to truth in interpersonal relationships tends to develop trust and deepen communication. People get better in psychotherapy when they are able to tell the truth about their experience in a safe space, without being judged. However, as a spiritual practice, this yoga requires a unilateral commitment. It does not depend on whether anyone else does it or not.

In his recent book *Living the Mindful Life,* psychologist Charles Tart points out that most of us lie automatically, without even knowing we are lying.[38] Deliberate lying is only a small part of the lying that goes on in everyday life. Tart suggests trying an exercise of deliberately telling a little white lie and noticing what happens in your body, as well as in general. Most people find the exercise of deliberate lying very difficult. One student who tried it said, "I tried telling a lie as I was talking now, but I couldn't do it at all while I was doing this sensing, looking, and listening work."

Usually we do not realize how much lying diverts attention and creates stress. Some common lies that we do not notice are those we tell to conform to others' expectations. For example, if I say, "I don't mind that you arrived late," when in fact I was annoyed at being kept waiting, I might not even notice it. On the other hand, if I practice being truthful and saying "I don't mind" only when I mean it, I notice the difference. The first step in the yoga of truth telling involves becoming more aware of how and when we lie, and the price we pay for it.

The yoga of truth telling is supported by discernment in knowing whom to trust and when not to talk. It means learning to express anger without attack and communicating genuine appreciation and gratitude in place of flattery. It also calls for containment of personal problems. While some people need to learn to express their emotions, others need to learn to contain themselves. Communication is enhanced and people report feeling lighter and less anxious when they make a commitment to stop lying. The yoga of truth telling can also be very illuminating about how often we lie because we are afraid to speak the truth and want to protect ourselves or others. Often we do not appreciate the fact that lying is usually hurtful rather than helpful to ourselves or others. The fact that one can always think of exceptions, such as in wartime when life is in danger, does not alter the fact that truth telling can be healing, empowering and liberating.

Ordinariness

The yoga of ordinariness is an antidote to specialness, both spiritual and egoic. It counteracts tendencies to ego inflation as well as ego deflation. Thinking of oneself either as specially gifted or specially deprived and miserable can prevent one from seeing oneself and others more realistically. To reconcile oneself to being nothing special, regardless of external circumstances, is an exacting spiritual discipline, similar to the traditional virtue of spiritual poverty.

At first the yoga or ordinariness may be experienced as an exercise in ego-reduction. Many children are taught by caring families to think of themselves as special. Unfortunately, parents are often unaware that this can become a heavy burden later in life when a person feels he or she cannot live up to these parental expectations. Other well-intentioned but punitive parents may contribute to making a child feel specially unworthy. Giving up claims to specialness can be a big relief, particularly for a perfectionist or one who is attached to melodrama. It can also free one to become more fully who one is, independent of idealized images. A yoga of ordinariness also counteracts self-indulgence and feeling sorry for oneself and helps prevent projection of the shadow onto others. Each one of us is unique and has special talents, but there is nothing special about uniqueness. Everybody is unique, although not everyone has had the opportunity to develop his or her talents.

Eye-level relationships

The yoga of eye-level relationships demands a willingness to relate to others as if they were equal, neither more nor less important than oneself. We tend to pay lip service to the idea of equality, but practicing equality can be a challenging discipline. The more insecure a person is, the more likely he or she will be to put some people down, while putting others up on a pedestal. The more comfortable one becomes with oneself, the more fully present one can be with others on an equal basis.

If I put a person on a pedestal, I feel separated and somehow less than him or her. Likewise, if I look down on someone, for whatever reason, I separate myself. It is possible to see others on the same level, not looking up or down. When I do this I can see others as equally valuable parts of the whole fabric of reality, of which we are all a tiny part. Meeting others in eye-level relationships requires courage and truthfulness. If I am trying to hide something about myself and do not want to be seen by another, I will find a way to put up barriers between us. Whatever barriers I invent to avoid meeting face to face and soul to soul keep me locked into my own prison of isolation.

One may start by meeting some people in eye-level relationships, but not others. Most of us have to keep working at this discipline. The temptation to idealize or devalue others who are not like us is ever present. Many people separate themselves from others by putting themselves down, thinking that they are not enough to warrant being seen or treated as equals by those they admire. This transference or projection gets in the way of whatever real contact might otherwise occur.

For example, when two people are attracted to each other in a romantic relationship, they may find themselves at a loss for words. Idealizing another makes communicating difficult. In some cases men and women project collective stereotypes onto each other, either idealizing or devaluing all members of the opposite sex. When this happens, intimacy and relatedness becomes impossible. Not until two people can meet in an eye-level relationship can they hope to have an authentic love relationship in which they see and accept each other as they are.

Attempting to practice eye-level relationships with everyone can be a demanding challenge. It is closely related to the practice of seeing everyone as a teacher and all events as lessons that awaken the soul. This attitude contributes to psychological and spiritual growth insofar as one is willing to accept mistakes and learn from their consequences.

Practicing eye-level relationships does not mean denying that some people are wiser than others or that you would rather be with some people instead of others. It does mean treating everyone, including yourself, with consideration and respect. Whereas the world of ego tends to accentuate differences, from the perspective of the soul we can focus more clearly on what we have in common.

Healing relationships

Spirituality in everyday life is reflected in the quality of our personal relationships. When spiritual practice was reserved for monastic settings, those who chose a religious life were not necessarily expected to be skilled in human relationships. It has become clear, however, that every walk of life involves relationships with others, and healing relationships is a yoga that has become an integral part of contemporary spiritual practice.

Healing relationships means letting go of resentments and guilt about the past. In a healthy relationship differences are communicated and boundaries are clearly defined. One is neither more important nor less important that the other. Equals treat each other with respect, and spiritual friends enjoy each other's company. When fear and anger preclude clear communication, relationships suffer from the burden of unexpressed feelings.

Some of the qualities that contribute to healthy relationships are authenticity, honesty, consistency, empathy and loving kindness. The golden rule about doing unto others as you would have them do unto you is a good basic principle for relationships, given the understanding that sometimes others would not want you to treat them exactly as you would want to be treated. For example, you might want somebody to give you honest feedback about your mistakes, whereas another person might not be ready to hear your feedback about theirs. Modeling behavior by correcting your own mistakes is usually more effective for healing relationships.

Listening to feelings that express either love or fear can help us recognize when love is hidden by anxiety and fear is covered by hostility. If I have not faced my own fears, I will probably not be able to listen to others very well, since I will be preoccupied by my own unresolved issues. If I find myself having trouble in relationships, it is a good indication that I need to do more of my own inner work. This does not mean that I should stay in a dysfunctional intimate relationship. In some cases it is better for both people to go their separate ways. It does mean that repetitive patterns in relationship indicate unresolved problems from the past.

The widespread tendency to blame others for whatever is troublesome in any relationship is bolstered by defenses such as denial, projection and repression. Blame is always unproductive and does not contribute to healing. Blaming oneself is as ineffectual as blaming others. When the tendency to assign blame can be replaced by self-disclosure and spiritual awareness, relationship problems diminish and friendships become a genuine source of joy and love, rather than a source of problems on the path.

Finally, the intention of healing relationships, instead of defending oneself against imagined threats, can affect everything we do and every relationship that we encounter, whether it be a casual interaction with a stranger or the most intimate love relationship. Whatever we think we must defend often turns out to be another illusion that casts a shadow on any relationship.

These four yogas reflect the basic virtues identified in the wisdom traditions as humility, charity and veracity. Veracity extends beyond truth telling to seeing things as they are, enabling us to see past the shadows of greed, hatred and delusion.[39]

REFLECTION

Wisdom without method is bondage. Method without wisdom is bondage.
—THE BUDDHA

Reflecting each day on the inner world of soul can be another way of deepening spiritual practice. Journal keeping, evening reviews or depth psychotherapy can offer access to the inner life that may be neglected under pressure from the world of ego.

Reflecting on where we have come from, what we are learning and where we think we are going is an effective way of increasing self-awareness. In this process it is important not to blame oneself or others for mistakes. Sometimes we learn more from our mistakes and failures than from our successes.

Support groups and co-counseling can also encourage reflection as spiritual practice if they occur in a context of spiritual inquiry with a commitment to truth telling and awakening the soul.

Psychotherapy that is oriented to developing self-awareness can be a powerful asset on the spiritual path if the therapist understands the value of practice and does not dismiss it prematurely as avoidance of relationship. Although one can use practice to avoid facing the world, practice also serves a purpose. A therapist who has no training or interest in spirituality and soul work may be helpful in other ways, but cannot be expected to assist in this process.

READING AND STUDY

Spiritual traditions point out that intellectual work alone is not liberating. It is possible to accumulate knowledge without increasing wisdom. My Zen teacher used to say, "In silence we learn what can never be taught." Studying the teachings can, nevertheless, be an integral part of spiritual practice. It supports other forms of practice as well as increasing our understanding of spiritual experiences.

Whereas the spiritual quest used to involve travel to distant lands and still does for some people, others find their path by exploring the literature of various traditions. Both exoteric and esoteric teachings from many traditions are readily available. I think Ken Wilber's books offer the best synthesis of psychology, philosophy and religion, East and West. For those who would like to deepen their understanding of traditions, *The World's*

Religions, by Huston Smith,[40] is a classic. *The Psychology of Religion,* by David Wulff,[41] is also an excellent text.

The history of transpersonal psychology is closely associated with contemporary efforts to reclaim the soul in psychology. The work of Ken Wilber, Stanislav Grof and others[42] brings a radically new perspective to psychology. There is so much relevant literature available today, the main problem is selectivity. Intellectual understanding is not the whole journey, but it can certainly be helpful on the way.

Literature, poetry, music, dance and all the arts may also be studied in the context of developing spiritual awareness. Although artistic expression does not always have a spiritual dimension, when it does it can be powerful in its effects. Even if one is not an artist, the appreciation of aesthetics and beauty in daily life is nourishing to the soul.

TEACHING AND LEARNING

Every tradition offers methods for teaching and learning. Some seemingly simple instructions can have a profound and long-lasting impact. The injunctions of the eightfold path in Buddhism are a good example of such teachings that have become popular in America in recent decades.

Buddhism teaches that all life is imbued with suffering. The root cause of suffering is said to be ignorance of our true nature and persistent clinging and attachment to what we find desirable in a world of impermanence and constant change. There is, however, a way out of this suffering. One who aspires to liberation is advised to follow the eightfold path, practicing the following principles in daily life:

1. *Right understanding.* Observing the changing, illusory nature of self-concept and understanding the laws of cause and effect is a strong motivation for spiritual practice. Right understanding affords insight into how ignorance creates suffering.

2. *Right thought.* Most of us are willing to take responsibility for our behavior, but few of us take responsibility for our thoughts. As we observe our thoughts, we can clarify them and free the mind from greed, hatred and delusion.

3. *Right speech.* This means telling the truth and not participating in malicious gossip. Speech reveals attitudes and intentions more than we realize. Practicing right speech can become a habit. It can also bring attention to dysfunctional patterns of self-abuse. For example, I might call myself stupid for making a mistake in situations in which I would not call

somebody else stupid for making the same mistake. Practicing right speech subvocally as well as out loud is a revealing practice.

4. *Right action.* This means a commitment to not killing and not harming others. Since we are not aware of the long-term effects of our action, we are advised to be gentle and peaceable in our behavior.

5. *Right livelihood.* This means engaging in work that is not harmful to others and does not involve killing, stealing or lying. Right livelihood means finding a way to live that does not exploit others or the earth and contributes to the benefit of the whole.

6. *Right effort.* This can be understood as an injunction to practice in a balanced way, without strain. We cannot force the process of spiritual unfolding. Effort is balanced by surrender.

7. *Mindfulness.* The practice of mindfulness means being aware of what is happening in the present moment, noticing body sensations, feelings and thoughts as they arise and disappear. Mindfulness is usually learned in meditation and then applied to everyday life. It is difficult to learn without focusing attention on mind/body processes to the exclusion of other activities.

8. *Right concentration.* This is the ability to hold the mind steady in meditation. This may be difficult at first, but any form of practice becomes easier when concentration is developed.[43]

According to *A Course in Miracles,* teaching is a constant process that goes on every moment of the day and continues into sleeping thoughts as well. To teach is to demonstrate, and from your demonstration others learn, and so do you.[44] One purpose of the *Course* is to provide you with a means of choosing what you want to teach and what you want to learn. It is a good example of a teaching method that is easily integrated with everyday life.

The *Course* is a spiritual self-study course that can be undertaken by anyone who is interested. I recommend working with the original material rather than someone else's interpretation of it. I usually suggest starting with the *Workbook,* since many people find the *Text* difficult at first. There is a big difference between reading the *Course* and putting the principles into practice. Even students who have been through it many times find practice challenging.

The *Course* is unique in offering a path that focuses specifically on healing relationships. It can be done alone, with a partner or in a group. You do not have to belong to any organization in order to be a student. All you need are the books.

SERVICE IN THE WORLD

I slept and dreamt that life was joy.
I awoke and saw that life was service,
I acted and behold, service was joy.

—TAGORE

Spirituality in daily life includes some form of service. Through service we can discover a lot about ourselves and our attachments. Service to an individual, the family, the community, the planet or God always involves being in relationship to something that is other than self. Many people find a sense of meaning and purpose in life through service.

However, if service is based on self-sacrifice, it can be detrimental to the one who is served as well as to the person doing the service. Furthermore, when service becomes a burden, it usually ends in burnout. Healthy people who have attained a degree of spiritual maturity are usually sincerely motivated to make a contribution to the well-being of others in some way, as an expression of their love, gratitude or compassion. Loving service stems not from a sense of obligation or duty, but from a genuine generosity of spirit. On the spiritual path service can become an integral part of whatever we do. If we are awake to our true nature and aware of self as soul, service seems to be a natural expression of who we are.

LETTING GO OF ILLUSIONS

Illusion is very strong, or it wouldn't be illusion. Illusion is not just a
property of what one desires, it's a property of the force of desire itself.[45]
—JACOB NEEDLEMAN

Our shadows walk beside us on the journey to freedom. Witnessing the play of illusion as Spirit in action, aware of the interdependence of opposites, we grow in wisdom and compassion. We can dream of infinite worlds of birth and death stretching through time *and* we can wake up to the eternal presence of emptiness, in which all dreams arise.

Many wise people have seen through shadows of the sacred and found the way to peace and liberation. But each of us has a personal shadow that demands attention too. Indulging the shadows or denying them, does not make them disappear. When we see the relativity of things and accept our shadows without mistaking them for reality, we can begin to make peace with them. Most of us are afraid to let illusions go. Long ago, Plato pointed out that when someone who escaped the prison of the cave realized that prisoners in the cave had mistaken shadows for reality, it was unlikely that those who were still in the cave would believe what they had not seen.[46]

As we begin to know ourselves and acknowledge our shadows and illusions, we begin to see that the spiritual path can be a gateway to freedom. Some people believe that there is no such gate, but there is no way of knowing except to go through it.[47] To believe that we ourselves, unlike others, are free of illusions and cast no shadow is to mistake our partial perceptions of reality for the whole. We shape the worlds that we inhabit by our desires, and they reflect our disowned shadows. If we refuse to look at them, we will never be free.

To let go of illusions is to forgive ourselves and each other for those blindspots that we have not yet recognized. To honor the sacred in spite of its shadows is to know ourselves better and to dispel the fear of darkness by listening to love and trusting the truth. As we open our hearts and quiet our minds, while making every effort to relieve the suffering rooted in ignorance and delusion, we can be grateful that we can learn to be kind, to let be and let go.

Shadows of the sacred are like dreams that disappear when we no longer value them. Behind the shadows and illusions, yet within reach, is joy. The path that leads from ignorance to understanding, from fear to love and through darkness to light invites our awakening. For the awakened soul perception is a mirror, and the play of light and shadow reveals the bright radiance of eternity.

Notes

Chapter 1 / Golden Chains on the Spiritual Path

1. C. Zweig and J. Abrams, eds. *Meeting the Shadow: The Hidden Power of the Dark Side of Human Nature* (Los Angeles: J. P. Tarcher, 1991).
2. Ibid., 4.
3. B. Walker, *The Woman's Encyclopedia of Myths and Secrets* (San Francisco: Harper and Row, 1983).
4. S. Taylor, *Positive Illusions: Creative Self-Deception and the Healthy Mind* (New York: Basic Books, 1989).
5. H. Smith, *Essays on World Religions* (New York: Paragon House, 1991), 123.
6. J. Robinson, ed., *The Nag Hammadi Library: The Gospel of Thomas* (New York: Harper and Row, 1977).
7. B. Devall and G. Sessions, *Deep Ecology: Living as if Nature Mattered* (Layton, Utah: Peregrine Smith Books, 1985), 67.
8. W. Fox, "Transpersonal Ecology: Psychologizing Ecophilosophy," *Journal of Transpersonal Psychology* 22(1):59–96.
9. L. Hixon, *Coming Home: The Experience of Enlightenment in Sacred Traditions* (Garden City, N.Y.: Anchor Press/Doubleday, 1978), 87.
10. A. Bergin, "Values and Religious Issues in Psychotherapy and Mental Health," *American Psychologist,* 46 (1991):394–403.
11. C. G. Jung, "Psychotherapists or the Clergy," in vol.11 *Collected Works* (Princeton, N.J.: Princeton University Press, 1932), 327–47.
12. A. Maslow, *The Farther Reaches of Human Nature* (New York: Viking, 1971).
13. S. Grof and C. Grof, eds., *Spiritual Emergency* (Los Angeles: J. P. Tarcher, 1989).
14. S. Grof, *The Adventure of Self Discovery* (New York: SUNY Press, 1988).
15. T. Byrom, ed., *The Dhammapada: The Sayings of the Buddha* (New York: Vintage, 1976), 70.

16. H. Luke, *Old Age* (New York: Parabola Books, 1987).

17. S. H. Nasr, *Knowledge and the Sacred* (New York: State University of New York, 1989).

18. Kalamas Sutra cited in S. Boorstein, ed., *Transpersonal Psychotherapy* (Palo Alto, Calif.: Science and Behavior, 1981).

19. S. E. Whicher, ed., *Selections from Ralph Waldo Emerson* (Boston: Houghton Mifflin, 1957), 21.

20. Sri Aurobindo, *Thoughts and Aphorisms* (Pondicherry, India: Sri Aurobindo Ashram, 1977), 6.

21. A. Deikman, *The Wrong Way Home* (Boston: Beacon Press, 1990).

22. S. Mitchell, *The Gospel According to Jesus* (New York: Harper Collins, 1991), 46–47.

Chapter 2 / Living in Two Worlds

1. C. Tart, "Perspectives on Scientism, Religion, and Philosophy Provided by Parapsychology," *Journal of Humanistic Psychology* 32(2):94 (1992).

2. Sri Aurobindo, "Thoughts and Glimpses," in *Sri Aurobindo and The Mother on Love,* ed. Pavitra (Pondicherry, India: Sri Aurobindo Ashram, 1973).

3. Tart, *Journal of Humanistic Psychology,* 74.

4. K. Wilber, *The Spectrum of Consciousness* (Wheaton, Ill.: Theosophical Publishing House, 1993).

5. M. Woodman, *Leaving my Father's House* (Boston: Shambhala, 1992).

6. T. Byrom, *The Dhammapada: The Sayings of the Buddha* (New York: Vintage, 1976).

7. F. Vaughan, *The Inward Arc: Healing in Psychotherapy and Spirituality,* 2d ed. (Nevada City, Calif.: Blue Dolphin Press, 1995).

8. Gyalse Ngulchu Thogmed, Quoted by Lama Surya Das in "The Secret Teachings of Tibet: An Interview with Catherine Ingram," in *Yoga Journal* (March-April 1993):65.

9. J. Callahan, "Leaving the Ashram," in *Common Boundary,* 10(4):32–39 (1992).

10. Byrom, *The Dhammapada,* 3.

11. S. Suzuki, *Zen Mind, Beginner's Mind* (New York: Weatherhill, 1980), 116.

Chapter 3 / Sex and Death

1. Sogyal Rinpoche, *The Tibetan Book of Living and Dying* (San Francisco: HarperCollins, 1992), 11.
2. K. Wilber, *The Atman Project* (Wheaton, Ill.: Theosophical Publishing House, 1980).
3. I. Yalom, *Existential Psychotherapy* (New York: Basic Books, 1980), 27.
4. S. Grof, *Books of the Dead: Manuals for Living and Dying* (New York: Thames and Hudson, 1994), 92.
5. R. Moody, *Life After Life* (Atlanta: Mockingbird Books, 1975).
6. K. Ring, *Life at Death* (New York: Coward, McCann and Geoghegan, 1980).
7. K. Ring, "Near Death Experiences: Implications for Human Evolution and Planetary Transformation," in *ReVision* 8(2):75–85 (1986).
8. H. Smith, *Forgotten Truth: The Primordial Tradition* (New York: Harper and Row, 1976), 143.
9. J. Campbell, *The Masks of God: Primitive Mythology* (New York: Viking, 1970), 178.
10. Ibid., 170–71.
11. S. Grof and H. Zina Bennett, *The Holotropic Mind: The Three Levels of Human Consciousness and How They Shape Our Lives* (San Francisco: HarperSanFrancisco, 1992), 60.
12. S. Grof, *The Adventure of Self-Discovery* (New York: State University of New York Press, 1988).
13. B. Walker, *The Woman's Encyclopedia of Myths and Secrets* (San Francisco: Harper and Row, 1983).
14. K. Wilber, "The Pre/Trans Fallacy," in *Eye to Eye* (Garden City, N.Y.: Anchor Books, 1983).
15. Ibid., 234.
16. Walker, *The Woman's Encyclopedia of Myths and Secrets*, 283.
17. M. Shaw, *Passionate Enlightenment: Women in Tantric Buddhism* (Princeton, N.J.: Princeton University Press, 1994).
18. R. Tigunait, "Upholding the Vedic Ideal," in *Yoga International* 4(2):22–28 (1994).
19. M. Eliade, "Sexuality: An Overview," in *The Encyclopedia of Religion*, ed. by M. Eliade (New York: Macmillan, 1987), 13:183–86.
20. Ibid., 975.

21. E. Pagels, Lecture on "The Gnostic Gospel of Philip," San Francisco, Calif., 1992.
22. M. L. von Franz, *On Dreams and Death* (Boston: Shambhala, 1986).
23. J. M. Robinson, ed., "The Sentences of Sextus," in *The Nag Hammadi Library* (San Francisco: Harper and Row, 1981), 456.
24. J. Singer, *Seeing Through the Visible World* (New York: Harper and Row, 1990), 261.
25. Robinson, *The Nag Hammadi Library.*
26. von Franz, *On Dreams and Death.*
27. C. G. Jung, "Letters," in *On Dreams and Death,* 155.
28. S. Grof and C. Grof, *Beyond Death* (New York: Thames and Hudson, Inc., 1980), 19–20.
29. Buddha, *The Parinirvana Sutra* cited in *Crazy Wisdom,* by Wes Nisker (Berkeley, Calif.: Ten Speed Press, 1990), 201.
30. F. Fremantle and C. Trungpa, eds., *The Tibetan Book of the Dead* (Boston: Shambhala, 1987).
31. *The Tibetan Book of the Dead,* cited in C. G. Jung, *Psychology and the East,* trans. by R. F. C. Hull (Princeton, N.J.: Princeton University Press, Bollingen Series, 1978).
32. Fremantle and Trungpa, *The Tibetan Book of The Dead,* 36.
33. C. G. Jung, *Psychology and the East.*
34. Walker, *The Woman's Encyclopedia of Myths and Secrets,* 749–50.
35. Grof, *Books of the Dead.*
36. Grof and Grof, *Beyond Death.*
37. Ibid.
38. Ibid.
39. Singer, *Seeing Through the Visible World,* 192.
40. A. Wallace, *Tibetan Buddhism From the Ground Up* (Boston: Wisdom Publications, 1993).
41. K. Kramer, *The Sacred Art of Dying* (New York: Paulist Press, 1988).
42. Sogyal Rinpoche, *The Tibetan Book of Living and Dying,* 14.
43. Ibid.
44. J. White, *A Practical Guide to Death and Dying* (Wheaton, Ill.: Quest Books, 1988).
45. T. Greening, "Awareness," in *Journal of Humanistic Psychology* 31(2):98. Reprinted with permission.
46. Chuang Tsu, quoted in *Crazy Wisdom,* by Wes Nisker (Berkeley, Calif.: Ten Speed Press, 1990), 201.

47. E. Warmington and P. Rouse, eds., "Phaedo," in *The Great Dialogues of Plato*, trans. by W. H. D. Rouse (New York: New American Library, 1956).

48. M. Murphy, *The Future of the Body* (Los Angeles: J. P. Tarcher, 1992), 456.

49. M. Harran, "Suicide," in *The Encyclopedia of Religion,* 14:125–31.

50. Ibid.

51. Namkhai Norbu, *Dream Yoga and the Practice of Natural Light,* ed. by Michael Katz (Ithaca, N.Y.: Snow Lion Publications, 1992), 48.

52. P. Rodegast and J. Stanton, eds., *Emmanuel's Book* (New York: Friends' Press, 1985).

53. Smith, *Forgotten Truth,* 144.

Chapter 4 / The Path of Love

1. L. Hixon, *Great Swan: Meetings with Ramakrishna* (Boston: Shambhala, 1992).

2. A. Peers, trans., "The Complete Works of St. John of the Cross," in *Forgotten Truth*, by H. Smith (New York: Harper and Row, 1976), 85.

3. H. Smith, *Beyond the Post-Modern Mind* (New York: Crossroads, 1982).

4. B. Metzger and R. Murphy, eds., *The New Oxford Annotated Bible* (New York: Oxford University Press, 1991), 34.

5. *The New English Bible* (Oxford University Press and Cambridge University Press, 1961), 296.

6. S. Mitchell, *The Gospel According to Jesus* (New York: Harper Collins, 1991).

7. Sri Aurobindo, *The Synthesis of Yoga,* 6th ed. (Pondicherry, India: Sri Aurobindo Ashram Press, 1976), 563.

8. D. Wulff, *Psychology of Religion* (New York: John Wiley, 1991).

9. Hixon, *Great Swan,* 17.

10. B. Long, "Love," *The Encyclopedia of Religion,* 9:38.

11. P. Tillich, *A History of Christian Thought* (New York: Simon and Schuster, 1967), 496.

12. Ibid., 122.

13. S. Mitchell, *The Enlightened Mind* (New York: Harper Collins, 1991), 40.

14. Ibid., 194.

15. H. Hendrix, *Getting the Love You Want: A Guide for Couples* (New York: Harper and Row, 1988).

16. A. Carotenuto, *Eros and Pathos: Shades of Love and Suffering* (Toronto, Canada: Inner City Books, 1980), 15.

17. A. H. Almas, *Essence: The Diamond Approach to Inner Realization* (York Beach, Maine: Samuel Weiser, 1986).

18. B. Metzger and R. Murphy, eds., *The New Oxford Annotated Bible*, 1 John 4:16–19.

19. K. Wilber, personal communication, 1991.

20. J. Campbell, *Transformations of Myth Through Time* (New York: Harper and Row, 1990), 156.

21. *A Course in Miracles* consists of a Text, Workbook for Students, and Manual for Teachers. It was channelled by two psychologists at Columbia Presbyterian College of Physicians and Surgeons who preferred to remain anonymous. It teaches that the Christ mind speaking through the *Course* is shared by everyone. It says that God is love and therefore so are we. The opposite of love is fear, which is rooted in the illusion of a separate, independent ego identity. For information contact The Foundation for Inner Peace, P.O. Box 598, Mill Valley, CA 94941.

22. Campbell, *Transformations of Myth Through Time,* 157.

23. K. Wilber, *Grace and Grit* (Boston: Shambhala, 1991), 410.

24. T. Moore, *Soulmates* (New York: HarperCollins, 1994) 258.

25. K. Kelly, *The Home Planet* (New York: Addison-Wesley, 1988), 38.

26. Ibid., 127.

27. P. Hopkins and S. Anderson, *The Feminine Face of God* (New York: Bantam, 1991).

28. Anonymous, *A Course in Miracles*, 2d ed. (Mill Valley, Calif.: Foundation for Inner Peace, 1992), WB(127):231.

29. F. Vaughan, *The Inward Arc* (Boston: Shambhala, 1986).

30. Rumi, unpublished version by Robert Bly, printed with permission of Robert Bly, 1994.

31. Anonymous, *A Course in Miracles,* T:339–40.

32. I. Yalom, *When Nietzsche Wept* (New York: Basic Books, 1992).

33. V. Solovyov, *The Meaning of Love* (West Stockbridge, Maine: Lindisfarne Press, 1985).

34. L. Kohlberg, *The Philosophy of Moral Development* (New York: Harper and Row, 1981).

35. C. Gilligan, *In a Different Voice* (Cambridge: Harvard University Press, 1982).

36. C. Kiefer, *The Mantle of Maturity: A History of Ideas About Character Development* (Albany, N.Y.: SUNY, 1988).

37. K. Wilber, et. al., eds., *Transformations of Consciousness* (Boston: Shambhala, 1986).

38. E. Fromm, *The Art of Loving* (New York: Harper and Row, 1956), 71.

39. R. McDermott, ed., *The Essential Steiner* (San Francisco: Harper and Row, 1984), 41.

40. L. Hixon, *Atom from the Sun of Knowledge* (Westport, Conn.: Pir Press, 1993), 101.

41. K. Kavanaugh and O. Rodriguez, trans., vol. 2 of *The Collected Works of St. Teresa of Avila* (Washington: D. V. L. Institute of Carmelite Studies, 1980).

42. M. Smith, "The Nature and Meaning of Mysticism," *Understanding Mysticism,* ed. R. Woods (Garden City, N.Y.: Doubleday, 1980), 20.

43. L. Hixon, *Great Swan,* 62–63.

44. Ibid., 75.

45. Anonymous, *A Course in Miracles,* WB(260):22

Chapter 5 / Awakening Soul

1. Anonymous, *A Course in Miracles,* 2d ed. (Mill Valley, Calif.: Foundation for Inner Peace, 1992), T:227.

2. A. Wierzbicka, "Soul and Mind: Linguistic Evidence for Ethnopsychology and Cultural History," *American Anthropologist* 9 (1989):41–58.

3. H. Zimmer, *Philosophies of India,* ed. by J. Campbell (Princeton, N.J.: Princeton University Press, Bollingen Series XXVI, 1951), 79.

4. A. Huxley, *The Perennial Philosophy* (New York: Harper and Row, 1944).

5. R. Walsh, *The Spirit of Shamanism* (Los Angeles: J. P. Tarcher, 1990).

6. J. Hillman, *Re-Visioning Psychology* (New York: Harper and Row, 1975), 174.

7. H. Smith, *Forgotten Truth: The Primordial Tradition* (New York: Harper and Row, 1976), 62.

8. Ibid., 74.

9. L. Hixon, *Coming Home: The Experience of Enlightenment in Sacred Traditions* (New York: Anchor Books, 1978).

10. Meister Eckhart, cited in K. Wilber, *Grace and Grit* (Boston: Shambhala, 1991).

11. K. Wilber, *A Sociable God* (New York: McGraw Hill, 1983).

12. Sri Aurobindo, *The Life Divine* (Pondicherry, India: Sri Aurobindo Ashram, 1982), 857.

13. Smith, *Forgotten Truth,* 89.

14. R. Walsh and F. Vaughan, *Paths Beyond Ego* (Los Angeles: J. P. Tarcher, 1993).

15. M. Harner, *The Way of the Shaman*, 2d ed. (San Francisco: Harper and Row, 1990).

16. S. Ingerman, *Soul Retrieval* (San Francisco: Harper Collins, 1991).

17. C. Spretnak, *States of Grace* (San Francisco: Harper, 1991).

18. R. Walsh, *The Spirit of Shamanism*.

19. A. Bailey, *The Light of the Soul* (New York: Lucis Press, 1955).

20. K. Wilber, *Sex, Ecology, Spirituality* (Boston: Shambhala, 1995).

21. J. Bremmer, "Soul: Greek and Hellenistic Concepts," in *The Encyclopedia of Religion*, ed. by M. Eliade (New York: Macmillan, 1987), 13:434–38.

22. E. Warmington and P. Rouse, eds., *Great Dialogues of Plato*, trans. by W. H. D. Rouse (New York: New American Library, 1956).

23. A. Shearer and P. Russell, trans., *The Upanishads* (London: Unwin Hyman Limited, 1989), 36.

24. W. K. Mahony, "Soul: Indian Concepts," in *The Encyclopedia of Religion*, 13:438–43.

25. Shearer and Russell, *The Upanishads*, 101.

26. C. Alexander and E. Langer, *Higher Stages of Human Development* (New York: Oxford University Press, 1991).

27. *Maharishi Mahesh Yogi on the Bhagavad-Gita* (London: Arkana, 1990), 443.

28. G. Feuerstein, *The Yoga-Sutra of Patanjali* (Rochester, Vt.: Inner Traditions, 1989), 50.

29. S. Collins, "Soul: Buddhist Concepts," in *The Encyclopedia of Religion*, 13:443–47.

30. T. Byrom, ed., *The Dhammapada: The Sayings of the Buddha* (New York: Vintage, 1976), 151.

31. Ibid., 97.

32. T. Wei-ming, "Chinese Concepts," in *The Encyclopedia of Religion*, 13:447–50.

33. J. White, "Martial Arts and the Path to Enlightenment: An Interview with Joe Hyams," in *New Realities* 10(1990):6, 20–24.

34. J. Bemporad, "Soul: Jewish Concepts," in *The Encyclopedia of Religion*, 13:450–54.

35. K. Kramer, *The Sacred Art of Dying* (New York: Paulist Press, 1988).

36. S. Kramer, *San Diego Jewish Meditation Institute Newsletter*, 1 (1992).

37. S. Kramer, "Introduction to Jewish Mysticism," Cassette tape (San Diego: Nogah Productions, 1992).

38. King James Translation, *Holy Bible,* Mark 8:36 and Matthew 16:26. Translated in *The New English Bible* as "What does a man gain by winning the whole world at the cost of his true self?" (Oxford University Press, 1961), 72.
39. King James Translation, *Holy Bible,* John 20:22.
40. G. MacGregor, "Christian Concepts," in *The Encyclopedia of Religion,* 13:455–60.
41. E. Pagels, *Adam, Eve, and the Serpent* (New York: Vintage Books, 1988).
42. M. Marmura, "Islamic Concepts," in *The Encyclopedia of Religion,* 13: 455–60.
43. L. Hixon, *Atom from the Sun of Knowledge* (Westport, Conn.: Pir Publications, 1993), 285.
44. Ibid., 93.
45. H. Corbin, *The Man of Light in Iranian Sufism,* trans. by Nancy Pearson (Boston: Shambhala, 1978), 68–71.
46. S. H. Nasr, *Knowledge and the Sacred* (New York: State University of New York, 1989), 147.
47. Hari Das, *The Yellow Book* (San Cristobal, New Mexico: Lama Foundation, 1973), cited in Fadiman and Frager, *Personality and Personal Growth* (San Francisco: Harper and Row, 1976).
48. K. Wilber, "The Spectrum of Transpersonal Development," in *Paths Beyond Ego,* 116–17.
49. F. Vaughan, *Awakening Intuition* (New York: Anchor Books, 1979).
50. K. Wilber, *Eye to Eye* (New York: Doubleday, 1983).
51. J. Hillman, *Re-Visioning Psychology.*
52. J. Singer, *Boundaries of the Soul* (Garden City, N.Y.: Anchor Books, 1971), 33.
53. R. Assagioli, *Psychosynthesis* (New York: Hobbs Dorman, 1965).
54. K. Wilber, *Grace and Grit,* 200.
55. K. Wilber, "Paths Beyond Ego in the Coming Decade," in *Paths Beyond Ego.*

Chapter 6 / Soul and Gender

1. A. Shearer and P. Russell, eds., *The Upanishads* (London: Mandala, 1989), 98.
2. S. Hoeller, *Jung and the Lost Gospels* (Wheaton, Ill.: Quest Books, 1989).
3. E. Pagels, *Adam, Eve, and the Serpent* (New York: Vintage Books, 1988).
4. E. F. Keller, *Reflections on Gender and Science* (New Haven: Yale University Press, 1985).

5. J. Borysenko, *Guilt is the Teacher, Love is the Lesson* (New York: Warner, 1990).
6. S. Colegrave, "The Unfolding Feminine Principle in Human Consciousness," in *To Be a Woman,* ed. by C. Zweig (Los Angeles: J. P. Tarcher, 1990).
7. R. Johnson, *We: Understanding the Psychology of Romantic Love* (San Francisco: Harper and Row, 1983), 160.
8. E. Neumann, *Amor and Psyche: The Psychic Development of the Feminine* (New York: Pantheon Books, Bollingen Series LIV, 1956).
9. J. Hillman, *Anima* (Dallas, Tex.: Spring Publications, 1985), 7.
10. Ibid., 19.
11. C. Douglas, "Christina Morgan's Visions Reconsidered: A Look Behind the Visions Seminars," in *The San Francisco Jung Library Journal* 8(4):5–27 (1989).
12. E. Whitmont, "Reassessing Femininity and Masculinity," in *Anima* 7(2): 125–39 (1981).
13. Ibid., 138–39.
14. C. Gilligan, *In a Different Voice* (Cambridge: Harvard University Press, 1982).
15. J. Singer, *Androgyny* (Garden City, N.Y.: Anchor Books, 1976).
16. C. Douglas, "Christina Morgan's Visions Reconsidered," in *The San Francisco Jung Library Journal* 8(4):5–27 (1989).
17. R. McDermott, *The Essential Steiner* (San Francisco: Harper and Row, 1984).
18. M. L. von Franz, *Projection and Re-collection in Jungian Psychology: Reflections of the Soul* (La Salle and London: Open Court, 1980).
19. Ibid., 166.
20. Shearer and Russell, *The Upanishads,* 98.
21. R. Metzner, "The Mystical Symbolic Psychology of Hildegard von Bingen," in *ReVision* 11(2):3–12 (1988).
22. von Franz, *Projection and Re-collection in Jungian Psychology,* 227.
23. J. M. Robinson, ed., "The Gospel of Thomas," in *The Nag Hammadi Library* (San Francisco: Harper and Row, 1981), 121.

Chapter 7 / Healing and Empowerment

1. E. Fromm, *The Art of Loving* (New York: Bantam, 1956), 21.
2. P. Young-Eisendrath and F. Wiedemann, *Female Authority* (New York: The Guilford Press, 1987), 1.

3. Fromm, *The Art of Loving,* 19.

4. Ibid., 38.

5. V. Frankl, "Salvation in a Concentration Camp," in *Soul: An Archaeology,* ed. by P. Cousineau (San Francisco: HarperSanFrancisco, 1994), 75–77.

6. C. Castaneda, *The Art of Dreaming* (San Francisco: HarperSanFrancisco, 1983), 81.

7. D. Elgin, *Awakening Earth* (New York: William Morrow, 1993).

8. Fromm, *The Art of Loving,* 18.

9. J. Needleman, *Money and the Meaning of Life* (New York: Doubleday, 1991).

10. L. Dossey, *Recovering the Soul: A Scientific and Spiritual Search* (New York: Bantam Books, 1989), 287.

11. R. Moore, *Care of the Soul* (New York: HarperCollins, 1993).

12. Anonymous, *A Course in Miracles,* 2d ed. (Mill Valley, Calif.: Foundation for Inner Peace, 1992), T:158.

13. S. Grof, *Adventures of Self-Discovery* (New York: State University of New York, 1988).

14. S. Grof, *The Holotropic Mind* (San Francisco: HarperSanFrancisco: 1992).

15. Ibid., 204.

16. S. Ingerman, *Soul Retrieval: Mending the Fragmented Self* (San Francisco: HarperSanFrancisco, 1991), 27.

17. J. Bradshaw, *Healing the Shame That Binds You* (Deerfield Beach, Fla.: Health Communications, Inc., 1988).

18. T. Moore, *The Planets Within* (Hudson, N.Y.: Lindisfarne Press, 1990), 53.

19. C. Grof, *The Thirst for Wholeness* (San Francisco: HarperSanFrancisco, 1993), 191.

20. Ibid., 185.

21. Thich Nhat Hanh, *Peace is Every Step* (New York: Bantam Books, 1991), 122.

22. R. Walsh, *The Spirit of Shamanism* (Los Angeles: J. P. Tarcher, 1990), 116.

23. W. James, *The Varieties of Religious Experience* (New York: New American Library, 1958), 389.

24. J. Hillman, *Re-Visioning Psychology* (New York: Harper and Row, 1975).

25. K. Wilber, *Grace and Grit* (Boston: Shambhala, 1991).

26. R. Tarnas, *The Passion of the Western Mind* (New York: Harmony Books, 1991).
27. F. Vaughan, *The Inward Arc: Healing in Psychotherapy and Spirituality* (Nevada City, Calif.: Blue Dolphin Press, 1995).
28. For further, more detailed discussion of these archetypes and some of their traditional representations, see Angeles Arrien, *The Fourfold Way* (San Francisco: Harper Collins, 1992).
29. R. Frager and J. Fadiman, *Personality and Personal Growth*, 2d ed. (New York: Harper and Row, 1984).
30. E. Pagels, *Adam, Eve, and the Serpent* (New York: Vintage Books, 1988).
31. D. Millman, *The Way of the Peaceful Warrior* (Tiburon, Calif.: H. J. Kramer, 1980).
32. J. Achterberg, *Woman as Healer* (Boston: Shambhala, 1990).
33. L. Dossey, *Healing Words* (San Francisco: HarperSanFrancisco, 1993).
34. A. Toynbee, *A Study of History* (New York: Oxford University Press, 1934).
35. R. Sardello, *Facing the World with Soul* (Hudson, N.Y.: Lindisfarne Press, 1992), 54.
36. A. Anthony, et al., *Spiritual Choices: Recognizing Authentic Paths to Inner Transformation* (New York: Paragon House, 1986).
37. Needleman, *Money and the Meaning of Life.*
38. Ibid., 136.
39. A. Shearer, trans., *Effortless Being: The Yoga Sutras of Patanjali* (London: Unwin, 1989).
40. W. James, *Principles of Psychology* (New York: Dover Publications, 1950), 1:424.
41. Fromm, *The Art of Loving,* 18.
42. Anonymous, *Meditations on the Tarot: A Journey into Christian Hermeticism* (Rockport, Maine: Element, Inc., 1985), 11.

Chapter 8 / The Myth of Enlightenment

1. L. Hixon, *Coming Home: The Experience of Enlightenment in Sacred Traditions* (Garden City, N.Y.: Anchor Books, 1978), 115.
2. A. Flew, *A Dictionary of Philosophy,* 2d ed. (New York: St. Martin's Press, 1979).
3. A. Wood, *The Encyclopedia of Religion,* 5:113.
4. S. Schumacher and G. Woerner, eds., *The Encyclopedia of Eastern Philosophy and Religion* (Boston: Shambhala, 1989).

5. Swami Prabhavananda and C. Isherwood, trans., *The Song of God: Bhagavad-Gita* (New York: New American Library, 1972).
6. Sri Aurobindo, *Thoughts and Aphorisms* (Pondicherry, India: Sri Aurobindo Ashram, 1977), 90.
7. Ibid., 4.
8. N. Norbu, *The Cycle of Day and Night: An Essential Tibetan Text on the Practice of Contemplation,* trans. and ed. by John Reynolds (Barrytown, N.Y.: Station Hill Press, 1987).
9. J. Campbell, *The Hero with a Thousand Faces* (New York: Meridian Books, 1967), 191–92.
10. D. T. Suzuki, "The Basis of Buddhist Philosophy," in *Understanding Mysticism,* ed. by R. Woods (Garden City, N.Y.: Doubleday, 1980), 132.
11. Ibid., 128.
12. Anonymous, *A Course in Miracles,* 2d ed. (Mill Valley, Calif.: Foundation for Inner Peace, 1992) WB(188):357.
13. Pir Vilayat Inayat-Kahn, *Toward the One* (New York: Harper and Row, 1974), 189–91.
14. S. H. Nasr, *Knowledge and the Sacred* (New York: State University of New York, 1989), 134.
15. Ibid., 135–36.
16. A. Huxley, *The Perennial Philosophy* (New York: Harper and Row, 1944).
17. D. Lukoff and F. G. Lu, "Transpersonal Psychology Research Review Topic: Mystical Experience," in *Journal of Transpersonal Psychology* 20(2):161–84 (1988).
18. R. Hood, "Differential Triggering of Mystical Experience as a Function of Self-Actualization," in *Review of Religious Research* 18 (1977):264–70.
19. A. Greeley, *The Sociology of the Paranormal* (Beverly Hills, Calif.: Sage Publications, 1975).
20. A. Maslow, *Religions, Values, and Peak-Experiences* (Columbus: Ohio State University Press, 1964).
21. F. White, *The Overview Effect: Space Exploration and Human Evolution* (Boston: Houghton Mifflin, 1987), 11–12.
22. Ibid., 40–41.
23. M. Murphy, *The Future of the Body* (Los Angeles: J. P. Tarcher, 1992), 456.
24. Ibid., 475.
25. M. Eliade, ed., "Mysticism," in *The Encyclopedia of Religion,* 10:245–61.
26. W. James, *The Varieties of Religious Experience* (New York: New American Library, 1958), 385.

27. Ibid., 386, 391.

28. L. Hixon, *Great Swan: Meetings with Ramakrishna* (Boston: Shambhala, 1992), 62.

29. James, *Varieties of Religious Experience.*

30. W. T. Stace, *Mysticism and Philosophy* (Los Angeles: J. P. Tarcher, 1960).

31. K. Wilber, *A Brief History of Everything* (Boston: Shambhala, 1995).

32. E. Underhill, *Mysticism* (New York: E. P. Dutton, 1955).

33. M. Fox, *The Coming of the Cosmic Christ* (San Francisco: HarperSan-Francisco, 1988), 51.

34. A. Shearer, trans., *Effortless Being: The Yoga Sutras of Patanjali* (London: Unwin, 1989), 79.

35. Anonymous, *Meditations on the Tarot: A Journey into Christian Hermeticism* (Rockport, Mass.: Element Press, 1991), 42.

36. Underhill, *Mysticism.*

37. Anonymous, *Meditations on the Tarot.*

38. Underhill, *Mysticism,* 401.

39. Plato, *The Republic,* trans. by F. Cornford (Oxford: Oxford University Press, 1945), 516.

40. Nasr, *Knowledge and the Sacred,* 146.

41. S. Hoeller, *Jung and the Lost Gospels* (Wheaton Ill.: Theosophical Publishing House, 1989), 189.

42. Ibid., 245.

43. K. Wilber, *Sex, Ecology, Spirituality: The Spirit of Evolution* (Boston: Shambhala, 1995), 327.

44. Swami Prabhavananda and C. Isherwood, trans., *Shankara's Crest-Jewel of Discrimination* (Hollywood, Calif.: The Vedanta Society, 1978).

45. Ibid., 7.

46. L. Hixon, *Great Swan,* 26.

47. C. Alexander and E. Langer, eds., *Higher Stages of Human Growth* (New York: Oxford University Press, 1990).

48. G. Feuerstein, *Encyclopedic Dictionary of Yoga* (New York: Paragon House, 1990).

49. Alexander and Langer, *Higher Stages of Human Growth,* 326.

50. D. Loy, *Nonduality* (New Haven: Yale University Press, 1988), 178.

51. D. T. Suzuki, *Mysticism: Christian and Buddhist* (New York: Harper, 1957).

52. K. Wilber, *Grace and Grit* (Boston: Shambhala, 1991), 399.

53. Hixon, *Great Swan,* 7.

54. Idries Shah, *The Tales of the Dervishes* (New York: Dutton, 1970).

---

55. D. T. Suzuki, "The Basis of Buddhist Philosophy," in *Understanding Mysticism,* ed. by R. Woods (Garden City, N.Y.: Doubleday, 1980).

56. Nasr, *Knowledge and the Sacred.*

57. Hixon, *Coming Home.*

58. T. Byrom, *The Dhammapada: The Sayings of the Buddha* (New York: Vintage Books, 1976).

59. Wilber, *Grace and Grit.*

60. K. Wilber, *No Boundary* (Boston: Shambhala, 1981).

61. Sengstan, *Hsin Hsin Ming: Verses on the Faith Mind* (Sharon Springs, N.Y.: Zen Center, 1976).

62. Hixon, *Great Swan,* 73.

63. Ibid., 7.

64. G. Feuerstein, *Sacred Paths* (Burdett, N.Y.: Larson Publications, 1991), 185.

65. Sri Aurobindo, "The Synthesis of Yoga," cited in "Satprem, Oneness and the Teaching of Sri Aurobindo," in *What is Enlightenment?,* ed. J. White (Los Angeles: J. P. Tarcher, 1984).

Chapter 9 / Spiritual Freedom

1. Hazrat Inayat Khan, in *Omega Institute Newsletter,* 1985.

2. R. Anthony, et al., eds., *Spiritual Choices: Recognizing Authentic Paths to Inner Transformation* (New York: Paragon House, 1986).

3. R. Fritz, *The Path of Least Resistance* (New York: Fawcett Columbine, 1984).

4. L. Booth, *When God Becomes a Drug: Breaking the Chains of Religious Addiction and Abuse* (Los Angeles: J. P. Tarcher, 1991).

5. Sri Aurobindo, *The Life Divine* (Pondicherry, India: Sri Aurobindo Ashram, 1970), 857.

6. F. Vaughan, *Awakening Intuition* (Garden City, N.Y.: Anchor Books, 1979).

7. D. Elkins, "On Being Spiritual," *Journal of Humanistic Psychology* 28(4): 5–18 (1988).

8. K. Wilber, *The Atman Project* (Wheaton, Ill.: Theosophical Publishing House, 1980).

9. C. G. Jung, "The Bill W.—Carl Jung Letters," in *Re-Vision* 10(2):19–21 (1987). Reprinted with permission from the Princeton University Press.

10. I. Yalom, *When Nietzsche Wept* (New York: Basic Books, 1992), 269.

11. Ibid., 233.

12. C. Grof and S. Grof, *The Stormy Search for Self* (Los Angeles: J. P. Tarcher, 1990).

13. Jung, "The Bill W.—Carl Jung Letters," in *Re-Vision.*

14. Yalom, *When Nietzsche Wept,* 233.

15. A. Deikman, *The Wrong Way Home: Uncovering the Patterns of Cult Behavior in American Society* (Boston: Beacon Press, 1990).

16. Anonymous, *A Course in Miracles,* 2d ed. (Mill Valley, Calif.: Foundation for Inner Peace, 1992), T:265.

17. J. Blofeld, *The Zen Teachings of Huang Po* (New York: Grove Press, 1958), 49.

18. D. Shapiro and R. Walsh, eds., *Meditation: Classic and Contemporary Perspectives* (New York: Aldine, 1984).

19. Blofeld, *The Zen Teaching of Huang Po,* 59.

20. Thich Nhat Hanh, *Peace is Every Step* (New York: Bantam, 1991).

21. J. Engler, "Therapeutic Aims in Psychotherapy and Meditation," in *Transformations of Consciousness,* eds. K. Wilber, J. Engler, and D. Brown (Boston: Shambhala, 1986) 17–51.

22. R. Niebuhr, *The Children of Light and the Children of Darkness* (New York: Charles Scribner's Sons, 1944), xii-xv.

23. Dogen, cited in F. Frank, *The Book of Angelus Silesius* (New York: Vintage, 1976).

24. S. H. Nasr, *Knowledge and the Sacred* (New York: University of New York, 1989), 150.

25. N. S. Xavier, *The Two Faces of Religion* (Tuscaloosa, Ala.: Portals, 1987).

26. Anthony, *Spiritual Choices,* 146.

27. T. Bielecki, *Teresa of Avila* (New York: Crossroads, 1994), 31.

28. S. Hoeller, *Jung and the Lost Gospels* (Wheaton, Ill.: Quest Books, 1989).

29. Anonymous, *A Course in Miracles,* T:11.

Chapter 10 / Spiritual Practice in Daily Life

1. R. Daumal, *Mount Analogue* (New York: Pantheon, 1960).

2. F. Vaughan, *Awakening Intuition* (New York: Anchor Books, 1989).

3. Anonymous, *A Course in Miracles,* 2nd ed. (Mill Valley, Calif.: Foundation for Inner Peace, 1992), WB (97):172.

4. Ibid., WB (188):357.

5. Thich Nhat Hanh, *Being Peace* (Berkeley, Calif.: Parallax Press, 1987), 5.

6. J. Sanford, *Dreams: God's Forgotten Language* (New York: Harper and Row, 1989), 170.

7. R. McDermott, ed., *The Essential Steiner* (New York: Harper and Row, 1984), 104–5.

8. Sanford, *Dreams: God's Forgotten Language.*

9. J. Campbell, *Transformations of Myth Through Time* (New York: Harper and Row, 1990), 162.

10. Anonymous, *A Course in Miracles,* T:376.

11. Namkhai Norbu, *Dream Yoga and the Practice of Natural Light,* ed. by Michael Katz (Ithaca, N.Y.: Snow Lion Publications, 1992), 42.

12. Sanford, *Dreams.*

13. His Holiness the Dalai Lama, Lecture on "The Nature of Consciousness," presented at the International Transpersonal Conference (Davos, Switzerland, 1983).

14. S. LaBerge, *Lucid Dreaming* (Los Angeles: J. P. Tarcher, 1985), 244–45.

15. S. LaBerge, "From Lucidity to Enlightenment: Tibetan Dream Yoga," in *Paths Beyond Ego: The Transpersonal Vision,* ed. by Roger Walsh and Frances Vaughan (Los Angeles: J. P. Tarcher, 1993).

16. Gackenbach and Bosveld, "Beyond Lucidity: Moving Toward Pure Consciousness," *Paths Beyond Ego.*

17. C. Castaneda, *The Art of Dreaming* (San Francisco: Harper Collins, 1993), 81.

18. A. Arrien, *Tarot Workbook: Practical Applications of Ancient Visual Symbols* (Sonoma, Calif.: Arcus Publishing Company, 1987).

19. A. Arrien, *Signs of Life* (Sonoma, Calif.: Arcus Publishing Company, 1992).

20. Ibid.

21. S. Hoeller, *Jung and the Lost Gospels* (Wheaton, Ill.: Quest Books, 1989), 211.

22. S. Suzuki, *Zen Mind, Beginner's Mind* (New York: John Weatherhill, 1980).

23. Ibid.

24. H. Benson, *The Relaxation Response* (New York: William Morrow, 1975).

25. S. Kiesling and T. G. Harris, "The Prayer War," in *Psychology Today* (October 1989):65–66.

26. J. Kabat-Zinn, *Full Catastrophe Living* (New York: Delacorte, 1991).

27. D. Shapiro and R. Walsh, eds., *Meditation: Classic and Contemporary Perspectives* (New York: Aldine, 1984).

28. Walsh and Vaughan, *Paths Beyond Ego,* 47–69.

29. R. Forman, "Grass Roots Spirituality," Paper presented at the World Parliament of Religions, Chicago, Ill., 1993.

30. J. Goldstein and J. Kornfield, *Seeking the Heart of Wisdom: The Path of Insight Meditation* (Boston: Shambhala, 1987).

31. Anonymous, *The Song of Prayer* (New York: Foundation for Inner Peace, 1978), 7.

32. L. Dossey, *Healing Words: The Power of Prayer and the Practice of Medicine* (San Francisco: HarperSanFrancisco, 1993).

33. R. Tagore, *Gitanjali* (New York: Collier Books, 1971), 80.

34. T. Keating, *Intimacy with God* (New York: Crossroads, 1994).

35. Anonymous, *The Song of Prayer,* 10.

36. D. Steindl-Rast, *Gratefulness: The Heart of Prayer* (New York: Paulist Press, 1984).

37. D. Steindl-Rast, personal communication, Thanksgiving Season letter, 1993.

38. C. Tart, *Living the Mindful Life* (Boston: Shambhala, 1994).

39. H. Smith, *The World's Religions* (San Francisco: HarperSanFrancisco, 1991).

40. Ibid.

41. D. Wulff, *Psychology of Religion* (New York: John Wiley, 1991).

42. Walsh and Vaughan, *Paths Beyond Ego.*

43. J. Goldstein, *The Experience of Insight* (Boston: Shambhala, 1983).

44. Anonymous, *A Course in Miracles,* Manual for Teachers.

45. J. Needleman, *Money and the Meaning of Life* (New York: Doubleday, 1991), 213.

46. A. Bloom, *The Republic of Plato* (New York: Basic Books, 1991).

47. R. D. Laing, *Knots* (New York: Pantheon Books, 1970), 86.

Index

Achterberg, Jean, 183
Addiction: causes of, 1, 33, 35, 42;
  soul loss and,168; feelings of
  possession and, 172; spirituality
  and 230–234, 238
Adler, Alfred, 50
Affirmations, 255–257
Alcoholics Anonymous, 173, 238
Almas, A.H., 91
Always/already, 11, 81, 100, 135,
  216
Altered states, 19, 114, 164–166,
  205, 206, 230, 233
Archetype,178–190; states in
  development: the warrior, 181–
  183; the healer, 183–186; the
  teacher, 186–188; the visionary,
  189–191
Arrien, Angeles, 168
Aurobindo, Sri, 26, 37, *The Synthesis
  of Yoga,* 87, 113, 198, 228

Becker, Ernest, 50
Benson, Herbert, 271
Bhagavad Gita, 71,121, 181, 198
Bohme, Jacob, 149
Booth, Father Leo, 227
Borysenko, Joan, 141
Bradshaw, John, 168

Breath, spiritual practice and,118,
  120, 124, 125, 129, 135. *See also*
  Holotropic breathing
Buddha, the, 26–27,46, 67, 218,
  284; nature, 7; story of, 199;
  teaching of, 42, 123
Buddhism, 226, 227; America and,
  122–124; Bodhidharma and,
  181; Bodhisattva and, 200, 219;
  death of ego and, 60; Four noble
  truths, 199; Mahayana and,
  123, 200; Noble eightfold path,
  199–200, 285–286; paths of,
  11–12; teacher and, 186, 190;
  Theravada and, 122, 123, 200;
  Vipassana and,123; Zen, 6, 13.
  See also Zen Buddhism; Spiritual
  awakening

Campbell, Joseph, 56, 93, 199
Carotenuto, Aldo, 90
Castaneda, Carlos, 181
Chinese cosmology, 124–125;
  Confucian and, 124; Taoist and,
  124; breath, 124; *I Ching,* 125;
  martial arts, 125, movement and
  meditation, 125.
Chakra, symbolism of, 12, 105,
  181, 183, 186, 189

Christianity: Jesus and, 186; Holy
Spirit and, 161; Resurrection
of Christ and, 59, 127; nature
of soul, 127–128; prayer and,
275–279; gnosticism and, 118.
See also Gnosticism
Chuang, Tsu, 75
Colegrave, Sukie, 141
Consciousness, unitive, 21, 205,
215, 222, 223, 230.
Contemplative life, 225
Course in Miracles, A; 93, 99,
100, 108, 163, 201, 241, 261,
286–287
Cults, abuse of power and, 239

Dalai Lama, His Holiness the, 62,
159, 174, 180
Dark night of the soul, 83, 164, 241
Daumal, René, 253
Death: anxiety and, 51–54; beliefs
about, 72; dreams of, 63–67; sex
and 49–79; Instructions for, 67–
68; making peace with, 71–75;
meditation on, 51; suicide and,
75–78; symbolic rituals, 56–60;
transcendence and, 58. See also
Tibetan Book of the Dead
Deep ecology, 9, 119, 228
Divine discontent, 20, 39, 47
Dogen, 247
Dossey, Larry, 161, 183
Douglas, Claire, 148
Dreams, 21–23, 135, 150, 189,
259–260; collective, 6; death and
63–66; lucid, 64, 179,180, 249,
264; precognitive, 114; symbols
and language, 8; yoga and, 63,
122, 262–263

Eckhart, Meister, 112
Eisendrath, Polly Young, 154
Emerson, Ralph Waldo, 26
Enlightenment: 196–224; Eastern
philosophy and, 197; experience
and beliefs about, 201–207;
illusion of, 222; mysticism and,
207–209; roadmap to, 197–200;
Western philosophy, 197
Ego, 31–37; death of, 75; desires of,
45; emotions and, 113, soul and,
39- 48; spirit, soul and 47–48;
transcendence and, 238
Exercises: forgiveness, 277;
lovingkindness, 278–279;
Imagination, 258; guidelines
for awakening, 136–137;
Interpretation of symbols: five
shapes, 266–269; five elements,
269–270. *See also* Archetype

Faith, 249
Feuerstein, Georg, 122
Forgiveness, exercise for, 277
Frankl, Victor, 158
Freud, Sigmund, 50
Fox, Matthew, 209
Fritz, Robert, 227
Fromm, Erich, 104, 152, 155, 158,
159

Gandhi, Mahatma, 229
Gilligan, Carol, 104
Gnosticism, 150; gnostics and,
63,118, 138; gnosis and, 93,
187, 212.
Greening, Tom, 73–74
Grof, Christina, 164–166, *The
Thirst for Wholeness*, 173

Grof, Stan, 54, 57–58, 164–166

Healing: confession and, 167;
cultural conditioning and, 177;
mind, body and,153; power of
prayer and, 183; psychotherapy
and, 153; Western medicine and,
168; women and, 183
Hillman, James, 40, 111, 133.
Hinduism: spiritual stages of
development and, 130. *See also*
Tantra
Hixon, Lex, 81, 105, 129, 130,
216, 223
Holotropic breathing, 58, 164–166,
203, 205. *See also* Breath.
Huang Po, 242, 244
Huxley, Aldous, 203

Inayat-Khan, Pir Vilayat, 202
Individuation, 163, 171
Ingerman, Sandra, 168
Intention, 243; clarifying, 253–254;
personal power and, 154
Intuition: imagination and, 254–
259; prajna and, 217; wisdom
and, 216- 219
Islam. *See* Sufism

James, William, 178, 193, 203,
207, 208.
Judaism, 125–127; 139, 140;
Spanish Kabbalism and 70
Jung, Carl, 24, 50, 63; shadow
side of spirituality 3–4; suffering
of the soul, 14; psychological
types, 24; love, 90; religion, 163;
symbols, 177; spirituality and
addiction, 230, 238

Kabat-Zinn, Jon, 271
Kalu Rimpoche, 7
Karma, 122
Keller, Evelyn Fox, 139
King, Martin Luther, 17
Kohlberg, Lawrence, 104
Kornfield, Jack, 245
Kübler-Ross, Elizabeth, 72
Kundalini: yoga and,12; energy
and, 19

LaBerge, Stephen, 263–264
Love: *agape* and, 60, 87, 88; barriers
to, 100–103; choosing a path
and, 103–104; divine, 83, eros
and, 60,87, 88; emotions and,
104; essence of, 81–83, 91, 92;
healing and, 104; nature of, 82;
philia and, 87, 94; relational
types of, 93–98; romantic myths
and, 89–90
Luke, Helen, *Old Age,* 23

Mahaarishi Mahesh Yogi, 121
Maslow, Abraham, 14, 162, 203
May, Rollo, 37, 50
Memories: false, 40; recovered, 165
Meditation, 16, 20, 45,135, 175,
243, 270–274, Buddhist, 201;
concentration and, 193; divine
guidance and, 126; instructions
in, 271- 273; objects of attention,
193–195; physical illness, 271;
transcendental, 121
Millman, Dan, *The Way of the
Peaceful Warrior,* 183
Mitchell, Edgar, 204
Mitchell, Stephen, 26, *Gospel
According to Jesus,* 86

Mind, power of, 193–195. See also Spiritual development.

Moody, Raymond, 54

Moore, Thomas, 170, *Soulmates*, 98

Mother Teresa of Calcutta, 17, 94

Muktananda, Baba, 19

Murphy, Michael, 205

Mystics, 99, 113

Mysicism: authentic, 205; characteristics of, 207–209, 222; magic and, 210

Mythology, 112; collective dreaming and, 179; concepts of the soul, 118; death, rebirth and resurrection, 69; Egyptian, 118; Greek, 58–59, 118, 147; Indian and Kali, 95. See also Love

Naess, Arne, 9, 228

Nag Hammadi Library, The, 63

Nasr, Seyyed Hossein, 202, 211, 248

Near-death experience, 54–55; 70, 78, 204

Needleman, Jacob, 192, 193, 287; *Money and the Meaning of Life*, 160

Neumann, Eric, 143

Niebuhr, Rhinehold, 247

Norbu, Namkhai, 79, 198, 262

Pagels, Elaine, 63

Patanjali, Yoga Sutra of, 122,193, 210

Peak experience, 203–204

Perennial philosophy, fundamental doctrines and, 203

Prayer, 243; Brother David Steindl-Rast and, 278; Buddhist blessing, 278- 279; forgiveness and, 276; gratitude and, 277- 278; Keating, Father Thomas and centering, 276; power of healing and,183; St. Francis of Assisi and intention, 275; The Song of, 274, 276; twelve step program and, 275

Psychology: archetypal symbols and, 178; hero's journey and, 15; humanistic, 162; analytical,142–143; depth,14; study of soul and, 162–163; transpersonal,162. *See also* Jung, Carl

Psychotherapy: authenticity and, existential, 164; 166; reclaiming feminine values and, 141–142; release from guilt and, 241; self-transcendence and, 238; soul work and, 96, 164; spiritual empowerment and, 161; The path and,10–18; unconditional acceptance and, 99

Ram Dass, 237, 242

Ramakrishna, Sri, 87, 94, 106, 205, 213, 222

Rank, Otto, 50

Religion, traditional: common themes in, 69, 85–88

Ring, Kenneth, 40, 54

Rituals, purification, 242

St. John of the Cross, 3, 83, 87,148

St. Teresa of Avila, 13, 105

Sanford, John, 262

Sardello, Robert, 187

Schlemihl, Peter, 4

Schweickart, Rusty, 204

Service. *See* Spiritual practice

Shadow: addiction and, 247; collective, 3, 4, 51; definition of, 3; denial of, 239–241; integration of, 241; projection of, 239; spiritual path and, 4, 5, 8

Shah, Idries, *Tales of the Dervishes*, 217

Shah, Miranda, *Passionate Enlightenment: Women in Tantric Buddhism*, 61

Shamanism: concepts of, 116–117; initiation and, 19–20, 176. *See also* Spiritual awakening

Singer, June, 133, *Androgyny*, 148; *Seeing Through the Visible World*, 65

Smith, Huston, 7, 56, 80, 83, 111, 115

Sogyal Rinpoche, 49, 71, 72

Solovyov, Vladimir, 103

Soul, concepts of: ancient mythology, 118–120; Buddhism, 122–124; Chinese, 124–125; Christian, 127–129; Egyptian, 119; Greek, 119; Gnostic Christians, 118; Indian, 120–122; Islamic, 129–131; Judaic,125–126; shamanism, 116–118; transpersonal psychology, 132-136; *Upanishads*, 121

Soul: beliefs about, 131; essence and, 113, 150; gender and, 138–151; guidelines for awakening visualization, 136–137; loss of, 158, 168- 170; meaning and, 177–178; spirit and,112–116; mystical union and, 218; retrieval of, 168; visualization exercise and, 267–269

Spiritual awakening, stages of, 16–24

Spiritual development, 11, 12; altered states and, 206; authentic, 247; 32; healthy, 30, 31; powers of mind and, 193–195; sexuality and, 61

Spiritual emergencies, 16

Spiritual freedom, 224; the middle way and, 235; obstacles to, 234–237; qualities of, 251

Spiritual maturity, 9, 11, 249–252; qualities of, 229, 230, 234

Spiritual practice: Buddhism and the eightfold path and, 285–286; *A Course in Miracles* and, 286–287; dreams and, 259–260; meditation practices and, 270–273; prayer and, 274–278; reading and study, 284; reflections, 284; service as, 287; support for, 26; yogas and four postmodern as, 279–284; zazen and, 270. *See also* Prayer

Spirituality: definition of, 5; illness and, 152; practice and, 253–254; qualities of, 228; search for meaning and, 3; universal experience and, 201–202.

Stace, W.T., 207, 208

Steindl-Rast, Brother David, 211

Steiner, Rudolph, 104, 176, 259

Sufism: mystics and, 63; story and, 216; teacher and, 186

Suicide, beliefs about, 75–77

Suzuki, D.T., 200, 217

Suzuki Roshi, 47, 270

Symbols: archetypal and, 171;
    interpretation of elements as,
    269–270 interpretation of shapes
    as, 266–267; metaphors and,
    7–8

Tagore, Rabindranath, 275, 287
Tantra, 61–63, 119, 124, 205
Tart, Charles, 29, 39, 280
Taylor, Shelly, *Positive Illusions:
    Creative Self-Deception and the
    Healthy Mind*, 7
Tibetan Book of the Dead, 67
Thich Nhat Hanh, 42, 174, 176,
    245, 259
Tillich, Paul, 88
Transmission, spontaneous
    experiences of, 19, 219–222

Unconscious, collective, 57, 133
Underhill, Evelyn, 106, 208, 211
Unitive consciousness. *See*
    Consciousness, unitive
Upanishads, 121, 149

Vision, spiritual, 40, 79–80, 83–85,
    99, 228, 251
Visualizations: *See* archetype
von Bingen, Hildegard, 150
von Franz, Marie Louise, 63, 66

Wallace, Alan, 71
Watts, Alan, 79
White, John, 73

Whitmont, Edward, 144
Wiedemann, Florence, 154
Wilber, Ken: spectrum of
    consciousness, 40,132–134;
    eros and unity, 51; spirit and
    unity, 60; unconditional love and
    healing, 96; stages of spiritual
    development,104; spirit, invo-
    lution and evolution,118,141;
    four types of mysticism, 208
    phenomenal reality and spirit,
    212; deity yoga, 215; unity
    consciousness, 222; spiritual
    freedom, 252
Wilson, Bill, 173

Xavier, N.S., *The Two Faces of
    Religion*, 249

Yalom, Irvin, 50, 51, *When Nietzche
    Wept*, 101, 232, 349
Yoga-Sutra of Patanjali. *See* Patanjali
Yoga, 193, guru, 247, psychology
    and, 181, 182, 186, 189; spiritual
    empowerment and, 161; three
    stages in deity and, 215
Yogas, four postmodern, 279–284;
    Indian philosophy and, 24

Zen, Buddhism, 6, 23,182; death
    awareness, 67; meditation and,
    67 123, 270; ox-herding pictures
    of, 13, 219. *See also* Spiritual
    awakening

QUEST BOOKS
are published by
The Theosophical Society in America,
Wheaton, Illinois 60189-0270,
a branch of a world organization
dedicated to the promotion of the unity of
humanity and the encouragement of the study of
religion, philosophy, and science, to the end that
we may better understand ourselves and our place in
the universe. The Society stands for complete
freedom of individual search and belief.
In the Classic Series well-known
theosophical works are made
available in popular editions.